AID AND POWER
VOLUME 1 ANALYSIS AND POLICY
PROPOSALS

The international recession of the early 1980s left many less developed countries in a precarious position as their exports collapsed, private capital flows were sharply reduced and interest rates rose. Major aid donors, in particular the World Bank, responded with fundamental changes in aid policy – the introduction of 'structural adjustment lending'. Under this new policy, financial flows to developing countries were made conditional on changes in policy, generally of a type that reduced the level of government intervention in the economy.

This book examines the implications of this change for both the World Bank and the recipients of aid. For the World Bank, there has been a serious conflict between the objectives of quick disbursement and enforcement of conditions. For developing countries, the Bank's conditions have often posed a political threat; but as the book shows, their governments have worked out ingenious strategies for countering this threat, even in countries where the economic predicament is desperate. As a consequence, the so-called 'counter-revolution' in development policy has found, in spite of the Bank's wishes, limited application in developing countries. The results of some economic reforms have been positive, particularly on external account, but their impact on economic growth and foreign resource inflows has been insignificant and on productive investment negative. Both donors and recipients have learned valuable lessons from the policy-based lending experience, and we move into the 1990s with a more modest and long-term view of what policy reform, and economic policy generally, can achieve in developing countries.

Volume 1 carries the analysis and policy recommendations. It examines the origins of policy-based lending and analyses the essential features of the bargaining process which is at its heart. Criteria for the assessment of the success and failure of programmes are developed, and the results of such programmes across a wide range of countries are examined. Proposals for reform of the system are made in the concluding chapter.

Volume 2 contains the results of nine case studies, involving countries in Asia, Africa, Latin America and the Caribbean. From this volume it becomes clear that each country's experience of structural adjustment is unique and that the relationship between the stimulus of a development loan and the recipient economy's response is conditioned by both donor and recipient bargaining strategies and the political and economic structure of the recipient country.

Paul Mosley is Professor of Economics at the University of Reading. Jane Harrigan, formerly Pricing Economist, Government of Malawi, is now Lecturer in Economics at the University of Manchester. John Toye is Director, Institute of Development Studies, University of Sussex.

AID AND POWER

The World Bank and Policy-based Lending

Volume 1   Analysis and policy proposals
Second edition

Paul Mosley, Jane Harrigan and John Toye

London and New York

First published 1991 by Routledge
11 New Fetter Lane, London EC4P 4EE
Second edition published 1995

Simultaneously published in the USA and Canada
by Routledge
29 West 35th Street, New York, NY 10001

© 1991, 1995 Paul Mosley, Jane Harrigan and John Toye

Printed and bound in Great Britain by Mackays of Chatham PLC, Kent

British Library Cataloguing in Publication Data
A catalogue record for this book is available from the British Library.

Library of Congress Cataloguing-in-Publication Data
A catalogue record for this book is available from the Library of Congress.

JK   ISBN 0–415–13209–6 (hbk)
ISBN 0–415–13210–X (pbk)

CONTENTS

Volume 1   Analysis and policy proposals

Part I   Background

Part II   The dynamics of policy reform

Part IV Conclusions

Volume 2   Case studies

Volume 1   Figures

Volume 1   Tables

PREFACE

The preface of a book offers its authors the opportunity to explain themselves. What is it that they think they have done? How did they manage it? And why did it seem such a good idea at the time? It also offers the casual bookshop browser, who may have thought that a book entitled *Aid and Power* was about artificial limbs, or safety in the workshop, the opportunity to discover immediately that this is not so, and to lay the volume down again with maximum speed and no undue loss of dignity. In fact, we have written a book about aid defined as official development assistance, and power in the sense of the relations of power that exist between donors of a certain kind of aid and its recipients.

The type of aid on which we focus is aid given by the World Bank, in the form of concessional loans, to which are attached conditions – but not just the usual conditions of repayment, rather conditions that the recipient government must fulfil by changing some of its previously chosen policies. Paul Mosley initiated the project, of which this book is the outcome, because he was dissatisfied with the two naïve explanations of how such loans came into being at the start of the 1980s. One of these explanations denied the existence of any link between such aid and political power. It held that loans conditioned on policy changes were made only when there was an unforced unanimity of views between the World Bank and the borrower about what the right policies were for the borrowing country. But if this were so, he argued, to make policy change a formal condition of the aid loan would be redundant.

The other naïve explanation was that the Bank was adopting the oppressive tactics of the International Monetary Fund and using Fund-type loan conditionality to lever financially distressed governments of low-income countries into conformity with its own preferred set of policies for them. But if this were so, the Bank's conditionality would have had to be identical with the Fund's, which it manifestly was not. Each of the present authors in turn became convinced that a better way to understand the offer and acceptance of policy-conditioned loans was as a dynamic bargaining process (Mosley, 1987; Harrigan, 1988a; Toye, 1989).

But herein lay an important difficulty. If the Bank was indeed engaged in bargaining – in effect offering loans in return for concessions to its vision of policy reform – it would be most unlikely to advertise this fact, or publish extensive analysis of its own institutional behaviour. No poker player cares to play with transparent cards. The truth of the dynamic bargaining hypothesis would never be endorsed by the Bank, especially if it were in fact true.

The present authors were not alone in detecting in the World Bank of the early 1980s a keen appreciation of the doctrine of useful and dangerous truths. Useful truths are those that support an institution's goals (or are believed to) and dangerous truths are those which threaten these goals (or, again, are believed to threaten them). The Bank's Research Department in the early 1980s responded to unorthodox thought defensively. To parody only slightly: 'We cannot be sure whether unorthodox thought A is true or not. If it is false it is dangerous, but if it is true, it is *even more* dangerous'. While this parody acquits the Bank of intellectual incompetence, it convicts it of the kind of intellectual protectionism that cannot be appropriate to a truly confident liberalism.

At all events, in the prevailing atmosphere of institutional defensiveness it seemed urgent to launch an independent enquiry into the Bank's use of policy-based loans. We were fortunate in securing a grant of about £100,000 from the UK Overseas Development Administration's Fund for economic and social research (ESCOR) in late 1986. Without this support, the research in this book might never have got off the drawing board, and all of us feel a deep debt of gratitude to the ODA for making our work possible. The applicants for the ESCOR grant were Paul Mosley and John Toye, and the grant made provision for a supporting research officer. Jane Harrigan was employed in that capacity on return from her ODI Fellowship in Malawi. But circumstances soon led to her taking an equal hand in the research work. Paul Mosley moved from a Readership in Economics at the University of Bath to a Chair in the University of Manchester and the Directorship of the University's Institute for Development Policy and Management (IDPM), and John Toye moved from University College, Swansea to direct the Institute of Development Studies (IDS) at the University of Sussex. Both moves entailed a distinct enlargement of administrative responsibilities. For this reason, the enhancement of Jane Harrigan's role from research officer to co-author was absolutely necessary and in no way overstates her contribution to the final product.

The aim of the research was to elaborate on and test the preliminary ideas set out in Paul Mosley's Princeton Essay, *Conditionality as Bargaining Process* (1987). Country case studies were intended to provide a range of empirical examples of the loan bargaining process, showing both the making of agreements, their partial implementation and what happens at the next round. These are presented under the names of their separate authors in Volume 2. We are grateful indeed to the 'guest authors' of the Turkey and Thailand studies for their eager co-operation with our plan of research. Their contributions provide additional coverage and insights beyond what would have been feasible for the three of us.

The country studies were designed to provide material for the analysis of particular issues to be discussed in Volume 1. Can the loan process be represented as a kind of game, and, if so, what kind of game is it? Can we measure the degree to which loan conditions are implemented? What political influences favour policy reform and which do not? Does administrative capability or the availability of alternative sources of finance have a separately distinguishable effect? Do countries which implement policy reforms turn in a better economic performance as a result?

This last question is a particularly intractable one, and attempts to settle it with an inadequate methodology have rightly raised controversy. Our research has pursued a series of partial methods, but tried to refine their applications. It has also explored the modelling approach, which in principle should be able to isolate the key correlations accurately, even though it cannot settle finally questions of causation. Two countries are treated through modelling – Malawi (with a model of the agricultural pricing system devised by Jane Harrigan) and Morocco (with a computable general equilibrium model devised by François Bourguignon). Again we are grateful to a 'guest author' for his contribution, especially as it had to be prepared at short notice and at considerable speed, and to the OECD for allowing us to use the model on which Professor Bourguignon's work is based. But generally we have striven for a synthesis that is stylistically uniform as far as possible, and which represents a consensus between us on matters of substance.

Anyone who tries to research a topic of current operational concern soon discovers that their target is a moving one. We originally intended to focus our enquiry on World Bank Structural Adjustment Loans (SALs). But we soon discovered other kinds of Bank loans which had many of the same features as SALs, and our enquiry widened to include other forms of adjustment lending. Our original focus on the Bank to the exclusion of the Fund was also somewhat misplaced. The idea had been to produce a study of Bank conditionality that would stand comparison with that of Fund conditionality produced by Killick et al. (1984). But the latter referred largely to the Fund in the 1970s and the Fund has developed significantly in the 1980s. We have had to spend much more time studying the evolution of Bank-Fund relations in the 1980s than we had originally intended.

The Bank also has not remained so opaque as it seemed to want to be in the early 1980s. It has conducted its own evaluations of adjustment lending and these have been put in the public domain. In a number of important respects, the results which we report are compatible with the Bank's own research on itself. We may then be asked: was your journey really necessary? Were not your fears of obfuscation exaggerated? To this last question, surely we have to answer that, as it turned out, the situation became much better than we had feared it would. But it is easy to be wise after the event. We would, however, strongly contest the suggestion that our labour has been superfluous. In the first place, we have much greater confidence in the Bank's own evaluations of its adjustment lending *precisely because* we have closely replicated the gist of their results using a separate research strategy and working quite independently. Second, it may not be entirely a piece of self-justifying vanity to suggest that the activities of independent researchers may have stimulated the more open and objective approach to research which the Bank has taken since 1986.

And the early 1980s psychology lives on in some bilateral donor agencies. The useful truths still have their champions. Aid bureaucrats still write position papers which rehearse this familiar litany: all developing countries' problems are internal ones; the aim of policy reform is to get the prices right and to roll back the government sector; this kind of reform increases equity as well as efficiency; conflict between stabilisation and structural adjustment goals is minimal, and so on. Admittedly, the 1990 document which said all of these things was sufficiently ingenuous to preface this litany with the statement that 'these propositions are in urgent need of truth-testing'. If that is meant seriously, this book may still have work to do.

Over the last five or six years many people have generally assisted us with their time and wisdom. In the UK, we have been guided by an Advisory Committee which was composed of Robert Cassen, Tony Killick, Stanley Please and various ODA officials including three successive Secretaries of ESCOR, William Kingsmill, John Hoy and Brian Thomson. Advice has also been given at different times by John Roberts, Peter Sandersley and Alan Coverdale of the ODA. Without wishing to implicate them in our conclusions, we hope that they all will recognise where their comments and viewpoints have influenced us and accept our thanks for giving us their valuable time and the benefit of their knowledge.

We made many friends in the World Bank whose valuable help we would also like to acknowledge. The number of Bank officials whom we consulted is too large for all to be listed here. But we are especially grateful to Vinod Dubey, Gene Tidrick, John Holsen, Nicholas Carter, Vittorio Corbo and William McCleary for the patient way in which they answered our questions, clarified our thinking when it became muddled and advised us how to maximise the intellectual benefits from our visits to the Bank. We also wish to thank Ernest Stern and Moeen Qureshi for granting us interviews when each was Senior Vice-President (Operations). Other Bank staff who helped us to complete the individual country studies in Volume 2 are named at the beginning of those studies. We do not wish to attribute any responsibility to any of the above named for what we have written, which is a distillation of information gathered from many and various sources. But we certainly would like to congratulate all of them for being good ambassadors for the Bank, helping us to understand its strengths and encouraging us to forgive its weaknesses.

We have other debts, too, owing across the Atlantic. Robert Wade wrote at our request a fascinating analysis of the working of the Bank, based partly on desk research and partly on his own observations made while an employee. To have included this long paper as an element in Volume 1 would have unbalanced it somewhat, so we have chosen instead to draw selectively on its insights, expecially in our Chapters 2 and 3. Apart from Robert Wade, we wish also to thank Joan Nelson and her colleagues, whose project on the politics of economic liberalisation has run broadly in parallel with our own research. We have had a number of workshops and conferences, both in the US and the UK, at which some or all of both teams have been present. The British team has derived great stimulation and encouragement from these exchanges and feels much obliged for the generosity with which research findings have been shared.

When the late Eric Stokes was preparing the manuscript for his posthumous book on *The Peasant and the Raj*, it became known to his family as *The Pheasant and the Rat*. In somewhat the same way, our project has given birth to a mythical researcher named Aidan Power, who has created a mighty manuscript. Many people have now got to know Aidan: some have even taken pity on him and befriended him. Since the manuscript has been prepared mainly at IDPM in Manchester, his friends are mainly there. Above all, he would like to thank Debra Whitehead, Lesley Bernardis, Margaret Curran and Pauline Whitehead for their tireless efforts to bring him into existence. But Aidan also has helpers at IDS, Sussex, and Jo Stannard and Lin Briggs are also to be warmly thanked on his behalf. Finally, Janet Toye, Helena Mosley and their respective children (two of whom were born during the period of this study) deserve our thanks for putting up with the absences and disturbances which its creation involved. We hope they will feel the fuss was worthwhile.

Manchester and Brighton
Easter, 1990

Paul Mosley
Jane Harrigan
John Toye

A NOTE ON TEXTUAL AMENDMENTS
IN THE SECOND EDITION

The amendments made in the text of the Second Edition fall into three categories. They are as follows.

Firstly, the story of the Bank's adjustment lending has been brought up to date. This has involved, apart from the inclusion of this new Introduction, revision of the text and tables of Chapters 1, 2, 4, 7 and 8. The bibliography has also been extended to incorporate relevant recent items.

Second, the analysis of adjustment lending has moved on by four years. We have attempted to take account of this both by revision of the Appendix to Chapter 3 on game theory, and by amending the summaries at the end of Chapters 7 and 8. Our aim has been to incorporate assessments of adjustment lending carried out since the publication of the first edition, in particular the three reports issued by the Bank.

Finally, some of the recommended actions originally included in Chapter 9 have moved from the world of ideas to the world of real life. We have great pleasure in amending the last section of this chapter to take note of these developments.

Paul Mosley
John Toye
December 1994

INTRODUCTION TO THE SECOND EDITION

SCOPE OF DISCUSSION

Even in the relatively short period since *Aid and Power* was first published in 1991, much concerning the World Bank has changed. A rueful sentence in the Preface to the first edition of this book declared that 'anyone who tries to research a topic of current operational concern soon discovers that their target is a moving one'. Events have now moved on again and policies, too, have struggled to keep up. This new Introduction has been written to report and comment on some of the most significant of those changes. A full account would, however, be well beyond its compass.

The Bank has been diagnosed by an astute ex-insider as an institution which suffers from a chronic ambiguity of, and conflict between, objectives. Over time it moves uneasily between four major roles. These are (i) a financial intermediary between world capital markets and its own borrowers, a role summarised as 'the Bank as a bank'; (ii) an instrument for the advancement of the interests of the rich countries who are its majority shareholders; (iii) an evangelist seeking changes in the beliefs and behaviour of developing countries' governments; and (iv) an agent for the net transfer of resources from rich to poor countries (Naim, 1994: 194–6). When looking at the changes that have occurred at the Bank in recent years, it may be helpful to have this taxonomy of objectives in mind as an organising framework.

In the last fifteen years, the Bank has placed increasing emphasis on role (iii), that of evangelist. The introduction of policy-based lending was an attempt to combine the earlier role of transferring resources to poor countries with a stronger effort to change the policy mix of certain borrowers. The story of *Aid and Power* in a nutshell is the story of the conflict between objectives (iii) and (iv) in the context of adjustment lending. The disappointing impact of policy reforms on economic performance, at least in sub-Saharan Africa in the 1980s, are detailed in Part III of the book. Notwithstanding this disappointment, one of the Bank's latest initiatives extends the scope of its evangelism still further.

The revival by the Bank of an active agenda on poverty is, for those with a strong commitment to humanitarianism, the most exciting Bank initiative. Without wishing to imply that the Bank abandoned all of its former interest in redistribution with growth during the 1980s, it is clear that the sharpness of its focus on the poverty issue and the scale of the effort and resources devoted to it have both very markedly increased in the period since 1987. This has affected both policy-based adjustment lending (the subject of *Aid and Power*) and other forms of lending such as investment projects. What has been done so far, and some of the strengths and weaknesses of the current poverty work, are the subject of the next section.

But other recent initiatives have responded to other objectives. The collapse of the state socialist regimes in Eastern Europe and the former Soviet Union have brought them much more closely into contact with the lending operations of the Bank and the International Monetary Fund (IMF). In this development, it could be argued that the Bank is operating in mode (ii), that is, as an instrument of the Group of Seven (G7) rich countries seeking to address a difficult and urgent geo-political problem. Such operations have brought new risks as well as new opportunities. They are bound to have implications for the Bank's asset portfolio in the future, which may threaten the Bank's ability to perform role (i), that of efficient financial intermediary. This set of problems is explored in the third section of this Introduction.

Finally, prompted by its fiftieth birthday, we speculate a little about where the Bank is going as an entire institution. Part of this is a question about the respective roles of the Bank and the IMF as international financial institutions. Some problems of the Bank–Fund relationship during the 1980s were explored in Chapter 2 of *Aid and Power*. How have they evolved, and how are they likely to evolve in the 1990s? But an equally fundamental question is that of the changing balance of power among the countries who are the stakeholders and the financial sponsors of the Bank, and whether they will be able to guide and direct the priorities of the Bank more effectively as it continues to try to fulfil multiple roles and achieve its multiple objectives.

THE BANK'S REVIVED POVERTY AGENDA

Aid and Power itself had little to say, in the original version, about poverty. That was not because the authors thought that poverty was a topic of negligible interest, or outside the proper agenda of development policy. Quite the contrary. The reason for the slight attention to the subject of poverty was simply the specifications of the research on which the book reported. The research was designed to provide an evaluation of the experience of World Bank-funded structural adjustment in the period from 1980 to 1988. As the beginning of Chapter 6 explains, the authors decided to use the Bank's own policy objectives as the appropriate criteria for the evaluation. At the relevant time, the Bank did not have poverty reduction as a major aim of adjustment lending. So the evaluation excluded poverty reduction as a criterion of the success of policy-based lending. If such a criterion had been included, our evaluation would have been open to the riposte that it criticised adjustment lending for failing to achieve something that it had never set out to achieve. It was judged more important to establish whether adjustment lending had succeeded on its own terms than whether it had succeeded when appraised against ideal criteria selected by outsiders to the Bank.

By the end of the 1980s, however, many of the expectations with which the Bank had embarked on the programme of structural adjustment lending were in need of revision. In particular it was then realised that in many countries, especially borrowers in sub-Saharan Africa, the time scale for an effective stabilisation and structural adjustment process could stretch beyond five years (Stewart, 1994: 128-9). This realisation undermined the doctrine that economic reform had to take absolute priority over social concerns, such as poverty alleviation. That ranking of priorities was just about tolerable to borrowing countries and other donors when the task of adjustment was thought to span two or three years. But the prospect of a much longer postponement of a policy agenda that directly addressed social welfare issues made the doctrine of absolute priority for economic reform politically vulnerable.

Leading critics of the Bank's structural adjustment lending argued that adjustment had had 'social costs' in terms of loss of employment and incomes, and had been accompanied by a series of adverse changes in social indicators such as school enrolments, maternal and child nutrition and the prevalence of certain diseases (Cornia, Jolly and Stewart, 1987). The adverse changes were usually real enough, as far as one could tell from the patchy data. But, in contrast with the methodology of *Aid and Power*, this critique did not (and did not claim to) separate out their causes, as between adjustment policies on the one hand and economic shocks like falling commodity prices and rising interest rates on the other. Nevertheless, these arguments launched a vigorous debate on the social aspects of adjustment. UNICEF took the lead in campaigning for what it termed 'adjustment with a human face'. This implied more gradual adjustment, greater attention to the composition of public expenditure and the design of specific forms of social safety-net to protect the poor and the vulnerable. The campaign to give adjustment a human face made a considerable impact in changing policy-makers' positions as well as their rhetoric.

Meanwhile, within the Bank, the fact that structural adjustment was proving a slower process than originally expected stimulated anxieties and possible 'adjustment fatigue' among borrowers. The concern was that the failure to achieve rapid results that were clearly beneficial would discourage borrowing governments from persisting in their commitment to economic reforms, and lead to the premature termination of some adjustment programmes. This worry was based not only on the suspicion that prolonged austerity would lead to accumulating unpopularity for governments, and that unpopularity would be more inconvenient to governments if (following the collapse of state socialist regimes in Europe) they were simultaneously trying to move towards more accountable and participatory forms of governance. It also took account of the even more uncomfortable perception that clear losers from the reform process were former government and parastatal employees, who tended to be concentrated in politically sensitive urban areas. This outcome was particularly evident in sub-Saharan African adjusting countries.

The Bank had generally resisted the idea put forward in Chapter 9 of *Aid and Power* that losers should be compensated, on the grounds that these urban losers had no right to the rents of which reform had deprived them. At the same time, the Bank was not opposed to general policy packages to mitigate the social costs of adjustment. These could include components of redundancy pay, retraining costs and special credit access for those who had been retrenched from public employment. While the Bank's principle of no right to compensation was preserved, the possible political dangers of entirely neglecting urban losers were discreetly averted.

This was done by means of a substantial programme on the Assessment of the Social Dimensions of Adjustment (SDA), which was started in 1987 jointly with UNDP and the African Development Bank. This was focused around the collection and analysis of data on living standards, through a series of national household surveys (the Priority Surveys). The SDA also contained objectives and assorted activities that were concerned directly with the design of improved poverty alleviation programmes and the strengthening of governments' institutional capacity to implement such programmes. These went under the title of Social Action Programmes (SAPs) and included programmes that were clearly adjustment-related as well as others that were not particularly targeted at the losers from adjustment policies.

The SDA rapidly ran into criticism. Some of this criticism identified weaknesses in management, leading to fast expansion, cost over-runs and lack of adequate reporting. Some focused on the excessive ambition of the aims and scope of the SDA. These included an attempt to make a major theoretical contribution through the document *Structural Adjustment: a Conceptual, Empirical and Policy Framework* (Report No. 8393-AFR, 1990), which attempted to distinguish conjunctural from long-term structural poverty. They also originally envisaged annual runs of the Bank's Living Standard Measurement Survey (LSMS) model to monitor progress in participating countries, a task which quickly proved much too cumbersome and costly. But perhaps the most damaging line of attack was the observation that the information component of the SDA was never properly articulated with the Social Action Programmes, so that the two main thrusts of the SDA developed largely independently of each other.

Many regard the cutting edge of the Bank as being its lending operations, that is, a combination of roles (i) and (iv). Country desk staff who manage these operations tended to resent the growth of the SDA on the grounds that they could make better use of the resources which it absorbed. When a 1990 UNDP report confirmed the widespread view that the information component of the SDA, having eluded management control, was foisting a single research instrument – the Priority Survey – on to the over-burdened statistical services of the participating governments, the top management of the Bank lost patience with the SDA in its original form. They decided that the SDA work had become too centralised and too separated from the everyday operational work. Their response was to reduce the scope of the programme, to split up what remained and to distribute it to a number of different parts of the organisation. The grandiose version of the SDA was thus very effectively humbled. The gloss that was put on this was that an opportunity was created thereby to mainstream the analysis of poverty and the design of anti-poverty policies (SDA Steering Committee, 1993).

The SDA experience showed that to concentrate scarce welfare resources on retrenched public sector workers, who were perceived rightly as less poor than many other people in both the urban and rural sector, was not defensible. However helpful it might be in keeping adjustment fatigue at bay, it was not equitable. The Bank came to the conclusion that the human face of adjustment required the issue of poverty to be addressed across a much broader front. During the internal vicissitudes over the SDA, the Bank had taken a major step towards raising the profile of the poverty issue externally when it published the *World Development Report 1990* on Poverty (World Bank, 1990b). The *WDR 1990* had a powerful impact in signalling to the wider development community that, from a position of relative neglect in the 1980s, structural poverty reduction had re-emerged as the central objective of development co-operation in the 1990s. In giving this signal, the Bank was in part responding to political change in the United States, the views of other donors and successful campaigning pressures from (mainly Northern) NGOs. In retrospect, it seems a bold move, because it raised external expectations at the very moment when, as just noted, the Bank's effects on conjunctural poverty were in some disarray.

Did the Bank really know how structural poverty reduction was to be achieved? The *WDR 1990* suggested that it did. The *WDR* anti-poverty strategy has three prongs. The first is the rekindling of economic growth. In poor countries poverty is too pervasive for it to be reduced significantly by redistribution of existing resources, so growth is indispensable. However, it is conceivable that economic growth could affect only those at the upper end of the income distribution and thus make no impact on poverty. In other words, growth may not trickle down to those at the bottom of the income distribution. So growth has to be labour-intensive in character, generating strong demand for labour, the resource with which the poor are most abundantly endowed.

The second prong concerns the composition of public expenditures. The ability of the poor to participate in labour markets depends on their stock of human capital. The government can and should help poor people to add to their stock of human capital by increasing the share of total government spending that goes on education and health and by increasing the share of education and health spending that reaches the poor. The third prong is the provision of social safety nets, that is, special government schemes targeted on the poor who are unable to enter the labour market. Some outside observers commented that perhaps the WDR strategy was better described as two-and-a-half pronged rather than three-pronged, because of the ambivalence expressed in *WDR 1990* about the appropriateness or feasibility of the social safety-net prong.

Having announced its poverty-reduction strategy, the Bank proceeded to develop some basic tools to implement it in the Bank's own operations. To follow up *WDR 1990*, a policy paper on 'Assistance Strategies to Reduce Poverty' (World Bank, 1991) recommended that Poverty Assessments (hence-forth PAs) be undertaken for almost all borrowing countries within three years from 1992 to check on the relation between government policies and the aim of poverty reduction, and between the Bank's assistance strategies and the government's efforts to reduce poverty. Other donors and UN agencies were to be involved in the task of improving the reliability of poverty data, and regular reports were to be sent to the Executive Directors on the progress of poverty reduction in connection with both adjustment and ordinary project lending.

Next, an Operational Directive on Poverty Reduction (O.D. 4.15) (World Bank, 1992a) provided detailed guidance on how PAs were to be prepared and how they were intended to mesh with the existing programmes of country economic and sector work, such as the Public Expenditure Reviews (PERs), the Country Economic Memoranda (CEMs), the Country Assistance Strategies (CASs) and, in the case of adjustment lending, the Policy Framework Papers (PFPs). The O.D. 4.15 allowed considerable latitude on the question of how the task of integrating the new PAs into existing programmes of country economic and sector work should be tackled. This should be decided by each country desk in the light of its country's circumstances. But it did establish some important criteria for monitoring the Bank's poverty-reduction efforts through its lending operations. In order to count as part of the programme of targeted interventions (PTI) to reduce poverty, projects should either contain a specific mechanism for targeting the poor, or the poor should figure disproportionately among the project's identified beneficiaries. The poverty-reduction components of adjust-ment lending were to be included with the PTI and a standard set of country poverty indicators in regular Progress Reports.

The Poverty Reduction Handbook (World Bank, 1992b) brought together for the benefit of Bank staff more detailed guidance on methods to estimate the prevalence, characteristics and causes of poverty, to analyse constraints on the effectiveness of measures to reduce poverty and then to devise a poverty-reduction strategy for the country concerned. Unlike the guidelines in O.D. 4.15, the methods in the *Handbook* were not mandatory in the preparation of PAs, but educational for staff who had to tackle this new and possibly unfamiliar task.

By the end of the fiscal year 1993, the Bank had produced some 28 PAs, five for Asian and Pacific countries, nine for Latin America and the Caribbean, four for South Asia, nine for sub-Saharan Africa and one for the Middle East and North Africa (Egypt). A further 74 were scheduled for completion by the end of the fiscal year 1997. This rate of completion represents some slippage on the timetable originally set out in 'Assistance Strategies to Reduce Poverty'. In early 1994, a further 24 countries were waiting for their PAs to be scheduled, while for a variety of others no plans were being made, either because of their political situations or because of their inactive status as Bank borrowers (World Bank, 1994d, Annex 4, notes). The question must be raised of whether the universal coverage of PAs, insisted on by the Executive Board in its effort to force the top management to take the poverty issue seriously, is either feasible or desirable. Selective concentration of resources on countries where there are genuine prospects of getting anti-poverty strategies launched seems to be a better idea.

Apart from the problem of slippage, the quality of the PAs that had been completed was distinctly variable. Some were excellent, but others were unsatisfactory. The variations in the quality had a number of causes. A few PAs were so designated retrospectively, indicating that they were produced before the documents that were intended to guide their production. In any case, even with advance guidelines, those responsible were on a steep learning curve. The learning that had to be done covered not just analytical methods, but also how to acquire the necessary resources to fund the work. Task Managers for the PAs are expected to be quite entrepreneurial, in that they must extract funding for the work both from higher-level management within the Bank and from a range of special Trust Funds set up by donors for particular purposes. There is no standard allocation for doing a PA from within the Bank, and it would have been surprising if all Task Managers had succeeded in tapping the Trust Funds to the extent necessary to make up an adequate resource package for the production of a satisfactory PA. It is an interesting question how far this state of affairs represents the effect of an absolute shortage of resources available to the Bank, and how far a low priority accorded to poverty reduction.

Inevitably, the unavailability of adequate data hampered what could be done, especially in the sub-Saharan African region. Often, considerable ingenuity was used to make the best of what was available but even then the outcome was usually a snapshot of the distribution of poverty rather than a moving picture of changes in that distribution over time. It is hoped, as PAs are up-dated in future, this will become less true. Most of the quantitative work revolves around the analysis of a household survey (usually the Priority Survey of SDA fame), plus demographic and nutritional survey data when available. The general picture derived from this approach is that a majority of people in poor countries are poor, and that the prevalence of consumption poverty is greater in rural than in urban areas. Given the paucity of regionally differentiated price indices, it is far from clear that these findings are reliable. They tend to confirm conventional views and thus to give little additional help to those trying to construct poverty-reduction policies.

One of the more encouraging recent methodological developments in the Bank's assessment of poverty is the emerging resort to more sociologically informative techniques of research. These include the cluster of methods that go under the label of Participatory Rural Appraisal (PRA), and Beneficiary Assessment which investigates the delivery of public services through focus groups and semi-structured interviews. They are important because they are able to illuminate a whole range of aspects of poverty on which the private consumption/nutrition/demography estimates remain silent. The gender division of labour within the household, the seasonality of poverty and the coping strategies of the vulnerable are three examples among many. PRA methods are also important because they can convey the preferences of the poor themselves on the policies which are intended to reduce poverty. But the use of PRA techniques and other types of special assessment needs to become still more widespread in the Bank.

Interdisciplinarity in the assessment of poverty was one of the requirements laid down by O.D. 4.15. The Directive states that 'analyses of the cultural constraints, sociological context, and/or political dynamics within which poverty persists contribute to understanding the process of poverty in a particular country and to evaluating the full costs and likely benefits of alternative measures to reduce poverty' (paragraph 8). In fact, the analysis of the process of poverty as contrasted with the state of poverty and in particular the political dynamics of this process, has been the weakest part of the Bank's poverty-assessment efforts to date. The explanation for this may lie in inhibitions arising from the non-political nature of the Bank's Charter, or in the under-representation of social and political analysts among the Bank's staff compared with economists, or in a combination of both. Whatever the causes, it is a critical area of weakness, given the boldness and ambition of the new poverty agenda. For the heart of the matter is that poverty reduction has been low on the domestic political agenda of many poor countries. Moreover, this low priority is often not a mere matter of oversight or neglect. It often is a result of the political and social arrangements inherited at independence from the colonial elite being deliberately retained and expanded as sources of rents for the indigenous elites who currently exercise power. This poses a very difficult problem for a Bank now committed to a poverty-reduction agenda.

It is perhaps not fully appreciated that the poverty-reduction agenda has received high political priority in the now developed countries only at particular historical moments and under well-defined conditions. Research shows that the attitudes of the elite were crucial. They took action on the poverty alleviation issue because they shared a consensus around three beliefs. They were that (i) the welfare of the elite and the welfare of the poor were interdependent, and the elite was not able to insulate itself from the living conditions of the poor; (ii) the poor did in fact have the means to affect the welfare of the elite, principally by three methods, namely crime, insurrection and epidemic disease; and (iii) some actions by the state would be efficacious in reducing the threat to the welfare of the elite posed by the behaviour of the poor (De Swan, 1988). In this context, it is evident that a fundamental scepticism about the capabilities of the state undercuts all efforts to give higher priority to poverty reduction within the political agenda.

If this historical interpretation is correct, then the Bank can only make progress by taking on, with the help of the donors, a quasi-political role. The logic of the situation seems to dictate that the Bank and the donors who subscribe its capital must initiate, and then carry forward as best they can, a participatory process aimed at changing elite perceptions in ways that raise the issue of poverty reduction to a much higher priority in the domestic political agenda. The best of the PAs have been conducted in an elaborately consultative manner, which is the essential groundwork for doing this. But the task now is to push the policy dialogue forward to the point where governments that have not already done so recognise and internalise the three propositions which should trigger their own active engagement with conditions of the poor. Hence our earlier comments about the extension of the Bank's role of evangelist.

It will be essential for the Bank's own credibility in pursuing this quasi-political approach that its own actions be seen to be in line with the policies that it is recommending to borrowing governments. The Bank's own lending programmes will have to have a clear orientation to reducing poverty. Undoubtedly, recent decisions about the future country lending programmes have been in the right direction. Looking at the distribution of total Bank (i.e. IBRD and IDA) lending by sector, loans for human resources development rose from 5 to 15 per cent between the early 1980s and 1991–3. For IDA lending to the poorest countries, the share was higher in 1991–3 at 26 per cent. Looking at investment lending, some 26 percent was within the PTI, i.e. was defined as poverty-alleviating in the fiscal year 1993, compared with 24 per cent in fiscal 1992 when the PTI categorisation was introduced. It could be argued that the Bank itself should not refocus its lending in this way, if it lacks skills in poverty-oriented projects which other donors possess. But this implies a degree of donor coordination that is still all too rare.

Within the sphere of adjustment lending, which is the primary focus of *Aid and Power*, some 24 out of 49 new loans in the fiscal years 1992–3 were defined by the Bank as poverty-focused. This means that just under half of the adjustment loans agreed in the last two years for which figures are available met at least one of the following five criteria. The loan either re-oriented public expenditure in favour of the poor; or it removed distortions or regulations that limited the poor's access to economic opportunities; or it supported safety nets for the most vulnerable; or it helped to gather data on or helped to monitor poverty; or it helped to develop poverty-reduction strategies (World Bank, 1994d: 9–12). The definition of poverty-focused loans here is evidently a broad one, and the unit is the number of loans and not the value of the loans, leaving open the possibility that the value of poverty-focused loans is on average less than the value of other types of loan. Nevertheless, the statistic indicates a considerable departure from the policy concerns of adjustment lending in the 1980s and should be welcomed.

To sum up, the Bank's revived poverty agenda which has been pursued since the publication of the 1990 *World Development Report* must count as the Bank's most heartening initiative since the first edition of *Aid and Power* went to press. During the Presidency of Lewis Preston, the Bank has transformed itself from a tardy follower (or sometimes outright critic) of the poverty agenda into a clear leader of important initiatives being taken worldwide to combat both long-term structural poverty and the conjunctural poverty which arises from shake-outs in the public sector and other adverse effects of particular structural adjustment policies. Even for this edition of *Aid and Power*, it has not been possible to evaluate the effect of this change of direction on levels of poverty. But certainly at the level of inputs, the Bank's project design and use of policy conditions are now much better attuned to the relief of poverty than they ever were before.

PORTFOLIO MANAGEMENT AND THE DRIVE TO THE EAST

Under the Preston presidency a review of the Bank's lending portfolio was set in train. But the real force behind this, as in the matter of structural adjustment lending, was Senior Vice-president (subsequently Managing Director) Ernest Stern. It is hard to be sure what pressures lay behind this move. But perhaps it was not entirely unconnected with the difficulties into which the Bank fell in the late 1980s over the environment issue. Preston's predecessor, Barber Conable, had tried to defuse mounting criticism of the Bank's lending practices by powerful US environmental lobby groups with a promise in 1987 that in future the Bank would do its upmost to ensure that its loans were environmentally friendly (World Bank, 1994b). The critics responded by publicising the loan to the large Narmada project in India that involved considerable population resettlement as a result of a complex irrigation and electricity-generation scheme. They argued that the Bank was breaching its own guidelines and failed to exert sufficient pressure on the borrower to comply with Bank policy on resettlement. This was awkward for the Bank, since India both absorbs substantial Bank finance and is not readily amenable to Bank leverage. While the Bank was not prepared just to pull out of the Narmada project and leave the Indian government in the dock, it decided to set up a general enquiry to identify unsatisfactory projects and failure by borrowers to comply with loan conditions. After the enquiry reported, in early 1993, the Indian government reportedly asked the Bank to withdraw its funding for Narmada.

The portfolio management review itself was carried out under the guidance of Willi Wapenhans, a retiring vice-president, whose report was published under the title *Effective Implementation: Key to Development Impact* (World Bank,

1992d). The startling thing about the Wapenhans Report was not what it said, much of which had been said before by external commentators, but that these same things were now being said and accepted officially by the Bank itself. In Chapter 2, under the heading of 'Lending versus Leverage', *Aid and Power* analysed the tension in the Bank's operations between the pressure to lend and the achievement of the development purposes of the loans, both in relation to investment lending and to adjustment lending. It suggested that better development performance was being inhibited by internal management practices designed to accommodate the pressure to lend. The Wapenhans Report confirmed the accuracy of this diagnosis. It is worth quoting the relevant passage in full.

> However, there are also aspects of Bank practice that either may contribute to portfolio management problems or are insufficiently effective in resolving them. Underlying many of these aspects is the Bank's pervasive preoccupation with new lending. In the eyes of Borrowers and co-lenders as well as staff, the emphasis on timely loan approval (described by some assistance agencies as the 'approval culture') and the often active Bank role in preparation, may connote a promotional – rather than objective – approach to appraisal.
>
> (Wapenhans Report, 1992d: iii)

Following this clear acknowledgement of the lending versus leverage problem, the Report made six principal recommendations, including that 'at appraisal, objective, realistic, experience-based assessments of likely results should supplant optimism and the temptation to promote' proposed loans. The Report also recognised that this would not be possible unless the internal environment of the Bank was changed to become more supportive of better portfolio management performance, including the provision of better recognition and rewards for staff who succeed in these tasks. This in turn requires the entire institution, including the Board of Executive Directors, to become 'pervaded with the necessary values and incentives'. That phrase gives some clue about the scale and difficulty of the transformation that the Report is seeking.

The Wapenhans Report noted 'a gradual but steady deterioration in portfolio performance' between the fiscal years 1981 and 1991 (ibid.: ii). Between those years, the share of projects with 'major problems' as defined by the Operations Evaluation Division increased from 11 to 20 per cent, these problems being especially severe in Africa. This overlaps almost exactly with the period (1980–8) for which *Aid and Power* analysed the impact of structural adjustment lending, and argued that it had indeed helped developing countries 'a little, but not as much as the Bank (had) hoped' (Chapter 9). The improvement of the environment for project implementation was, we argued in Chapter 2, one of the objectives of the Bank when it devised policy-based lending in the late 1970s. The deterioration of the portfolio between 1981 and 1991 is powerful additional evidence that the Bank's hopes in that regard were disappointed. In fact, the Wapenhans Report cites structural adjustment as one of the factors, along with worsening global conditions, that contributed to the decline in the quality of the portfolio. It concluded that 'policy responses (to worsening global conditions), including structural adjustment, have often changed priorities and restrained outlays for public investment programmes' (ibid.: iii).

In the light of that comment, it becomes easier to understand Wapenhans' subsequent criticism of *Aid and Power* for suggesting that the Bank had intended structural adjustment to 'demolish those structures of policy which it blamed ... for the increasing incidence of failure of its projects' (Wapenhans 1994: 37). There was no such hidden agenda, he protests. Given the findings of his own team's Report, it would certainly be less embarrassing for the Bank if he were correct. The original suggestion is, however, maintained in the current edition, based on interviews with other Bank officials. Motives were no doubt mixed. Concern for an improved policy environment for projects was only one stimulus, alongside a desire to push out more money more quickly in accord with the 'approval culture' that the Wapenhans Report subsequently rebuked.

In any case, the central point is that the Bank continues to have difficulty in preserving the quality of its portfolio, and until very recently that difficulty has increased rather than diminished. To the extent that the percentage of problem projects registered a slight decline in fiscal years 1992 and 1993, this was mainly the result of a special portfolio restructuring exercise which led to the closure or cancellation of 115 problem projects in those two years (World Bank, 1994a: 76, n. 5 and n. 6). This included the end of the Bank's involvement with the Narmada project. It is not, therefore, evidence that internal changes designed to curb the 'approval culture' are being effective in raising project quality at the point of entry into the portfolio. They may indeed be, but it is still too early to say.

It is in this context that the Bank's expanded involvement in Eastern Europe and the former Soviet Union must be considered. This substantial eastward thrust – possibly the last extension of its frontier that will ever occur – typifies both the problems and the opportunities that the Bank currently faces. Since 1990, Bank lending to the region has been running at about $4 billion a year. Just under 30 per cent of Bank lending to Eastern Europe and Central Asia consists of sectoral and structural adjustment loans. This is a high proportion, compared with the average for all regions. Investment lending has been directed to the energy sector (22 per cent), transport and agriculture (10 per cent each). The largest borrowers have been Poland (28 per cent), Russia (21 per cent, including an enormous $600 million rehabilitation loan made in August 1992) and Hungary (12 per cent) (Wallich, 1994).

All of this lending is on near-commercial IBRD terms. But, in many cases, the borrowers are countries which at the end of the 1980s had already taken on as much external debt as they could prudently afford. The adding of a new burden of debt service on top of existing obligations makes it imperative that adjustment takes place quickly, or countries may fall into repayments arrears. In late 1994, the fate of these adjustment efforts was in the balance. Only Poland, Albania and the Czech Republic had returned to positive growth. The Bank is limited both legally and politically in what it can do to revive the private sector and remove international obstacles to the growth of the region's exports. It could therefore be argued that it risks being sucked into the quicksand of underwriting other lenders' rescheduling operations, as it was in South America in the 1980s. Worse than this, poverty has sharply increased in Eastern Europe, contrary to the experience of China and other non-European transitional economies, as brilliantly documented by Cornia (1994). Whereas ten years ago Bank staff might have brushed aside such a trend as a blip, in the 1990s they could not and would not wish to do so.

In 1994 the Bank's commitments to the whole of Europe and Central Asia since 1990 amounted to about $16 billion, of which rather more than half remained to be disbursed. Since the Bank's entire portfolio was $148 billion, it is clear that dangers are prospective rather than immediate. Much depends on how lending to other regions is handled. For example, will an effort be made to repackage IBRD finance more imaginatively, so that it will continue to be attractive to highly creditworthy countries like Thailand and South Korea, which otherwise might be inclined to move away to other sources? Even without new loans, such countries will disappear from the portfolio only gradually, since the average remaining terms of their existing loans is quite long. So they will continue to balance the Bank's portfolio, albeit on a slowly declining basis, for many years to come. Also, it is easy to forget that 30 years ago the decision to start lending to South Korea looked about as risky as the decision to lend today to some of the countries of Eastern Europe and the former Soviet Union.

The Bank has admitted that the risks associated with its loans to borrowers who are at an early and difficult stage of transition to a market economy are 'significant' because of the 'institutional and economic flux' which characterises them (World Bank, 1994a: 77 and 106). But that is only one aspect of the problem: there is another. It is the geopolitical importance of region itself, especially to the single largest shareholder of the Bank, the United States. In *Aid and Power*, previous attempts by the US to pressure the Bank to make unsound loans for political reasons in Latin America (especially to Argentina in 1988) were noted. It seems highly probable that similar pressure both already has been, and will continue to be, exerted in favour of more lending to Eastern Europe and Central Asia, as a means of calming political turbulence. To its credit, the Bank has often tried to resist such pressures. But the Bank's need for US government support for General Capital Increases and the replenishment of IDA is a powerful weapon which has proved its effectiveness in the past. The G7 countries have already successfully exerted pressure to step up loans to Russia for this reason, leading to complaints from other borrowers in the region that they are being treated less favourably (Wallich, 1994: 55). In fact, disbursements to Russia have been much lower than commitments. But a doubt remains about the adequacy of the Wapenhans reforms to protect the Bank against future pressure of this kind.

BROADER INSTITUTIONAL ISSUES

In its *drang nach Osten* since 1990, the Bank has worked closely with the IMF. This is a reflection of the general improvement in Bank–Fund working relations which began in the mid-1980s and was more or less consolidated by 1989. The occasion of this consolidation was the aftermath of the 1988 Argentinian loan just mentioned. It had been made despite the Fund's unwillingness to agree a new stand-by arrangement with Argentina. The Fund's judgement was vindicated a few months later when Argentina failed to deliver the changes in fiscal policy which had been the condition of the Bank's loan. As a result, Ministers of the Group of Ten demanded and secured a new and stricter Enhanced Collaboration Agreement between the Bank and the Fund.

The term 'convergence' has been used to describe the trajectories of the two Bretton Woods institutions. This is useful in indicating that the Fund's invention in the 1980s of its Structural Adjustment Facility and its Extended Structural Adjustment Facility (SAF and ESAF) involve it in financial activities which are scarcely distinguishable from the Bank's structural adjustment lending. But the idea of 'convergence' becomes misleading if it obscures the fact that the Fund continues to do many other things besides manage SAF and ESAF and that each institution retains its distinct mode of working. While a formal reconciliation of the two institutions' separate policy models has been done, it has had no impact in unifying their individual analytical perspectives. The Fund applies its stabilisation prescriptions more uniformly than the Bank applies its structural adjustment prescriptions. The Fund continues to maintain a harder form of policy conditionality than does the Bank. The consolidation of Bank–Fund relations is as much a matter of delineating spheres of influence and avoiding transgression of mutually agreed boundaries, as it is of convergence.

The Fund for its part has recognised that structural reforms help to make macroeconomic stabilisation sustainable, and is ready to make sympathetic noises about mitigating the social costs of adjustment, although in practice very little follows from this new rhetoric. Meanwhile, the Bank has accepted the absolute priority of stabilisation and has scaled back its own work on macroeconomics in order to leave the Fund a clear run in this policy area. This division of labour has been maintained by increasing the number of joint Bank–Fund country missions, leading to more shared assessments of country policy packages, often embodied in Policy Framework Papers. The experience of working together in Eastern Europe and the former Soviet Union has helped to reinforce the Bank's agreement that stabilisation had to be undertaken before anything else could be done.

The complaints of the developing countries against Bank–Fund cross-conditionality in adjustment lending have largely gone unheeded. Both Fund and Bank have continued to avoid formal cross-conditionality, in the sense of incorporation of conditions agreed between the borrowing government and the other institution into its own agreements. The sole exception is that neither will lend when arrears are owing to the other. Each has to do this to prevent its own debt from being rescheduled. But informal or indirect cross-conditionality has not only survived but has intensified as the Fund and the Bank have worked harder to define a joint package of policy advice, and as third parties have increasingly looked to performance criteria set by the Fund and the Bank as the trigger for their own lending.

Such informal cross-conditionality, although often supported and attacked as a matter of principle, is not right or wrong in principle. Its rightness depends on whether it is applied to a policy condition that is itself right. Many of the policy conditions to which it is applied will be right beyond a peradventure. The danger lies, as was argued in *Aid and Power*, in the excessive multiplication of policy conditions and the use of informal cross-conditionality to enforce large aggregated policy packages, many of whose conditions will be right but some of which will be wrong. Rather than the outlawing of cross-conditionality, what is needed is a self-denying ordinance to limit its use to a small number of crucial policy reforms whose benefits are as unambiguous as possible.

Simple observation would seem to bear out the view that opinion about appropriate economic policies for developing countries is now less divided and narrower in range than it was one or two decades ago. Consensus on this question has increased, as a result both of sustained debate and of world events. At the same time, it is contrary to the spirit of this emerging consensus to try and capture truth once and for all in the ten points of a Washington Consensus or a Universal Convergence or whatever. The small number of crucial policy reforms whose benefits are as unambiguous as possible cannot be taken lock, stock and barrel from lists such as these, however convenient it might be to believe otherwise. Successful economic policy-making is the art of applying complex analytical insights to particular complex circumstances, and it is mischievous nonsense to suggest that this can be reduced to following a short recipe. Such lists may give broad indications of policy areas where policy action is appropriate, and even desirable directions of change in many cases. But it is a long way from this to the definition of policy conditions that will unambiguously benefit a specific economy. Bridging that gap will always be a special act of economic skill tempered, hopefully, by prudence and pragmatism.

Although the range of the debate on development policy has undoubtedly narrowed, one important dissenting voice has made itself heard within the narrower range. Japan has discovered its voice within the Bank, and one element of its message is scepticism about the efficacy of policy-based lending. In 1993, Japan's Overseas Economic Cooperation Fund published its thoughts about adjustment lending in its Occasional Paper No. 1 entitled *Issues Related to the World Bank's Approach to Structural Adjustment: Proposals from a Major Partner* (OECF, 1993). This argued in favour of infant industry protection and of credit subsidies for selected industries that are believed to have export potential, in opposition to the Bank's approach of blanket liberalisation. The Japanese government also proposed and financed a research study by the Bank on the causes of the very rapid economic growth in Japan and its neighbouring region, which was published as *The East Asian Miracle* (World Bank, 1993).

A major motive behind both of these initiatives was to persuade the Bank to admit to the weakness of the empirical reasoning underlying its claim that state intervention in the markets of developing countries acts to undermine economic performance. The Japanese government was anxious to demonstrate that the hypergrowth experienced in the Far East since World War II was associated with a significant measure of state control over the economies of Taiwan, South Korea, and more recently also of Thailand and Indonesia, involving precisely the methods of performance-contingent state support commended in the OECF's Occasional Paper (Chang 1993; Wade, 1990; Amsden, 1989). The discrepancy between the historical record of the most successful developing countries and the Bank's advice to poor countries to continue along the path of liberalisation (in, for example, World Bank, 1994c: 184 and 192) was something which the Japanese government was extremely keen to expose to public scrutiny. This keenness had more than intellectual motives. It also served to vindicate and protect the time-honoured Japanese practice of providing soft loans to leading sectors of developing economies through its aid programme.

The awakening of the sleeping Japanese giant has by no means compelled the World Bank – yet – into major departures from its approach to economic policy reform. The *East Asian Miracle* study, in the version that was finally approved for publication by the Bank, endorsed selective state intervention only for export promotion. It argued explicitly against import protection and credit market interventions of the East Asian type being applied in other developing economies, arguments which the OECF have again contested (World Bank, 1993: 20–3; OECF, 1993b: 5–6). Nevertheless, this episode has cast further doubt on the rightness of the Bank's policy advice, and of the Washington Consensus which stands behind it. Most now agree that it will be far from easy to assemble in very poor countries all of the elements which made selective state intervention effective in the Far East. But the proposition that only one technology of economic reform exists is one that can no longer be seriously sustained.

Japanese assertiveness on the design of policy-based lending can be placed in the context of changes in the balance of power among the leading developed country shareholders of the Bank. In 1991 Japan overtook the United States as the world's main aid donor. Although Japan's share of votes in the IBRD and IDA was by 1993 still only 7 and 10 per cent compared with 17 and 16 per cent respectively for the US, that share has in recent years gradually increased with each relative increase in Japan's financial support for the Bank. As is often said, the Bank is not a 'democratic' institution, but the balance of power as between different stakeholders does change over time according to their financial contributions. In turn, this can be expected to have some effect on the way in which the Bank balances between its different roles.

But Japanese frustration with economic liberalisation policies as the core of structural adjustment also points to another less visible structural problem of the Bank. It is that all stakeholders collectively have difficulty in governing the top management of the Bank. Chapter 2 of *Aid and Power* recounts the reluctance of the Board of Executive Directors to support the move to policy-based lending, and the success of top management in making the move anyway. The weakness of the Board in relation to top management has continued. This is due partly to the size of the Board. Its membership of 24, at double the original size of 12, is too large and unwieldy for effective decision-making. Executive Directors stay in the job for very short periods, so that no sooner have they understood the job than they leave. Their work is mainly that of scrutinising a large number of individual loan proposals, leaving little time for resolving strategic issues.

The limitations of the Board as an instrument of effective governance of the Bank are thus structural in character. They would act as effective constraints even in the absence of other factors which also push in the same direction. Some have noted a decline in the stature of those appointed as Executive Directors. Insiders to the Bank have also commented on the tactics used by top management to baffle strategic intervention by the Board. Noteworthy in this connection is top management's 'mushroom treatment' of the Executive Board – that is, keeping them in the dark and feeding them garbage (*Financial Times*, 28.9.94). Even supposing that such imputations are unfair and unwarranted, the problem of governance would remain serious.

These structural weaknesses of governance go some way to explain the way in which the Bank has developed. Unable to focus on a clear strategy which is based on assigning priorities to different goals, the Bank has tended to add to its ambitions and respond to problems simply by promising more and different outputs. The Bank has an increasing tendency to try to address all the world's problems – gender discrimination, environmental degradation, governance, militarism, human rights and so on. There is an uncomfortable truth in the jibe that 'the way that history is moving, the way the institution is playing its cards, the Bank is the prime candidate for the Ministry of Everything Else' in a future global technocratic government (George and Sabelli, 1994: 160–1). Will the Bank prove itself able to be sufficiently selective in its interventions to keep them manageable enough to deliver the 'on the ground results' which the Wapenhans Report calls for? It would be the unhappiest irony if the Bank, which has railed so long and loud against over-extended government, cannot find a way to avoid over-extending itself.

Following through on each new goal increases its internal rules and guidelines at a geometrical rate. Continued management in this style can only lead to a creeping form of operational paralysis, because it will become impossible to list all the appropriate checklists, let alone comply with them. The implication of this diagnosis is that, unless the Bank's shareholders find a way of cutting into the present organisation of the Bank and reforming its governance, not only will conflicts between the Bank's four main roles multiply, but also the effectiveness with which the Bank performs all of them will decline. Since, for all its deficiencies, the Bank is still the best of the multilateral development institutions, this is an outcome which no-one concerned with world development could reasonably welcome.

Part I

BACKGROUND

1

WORLD DEVELOPMENT AND INTERNATIONAL FINANCE SINCE 1970

1.1 INTRODUCTION

Aid and power is our theme. We are interested in assessing the power which international organisations dispensing concessional development finance can exert over the domestic decisions of developing countries. Developing countries, like countries generally, are jealous of their political sovereignty. In practical terms this means that they wish their governments to exercise full independent control over all major policy decisions, unless that control is willingly and voluntarily delegated to others. They do not wish to lose the independence which they have gained relatively recently, sometimes after having to resort to an armed struggle against colonising powers. In the immediate aftermath of decolonisation, most leaders of newly independent nations saw intuitively that political independence could be consolidated only if they could preserve substantial control over the economic forces that can be used to subvert it – the trading companies operating from ex-colonising countries, foreign investors whose priorities care little for national development aspirations, and the domestic economic interests whose resources and ambitions were strengthened by their close foreign connections. The notion of economic independence as the final guarantor of political independence gained ground. Many developing countries adopted a set of regulations governing trade, industrial investment and money and credit whose broad thrust reflected their perceived vulnerability as both political ex-colonies and economic late developers. Weakness, both real and perceived, was the origin of the wide spread in the developing world of the policies of economic nationalism.

In the 1980s, the economic weakness of many (but not all) developing countries has been vividly demonstrated by events. At the same time, the economic policies of nationalism have come under growing challenge. As we shall see, there are some analysts who connect these two in a single theory of cause and effect. Economic nationalism had led to incorrect economic policy, they say, and this had caused the poor economic performance. It was therefore both predictable and right that bad policies should be challenged at a time when economic outcomes were disappointing. This is not a perspective which the present authors share. We do not believe that economic nationalism is necessarily irrational; nor that policy errors were the major source of developing countries' economic distress; nor that it is always obvious that policies focused on liberalisation and widening the scope for the operation of market forces are sufficient to improve economic performance – or that, in some circumstances, they will not make it worse.

But, increasingly, conventional wisdom has come to deprecate such doubts. International organisations like the World Bank – which is the major focus for this study – came to see liberalisation and the release of market forces as the key to unlocking the future development prospects of the developing countries. Further, instead of relying merely on dialogue and the force of rational persuasion to advance the application of these ideas, the Bank, in co-operation with other international organisations (like the International Monetary Fund), decided to make an initially small, but now growing proportion of its new lending to developing countries conditional on their changing their economic policies to those favoured by the Bank and the Fund. The emergence of policy-based lending in the 1980s as a tool for reforming the policies of economic nationalism is the particular subject of this study. We shall discuss not only the adoption and refinement of this form of aid and the reasons why some developing countries have accepted it while others have either not accepted it or not been offered it. We shall also try and examine the factors which influence whether or not the agreed policy changes are in fact made, and perhaps most important of all, whether economic performance has actually improved because of the implementation of agreed policy changes. To the extent that the consequences are good, doubts about the modalities diminish.

But first it is necessary to describe the economic background against which the Bank decided to link its loans with policy reform; and also the intellectual background out of which the Bank's preferred policies for economic development were distilled.

1.2   THE INTERNATIONAL ECONOMIC CONTEXT

What was the international economic context within which this innovation in aid-giving was developed? Is it plausible to represent domestic policy failures as the major cause of the economic problems of developing countries in the 1980s? To throw some light on these questions, let us begin by looking at some key indicators of developing and industrial country performance over the period 1965–92, set out in Table 1.1.

4

Table 1.1 Economic performance of developing and industrial
countries, 1965–92
(annual average percentage change)

	1965–73	1973–80	1980–92
Developing countries			
Real GDP	6.5	5.4	2.8
Low -income countries	5.5	4.6	5.9
Middle-income countries	7.0	5.7	1.7
Oil exporters	6.9	6.0	0.8
Exporters of manufactures	7.4	6.0	6.0
Highly-indebted countries	6.9	5.4	1.0
Sub-Saharan Africa	6.4	3.2	2.2
Industrial countries			
Real GDP	4.7	2.8	1.6

Source: Adapted from World Bank, *World Development Report* 1994, Appendix Tables 1 and 25.

The evidence of growth rate statistics shows that the whole of this period has been one of the gradual deceleration of growth in almost all parts of the world. The only significant exception was in China and the countries of South and South-East Asia in the 1980s. Within this general deceleration of growth, two aspects are worth noting. One is that the developing countries have consistently grown faster than the industrial countries by a margin of nearly 2 percentage points of growth, shrinking to 1.2 as the deceleration proceeded. The other is that within the developing countries, the dispersion of growth rates has widened, with sub-Saharan African economies actually contracting in the early 1980s while China and India were improving on their historic growth performances. The differences in the rates of population growth between countries are included in Table 1.2 to give statistics of real GDP per capita. Once this is done, the picture changes in two ways. The faster growth of real GDP in developing countries is by and large cancelled out by their faster population growth, so that the growth of real income per head no longer differs much between the developing and the industrial world. Apart from that, the effect is to show that real income per head contracted in other parts of the developing world as well as sub-Saharan Africa. Highly-indebted middle income countries and oil-exporters also suffered declines, although not so severely, in the period 1980–92.

The twenty-year-long slow-down of world economic growth is best understood in terms of two critical events. These are the two great oil price rises of 1973 and 1979–80 and the consequent debt crisis which erupted in 1982. They are linked together in a single chain of turbulent events. The governments of the industrial countries allowed an expansion of aggregate demand that provoked a strong bout of inflation in the industrial world in 1972–3, which in turn triggered off a brief boom in non-oil primary commodities in 1972–4.

Table 1.2 Growth of GDP per capita, 1965–92
(average annual percentage change)

	1965–73	1973–80	1980–92
Developing countries	3.9	3.2	0.9
Low-income countries	2.9	2.5	3.9
Middle-income countries	4.4	3.3	−0.1
Oil exporters	4.3	3.2	−1.8
Exporters of manufactures	4.8	4.1	4.3
Highly-indebted countries	4.2	2.9	−1.0
Sub-Saharan Africa	3.6	0.3	−0.8
Industrial countries	3.7	2.1	2.3

Source: Extracted from World Bank, *World Development Report* 1994, Table 2.6.

The organisation of Petroleum Exporting Countries (OPEC) took advantage of the prevailing shortage psychology to raise the price of petroleum threefold. This shock cut back real growth of output in OECD countries, although inflationary conditions persisted until the end of the decade. A further tripling of the oil price in 1979–80 pushed the OECD economies towards serious recession. At the same time, the arrival of conservatively inclined governments determined to squeeze inflation out of the world system at any cost in terms of unemployment reinforced the already strong recessionary tendencies. Negative, or very slow growth persisted in the industrial countries until the real oil price (which had been eroding slowly because of remaining inflation) finally retreated to a more realistic level in 1986 – see Table 1.3.

On top of all this, a huge debt crisis erupted in 1982. This was a direct consequence of the decision by OECD governments to leave the intermediation of the large OPEC balance of payments surpluses, caused by the oil price rises, to the private banking system. The recycling of these surpluses was believed wrongly to be a profitable (because riskless) form of lending, because the borrowers were mainly Third World governments who would never willingly default on sovereign debt, however the loan money was actually invested. The bankers were right in the sense that no Third World government has formally defaulted on what it borrowed in the 1973–82 period. They were wrong in the sense that few of these loans have been serviced in accordance with their original terms, and so many have had to be written off or very heavily discounted in the banks' portfolios. If the bankers failed to forecast the results of their lending decisions, so did the borrowing governments fail to foresee the results of their borrowing decisions. At the time, it seemed to them that they were getting access to cheap money, vital to bridge growing balance of payments gaps and unlikely to cause them serious repayments problems. Many allowed the money to be spent without much attention to the question of whether the

6

Table 1.3 Change in export prices and terms of trade, 1965–92
(average annual percentage change)

Country group	1965–73	1973–80	1980–5	1986	1987–92
Export prices					
Low- and middle-income economies	6.1	14.8	–4.3	–8.3	..
Manufactures	6.4	8.2	–3.7	9.4	..
Food	5.9	8.6	–4.1	7.2	..
Non-food	4.6	10.2	–4.9	0.0	..
Metals and minerals	2.5	4.7	–4.5	–4.8	..
Fuels	8.0	26.2	–4.1	–46.7	..
High-income OECD members					
Total	4.8	10.3	–3.1	12.0	..
Manufactures	4.6	10.8	–2.8	19.6	..
Terms of trade					
Low- and middle-income economies	0.1	2.6	–2.0	–9.3	–5.0
Low-income economies	–4.8	4.0	–1.1	–16.8	–10.0
Middle-income economies	1.7	2.1	–2.4	–6.7	–2.0
Sub-Saharan Africa	–8.5	5.0	–2.3	–23.2	–12.0
East Asia	–0.6	1.2	–0.6	–7.0	3.0
South Asia	3.7	–3.4	1.7	2.8	–9.0
Europe, Middle East, and North Africa	..	..	..	..	..
Latin America and the Caribbean	3.9	2.4	–1.9	–14.0	–5.0
17 highly indebted countries	1.4	3.5	–1.3	–13.7	–8.0
High-income economies	–1.2	–2.0	–0.4	8.7	–1.0
OECD members	–1.0	–3.3	–0.2	12.4	..
Oil exporters	0.3	9.6	–2.2	–47.5	..

Source: World Bank, *World Development Report 1994*, appendix tables.

'investment' would create a surplus, and whether that surplus could be realized as additional foreign exchange for debt service. They, too, were spectacularly wrong.

What brought these mutual miscalculations out into the open at the beginning of 1980 was the course of real interest rates. The years 1979–80 saw the arrival in office in the major industrialised countries of political parties of the right, convinced – or claiming to be convinced – of the simple proposition that inflation can be manipulated by the control of the money supply. In the UK, the USA and the Federal Republic of Germany in quick succession, new administrations arrived with the aim of putting this monetarist doctrine into speedy and effective practice. The reining back of the money supply implied a rise in nominal interest rates, and this certainly occurred, as shown in Table 1.4. But this coincided with the effect of the second 1979 oil price shock which itself was having a powerful effect in undermining demand and economic activity. So the policy-induced monetary contraction came on top of the existing deflationary

Table 1.4 Interest rates, 1965–86

	1965–73	1973–80	1980–6
Nominal interest rate[1]	6.8	9.3	11.1
Inflation rate[2]	6.1	10.1	1.7
Real interest rate[3]	2.3	1.3	5.9

Notes: 1 Average annual rate.
       2 Industrial countries' GDP deflator expressed in dollars.
       3 Average 6-month dollar-Eurocurrency rate deflated by the US GDP deflator.
Source: World Bank, *World Development Report 1987*, Table 2.5 (adapted).

impact of an oil price at $30 a barrel. The inflation rate as well as the growth of real output fell dramatically.

The economic crisis of the 1980s, which was the most serious world economic setback since the Depression of the 1930s, spread through the Third World by a variety of channels. Those Third World countries who had borrowed heavily the recycled petro-dollars had done so at *variable* interest rates. When nominal interest rates remained low relative to inflation, this borrowing was cheap in real terms: for some periods in the 1970s, real interest rates were negative, so the borrowers were being paid to borrow, rather than having to pay for their borrowing. But the combination of a rising nominal interest rate with a falling rate of inflation (consequent on slower growth plus monetary restriction) created an alarming increase in the real cost of borrowing. It was this, in the deteriorating economic conditions of the early 1980s, that the Third World debtors had to pay contractually, but could not pay in fact.

The reason that they could not pay was that the prices of almost all developing country exports began falling, as indicated in Table 1.3. Under the impact of recession in the industrial countries and a much higher oil price, their terms of trade, which had remained broadly favourable in the 1970s, began a sharp decline. Declining terms of trade combined with higher (and unexpected) financial outflows for debt service constituted sources of acute pressure on developing countries' balances of payments. The widening payments deficits either had to be financed, or their economies had to be adjusted in order to bring demand for foreign exchange into better balance with the decreased supply.

What were the sources of balance of payments finance? Table 1.5 presents the picture of external financing flows for the period 1973–86. Before the first oil shock in 1973, official development assistance (i.e., foreign aid, both bilateral and from multilateral aid donors like the World Bank) provided the principal means of bridging developing countries' balance of payments deficits. Between 1973 and the early 1980s when the debt crisis broke, the principal source of external finance became private

Table 1.5   External financing by type of flow, 1973–86
(billions of dollars)

	1973	1980	1986
Developing countries[1]			
Deficit on goods, services and			
private transfers[2]	9.0	69.1	35.5
Official development			
assistance (net)	8.7	22.8	21.7
of which: Grants	4.7	11.5	14.1
Concessional loans	4.0	11.3	7.6
Direct private investment	4.9	10.0	12.4
Non-concessional loans (net)	11.6	47.0	18.1
of which: Private	9.6	30.0	13.3
Official	2.0	9.0	4.8
Other capital	−5.0	1.6	−0.7

Note: 1   Based on a sample of 90 developing countries.
    2   Difference between the deficit figure and the sum of external finance results in changes in foreign reserves.
Source: World Bank, *World Development Report 1987*, extracted from Table 2.9.

non-concessional loans, the petro-dollars on-lent by the private commercial banks. Once the debt crisis arrived in 1982, however, this source of funding dried up overnight for all developing countries that were already highly indebted. By 1986, as Table 1.5 shows, it had fallen back to one-third of its 1980 level, with new flows directed to countries like India which had remained creditworthy through the 1970s. But foreign aid was not able to expand to fill the financing gap created by falling levels of new bank lending. The new governments in the lending industrialised countries began cutting foreign aid, as an easy target in the campaign for greater fiscal tightness, so that the expansion of aid from other industrial countries such as Japan and Italy was necessary merely to keep the aggregate flows roughly constant. In the 1980s, then, the global economic context placed a premium on finding ways of bringing down developing countries' payments deficits to the level that could be financed by stagnant aid flows plus rapidly dwindling private commercial lending. In essence, that is what 'structural adjustment' of the developing countries' economies is intended to do.

1.3   THE INTELLECTUAL BACKGROUND

The same bout of inflation in the OECD countries in 1972–3 which paved the way for the first oil price shock also sparked off what turned out to be a major reversal of academic perceptions and political attitudes. In the late

1960s, monetarism was still a somewhat esoteric cult among academic economists, although the work of Milton Friedman in the United States was a little better known than was that of his followers like Alan Walters in the UK. The mid-1970s saw a vigorous public debate among economists, economic journalists, political pundits and politicians about the possibilities of macro-economic regulation by means of money supply control. Inflation gradually eclipsed unemployment in the ranking of economic problems, and reliance on variations of monetary manipulation came to be seen as superior to the attempt to fine-tune aggregate demand by fiscal means. The mission of the International Monetary Fund (IMF) to the UK in 1976 raised the salience of monetarist approaches to economic policy, and between 1976 and 1980, the need for monetarism became a major campaign plank of conservative oppositions.

Enclosed in the monetary versus fiscal policy debate was the idea that government should not attempt to do too much by way of economic management. The control of the money supply (which had not been seriously attempted as such for forty years) was presented as a simpler and more straightforward policy task than the familiar methods of fiscal demand management. It is not at all clear that this is true, but the assertion indicates the spirit of the times – a weariness with complexities and multiple and conflicting responsibilities for governments. Fiscal demand management was a tricky business, and could be used counter-cyclically, exaggerating booms and slumps instead of smoothing them out. But this was in fact as much to do with the politicians of all parties creating a political business cycle for electoral advantage as it was with the inherent difficulty of such a style of management. However, one important difficulty, long vaguely perceived, was not formalised in economic theory – the problem of countervailing action. Economic agents can and do react to government fiscal stimulation and dampening in ways that neutralise its effects. Keynesian demand management works best with passive economic agents; once they have learned the rules of the game they will play it for all it is worth to them, and its initial effectiveness will be eroded. This was an important point to clarify, even if one finds the assumption of fully rational economic expectations incredible (Killick, 1989: 11).

The breaking up of the consensus around neo-Keynesian macroeconomics in the 1970s spilled over into debates about the validity and utility of development economics. This was, at one level at least, quite odd because logical similarities between macroeconomics and development economics were not very great, the latter having been conceived beyond and outside the conventional neo-Keynesian schema. Nevertheless, such similarities as could be found or invented by ingenious minds, such as those of Harry G. Johnson or Peter Bauer, were duly flourished and criticised. A fetish about physical investment, over-reliance on central planning, and a mistaken analysis of the underemployment of labour and its transfer out of agriculture were some of the 'Keynesian' features of development economics which were identified in order to be condemned. The mood of disenchantment with neo-Keynesianism did not come only from economists of neo-liberal persuasion. It was shared by others, like Dudley Seers, who wanted a more structural, disaggregated analysis in order to tackle problems of maldistribution of income, poverty and inadequate employment. But, in the end, the effect of the discrediting of neo-Keynesian ideas in the development debate was to open the way for the neo-liberals to establish their agenda and their policy preferences. These were eagerly picked up when the political mood decisively shifted to the right at the end of the 1970s.

What then was the neo-liberal agenda and what were its policy preferences? Any attempt to summarise them into one coherent and consistent package is bound to be misleading, and invite cries of 'straw man'. Even with much lengthier presentations than are possible here, such as Toye (1987) or Colclough and Manor (1990), no attempt at definition will succeed in making adequate allowance for all the complex variants which are to be found. But since one may as well be hung for a sheep as for a lamb, let us suggest that neo-liberals have a strong policy preference for economic liberalisation. This implies the roll-back of the state, both in terms of its ownership of industries, financial institutions and marketing agencies and of its regulatory activities in trade, industry, agriculture, credit and foreign investment. The economic arguments centre on the failure of the state to create the right system of incentives for an efficiently operating economy. This is sometimes expressed as the state's preference for macroeconomic policy instruments which are exercised at the expense of microeconomic rationality. The corrective measures are then privatisation and extensive deregulation, recommended in the belief that freely operating markets will conduce to the more efficient use of the scarce resources of poor countries.

This efficiency argument was augmented at times by various equity arguments. Lipton's (1977) account of urban bias was incorporated to suggest that liberalisation would merely counteract the existing engineered economic biases in favour of a richer 'urban class'. Poor peasants in the rural areas would gain from liberalisation, while parasitic urban rent-seekers would find their incomes being levelled down. Thus the income distribution would become more equal and greater efficiency go hand in hand with greater equity. Another similar argument for this congruence suggested that the poor (whether rural or urban) suffered most from rapid or accelerating inflation and from the widespread existence of parallel markets. The poor were seen as relatively more vulnerable to economic instability and market distortion: less able to defend the real value of their incomes and less adept at parallel transactions. 'Hard' and 'soft' liberalisers were united in their general approach to economic policy. The 'soft' approach was to add equity reasons to efficiency reasons by way of justification. The 'hard' approach was not to bother. But in either case, proposals for government interventions to protect the vulnerable during the process of stabilisation and adjustment fell on deaf ears. That whole agenda had to be politically relaunched by UNICEF and others in the mid-1980s, after being sunk without trace by the neo-liberals at the end of the 1970s.

Such strong antipathy to the role of the state in economic development rested in part on nothing more intellectual than a populist gut prejudice. A strong undercurrent of anxiety about the implementation performance of the state had run through the literature on economic planning from the early 1970s and even before (e.g. Lewis, 1966: 100; Faber and Seers, 1972). Accumulating disappointments, as developing country governments implemented plans and projects cack-handedly and then seemed to lapse into near inertia as the external economic turbulence strengthened, fed an anti-statist mood. At first this went largely untheorised, except by Marxist writers. Economists stretched the apparatus of welfare economics to try and prove the proposition that government interventions in the economy would necessarily produce worse results in terms of welfare than leaving matters to be determined by free markets. Such a strong conclusion could not, in fact, legitimately be extracted from such a weak technique. Nevertheless, so strong was the anti-state mood that many intelligent people swallowed it. 'Market failure is better than government failure' became a byword of the liberalisation school.

We have already noted that one pattern to be found in world development during the 1970s was the growing disparity in the economic performance and achievement of developing countries. The newly industrialising countries (NICs) of South Korea, Taiwan, Hong Kong, Singapore and Brazil had shown growth rates of manufactured output and exports in double digits in the 1970–7 period. Whatever one might think about the quality of the growth by criteria of labour conditions, environmental stress and equitable income distribution, it was clear that these NICs had escaped from economic stagnation with a vengeance. By contrast, most of sub-Saharan Africa was lapsing into economic stagnation (see Table 1.2) with investment and per capita income levels actually falling in many countries. It was natural that neo-liberals should claim the successes of the NICs as proof of the efficacy of liberalisation, and the failures of sub-Saharan Africa as evidence of the deadening effect of excessively powerful states. It was equally natural that this should be strongly contested, because there is indeed plentiful evidence that governments of the NICs possess and exercise strong powers of direction over their economies. Their success is due to the sophisticated and economically intelligent manner in which this is done. They are not, and never have been, models of a *laissez-faire* approach (World Bank, 1993). Thus empirical case studies, no more than the theory of welfare, economics, provided the intellectual underpinning which the neo-liberals sought. Something grander and more robust than either was called for, a new whole social science paradigm based on applying economic methods to the study of politics.

1.4 A DIGRESSION ON THE NEW POLITICAL ECONOMY

This New Political Economy of development uses the assumptions of neo-classical microeconomics − methodological individualism, rational utility maximisation and the comparative statics method of equilibrium analysis − to explain the failure of governments to adopt the 'right', i.e. neo-liberal, economic policies for growth and development. In this way, neo-liberalism presents not merely 'a body of settled conclusions immediately applicable to policy', but also, in the form of the New Political Economy (NPE), an account of *why* its own prescriptions over the previous forty years of the practice of development have until recently found so little political favour. At their most ambitious the neo-liberals strive for the unification of economics and politics − both in normative and in positive modes under the banner of rational choice theory (Grindle, 1989).

The NPE takes a profoundly cynical view of the state in developing countries. To say, as exponents of the NPE do, that people in political positions are typically motivated *only* by individual self-interest is, and should be, shocking. However one defines the public interest, and however much scope one grants to the protection of private interests as part of the definition of the public interest, the unbridled pursuit of self-interest by rulers belongs to the pathology of politics − to tyranny or dictatorship or, ultimately, to anarchy.[1] To attribute individual self-interest as their exclusive motive to politicians in developing countries is to deny their sincerity, their merit and, ultimately, their legitimate right to govern. While this is appropriate criticism for particular rulers or regimes, in the developing no less than in the developed areas of the world, as a general characterisation of the state in developing countries, it is breathtaking in its scope and pretension. The NPE is not merely saying unflattering things about Third World politicians − that they are misguided, myopic, or cowardly. Its claims are much more extreme: that their unbridled egoism makes them constitutionally unfit for any political role whatsoever.

The political hypotheses of the NPE are too cynical, too extreme, and it is this extremism which creates the second major feature of the NPE, its pessimism. For the major prediction of the new political economy in its positive mode must be that significant changes towards the 'right' neo-liberal policies will not, or will hardly ever, take place. Where the interests of rulers and ruled conflict, personally self-interested politicians will not make arrangements which secure the legitimate interests of citizens. In the absence of a natural harmony of interests, rulers serve themselves better by using their power to exploit others, and political arrangements which limit rulers' pursuit of self-interest are the only constraint on this exploitation. If such arrangements do not exist or have been subverted – which is the scenario in developing countries, according to the NPE – then the adoption of 'good' policies becomes an impossible dream. An inherent inability to implement policies that are taken to be obviously socially desirable amounts to more than just gloom about the prospects for reform. It is much more deterministic and much more pessimistic than this. It is (as it has been dubbed elsewhere) 'an economistic hypothesis of equilibrium unhappiness' – or an EHEU theory (Toye, 1987: 122–7). The same point is made by Grindle (1989: 31–2), who states that:

> while the new political economy provides tools for understanding bad situations and for recommending policies that will engender better situations, it provides no logically apparent means of moving from bad to better. . . . Locked into an ahistorical explanation of why things are the way they are and the notion that existing situations demonstrate an inevitable rationality, it is hard to envisage how changes in such situations occur.

In an interdependent world with an unequal distribution of political power, it is only to be expected that some of the dynamics of policy changes in poor, developing countries will be international in character. But the NPE typically pays much less attention to international influences on public policy in less developed countries (LDCs) than to national influences. Its frame of reference for analysis is the individual developing country. This is either analysed as a unitary entity, as in theories of 'the predatory state' (or 'the Leviathan state') which has its own rational self-interest; or as an arena in which outcomes result from the pursuit of rational self-interest by individual LDC politicians, bureaucrats and other actors. In the best examples of the NPE, for example Repetto's analysis of irrigation projects (Moore, in Colclough and Manor, 1990: Chapter 14) other actors do include international influences like multinational construction companies and international aid agencies. But this is not usually the case. The international actors are kept typically beyond the framework of analysis. The desirable policies are desirable domestic policies for developing country governments. Usually no complementary policy changes are demanded by NPE theorists from the developed countries' governments, or from the international institutions which they largely control. Ironically, in view of its heavy emphasis on international trade and investment, the NPE usually takes a very 'closed economy' approach to policy-making in developing countries.

The NPE is an economic theory of politics, and uses the assumptions of neo-classical microeconomics. But nothing in those assumptions, or in the economic theory of politics as such, requires or determines the three major features of the NPE that have just been identified. In the transposition of the economic theory of politics from its earlier reference to developed countries (and particularly, the United States) to its present reference, via the NPE, to developing countries, a number of significant component parts have been removed and replaced with something different. Such flexibility of the content of the economic theory of politics emphasises that neo-classical microeconomics is not so much a doctrine as a method. It is a particular brand of logic, within which a great variety of different models of reality can be constructed, but not *any* model of reality. It is even more like a set of Meccano or Lego than the 'toolkit' with which it is usually compared. It is worth noting just how flexible the economic theory of politics has been over the years, in order to avoid the mistaken view that the conclusions of the NPE can simply be read off from its neo-classical starting points. Three examples are discussed, concerning the nature of interest group pressures in the political process, the origin of social rigidities and the optimal size of the government sector.

Originally, the pressures of interest groups in the political process were evaluated positively: they were a good thing. Interest group pressures were interpreted as equivalent to a competitive process in the political arena. The political need to achieve a broad consensus for the government's programme of measures ensured that extreme demands would be moderated by compromises, while the reasonable expectations of minorities would be respected in the process of coalition-building. The political competition of interest groups thus served not only to protect, but actually to construct the public interest. In the NPE, all this has changed. Interest group competition has become *destructive* of the public interest (identified with liberalisation policies) and symptomatic of a political fragmentation which occurs when politicians and administrators (illegitimately) as well as ordinary citizens (legitimately) pursue their individual self-interest (Grindle, 1989: 13).

An even more dramatic change has occurred on the question of the origin of social rigidities, because here the shift of emphasis occurs between the earlier and later works of the same author – Mancur Olson. In the revised edition of his path-breaking *The Logic of Collective Action*, Olson summarises its key finding as follows:

> even if all of the individuals in a large group are rational and self-interested, and would gain if, as a group, they acted to achieve their common interest or objective, they will still not voluntarily act to achieve that common or group interest.
>
> (Olson, 1971: 2)

This finding that, paradoxically, rational individuals will not organise themselves to achieve their common interests is then used as a critique of writers in the pluralist tradition who assumed not only that interest group pressures were benign, but that they would indeed manifest themselves. It was not the benign nature of interest group pressure which Olson questioned in 1971, but the logical inconsistency of assuming that self-interested individuals will voluntarily sacrifice in order to promote group aims (1971: 126). But a decade later, the story line has been completely reversed. In *The Rise and Decline of Nations* (Olson, 1982), notwithstanding the difficulties of group collective organisation, such groups are argued, not only to exist, but also to 'reduce efficiency and aggregate income in the societies in which they operate and make political life more divisive' (1982: 47). Interest groups' activity is then used to explain the relatively slow growth performance of Britain, India, China and the South African apartheid system. Not only have interest groups changed from being unproblematic to being the critical source of socio-economic ills, but the logical flaw which Olson originally spotted in interest group theory has dropped progressively out of sight.

A third example of the changing content of the economic theory of politics concerns the role of government. Anthony Downs, the pioneer of the economic theory of politics, used the theory to argue that the government sector would be inevitably *under*-extended (1960: 341–63). His argument turned on the cost to citizens of acquiring information about remote dangers which could, if they occurred, cause massive damage, and which the government could potentially prevent. His example was the possible threat from improved Soviet space capability, but global environmental problems would be a clearer contemporary illustration. However, by the 1980s, the NPE is concerned exclusively with the *over*-extension of government, and the argument used is the power of interest groups to vote themselves increases in public expenditure while diffusing the resultant costs through rises in general taxation.

The purpose of indicating these three major *voltes-face* in the content of the economic theory of politics is not to pass an opinion on whether the early version is better than the later one, or vice versa. Two points are relevant to our argument about the NPE. One is well put by Hindess (1988: 20–1), who remarks 'how radically different conclusions can be generated from the same set of abstract principles as a result of different assumptions about the conditions in which they are supposed to apply'. The other is that all three changes are consistent with each other. They together represent a dramatic shift away from a pluralist, participatory ideal of politics and towards an authoritarian and technocratic ideal based not on big government but on small and highly efficient government. In the longer perspective, they signal the return in the 1980s to dominance of the non-participatory strand of western liberal political theory (Hexter, 1979: 293–303).[2]

Surprisingly perhaps, there is also nothing in the theory of rent-seeking which drives one inevitably towards the cynicism, pessimism and

16

contracted focus of the NPE. The original analysis of government economic controls did not provide a new political economy. Its author, Anne Krueger, explicitly declined to draw any political conclusions from her discussion of rent-seeking (1974: 302). Its significance in the doctrines of neo-liberalism was economic, not political. It was aimed at showing that trade controls are much more costly in terms of economic welfare than they had previously been taken to be. Empirical estimates of the size of the loss inflicted by the use of trade restrictions have, over the years, normally been small. Typically the gain in efficiency to be derived by the removal of trade controls has been estimated to be around 3 to 5 per cent of GNP – an amount equivalent to one year of growth in the case of many developing countries. If governments of LDCs believed that trade controls could be used to improve their growth rate in the medium and long term, they might well be willing to trade-off static efficiency losses of this kind of size against their expected increase in long-run growth. Trade liberalisation as a policy was handicapped because its pay-off was stated, even by its own advocates, to be relatively small. Krueger's rent-seeking theory was an attempt to address this problem, in the belief that the true economic costs of protection must be higher than had previously been calculated.

Krueger identified an additional source of static welfare loss from protection, namely the resources which are used up by economic agents in competing for an allocation of administratively allocated import licences. Such resources produce nothing and, at the limit, could equal in size the economic rents which the licensing regime creates. Thus the *potential* costs of using quantitative restrictions on imports were shown to be much greater than had previously been considered. This was a fundamental neo-liberal insight and it has not been gainsaid. But its implications for political economy remain to be fully assessed. They are not at all as straightforward a confirmation of the tenets of the NPE as it might appear at first blush.

The additional welfare losses arising from a quantitative restriction (QR) regime result from an unproductive, but resource-consuming, competitive scramble for import licences that bring windfall gains to those who acquire them. For these additional losses to be realised in practice requires such a process to exist. But does it exist? It does not exist when the competitive scramble which we actually observe in developing countries is conducted by those who would be otherwise unemployed; clerks who fill in forms, leg-men who stand in queues at government offices are consuming largely their own time and effort, and it is often sadly true in developing economies that these do not have any alternative productive use, and therefore no economic value. Nor does it exist in a political economy such as Malawi (see chapter 15) in which the ruler's allies are rewarded purely through the award of political influence and not through the offer of economic rents. But more importantly for the NPE, a competitive rent-seeking process does not exist when licences are allocated by a process of pure patronage of the sort which self-interested political leaders use to reward their cronies. When a military ruler instructs officials of the Foreign Trade Ministry to issue import licences to his chief henchmen and lieutenants, there is *no* competitive process and *no* resource cost involved. This point is usually overlooked. In neo-liberal discussions of 'the politicisation of economic life', the scramble for spoils and corrupt practices are lumped together as if they were slightly different aspects of essentially the same phenomenon, whereas for the purpose of gauging the real significance of rent-seeking theory they have diametrically *opposite* implications.

The cynical view of Third World states, that self-interested state rulers, lacking much in the way of institutional constraints, maximise their own welfare at the public's expense, fits most easily with the scenario of corruption, rather than with that of the competitive scramble for spoils. The competitive scramble theory assumes that rulers are indifferent about the identities of the winners of the spoils. If this were true, it would be difficult to explain why the authorities would continue to oppose an auction of import quotas. An auction, after all, captures the rents of the import licences for the ruler's own treasury, while eliminating their dissipation on unproductive activities. Its crucial disadvantage, from the self-interested politician's viewpoint, is that it also abolishes clandestine political control over the distribution of unearned benefits. And, on that criterion, the competitive scramble is no different from an auction. It is difficult to argue, in the light of these considerations, that it is the logic of the theory of rent-seeking that has produced the characteristic features of the NPE. The theory of rent-seeking has no specific theory of political economy built into it, and, to the extent that it is based on the idea of impersonal competition for rents, stands at some distance from the cynical account of Third World rulers' behaviour which the New Political Economy offers. Nevertheless, they were conflated in a new conventional wisdom that trade controls are the underpinning of corrupt and inefficient regimes.

To elucidate the NPE solely in terms of its genealogy in economic science would be inadequate and confusing. The rhetorical uses of economic theory must also be brought into any explanation of why the NPE is as it is. Economic theorising always takes place within a specific changing historical context. Our assumption here is that two-way interaction can take place between economic theories and their changing context. Larger-scale change in the political mood, such as occurred in the 1980s, can affect what is theorised and the substance of the conclusions of theory. Influence can also flow in the reverse direction, as theorists deliberately seek to alter the stances of public policy-makers. If these assumptions are valid, one should not expect to be able to confine the intellectual history of the NPE just to its lineage in logic: there may well be strange logical leaps of the kind which have been noted above. We need to turn elsewhere to investigate why one kind of intellectual tool is produced from the tool-kit at one moment, and another kind of tool at another time, or why the same tools produce opposite policy conclusions in succeeding periods.[3]

What was the historical context of the emergence of the NPE, and what were the extra-scientific factors that shaped its development? Let us start from one further puzzle of the 'new political economy', its title. Why does the NPE refer to itself as 'new'? The standard answer to this is that it is new because it rejects the naïvety of the development economists and others who in the 1950s and 1960s believed that the state was an agency that promoted social welfare – the assumption of the benevolent or do-gooding state. But this is to respond to one naïvety with another. To suggest that all that was needed to give birth to the NPE was a process of gradual disillusion with the benevolence of the state in developing countries has the same simple-minded quality as the benevolent state assumption has itself.

One could put another case. It is that very few development economists forty years ago believed that the state in developing countries was concerned unreservedly to maximise social welfare. Quite a lot of economic work is technical and requires no particular view of the state. The assumption of the benevolent state, when it appeared without qualification, was usually more a matter either of pure diplomacy or of 'reformist hope'. It is vital to recall that the development economists of that time were largely foreigners to the developing countries, where they operated with either explicit or implicit sponsorship of their home governments. They wanted to assist their adopted country in their capacity as professional 'improvers', but not to get entangled with local politics. As professional economists seeking to promote reforms, they assumed the existence of certain institutions and attitudes, as it were trying to coax them into life while aware that they were often not in fact there. *Saying* that there were not there in public would, however, have been easily interpreted as a political act. The benevolent state assumption in developing countries was thus a convenient myth for those in a false position, not their firm belief. Many felt morally uncomfortable in their inability to explore openly the reasons for their professional frustration, but most of these loyally respected the diplomatic imperative.

What the orthodox could not acknowledge publicly in the 1950s and 1960s surfaced as dissent. Specifically, it appeared in the neo-Marxist political economy of development. In the work of Paul Baran (1973), this combined a cynical view of the LDC state with strong and critical emphasis on the role of foreign capital in frustrating rational development. Gradually this tradition bifurcated, with some neo-Marxists retaining the stress on the determining pressure of foreign capital ('capital logic') and others locating the source of distorting pressures in the domestic class sytem above all ('class logic'). The class logic version of the Marxian political economy of development is morphologically almost identical with that version of the

NPE which concentrates on the problematic role of interest groups. Both have political processes which guarantee economically irrational outcomes. The only important difference is that the former attributes the pressures for economic irrationality to an exploitative class, while the latter attributes it to the activities of self-interested groups. And both, of course, keep out of sight the international pressures which a capitalist system generates on developing countries. It is thus highly misleading to ignore the influence that neo-Marxism exerted on the NPE. The success of neo-Marxism in discrediting the assumption of the benevolent state paved the way down which the New Right moved triumphantly in the 1980s. The NPE is new specifically in succession to the 'old' political economy of neo-Marxism.

As we shall see in Chapter 2, the decisive events in ensuring this succession took place, as usual, in the sphere of high politics. Some time at the end of the 1970s, at the end of McNamara's time as President of the World Bank, diplomacy no longer seemed to require tact and tongue-biting, but instead a justification for a much more active intervention in the local politics of developing countries. Neo-classical economists, many of whom were then still producing project appraisal manuals with shadow prices and income-distribution weights, went back to the box of Lego and produced instead various sanitised versions of neo-Marxian political economy, sanitised in that they were deducible from individual rational self-interest rather than anything so unorthodox as 'class'. (The neo-Marxists were having sufficient difficulty with class themselves!)[4]

The revamping of the neo-Marxist class logic story with the aid of methodological individualism left its major rhetorical features unaffected. The introduction of rational self-interest as the sole motive of politicians and bureaucrats did not change the neo-Marxist view of the state as an entity merely pretending a real concern for the public interest and national welfare. Like neo-Marxism, the NPE makes strong normative claims, essentially taking it as obvious that a certain set of social and economic arrangements is right. The conjunction of a cynical view of the politics of existing regimes and strong normative claims leads both to produce a bleak and deeply contradictory pessimism about the possibilities of progress. But the aim in both cases is not so much to interpret the world as to change it, and for that purpose cynicism and pessimism (when further combined with a vision of a liberating crisis) are powerful ideological instruments of persuasion.

The NPE found in the profound economic shocks of the 1970s, which we have sketched in section 1.1, a catastrophe that served as a revolutionary crisis. The liberation was to be provided, not by classless intellectuals, but by international economic experts. Dudley Seers who postulated (1979) 'the congruence of Marxism and other neo-classical doctrines' provided the clue to these and other parallels. For in both neo-Marxism and the NPE, what is attempted is nothing less than the unity of theory and practice.

On this interpretation, it makes no sense at all to try and refute the cynicism and pessimism of the NPE about the governments of developing countries by pointing to current examples of successful reform programmes in Africa and Asia (as Grindle, 1989, does). For it is here that the economic catastrophe has taken place, and here that the international economic experts of structural adjustment have arrived. Most of the empirical evidence from the 1980s on internal ability to undertake policy reform is contaminated (from a scientific point of view) by the very rhetorical success which the NPE theorists have achieved in underwriting international action in support of liberalising reform. It is quite impossible, for example, to judge whether Turkey or Ghana would have achieved their abrupt liberalising shifts of the 1980s in the absence of external finance conditional on those shifts. The appearance of contrary cases may represent failure for the scientist, but it signals success for the soothsayer.

1.5   THE WORLD BANK'S CHANGING VIEWS

In the middle of the 1970s, the World Bank, in the person of Hollis Chenery (then Vice-President for Development Policy) commissioned a study of the previous twenty-five years of development effort. Its broad conclusions were that economic growth had been surprisingly rapid, but that the distribution of the benefits of that growth remained unsatisfactory. Additionally, some one billion people's poverty could be attributed to economic stagnation and very low productivity. By implication, continuing international action would be needed, both by means of aid and by means of trade reform, to tackle these massive problems of income maldistribution and technological change. This study of post-war development experience (Morawetz, 1977), although undertaken by an independent consultant to the Bank, managed to crystallise the official viewpoint of the bank as an institution during the Presidency of Robert MacNamara (1968–81), It was a viewpoint compounded of concern and complacency, in about equal measures, and it was maintained with a rare consistency throughout the economic turbulence of the 1970s.

MacNamara's Presidency not only saw the rapid expansion of Bank lending, but it produced a new emphasis on the alleviation of poverty as a Bank objective. New areas of lending were opened – rural development for small (usually *fairly* small or even middle-sized in practice) farmers; urban infrastructure, including housing and education and health (Ayres, 1983: 4–11). The sheer scale of world poverty, which had been the stick with which radicals had beaten the Bank in the 1960s, became in the 1970s the basic justification for the continuation and indeed the expansion of the MacNamara Bank. Nor was this just a cynical manoeuvre: undoubtedly MacNamara himself felt profound concern for world poverty. He also felt that the industrial countries had heavy responsibilities to take action to meet these poverty concerns. Not only were aid flows inadequate, the protectionist trade practices of the industrial countries were highly objectionable and detrimental to global welfare. Another facet of the Bank's institutional viewpoint in the 1970s was its willingness to speak out against the policies of OECD countries in the interests of poverty alleviation – something which became very muted indeed in the early 1980s. At this time, the term 'structural adjustment' was used by the Bank to mean the restructuring of industry in OECD countries after they had dismantled protectionist devices like the Multi-Fibre agreement and the European steel price ring (World Bank, *World Development Report* 1978: 17). As the degree of protectionism in industrial countries continued to increase through the 1980s, the term 'structural adjustment' acquired a different application, to the developing countries struggling with rising balance of payments deficits and huge stocks of debt.

But mixed in with the compassion and the courageousness in public debate, the MacNamara Bank also suffered from a certain complacency. The Morawetz study, with which the Bank was very closely identified, included some curious blind spots. It thought that future mortality from famines would be small, something which the Ethiopian and Sudanese famines of 1984–5 were most shockingly to disprove (Morawetz, 1977: 46). It thought that the problems of monoproduct economies would greatly ease, overlooking the 'Dutch disease' just about to afflict the OPEC countries when oil prices fell (ibid.: 65). It was convinced that 'the recent heightened concern with the eradication of poverty is not likely to be just another fad' (ibid.: 7). The Bank of the 1980s was to try very hard to disprove that prediction, as poverty-alleviation was demoted to priority zero so that the 'structural adjustment' of the developing economies could take place. Even in the middle of an unprecedentedly volatile decade, the MacNamara Bank was not expecting the unexpected.

The Morawetz study also thought that preoccupation with problems of debt was overdone (ibid.: 65). That seems to have been the Bank's view, too. In his 1977 Presidential Address, MacNamara continued to argue that the large growth in private commercial lending to developing countries did not make a debt crisis inevitable, and that it could be staved off by appropriate corrective actions. Such danger as was foreseen was that an individual developing country might be faced with a liquidity crisis which, if not promptly dealt with through a debt rescheduling, could damage confidence in the recycling mechanism. That the whole mechanism would seize up because a whole set of countries were borrowing beyond their ability to repay was not foreseen by the Bank in the 1970s. In 1977, the Bank was 'even more confident today than . . . a year ago that the debt problem is indeed manageable'. It was not until after the second oil price shock in 1979–80 that the Bank publicly revived 'questions about the international financial system's ability to recycle enough funds . . . to

22

maintain import levels and economic growth rates' (World Bank, World Development Report 1980: 3).

The sudden change of stance at the very end of the MacNamara Presidency was influenced not just by the second oil shock. The accompanying 'strong deflationary measures' by the new conservative governments of leading OECD countries were also cited as producing an outlook for growth which caused 'deep concern'. A third factor was the belief in the Bank that the real price of energy would rise even further throughout the 1980s – a forecast which (at least for oil and coal-based energy) has proved erroneous. All three factors together convinced MacNamara, in his 1980 Presidential Address, that what had occurred constituted a 'permanent change in the world economy, not . . . some temporary phenomenon which will later automatically reverse itself'. Hence the need for the developing countries to structurally adjust their economies. Developing country governments were now publicly criticised by the Bank for failing to recognise the need for structural adjustment during the 1970s. The fact that the Bank itself had only just arrived at this analysis did not seem to be allowed as a plea in mitigation of the offence. Throughout the 1970s the Bank had not been much concerned about adjustment, and it did not oppose large-scale commercial borrowing in order to maintain economic growth rates. In fact it saw high growth as the guarantee of the continuing creditworthiness of developing countries, and it had repeatedly soothed fears about the sustainability of the recycling operation.

Once the perception of a permanent change in the world economy took hold of the Bank in 1980, various other policy conclusions followed. If in the past external finance had been used as a substitute for structural adjustment, it now had to be used to support structural adjustment. Here is the first public glimmer of the phenomenon which is dissected in this book – World Bank policy-based lending. If growth in the 1970s had been pursued regardless of stability, stability must not now be pursued regardless of growth: hence the new policy objective becomes structural adjustment with growth – as much growth as is consistent with stability. Finally, the private banks were themselves unable to carry out the whole recycling task on their own; the Bank must no longer stand on the sidelines giving a running commentary designed to encourage the players. It must plunge in itself. The 1980s would require 'a major re-examination of the functions of the Bretton Woods institutions in the recycling of financial flows'. The World Bank, the IMF and the private banks would all have to reorganise themselves to work together better in complementary forms of financial intermediation. As Chapter 2 shows, such changes have indeed been taking place in the 1980s, and the Bank's adjustment lending has had to be developed continuously through the decade.

During the Clausen Presidency (1981–6), the MacNamara interpretation of the world was largely swept aside. The change is best symbolised by the Bank's Report on *Accelerated Development in sub-Saharan Africa*. Responding to the real economic stagnation in SSA during the 1970s, this report ('the Berg Report' after its author Elliot Berg) used the doctrines of the new political economy to analyse the policy and performance failures of African governments. After explaining its view of the social and political interests at work, it showed how they produced perverse outcomes in policy-making (World Bank, 1981: 24–44). The recommended remedy was the retreat of the state from economic life and the opening up of economic activity – especially in agriculture – to the free play of market forces. While clearly saying some things that were relevant and true, and which had not been said publicly by the Bank before, the naïvety of political analysis and the sweeping nature of the liberalisation proposals was startling, and signalled a major change of course.

It would be wrong to suggest that the Bank was united during the Clausen period behind the brash doctrines of the Berg Report. In some ways, the Bank became more diversified and fragmented in its policy approaches than it had been under the hand of MacNamara. The Bank's research department represented the extreme version of neo-liberal commitment. For different reasons, dissent there was little tolerated. The Bank's research was reorganised more tightly around large projects designed to substantiate what everyone knew in their hearts already: that economic liberalisation was right. The real work of the Bank was not done there, however. Undoubtedly, staff on the operational side remained more pragmatic in their beliefs about developing countries and their prescriptions for them. As a result, the Bank never became a neo-liberal monolith, even in its most doctrinaire years. For every research report vindicating the neo-liberal position, one could find another Bank publication which looked more soberly at the social and technological constraints on development and contemplated – without any sense of guilt or incongruity – some appropriate piecemeal social engineering. For the agricultural sector, the division between the price reformers and the structuralists within the Bank was illustrated by Lipton (1987). Our case studies suggest that in the area of adjustment lending, the philosophy of economic liberalisation is strongly present, but not embodied in a wholly procrustean model of policy reform.

However, the Clausen Bank does contrast quite strongly with the emerging shape of the Bank under Barber Conable and Lewis Preston. The ideologues in the Research Department have left and the department itself disappeared as a separate Vice-Presidency in the reorganisation of 1987. The Bank's public style is much more consensual. The Bank now not only admits to its mistakes, but has enshrined learning from them as part of its corporate philosophy. Certain priorities – such as poverty alleviation and mitigating the social costs of adjustment – have again been elevated, and incorporated into the conditionality of policy-based lending itself. Their neglect during the early

24

1980s is now acknowledged as disastrous. New priorities have been specified, especially a greatly increased concern with environmental stress, 'governance' and gender issues.

Despite all of these recent welcome changes, the Bank's political economy analyses remain weak and over-influenced by the new political economy approach criticised in section 1.4. There are some obvious reasons for this. Its own status as a political actor is one: not only are there diplomatic niceties to be observed, but room for manoeuvre is objectively constrained by its own need to have its funds replenished and its capital increases subscribed. Nevertheless, how we think about things does influence what we want to do, and thus what constraints we decide to try and shift. The new political economy of development produces a much too mechanical understanding of the political process in developing countries – and indeed in industrial countries and in the Bank itself. Too much of politics is concerned with forces which theories of individual or group self-interest cannot adequately explain. The nationalism which underpins many of the economic policies of developing countries is one, but an important, example. The political institutions whose absence or presence is often vital to the good performance of certain policy tasks is another. A better understanding of political economy may, therefore, be the Bank's next new frontier.

But in contemplating the attractive prospect of a kinder, gentler and greener World Bank at the end of the twentieth century, we have advanced too far. Much had to be learned through the 1980s, and learned the hard way, in order to make this possible. It is time to go back to the beginning again, to look in more detail at the origins of the scheme for structural adjustment lending which the Bank launched in 1980.

NOTES

1 It may be of interest to explain why the statement that 'politicians and bureaucrats are motivated only by individual self-interest' is shocking. First, it is assumed that the proposition is not tautological, that is, it does not mean that whatever these actors do must be self-interested in some sense, because otherwise they would not do it. Second, if the statement is not empty because tautological, it means that these actors when faced with any conflict between their own individual interest and the interest of any other person will infallibly prefer the former. Third, it is assumed that conflicts of interest do occur, and that a natural harmony of individual interests does not prevail. When conflicts of interest occur between individuals in economic life they are arbitrated in the market place by the 'invisible hand' of the price mechanism which, on given assumptions, can achieve an 'efficient' reconciliation of conflicting interests. But even Adam Smith did not suppose that market-generated outcomes could be efficient without an over-arching framework of law and regulation to maintain the socio-political parameters within which markets can work efficiently. Now if the politicians and bureaucrats, who are responsible for enacting laws and enforcing regulations, use their political power to advance personal and private interests when they conflict with the public interest, they betray their duty to the general public and that is, and ought to be, shocking. The application of the neo-

classical self-interest assumption to politics is, therefore, something much more fundamental than the simple 'extension' of a behavioural assumption from one arena of social life to another.

2 The participatory strand in western political theory starts from Aristotle and runs through Machiavelli and Guicciardini, Harrington, Ferguson and Rousseau. The non-participatory strand starts with the Stoics and runs through the Roman legists, Magna Carta, Coke, Blackstone, Bentham and James Mill.

3 For an earlier attempt to discuss the basic logical difficulties of certain economic theories of politics, see Toye (1976).

4 In this regard, they follow closely in the footsteps of Marx himself. The *Communist Manifesto* speaks of two classes, bourgeoisie and proletariat, but in his other writings three-layered and other multilayered models of class structure are to be found; and when Marx discusses class in what was later to become Volume III of *Capital*, the manuscript breaks off before the definition has properly begun (Prawer, 1978: 146–7).

2

THE WORLD BANK'S MOVE TO POLICY-BASED LENDING

2.1 THE EARLY HISTORY OF POLICY-BASED LENDING: INDIA

This study focuses on the World Bank's experience with policy-based conditional lending during the 1980s. When structural adjustment loans (SALs) made their first appearance in 1980, they seemed to represent a major departure from the Bank's established philosophy and practice. That perception was not wrong. But at the same time, it came without much general public understanding of how the Bank's pre-1980 philosophy and practice paved the way for such a departure. What should that understanding have been?

Unsurprisingly, perhaps, the World Bank has never made unconditional loans. Even when virtually all of its loans were for development projects – that is, discrete chunks of physical investment – these loans carried conditions to which the borrower had to agree; and, more importantly, some of these conditions required policy changes. An obvious and familiar example would be a power station project, for which the Bank might not agree to lend unless the developing country borrower agreed to an overhaul of its electricity tariff. The basic rationale for this was not only that the loan had to be serviced, but also that projects should not be supported when pricing encouraged wasteful consumption. Certainly in the 1950s, if not earlier, the Bank exchanged development finance for this kind of policy reform. But a specific project was also still involved at this time; the required policy change could be interpreted as one designed to facilitate the success of that project; and the extent of the policy change was sectoral or sub-sectoral in scope.

Three important steps were involved in the move towards 1980s-style SALs. One was the use of non-project, or programme lending. Programme lending divorces development finance from specific items of investment; it is given as general support for a deficit balance of payments to facilitate imports that should increase economic growth and, hopefully, development. Another vital step was the combination of programme lending with policy change conditions. The third step was the broadening of these conditions from the sectoral or sub-sectoral to the national, macroeconomic level.

Programme lending with policy reform conditions that are economy-wide thus provides us with the definition of the Structural Adjustment Loans of the early 1980s. If we wish to find the major precedent for Bank lending of this character, we have to go back to the middle of the 1960s, when, in fact if not in name, it was used briefly in India. This episode is well-known, and has been much studied (e.g. by Bhagwati and Srinivasan, 1975: 83–172, and Lipton and Toye, 1990: 80–116). The story, in summary, is that from about 1963–4, a rapidly increasing share of the Aid-India Consortium's aid to India came as non-project loans for general balance-of-payments support. At the same time, starting with the Bell Mission from the Bank, the Indian government received strong advice in favour of major changes of economic policy including agricultural strategy, the liberalisation of controls over trade and industry and the devaluation of the rupee. In the period 1965–6 the Indian Government accepted (in the Woods-Mathur Agreement) and then implemented the required policy changes (including the June 1966 rupee devaluation). But the results for trade and industry were unsatisfactory and the liberalisation process was halted; the devaluation was seen as both externally imposed and ineffective; promised aid failed to arrive and much resentment at the Bank's and the US Government's leverage tactics was provoked inside India.

The legacy of this episode was varied, and highly relevant to the evolution of SALs. In India itself, the Bank, the US government and other members of the Aid-India Consortium retired hurt, not admitting the full extent of their involvement in the aid leverage on policy, but not trying to repeat the manoeuvre either. In any case, a repetition became increasingly less feasible as the relative importance of aid flows to the Indian economy fell in the 1970s. But the frustration experienced by the Bank at the half-success, half-failure of the Indian devaluation saga did not obliterate all thoughts of repeating the exercise elsewhere, should the need arise.

The other results, providing specific threads of continuity between the Bank's Indian imbroglio of the mid-1960s and the later history of policy-based lending, are also worth noting. Programme lending for general support to the Indian balance of payments continued throughout the 1970s, although at a reduced level and without any policy change conditions. It also continued – on grounds of parity of treatment – in Pakistan and, after the 1971 secession of East Bengal, in Bangladesh. This programme lending was not linked with any policy change conditions. But the absence of policy conditions came to be seen in the late 1970s as anomalous, at least in Bangladesh where the policy environment was regarded by the Bank as unfavourable for development, and where the

28

dominant role of aid in the economy provided the kind of prospect for successful aid leverage on policy that no longer existed in India. At the very end of the 1970s, and just before the introduction of the SAL as a lending instrument, conditions relating to food policy were in fact introduced into non-project (programme) lending to Bangladesh.

Certain personal histories also link the Indian episode of the 1960s to the invention of the SAL in 1980. Ernest Stern, who became the Bank's Vice-President for operations and who spearheaded the move towards SALs, had worked on South Asia for USAID before moving to the Bank in 1973. Stern's Senior Advisor on SALs between 1980 and 1983 was Stanley Please, who had started his career in the Bank as the fiscal economist on the Bell Mission to India. It would be surprising if their early professional experience of the Bank's partially abortive attempts to secure economic liberalisation through aid leverage had not influenced their subsequent judgements and decisions in this area. If one had to summarise what the 'Indian lesson' for them amounted to it would be this. Economic liberalisation remains a sound, and indeed necessary, set of policies for development; the power to grant or to withhold aid money can be used, and should be used, to induce governments to liberalise their economies; but not, perhaps, in India.

2.2   THE PROBLEMS OF PROJECT LENDING IN THE 1970s

The shocks to the international economy which are sketched in Chapter 1 came at a time when the World Bank's transactions with developing countries consisted overwhelmingly of project lending – the long-drawn-out cycle stretching from an initial project idea, through an average two years of project preparation to appraisal, negotiation of terms and conditions, implementation and eventual evaluation some five years after implementation has begun. This style of development lending came to look increasingly problematic after the first huge oil price rise of 1973.

The project mode reflected the early dominance of professional engineers within the Bank. It is natural for engineers to think of development as being a sequence of new physical structures which have to be put in place – i.e. projects. Economists, who were just beginning to have an impact on Bank policies in the 1960s, tend to be more sceptical of the project mode. In the 1960s debate over project versus non-project or programme aid, some of the economists' doubts about projects surfaced. One major worry was called 'the fungibility problem': it was that, if aid finances a project which the recipient government would have undertaken anyway – aid or no aid – then the aid money is actually financing some other, unidentified project which the aid agency does not know about and might not like. Project aid can thus create a misleading sense of certainty about the impact of aid on development.

The countries worst affected by the economic turbulence of the 1970s were those of sub-Saharan Africa. They were more open to the effects of deteriorating terms of trade implied by oil price rises and the collapse of the inflation-fuelled commodity boom after 1973. In addition, their political and administrative structures showed less flexibility in coming to terms with the need for adjustment. In sub-Saharan Africa, the economist's fungibility problem did not apply strongly: when aid plays such a large part in financing investment and imports as it did in Africa at that time, the possibility that the aided projects would have been undertaken anyway – aid or no aid – becomes much smaller than when the relative importance of aid in the economy is much less.[1]

Nevertheless, the economists of the 1960s had pinpointed another set of reasons why aid-giving in the project mode was problematic. These reasons concerned the general economic environment in which every project has to operate, and the fact that many governments in the sub-Saharan Africa region were finding it increasingly difficult to organise an environment that was generally favourable to project success. When economic policies are not well ordered (and that includes the ability to change policies appropriately in the face of fast-changing external conditions), a number of serious consequences for project success arise.

One is that project identification and appraisal become more difficult. For example, when internal prices depart in many cases and to a major degree from true scarcity values (for which world prices may or may not provide a good proxy), it becomes much harder to spot a project that will be economically worthwhile, and not just financially lucrative to its owners and operators. Many of the projects which appear to entrepreneurs to be sound will not be economically valuable, or sufficiently economically valuable to tie up resources in them. Appraisals on the basis of 'shadow' or 'accounting' prices will reject many projects as unsatisfactory and the shelf of economically worthwhile projects will get shorter and shorter. Alternatively, if the complex appraisal methods using 'shadow' prices prove too burdensome for weak administrations to use, uneconomic projects will continue to be chosen and put up for funding – with disastrous results if they secure it.

Most projects require some domestic resources to complement those coming from aid donors. Usually these complementary domestic resources, or counterpart funds, are used to finance initial civil engineering and construction works and the recurrent expenditure arising from the operation of the new facility – power station, road, hospital, school, etc. When the government's macroeconomic policies are in disarray, however, these counterpart funds may simply dry up. If state utilities fail to charge appropriately or recover consumer debts, and if tax effort is also insufficient to cover the implied claims on public expenditure arising from new projects, many capital investments will be halted in mid-construction and projects recently undertaken will begin to fail. Underutilisation of the capital will occur first; then, if maintenance is also neglected, will come physical collapse. This was the common experience in Africa in the 1970s – many relatively new structures half-built, underused or falling apart.

It therefore made little sense to continue with ever more schemes for new projects. Existing projects demanded completion or rehabilitation first; the government budget needed reform before it could support counterpart funding adequately; the pricing structure needed reform directly because many projects which were rational on the basis of scarcity prices could not be undertaken unless the operators were subsidised – i.e. unless new industrial subsidies were added on to an already over-burdened government budget. Programme aid, by contrast, strengthens the government budget. It provides foreign exchange which is sold by the government to importers in exchange for domestic money.

It would be wrong to imply that the Bank had not, to some extent, foreseen these kind of problems before they were felt so acutely in the case of Africa in the 1970s. It had already devised a way of linking (partially) project aid allocations to more general indicators of economic performance. When highly concessional aid, in the form of IDA funds, was introduced by the Bank in 1964, it began to devise normative criteria to ration IDA funds between countries and to calculate IDA/IBRD funds mixes for certain countries which borrowed from both windows of the Bank. Alongside population size, per capita GNP and a country constant representing a minimum allocation for small countries, an indicator of 'performance' on a scale of 1 to 5 was incorporated as an allocation criterion.

Economic performance therefore entered as a determinant of aid flows as early as the 1960s and 1970s. But its role was as one of the factors shaping a country's quota of available Bank funds, which was then absorbed through a sequence of project loans. It is worth noting that the performance criterion did have a quantitatively powerful influence on the overall allocation, and that the scaling of performance was based on a detailed set of sub-criteria relating to macroeconomic performance, adjustment experience, the pricing environment, the performance of public institutions and of public policies in the welfare and poverty alleviation area. By 1977, the normative criteria had been formalised to a high degree, and allocations were calculated by computer programme. Despite this system of allocating more funds to countries with *ceteris paribus* a better economic performance, the project mode did not remain viable as the exclusive vehicle for the transfer of Bank aid.

Why not? Partly it was because project aid could not be made to respond as quickly as Bank staff would have liked when major external shocks threw developing countries off their charted course. When sudden large gaps opened up between export proceeds and import costs, the Bank often wanted to give immediate financial support to smooth the path of adjustment. Quick- disbursing aid was at a premium, and the project mode was notorious for the slowness with which it was disbursed. Partly also, some Bank officials were dissatisfied by the rate of change of economic performance. It was well enough to reward the better performers through large allocations, but the real problem was to raise the overall standard of performance. Only by doing so were economic conditions likely to improve sufficiently to allow increases in project aid itself. Yet policy conditions attached to project finance were regarded as a non-starter, because the extra pain of foregoing the project finance in a badly managed economy would be perceived by the borrower as less than the pain of making the policy changes.

2.3 THE INVENTION OF STRUCTURAL ADJUSTMENT LENDING

Against this background, programme lending combined with policy change conditions was revived in the early 1970s for the first time since the Indian incident of the mid-1960s. This revival was hasty and reactive: the trigger was the great oil price shock of October 1973, which at the end of 1973 began to produce a sudden rapid deterioration in current accounts of the balance of payments in (among others) several East African countries. Between 1973 and 1975, three of these – Zambia, Kenya and Tanzania – were offered programme loans with policy conditions attached. The policy conditions included changes to the existing organisation of agricultural marketing and prices, amongst other issues.

The Bank was clearly acting under the pressure of external events. It has been observed that

> the donors have . . . lurched into [conditional programme aid] as a matter of urgent necessity, with a sense on the part of some agencies at least that it is temporary, and that the 'normal' preponderance of project lending will resume when circumstances are 'normal' (Cassen, *et al.*, 1986: 150–1).

In the mid-1970s, the Bank's top management took this view. Only one programme loan was sanctioned for Kenya, and two for Tanzania. In 1978, one programme loan ($150 m.) was sanctioned for Turkey, and it was, interestingly, accompanied by a 'letter of intent' declaring that the Turkish government intended to reform major aspects of its trade strategy. But the general stance of the Bank was not yet favourable to the birth of the structural adjustment loan. There was still much suspicion within the Bank of programme lending as inherently irresponsible, and as something that had to be stringently limited.

The view that conditional programme lending was something exceptional became harder to preserve once the second great oil price shock arrived in May–November 1979, although the phrase 'structural adjustment loan' itself still embodied it. Yet it is important to insist that the invention of 'structural adjustment lending' was *not* simply a reaction to the second oil price shock. It pre-dated it, just as it also pre-dated the political shift which returned to power conservative governments in the UK (May 1979), the US (November 1979) and the Federal German Republic (1980). Economic and political changes may have strengthened the move towards SALs, but they did not create it in the first instance. The original pressures for the second revival of conditional programme lending came from inside the Bank itself, as it reassessed its own effectiveness. This reassessment involved the President, Robert McNamara and a small and disparate group of senior officials. As we shall see, the Executive Board itself[2] did not take the lead, and in fact was hostile.

The internal pressures for change derived from a number of not entirely convergent considerations. McNamara himself was reaching the end of his presidency, in which he had done so much to expand the Bank's operations and to increase the salience of poverty alleviation as an objective of policy. He seems to have come to doubt just how successful these changes in strategy had been. Some critics within the Bank regarded its move to poverty-based lending as little more than a gesture, an example of tokenism. Mahbub ul Haq was one of these critics, who argued that the size of Bank poverty-based lending was too small to have more than a negligible impact either on the productivity of the poor or on the amount of productive employment available to them. His solution to this was a new programme of *long-term* programme lending, that would finally discard the official view that this was necessarily abnormal or exceptional. A paper was written in this sense which had some influence with McNamara. Indeed, this was a proposal which had been propounded as long before as 1969, in the Pearson Report,[3] but without leading to much accumulation of political support.

The operational side of the Bank, headed since 1978 by Ernest Stern, had rather little patience with what it regarded as an 'intellectual' (in the pejorative sense) approach to Bank policy. For them the concern was less with ways of improving the poverty-impact of lending and more with ways of persuading borrower governments to put their houses in good economic order: once this was done, it was maintained, poverty would look after itself. The operators had become increasingly disillusioned with the current method of persuasion – policy dialogue with the borrowing government combined with control over the flow of project funding. It is quite possible for project funding and an ineffective policy dialogue to coexist for a long time. The project mode provides a 'safe' format of aid-giving when donors and recipient disagree about priorities and general economic policies. As long as there are projects in the pipeline in sufficient number, the policy dialogue does not *need* to succeed. But by the late 1970s, sub-Saharan

Africa was in danger of having neither projects nor acceptable economic strategies to be aid-financed. When projects dry up, the policy dialogue suddenly needs to succeed, and succeed very quickly. A new kind of development 'plan' which the Bank could feel positively enthusiastic about, was urgently needed, if its aid was to continue to flow at anything like the accustomed levels.

The announcement of the new move to make long-term non-project assistance available to countries which were prepared to embrace economic policies which the Bank regarded as necessary for development was made by McNamara at an UNCTAD meeting in Manila in April 1979. The first operational effect was the conversion of some sector lending to the new policy-conditioned basis, for example in the Philippines. This was a mode of lending which followed up the example of the 1978 Turkish programme loan, and which eventually came back into favour as the SECAL – the sector adjustment loan – from 1983–4 onwards. But in 1979 it was regarded only as a hesitant first step towards the SAL – the structural adjustment loan. At this time, the sectoral basis of lending was regarded as too slender to gain the Bank the entrée which it thought it needed to top-level policy-making in developing countries. If the whole environment were to be switched permanently to a more orthodox economic mode, the Bank felt that it needed to have a place at the top policy-making table. To secure that, it wanted loans that were large enough to matter at the highest level of authority, and policy conditionality that was economy-wide in scope. Normally both characteristics were present in SALs.

The step which initiated SALs themselves came in early 1980, when a very brief proposal document was put to, and approved by the Executive Board. But this formal blessing by no means indicated unanimity within the Bank on the desirability of the new SALs. The Board had bowed to the wishes of the management of the Bank, but remained sceptical about the utility of SALs for several years. This scepticism had several sources and it is interesting to evaluate these in the light of more recent developments in policy-reform lending. Some of the scepticism was undoubtedly the consequence of the lack of preparation or persuasion of the Board on the merits of the new SALs. A major policy shift was presented abruptly, with a minimum of argumentation. This manner of doing business provoked resentment and informal dissent. This would be hardly worth commenting on if it did not illuminate similar reactions among developing country officials when faced with the negotiating style of some Bank officials. It is easier to credit some of the developing countries' complaints about World Bank 'arrogance' when the manner in which the Executive Board itself was treated by the Bank management at this time is appreciated.

Apart from the question of style, the Board collectively had a number of concerns. One was presentational. The introduction of SALs implied a reversal of the Bank's previous claims about the effectiveness of past efforts at securing reform by policy dialogue in combination with project lending. If SALs were really needed to secure policy reform, the previous policy was shown up as a failure. The proper decision, even though embarrassing, would have been to make a clean breast of it. But the presentational problem was aggravated by the Board's doubts about whether SALs themselves really would be more effective than project lending plus policy dialogue. Failure is always relative, so unless SALs were indeed superior in achieving policy reform, it would be counter-productive to cry, even implicitly, *mea culpa*. The Board harboured real doubts.

Would SALs be more effective in promoting policy reform? Board members spotted two central flaws in the logic behind the SAL scheme. One of these concerned the validity of the rationale for linking non-project assistance with policy reform conditions, thus questioning the very essence of the SAL concept. The other concerned the division of institutional labour between the Bank and the IMF, a co-ordination problem which in fact has rumbled on throughout the 1980s, with a variety of unfortunate results. Because these two areas of concern have proved to be so important in the subsequent development of policy-based lending, it may be worth interrupting the narrative of events at this point to expand somewhat on the nature of the two problems. In doing so, however, it would be wrong to give the impression that members of the Executive Board understood all their ramifications in early 1980. It is necessary then to distinguish the Board's foresight from what can now be seen with hindsight.

The Board certainly did question the rationale for combining non-project assistance with conditions requiring major policy changes. They accepted the policy of restricting programme lending to countries whose policy environment was, in the Bank's assessment, favourable. But they did question why countries which had *not yet* succeeded in creating the 'right' policy environment should be given loan finance. What function did the loan finance play in the process of getting major policies right? Unlike a physical investment project, policy reform did not require money: either policies were reformed, or they were not. Finance was needed, in the Board's view, for two quite different purposes: either in order to allow reform to proceed more *gradually*, so that phasing and sequencing problems could be handled, or as an *insurance* policy if reforms failed to work (as in the Indian episode of 1966–7). Neither of these considerations was given much weight in 1980: sequencing was not seen as a major challenge and no one in the Bank was prepared to contemplate that the 'right' policies might turn out, at a particular time and place, to be 'wrong'. So what was the SAL money for?

The Board did *not* want to use loans to 'buy' policy change, to persuade reluctant developing countries to undertake reforms, to induce waverers to do what they feared would be politically painful or to strengthen the hands of reforming groups in developing countries at the expense of their opponents. Using loans for leverage in this way was meddling in developing countries' internal politics: it would damage the Bank's stance of political neutrality and, to be successful, it would require political skills which the Bank did not possess. However, the prospect of exerting leverage may be supposed to have been quite definitely in the mind of the management of the Bank when inventing the SAL instrument. But several years had to pass before the aim of leverage, and the problems associated with trying to exercise it, surfaced in official Bank pronouncements.

The question 'what is the money for?' has as its logical counterpart the question 'what is the conditionality for?'. Policy conditionality attached to loans does not make sense if both the Bank and the borrower are truly like-minded about the need for reform and the right methods to go about it. Only when real differences exist in objectives or perceptions about how best to achieve those objectives does the device of policy conditionality become relevant (Harrigan, 1988a; Streeten, 1989: 16–18.) If that is so, the official Bank doctrine that SALs are for countries that have previously independently decided to pursue policy reform suggests one of two things. Either conditionality *is* indeed redundant and need never have been invented, or the official doctrine is misleading and SALs are the product of a bargaining process – this much money being exchanged for that much policy reform. Where the balance lies between these two explanations is an empirical matter. From the countries examined in this study (see Volume 2), Thailand comes close to the first extreme, while Jamaica comes close to the second.

The second major problem with policy-conditioned programme lending which troubled the Executive Board of the Bank focused on its implications for Bank relations with the IMF. The creation of two *separate* international financial institutions had been made deliberately in the mid-1940s in order to avoid 'loss of effectiveness . . . overcentralisation of power and the danger of making costly errors of judgement' (Feinberg, 1986: 2). Bank-IMF tensions arose, however, from time to time about how far the responsibilities of each extended, where overlaps occurred, and who was entitled to do what. By the middle 1960s, the tensions were sufficiently irritating to prompt the negotiation of a new concordat on the division of labour. In December 1966, it was agreed that the IMF should lead on 'exchange rates and restrictive (trade) systems, . . . adjustment for temporary balance of payments disequilibria and . . . stabilisation programmes'. The Bank was to lead on '. . . development programmes and project evaluation, including development priorities' (Feinberg, 1986: 5). Financial institutions, capital markets, domestic savings and domestic and foreign debt remained as overlapping responsibilities. Even in 1966 the demarcation lines could not be drawn with absolute precision, so in practice much depended on good communications and mutual restraint in sensitive areas. Although joint meetings of officials became more regular, restraint was not always mutual, with the Fund often asserting its assumed prerogatives as the 'senior' of the two institutions.

During the 1970s, the sensitive areas within the concordat included the management of foreign exchange rates and public expenditure. The Bank found the Fund too restrictive in its approach to developing countries' exchange rates and insufficiently directive with regard to priorities for public expenditure. The Fund's stance was in line with its own institutional objectives, but the Bank's inability to secure consideration for *its own* institutional concerns in these two areas was frustrating. These frustrations increased with the creation of the Fund's Extended Fund Facility (EFF) in 1974. Though welcomed for the increased and more flexible finance which it brought to the first oil shock crisis, the EFF was unwelcome to the Bank because it took the IMF into medium-term (up to 10 years) lending, which had previously been an exclusive province of the Bank. The Fund thereby spread out into areas of development policy with which it had not connected previously, threatening the Bank with loss of institutional identity and an increase in demarcation disputes.

The Executive Board might have grasped the 1980 proposal for SALs as an opportunity to countermarch on to traditional IMF territory – conditional, quick-disbursing non-project lending. But it did not. Instead it was inclined to the view that this would make institutional confusion worse confounded, and that one agency – the IMF – using conditional loans to support policy reform was quite sufficient. The Bank's senior management not only believed otherwise, but, in deference to internal worries about SALs becoming a channel for irresponsible lending, tied them as tightly as possible to the simultaneous existence of an IMF lending operation in the borrowing country. The Bank had bound itself, under its Articles of Agreement, to make programme loans only in 'exceptional' cases. To receive a SAL, exceptionality was now defined as a borrower country already having an IMF stabilisation programme. This decision ensured that the problem of co-ordinating Bank and Fund conditionalities would swiftly arise, and that new concordats on the subject of conditionality would soon be urgently required to save externally-directed policy reform from incoherence. It also proved to restrict too severely the Bank's own use of the SAL instrument. The Bank soon wanted to break its own rule.

The scepticism with which the Executive Board greeted SALs was widely shared in the Bank. They were seen as a radical departure from lending principles which, whatever their other deficiencies, were at least sound. The country-desk officers were perhaps the most welcoming to the new instrument, which they could use to bring rapid relief to countries that were very distressed by external forces – severe worsening of terms of trade and rapidly rising real interest rates. But that was only one side of the SAL coin. The other was the finding of willing takers, particularly given the newly attached policy conditions. That task was not as straightforward as it might have appeared, because embedded in the new SAL instrument lay a curious example of moral hazard.

One of us, Mosley (1987: 2) has argued that policy reform conditionality has two features which create an opportunity for borrowers to cheat – that is, to avoid fulfilling the promised programme of policy change. First, the policy changes are often numerous and disparate in nature, and loosely linked with capacity to repay the loan. Second, the fulfilment of the conditions cannot be achieved in a short period of time, and often stretches out over quite a few years. SAL policy conditions are, in a word, broader and longer than conditions attaching to IMF drawings and are *ipso facto* easier to evade. The moral hazard of SALs was that some hard-pressed developing countries would be tempted to take a short-sighted view of their national interest and accept a SAL without having any serious intention of fulfilling the policy conditions. Indeed, that this was a very real possibility was demonstrated very quickly with the Bolivian SAL of May, 1980, a $50 million loan which was made with very little preparation and which produced nothing by way of policy change in Bolivia. That this *could* happen did not imply that it *would* happen, necessarily and inevitably. Another early SAL to Turkey in March, 1980 for $275 million had a very different outcome. Here there had been some preparation in the form of the 1978 programme loan (with letter of intent) and the new military government was committed to policy change. It was not interested in exploiting the loopholes which at that time existed in the SAL lending instrument. But an unexploited loophole is still a loophole.

The invention of structural adjustment lending thus immediately raised a number of unresolved questions. Although the SAL was devised before the electoral successes of conservative parties in Europe and the United States, it quickly began to be seen as the instrument which could exert pressure on developing countries to follow orthodox liberal economic prescriptions of price reform and privatisation. Yet division remained within the Bank both about how much such leverage should be attempted and how much, if it were attempted, such leverage should be publicly acknowledged. Another question which had clearly emerged by late 1980 was whether SALs were properly designed to exert leverage at all, particularly after the Bolivian fiasco.

Again, although the SAL was not devised as a means to cope with the economic blizzard which began in mid-1979, its ability to provide quick-disbursing balance-of-payments support made its arrival and expansion seem very timely in 1980. But from this point of view, policy conditionality became an element of awkwardness, which Bank staff hoped would be resolved by developing countries' willing compliance with the stated conditions. In short, the new SAL soon revealed itself as the offspring of Janus, smiling with one face as it delivered welcome foreign exchange, frowning with the other as it insisted on the performance of politically dangerous and administratively complex tasks.

2.4 SALs IN PRACTICE: 1980–6

Between 1980 and 1986, some thirty-seven SALs were negotiated by the Bank, with a value of US $5,259 million (see Table 2.1). SAL activity built up slowly in the first three years of operation, reached its apogee in 1983 and fell away rapidly in the period 1984–6. The figures in Table 2.1 reveal some interesting features of the Bank's experience with SALs. Three in particular are relevant for an account of the practical history of SALs.

The slow start in 1980–2 reflects the hesitations and uncertainties within the Bank about the proper role of the SAL instrument, and particularly the reluctance of Board members, who had to approve each SAL, fully to endorse the senior management's strategy of using SALs for leverage on policy reform. By 1983, this reluctance had evaporated, because by this time SAL lending to Turkey, which had absorbed 35 per cent of all SAL lending between 1980 and 1984, appeared to be producing a major success story of economic reform in a country which had been used to state control of economic life for many decades, but whose major exports after fifty years of industrialisation remained raisins, hazelnuts, cotton and tobacco. The burst of confident SAL activity in 1983 soon tailed off, however. This was partly because of the detection by the Bank of design flaws in the SAL instrument, and a felt need, if not to replace it entirely, at least to gain operational flexibility by adding new forms of conditional programme loan to carry forward the task of policy reform. With effect from 1984, the structural adjustment loan was overtaken by the *sectoral* adjustment loan (SECAL) as the vehicle for the majority of what the Bank terms 'adjustment lending' (World Bank, 1988a: 66). In a sense, this was a

Table 2.1   Structural Adjustment Loans by Value, 1980–6 (US$ millions)

Year	Number of SALs	Value	Of which: Turkey
1980	4	580	275
1981	6	782	300
1982	4	670	304
1983	12	1927	300
1984	2	431	376
1985	4	388	–
1986	5	481	–
Total	37	5259	1555

Source: Calculated from Mosley (1987), Table 3.

move back to the model of the 1979 industrial sector loan to the Philippines. But the two forms of policy-based lending between them now account for about a quarter of all World Bank disbursements.

The hesitations of the 1980–2 period were considerable. The Executive Board scrutinized each SAL proposal very carefully and their approval was quite difficult to obtain. The Board was moved by conflicting considerations. On the one hand, it had set its face against using SAL money to persuade reluctant governments to undertake policy reform. On the other hand, it did not want to withhold balance-of-payments support to governments who wanted to pursue reform programmes and had just been knocked off course by large external shocks. But telling the former case from the latter required a long and difficult effort of discrimination.

The public presentation of the new SAL instrument followed closely the Board's view of what it was for. SALs were needed, the Bank said, 'to assist countries . . . prepared to undertake a program of adjustment to meet an existing or to avoid an impending balance of payments crisis' (World Bank, *Annual Report* 1988: 22). What was stressed initially was that the SAL was a response to a once-for-all, exceptional crisis in the balance of payments, albeit one that would require assistance over a longer time period than that for which IMF stand-by finance was available. Such assistance was to be confined to countries both willing and able to make progress on policy reform. As a further limitation on the spread of this form of lending, the Board was assured that it would not exceed 10 per cent of the Bank's annual lending, and that no one country would receive more than five SALs at intervals of twelve to eighteen months.

The country ceiling on the number of SALs was adhered to, and Turkey alone ran the full course of five SALs. But both the 10 per cent of annual lending limit and the initial rationale of SALs did not last. By 1983, SALs were increasingly defended as a means of persuading more governments to change their economic policies, with internal factors being given a greater prominence than external factors as causes of poor development performance. Reforms were increasingly sought in areas, e.g. institutional arrangements, where, even if successful, they would have little immediate impact on the balance-of-payments. Instead of providing balance of payments assistance to countries willing to undertake structural adjustment, the Bank increasingly saw itself as using SAL money to facilitate the countries' decision to adopt a broad programme of economic reform (Berg and Batchelder, 1984: 23–32). Thus the top management's 1979 view of the potential of SALs had finally emerged and the Board's original view finally submerged.

The continued deterioration of developing countries' *external* environments in the early 1980s – worsening terms of trade and rising real interest rates featuring strongly – became a reason why it was especially important for the new, more ambitious conception of adjustment lending to succeed

40

in the task of persuading more countries to change their *internal* policies. (This simply reversed the radical argument of the 1970s that policy inflexibility in LDCs made reforms of the international order especially important.) The worsening international economic climate of the 1980s was also used to justify an expanding volume of adjustment lending and a lengthening of the period during which policy reforms would be required.

But the Bank's attempt to use SALs as a ticket to 'the top policy table' inside developing countries misfired in various important ways. Presumably, one criterion of the success of this attempt would be how many countries were induced to change their economic policy ways as a result of receiving an SAL. If one inspects the country distribution of the early SALs, one finds – always disregarding the 'model' instance of Turkey – two kinds of recipients, neither of which represent great success in targeting SALs on countries switching from long-entrenched *dirigisme* to the orthodox liberal path. One such group are countries whose basic forms of economic organisation were already conducive to growth and export-orientation (although not in any very orthodox manner). These are exemplified by Thailand, South Korea and Malawi, who between them received seven of the early SALs. The other group, while much more in need of conversion to better policies, on the Bank's assessment, evidently found it difficult to change, and the course of treatment was discontinued after (or, in one case, during) the first or second SAL. Apart from Bolivia, Guyana, Pakistan, Panama, Senegal and Yugoslavia fall into this second category. So, in fact, do the initial loans of certain countries which were permitted to continue the SAL treatment, for example, the 1980 SAL for Kenya and the 1980 SAL for the Philippines. In these circumstances, it is not surprising that the Bank itself has found no correlation between the intensity of policy reform carried out under SALs and the pre-existing level of economic distortions as measured by the Bank (Gulhati, 1987: 10; see also Chapter 4). Those least in need of the policy reform medicine swallowed it most readily, while those most in need (on the Bank's criteria) swallowed very little at all.

The shift from about 1982 towards a more open attempt to use SALs to persuade at least half-reluctant governments to embrace policy reforms compounded this problem. The Bank's willingness to 'buy' policy reforms with SAL money tended to place policy reform in a context of bargaining: how much reform should be exchanged for how much programme finance? But in a bargaining context, those with the weakest bargaining strength will be most likely to accept conditional loans, even if they are unhappy with some of the conditions, and they are also likely to accept more heavily conditioned loans than those agreed with better placed bargainers. Conditions for policy reform thus tended to be disproportionately loaded on to countries that needed balance-of-payments support money. These were not necessarily the countries that most urgently needed policy reform –

although in some cases the two distinct needs were both present, and one could cite Ghana as an example here (see Table 2.2).

In this failure to target policy-reform loans effectively on developing countries which are perceived as needing policy reform most urgently, can we detect a result of the Janus-faced character of the SAL? Countries which need the foreign exchange also have to have heavy doses of policy reform, while countries which need the policy reform may not sustain it for long even if they borrow the extra foreign exchange (or, much more disturbingly, precisely because they borrow the extra foreign exchange). In short, the yoking together of money and conditionality may actually make it more difficult to set up a loan with an appropriate borrower – i.e. a country which is independently committed to undertaking policy reform and which has good reason to borrow more.

The progression from SALs to SECALs which has already been noted seems to be a consequence also of design problems in the original SAL concept. Retrospectively, the Bank portrays the progression as a natural one that is related to an 'adjustment cycle' – an initial concentration on the reform of overall incentive structures followed by detailed sector-specific reforms (World Bank, *Annual Report 1988*: 66). This naturalistic explanation is something of an *ex post facto* rationalisation. The first SECAL

Table 2.2 Status of policy and institutional reforms in sub-Saharan Africa

Intensity and duration of reforms 1980–6	*Magnitude of policy and institutional distortions, end of 1970s*		
	High	*Medium*	*Low*
High	Zambia Ghana Zaire	Côte d'Ivoire Togo	Malawi Mauritius
Medium	Somalia Senegal Madagascar	Kenya	
Marginal or none	Liberia	Mali Burkina-Faso Zimbabwe Ethiopia	
Aborted	Sudan Uganda		
New entrants	Guinea Nigeria Tanzania Guinea-Bissau Sierra Leone	Burundi Niger Mauritania	

Source: Gulhati (1987), Table 3, p.10.

was given to Pakistan in 1983–4 at a time when it had exhausted its EFF drawings: it was essentially a device to avoid the requirement of an IMF stand-by programme that the Bank attached to SALs. A number of other early SECALs were made where there was no IMF presence. But that is not the whole story. SECALs were preferred to SALs because of important design flaws in the latter. Further, the growing popularity of SECALs in the late 1980s then raised again the question of whether they should continue to be used in the absence of an IMF stabilisation programme.

We hypothesise that the SAL format was determined by the 'big deal' mentality of the Bank's management in the early 1980s, and that from this its design flaws stemmed. The aim was to gain a purchase on high policy, to do so through direct negotiations at the highest level and to be offering enough resources to justify the attention of the country's top policy-makers. A sum like the $1.5 billion which Turkey was able to borrow under the SAL arrangements would be much more likely to achieve this than the normal project loan. However, in the pursuit of the big deal, the moral hazard problem was lost sight of. The size of the conditionality sought was related to the size of the money available – both had to be big. The early SALs were extravagant and naïve in their conditionality. The conditions were spread out across a broad range of policy areas including trade policy, public finance, price reform in agriculture and in energy and institutional change in the civil service, parastatals and public corporations. In order to indicate this, Table 2.3 shows the high percentage of SALs that included conditions related to nineteen typical policy measures.

The average SAL had conditions in ten of these nineteen policy reform areas, and a particular SAL could have as many as one hundred separate policy conditions. (The second SAL in Thailand boasted *over* one hundred conditions.) Once a SAL was being negotiated, a temptation existed (and was not always resisted) for each different division of the Bank to add some extra conditions that related to their own areas of current policy concern. The SAL often became a 'Christmas tree' decorated with enough conditions to please everyone. This had various quite serious implications. The obvious one is administrative overload on the borrowing country, which may often, like Ghana, have just suffered a large out-migration of skilled and educated labour during the prior phase of economic crisis. Even when firm political support existed for policy reform, the conditions could easily make demands that were beyond the weakened administrative capacity of the country. This was especially ironical because one of the difficulties with project loans (which programme aid was supposed to overcome) was the strain which too many new projects placed on local administrative capacity. A second, less obvious, problem was that the plethora of conditions caused confusion in the mind of the borrower. Which conditions were the ones that *really* mattered to the Bank? Since it was unlikely that all the conditions could be attended to, it was important that the borrower should

Table 2.3 Types of policy measure requested in return for SAL finance, 1980–6

Measure	Percentage of SALs subject to conditions in this area
Trade policy:	
Remove import quotas	57
Cut tariffs	24
Improve export incentives, etc.	76
Resource mobilisation:	
Reform budget or taxes	70
Reform interest rate policy	49
Strengthen management of external borrowing	49
Improve financial performance of public enterprise	73
Efficient use of resources:	
Revise priorities of public investment programme	59
Revise agricultural prices	73
Dissolve or reduce powers of state marketing boards	14
Reduce or eliminate some agricultural import subsidies	27
Revise energy prices	49
Introduce energy-conservation measures	35
Develop indigenous energy sources	24
Revise industry incentive system	68
Institutional reforms:	
Strengthen capacity to formulate and implement public investment programme	86
Increase efficiency of public enterprises	57
Improve support for agriculture (marketing, etc.)	57
Improve support for industry and subsectors (including price controls)	49

Source: Mosley (1987), Table 2, p.5

not be allowed to pour scarce administrative resources into complying with relatively trivial conditions. Yet a Christmas Tree SAL would allow that to happen.

The practice of piling condition on condition in the SAL agreements was presumably underpinned by a sense within the Bank that this guaranteed value for money in the exchange of loans for promises of reforms. If so, this view was quite illusory. The multiplication of conditions made their implementation harder to monitor and complicated the decision which the Bank had to make about whether or not to proceed with a further SAL in the event that the borrowing country failed to comply with the agreed conditions. Some conditions needed for their performance very little time and administrative effort, and their performance or non-performance was readily inspectable. But many others, especially in the area of institutional reform, but also concerning changes in the vital foreign exchange and domestic budgetary arrangements were not so inspectable, nor would it be reasonable to expect them to be accomplished without a lengthy period of study, consultation and planning. Given the complex interaction of policy instruments, it is often possible to fulfil the stated condition, but simultaneously or shortly afterwards also to take some further action that neutralizes the effect of the fulfilling action. It is also possible to embark on an energetic programme of expert study groups, provisional policy documents and advanced personnel training with the intention of prolonging these activities, in one form or another, until the Greek Calends. Such is the wickedness of the world. The 'toughness' of loan conditions has two aspects – the number and scope of the conditions is one; the severity with which non-compliance is punished is the other. With the SALs, too much toughness in the first sense sabotaged toughness in the second.

For the purposes of policing SAL agreements, therefore, it is more in the interests of the Bank to be dealing with smaller amounts of money, and to have a smaller number of high-priority conditions attached to each loan. In the second half of the 1980s, we see three developments in the design of structural adjustment lending which are essentially a belated response to the problem of policing SALs. One is the growing popularity of the SECAL, and the move away from the initial idea of a set of five SALs, which would follow on from each other, given 'good behaviour' on the part of the borrower. A second is the increased use of 'tranching', the slicing of a given loan up into smaller and smaller elements, the release of each tranche being made dependent on the performance of certain conditions. The third goes even further than tranching. It is the 'front-loading' of conditionality, i.e. the requirement that key conditions are fulfilled in advance of the release of any part of the loan. Front-loading is significant because it is a move back towards the original perception of the Executive Board that reform does not itself cost money, and that money should be channelled to countries that have already undertaken reforms, not those who say that they are about to. These three moves taken together respond to anxieties about adjustment lending expressed in 1986 by the Joint Audit Committee's Sub-committee on Project Performance Audit Results.

2.5 LENDING VERSUS LEVERAGE

But how far can the development of better techniques of policing loan conditionality by itself overcome deeper and more systemic tendencies within the Bank to lend more, even in the face of poor compliance? After all, only one country, Senegal, has in the 1980s been refused the release of the second tranche of an adjustment loan. In numerous other cases the Bank has insisted on delaying the release of loan tranches, but in the end the money has been sanctioned. Either one can argue that virtually all borrowers respond positively to the use of delays, or one has to conclude that Bank conditionality has been of the relatively 'soft' variety, with the carrot more in evidence than the stick. Does this reflect strong systemic pressures to lend, which in turn undermine the Bank's ability to exert leverage on policy reform?

Many of the management problems arising in the Bank's internal organization are connected with the attempt to find the right balance between lending and achieving the developmental purposes of lending. The pressure to lend arises because the Bank commits itself in advance to a view of the borrowing needs of the developing countries, on the basis of which it invites additional capital subscriptions from its members and itself borrows on world money markets. Once the size of its planned activity is declared in this way, there is a natural internal pressure for the fulfilment of aggregate lending plans. Coupled with this is the Bank's status as a preferred creditor: repayment of its loans is guaranteed by the government (rather than the actual beneficiary organisation) in the borrowing country; and if and when the government has to request a debt rescheduling, Bank loans are accorded privileged treatment. This protects the Bank financially against some of the worst consequences of unsound lending, and makes it very important that its own internal mechanisms compensate for the lack of financial penalties for poor quality loans.

In the pre-SAL era, when loans were all still mainly for project finance, the conflict of objectives can be illustrated by considering the use that was made of project appraisal by the Bank. Ideally, project appraisal should be used to rank projects according to their calculated social rate of return, and all those projects should be undertaken whose rate of return exceeds the marginal social cost of funds; or, if funds are constrained, projects should be undertaken in rank order until the investment budget is exhausted. The Bank did not follow these ideal investment rules. Rather, it first made its own sectoral allocations of available funds, and then within sectors set a minimum rate of return which each project undertaken had to satisfy. This sub-optimising treatment of projects was used *despite* the Bank's own considerable investment in developing the methodology of project appraisal (Leff, 1985). The Bank's practice in this matter represents an evident compromise between the desire to facilitate lending, and the desire to maintain control of the quality of the projects financed. Project evaluations show that Bank projects in India, for example, achieved healthy rates of return, in the range from 10 to 50 per cent. But it is quite possible that even better results could have been achieved, especially since actual results were often the product of a redesign process which was undertaken *after* projects were started, and which imposed considerable delays on the planned schedule of work (Lipton and Toye, 1990: 149–61).

The development goals of the SALs, which are intended to flow from sustaining or promoting policy reform, are in essentially the same tension with the pressure to lend. The rapid expansion of the McNamara Bank in the 1970s had internalised this pressure with the setting of country lending *targets*, and a staff appraisal and promotion system which judged officers on their skill in meeting such targets, given the internal checks and balances aimed at preventing irresponsible lending. In the 1980s, although expansion became much less rapid, the very deterioration of the external economic environment of developing countries has strengthened the pressure to lend. This must have weakened the Bank's use of conditionality in some areas of its lending. The additional pressures can be looked at on two levels, that of the global debt crisis and that of the Bank's own financial situation.

As indicated in Chapter 1, the Bank was slow to anticipate the emergence of the global debt crisis of 1982, and found itself facing a situation in which new commercial bank lending to developing countries suddenly almost ceased while the interest rate on existing debt rose. Net transfers to developing countries reached zero by mid-1983 and reverse transfers *from* developing countries reached $30 billion by 1987, the same year in which the Bank itself began to receive more in financial inflows from developing countries than it was able to lend to them. Table 2.4 shows a $700 million *positive* net transfer for 1988, but this relates only to countries who were current borrowers at that date and the overall position was much worse than this indicates. Negative net transfers have continued in 1989 and 1990, and are now over $50 billion. The pressure to lend is both general, to return the Bank toward being again a positive net lender to developing countries, and particular, to give special assistance to highly indebted Latin American borrowers where US commercial banks had dangerously large exposures. The Bank's top management does not admit that its decisions are influenced by the net transfers situation, but that is only to be expected in the circumstances.

In terms of the Bank's own financial health, the pressure arises from its policy of rarely retrospectively softening the terms of its own loans. Twelve loans were, exceptionally, rescheduled in 1968 as part of the Indian saga

Table 2.4   World Bank net transfers in 1988 (US$ millions)

	Africa	Asia	Europe, etc.	L.A. + Caribbean	Total
Gross disbursements	1873	6009	2820	4257	14959
Repayments	555	2732	1672	2460	7419
Net disbursements	1318	3277	1148	1797	7540
Interest and charges	736	2363	1573	2158	6830
Net transfer	582	914	−425	−361	711

Source: Calculated from World Bank, *Annual Report* 1988
Tables 6.4, 6.7, 6.10 and 6.13.

already mentioned, and other exceptions include Haiti, Lebanon and Chile (pre-1968); Bangladesh (1975) and Nicaragua (1979). Thus as more countrie˙ built up arrears on their existing repayments and debt service – something which the Bank, for other reasons connected with its own creditworthiness, wishes to minimise – the Bank's only recourse is to arrange fresh lending. Formally, its policy is not to allow fresh loans to countries in arrears on past loans. To permit this to happen, an elaborate ritual can be performed involving borrowing from a third party to pay off the Bank's arrears, in the knowledge that forthcoming Bank lending will allow the third party to be promptly repaid (Faber, 1990). Since the Bank also refuses to make unconditional programme loans, the new loan has to embody policy conditionality, even if the main purpose is simply to reduce the build-up of its own arrears. In this case, the required conditionality is merely window-dressing.

Apart from financial pressures, the Bank also has to contend with straight political pressures from its major shareholders to lend for non-economic reasons. A blatant recent example of this was the huge composite loan of $1.25 billion to Argentina in October, 1988. Highly indebted both to US commercial banks and to the World Bank, Argentina received very rapid approval for this huge new loan, despite the absence of an IMF stabilisation programme (hitherto regarded as an absolute *sine qua non*) and despite a reputation for poor compliance with Bank conditionality. Belatedly, the Bank is trying to limit the damage caused by its capitulation to US government pressure by cancelling large chunks of this loan[4]. But a consequence of high risk lending is that the Bank must try hard to balance its portfolio by lending more to low-risk, low-indebtedness countries such as India, Thailand and Botswana where conditionality is either impossible to secure or largely unnecessary (Wade, 1989: section 3.4). Thus the use of conditions as window-dressing for what are essentially balance of payments support loans tends to erode the legitimacy of conditionality in those other cases where it is intended seriously.

Within the Bank's organization, the various sources of pressure to lend have to contend with inbuilt checks against unsound lending. The Executive Board itself does not help very much in this regard. Its practice of scrutinising every loan, though it sounds like a good safeguard, does not quite work in that way. The Board concerns itself with rather few other aspects of the Bank's operations, and is distanced from the analytical background information which provides the necessary context for individual loan proposals. At the same time, loan proposals are so numerous that success depends on making them 'acceptable' to the Board at the precise moment of their pre-programmed window of opportunity – one of the 247 slots into which all proposals must be fitted in the course of the year. A lot of massaging of proposals goes on to ensure their momentary acceptability, by such means as excessively optimistic primary product price forecasts.

The spending of extra time to improve the quality of the loan is discouraged, because 'missing the slot' imposes serious delays before the opportunity for Board consideration will recur.

At lower levels in the Bank, the preparation of an adjustment loan passes through various stages of internal scrutiny. When a new loan is proposed, an initiating memorandum is considered by the Operations Committee (previously the Loan Committee) and, if the decision is favourable, a loan appraisal mission is dispatched to the intended borrower country. Any substantial changes in the proposal after its approval by the Operations Committee have to be approved by the Senior Vice-President (Operations). Once the appraisal mission's report has been received, a second stage of decision-making occurs: the granting of permission for a direct negotiation with the borrowing government. The final stage takes place once a loan agreement package has been negotiated. Since there is a premium on speed and flexibility of response, the Senior Vice-President (Operations) makes the final decision on behalf of the Bank on the commitment of funds to the loan.

This decision-making procedure for adjustment loans has altered very little since 1980. The only major change has been that since 1986, second-stage approval has normally been conducted by circulation of Operations (Loan) Committee members, rather than by decision in full committee. Thus adjustment lending has been little affected by the upheavals of the Bank's reorganisation in 1987, which took place just after Barber Conable succeeded A.W. Clausen as its President. (The Bank's structure following this reorganisation is set out as Figure 2.1.) The Bank's Annual Report for 1988 (p.45) admits guardedly that 'the short-term, intangible costs of the reorganisation were perhaps higher than had been expected'. The short-term effects were the disruption of normal business and the massive droop in staff morale. In the longer term it has been asked whether the reduction of staff and the streamlining of organisational structure has not reduced the ability of specialist staff to run independent checks on the quality of loan proposals (Wade, 1989). If this is so, however, it seems that it will concern project lending and not adjustment lending, where the internal checks and balances have survived more or less intact.

The phenomenon of 'hitting the target', i.e. fulfilling management-set lending plans, does seem to affect adjustment lending to some degree. Each country does have a preplanned lending programme which includes adjustment loans: it looks forward three years and is part of an envelope of projections stretching five years ahead. The country programme, however, is expressed in terms of a *range* of amounts. The existence of this range means that the target for lending can be hit even if there is some last-minute delay or cancellation of lending as part of the enforcement of conditionality in a particular country. There is, by contrast, much less substitution between regions than there is between countries. Limited

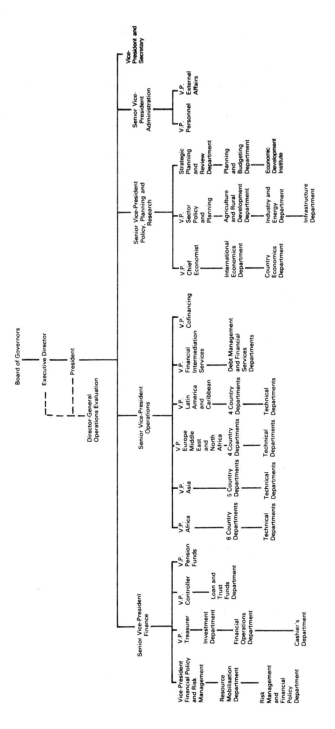

Figure 2.1 World Bank organisation chart since 1987 reorganisation

freedom to switch lending between countries when this has to be done is not paralleled by the same freedom at the level of regions. It may be that financial resources which ideally should be switched from Africa to Asia at the margin do not get switched in this way. The consequence of this regional-level rigidity in allocations is that, while conditionality can be enforced on one or two countries in a region at any one time, it could not be enforced on all. When some countries in the region are being disciplined, others will necessarily find that a more lenient and charitable view is taken of their economic performance. In this kind of system, the Bank's leverage for the enforcement of policy reform conditions will necessarily remain partial.[5]

2.6 THE WORLD BANK/IMF RELATIONSHIP

After the question of leverage, the second major flaw in the SAL concept which the Executive Board identified in 1980 was the complication which it introduced into the already touchy relations between the Bank and the IMF. The SALs at one and the same time launched the Bank on a career of conditional programme lending and yoked Bank conditionality to situations in which Fund conditionality was already operating. From this, the problems of Bank/Fund cross-conditionality emerged. They fall into two main categories – problems arising from the different nature of the two conditionalities, and problems arising from the need to harmonise the content of the two kinds of conditionality.

The first difficulty is that Fund and Bank conditionality work quite differently. Fund conditions are quantified and precise, relating to macroeconomic performance indicators which are already in place. The consequences of failure to meet conditions are non-negotiable and serious, resulting in a cessation of further lending until it is reinstated by the IMF Board. Bank conditionality, by contrast, runs a spectrum from quantified to highly qualitative; compliance is not always easy to judge and thus becomes negotiable; and established failure may or may not be reacted to severely by the Bank – all that may happen is that a reaffirmation of good intentions by the borrower is sought. These differences may be quite confusing for developing countries' policy-makers. In the day-to-day bustle of policy- making, it is quite easy for developing country governments to neglect the question of *whose* conditions apply to a particular action, and to be surprised and disrupted by the discovery that what was assumed to be a negotiable Bank condition is, in fact, a Fund condition with strict punishment following. Of course, LDC governments ought not to get confused about these technicalities, any more than they should fail to compile a central record of their external debt, or not know how many people they employ. But the fact is that they do and the consequences to them can be costly in terms of delayed external finance.

The second type of problem is one of consistency. Conflicting advice from international experts is bad enough if one's policy-making abilities are weak, as is true *ex hypothesi* for countries receiving structural adjustment loans. But to be mandated to do contradictory things, and so to be vulnerable to sanctions (admittedly of different degrees of hardness or softness) whatever one does is double jeopardy, and it ought to be as outlawed in the practice of international financial institutions as it is in the US constitution. There are structural reasons why – unless something is done to prevent it – the double jeopardy of conditionality will occur. The Bank and the Fund have differing institutional objectives in their dealings with developing countries, and, armed each with its own condition-making power, may easily either directly or by implication require actions which frustrate the objectives of the other. The Fund's setting of values for key macroeconomic variables will notoriously constrain what can be done in the Bank's realm of microeconomic supply side changes.

It might be inferred that this conflict opens up additional room for policy manoeuvre for the borrowing government. This is not the typical result. If an LDC government wishes to play the Bank off against the Fund, it will try to do this by dealing with them in sequence, not in parallel. When both are present, it is much more likely either that the Fund conditions will simply undermine the growth-orientated strategies of the Bank (as in Jamaica under Seaga) or that the Fund and Bank will negotiate away their differences over the head of the developing country government (as tended to happen in Malawi).

In the mid-1980s the Bank itself had occasion to conclude that the strict tying of adjustment lending to the presence of an IMF stabilisation operation was too constraining and inflexible. The new *sectoral* adjustment loan (given first to Pakistan in 1983–4) was an initial step towards a more flexible style of adjustment lending. A narrower focus for policy reform plus a different name made it legitimate in the Bank's eyes to sidestep its own rule (which has been broken only in the cases of Honduras and Argentina) that a SAL must be accompanied by an IMF programme (or a programme agreed with the IMF, even if the programme itself was not being implemented, as in the case of Nigeria[6]). Some nine SECALs were agreed with developing countries on a non-IMF basis. Others were agreed on the same with-IMF basis as the normal SALs. But the non-IMF-linked SECALs themselves proved problematic, both from the Bank's and from the borrowers' viewpoints. What were the problems?

One concerned the feasibility of securing sectoral adjustment in conditions of macroeconomic instability. The classic example is the difficulty of securing a realignment of relative prices in one economic sector when the economy as a whole is experiencing the acceleration of inflation. Unless the macroeconomy is 'on track', sectoral adjustment becomes very much more difficult. The acknowledgement of this difficulty has produced, on the one hand, a shift back towards the Bank's use of SECAL in conjunction with IMF programmes and, on the other, an internal debate about whether the existence of an IMF programme itself necessarily guarantees that the macroeconomy *is* on track. The sceptics argue that an IMF programme may be in place, but not (or not yet) working; and that the Bank's own macroeconomic diagnosis and prescription has on occasion (especially in Africa) proved itself superior to the Fund's. One hears, therefore, some talk of the Bank adopting, as a condition of all its adjustment lending, the requirement that 'overall the adjustment programme is on track' and leaving open the precise modality of how that condition is to be verified.

This may not last long, however, for two very practical reasons. One is that, if the Bank lends in the absence of the Fund, and if the borrower country is indebted to the Fund, the Bank's loan will merely 'cross 19th Street', i.e. be used by the borrower to pay old Fund debts – something which the Bank does not want to be seen doing. The other reason is that, as external conditions of LDCs have worsened in the 1980s, more borrower countries have sought debt rescheduling at the Paris Club, or elsewhere. In order to secure it, they need to have a Fund programme in place. Since the value to them of a debt rescheduling is likely to be much more than the value of an adjustment loan from the Bank, the development of a non-IMF-based adjustment loan is not likely to seem especially attractive to poor and debt-distressed LDCs.

But to combine an IMF programme with a SECAL tends to create more Fund/Bank conflicts than a Fund programme combined with a SAL. When the Bank is concentrating on the reform of one sector, it can become less aware of, or patient with, the Fund view of the macroeconomic constraints. So, at the end of the 1980s, the issue of Bank-Fund co-ordination remained on the agenda of adjustment lending, and produced two important innovations in their relationship – the 'Policy Framework' and the 'New Concordat' of early 1989. The Policy Framework Paper (PFP) is a document drafted by the Fund, and amended and agreed by the Bank and the borrowing government, which sets out a joint understanding of the economic situation of the borrowing country and the policies necessary for successful stabilisation and adjustment. It is the bare bones of an economic development plan, containing agreed projections and planning assumptions about future policies.

The origin of the PFP lies in the Fund's establishment of a new Structural Adjustment Facility in 1986 (the SAF). In the early 1980s, the Fund decided that (following the precedent of its EFF), it would further expand its medium-term lending, but now would do so on concessional terms (which the EFF had not featured). The reason why the Fund did not want to leave this type of lending to the Bank is not very clear. But the opportunity for the Fund to move into concessional structural adjustment lending was provided by the repayments that had flowed back from its earlier Trust Fund lending. SAF lending raised the problem of consistency of policy reform conditions between the Fund and the Bank in an acute and obvious form, and the PFP was the result. When the Fund introduced the Enhanced Structural Adjustment Facility (ESAF) in 1987 for poor indebted LDCs pursuing stabilisation and adjustment policies, the agreement of a PFP was made a prerequisite for access to this very favourable $8 billion facility.

Although the PFP has proved itself as a useful way of limiting the damage done in the borrowing country by conflicts of policy between the Fund and the Bank, it is not, and cannot be, a method of eliminating these conflicts. The two organisations pursue different institutional objectives, and these are likely to continue to result in conflicts of viewpoint and *conjunctural* judgement. The Bank, for example, will always want to show that a country has a financing gap in its macroeconomic accounts – a gap large enough to require Bank and other donor finance, but not so big as to frighten away co-financing donors. The Fund remains basically concerned with the required internal changes for restoration of a sustainable macroeconomic trajectory. The recent statements of its Managing Director, M. Camdessus, about social aspects of adjustment and excessive defence expenditure almost certainly exaggerate the extent to which the Fund at the operational level has moved or will move away from this traditional brief.

Second, although the PFP provides a solution to the problem of conflicting conditions, it does bring another problem in its wake. Has Bank/Fund cross-conditionality become too strong? We need not delay long with the technical response that formal cross-conditionality between Bank and Fund loans does not exist. This is correct: a breach of a Bank condition still does not jeopardise a Fund loan or vice versa. But effectively there has been a great deal of informal cross-conditionality (although with the conspicuous exception of the 1988 Argentina loan already mentioned). This arises because Bank adjustment lending normally requires an IMF stabilisation loan to be in place. If the conditions of both loans are then co-ordinated through a PFP – and if bilateral donors then follow suit by making their aid subject to the conditionality of the Fund and Bank being observed – does this not become an intolerable strait-jacket on the borrower's freedom of action in policy-making?

That it constitutes more of a strait-jacket than the previous arrangement seems undeniable. The room for independent policy manoeuvre *is* more restricted, both in terms of the measures to be adopted, and of the sequencing and timing of their adoption. Whether this is intolerable depends on one's opinion of the policies which informal cross-conditionality now makes it more difficult for the borrower to avoid. If they are undeniably right, then increased constraint must logically be a good thing, and, if not, not. What is worrying about the new situation is that it effectively creates a managed duopoly of policy advice. Once the officials of the Bank and the Fund have made up their minds, there is usually little material contribution from the officials of the borrowing government, at least in the case of the poor, indebted countries where conditionality already bites hardest. Since the Bank from 1986 has begun to speak publicly of the political aspect of structural adjustment lending, and has acknowledged its efforts to build up internal coalitions in borrowing countries in support of its policies, it is perfectly clear that the tightening of cross-conditionality has direct implications for the political future of borrowing countries. On these grounds alone, a concern for liberal values would seem to indicate the need to break the duopoly of economic advice which at present is co-ordinated between the Fund and the Bank, and to widen considerably the circle of advisers available to governments for the process of deciding economic policy and for negotiating external finance in a chosen policy context.

The Argentine loan of September, 1988 represented a low point in the co-operation of the Bank and the Fund. In an attempt to repair the damage that was done at this time, a 'new concordat' was devised and agreed by Messrs Conable and Camdessus in early 1989. In the light of what has been said already about enduring differences of objectives, it would not be reasonable to expect that this new concordat has resolved all disagreements, or that its terms will be immune to future differences of interpretation. However, some renewal of co-operation has been achieved around the following decisions.

Where disagreements exist between the Bank's and the Fund's approaches to adjustment, attempts should be made to resolve them at the earliest possible stage, and in particular before conflicting advice is given to the developing country that is involved. The PFP mechanism is a way to do this, but at present it is used only in very poor countries borrowing from the SAF or the ESAF. The question arises whether PFPs should be used also when both Bank and Fund are involved in operations to highly indebted middle-income countries. This would be a politically contentious move, and has not yet been brought to the centre-stage of debate. It clearly would restrict the room for manoeuvre of middle-income borrowers. At the same time, it has also to be said that these countries have typically much greater sources of skilled, professional personnel who could contribute to the policy-making debate. So there should be less chance that the content of the PFP will represent a Fund-Bank policy *diktat* than is currently the case with SAF and ESAF low-income borrowers.

Even if this extension of the PFP mechanism does take place, and Fund–Bank co-ordination becomes still tighter, the 1989 concordat (which is, technically, only a 'joint memorandum') does not envisage any institutional merging. Each institution will retain its own identity and independence of decision. There will be no joint Fund/Bank missions, although Bank staff may be invited – as has happened frequently before – to accompany a Fund mission, or vice versa. There are many practical ways in which close co-operation can be maintained, through regular consultation meetings, through exchange of briefing papers, memoranda and forecasts and through willingness to interpret functions flexibly when it would assist the other institution for this to be done. But none of these go even as far as the notion that either the Fund or the Bank act as the 'lead institution' in a country, let alone the idea floated in the mid-1980s for a merger between Bank and Fund (Please, 1984: 69–74). From the viewpoint of encouraging a more vigorous and more transparent debate about adjustment, policy reform and concessional finance, the continued absence of a merged Bank/Fund or Fund/Bank is surely to be welcomed.

APPENDIX. A SAMPLE POLICY-BASED LENDING AGREEMENT
(dated February 1987)

Proposed structural adjustment programme: issues and scope

Structural issues	Measures taken by government	Conditions of Board presentation	Prior to second tranche disbursement
MACROECONOMIC AND EXPORT PROMOTION			
Maintain competitiveness of exports, especially non-traditional exports.	Renewal of Copper Stabilisation Fund established in 1985.	Maintain Copper Stabilisation Fund.	Strengthen Cooper Stabilisation Fund in 1988 by narrowing bands that activate fund and substitute quarterly for annual averaging.
	Attractive real exchange rate.	Continue present policy of nominal adjustments in the exchange rate to maintain the real effective exchange rate.	Continue present policy of regular adjustments in the nominal exchange rate to maintain the real effective exchange rate.
Promote non-traditional exports to continue efforts of diversification.	Legislation that provides incentives to small non-traditional exporters.	Modify incentive framework if non-traditional exports are projected to grow by less than 6% in real terms in 1987.	Modify incentive framework if non-traditional exports are projected to grow by less than 7% in real terms in 1988.
			Evidence that programme of external financing will continue to be adequate.

Structural issues	Measures taken by government	Conditions of Board presentation	Prior to second tranche disbursement
Offset disadvantage of tariff system for exports.	Unified 20% tariff rate for imports. Established limited drawback programme for exports.	Revise Decree Laws 1226 and 409 to expand tariff rebate system to include indirect exporters in drawback system.	
		Promote non-traditional exports by establishing legal framework for export credit insurance system and partial guarantees for small exporters.	

PUBLIC FINANCE AND INVESTMENT

Structural issues	Measures taken by government	Conditions of Board presentation	Prior to second tranche disbursement
Increase the contribution of the public sector to domestic savings.	Publication of 1986–9 development programme.	Increase public savings to a projected 4.8% of GDP in 1987.	Increase public savings to a projected 5.0% of GDP in 1988.
Maintain performance of overall public sector consistent with sustainable growth.			Maintain current programme of public expenditure restraint to limit overall deficit of non-financial public sector to 1.6% of GDP for 1987 and less for 1988.
Improve social returns to public investment.	Prepared public investment programme 1987–9.	Prepare an investment programme with investment levels of 7.5% of GDP in 1988 consistent with sustainable increases in overall investment.	Prepare a public investment programme for the years 1988–90, including investment of 7.5% of GDP in 1988; review with the Bank the execution of the 1987 and 1988 public investment programme.

FINANCIAL SYSTEM

Structural issues	Measures taken by government	Conditions of Board presentation	Prior to second tranche disbursement
Continue rehabilitation of the banking system.	Recapitalisation process for intervened banks. Completed privatisation of intervened banks.	Continue banking sector rehabilitation, augmenting monitoring, and improving public disclosure of deposit limits.	Complete a study of banking sector efficiency and competition.

Structural issues	Measures taken by government	Conditions of Board presentation	Prior to second tranche disbursement
	Enacted new banking law of 1986, including deposit insurance scheme.		
Improve efficiency of intermediation in long-term financial markets, enhance security of pension funds, and develop capital markets.	Income tax reform in 1984 to encourage reinvestment of corporate profits and private savings.		Modify tax law to encourage equity investments and reduce stamp tax from 2.4% to 1.2%
	New corporate legislation improving transparency of controlling stockholders and reducing crossparticipation between firms.	Amend DL 3500 to permit enhanced participation of pension funds in equity markets. Strengthen regulation of insurance companies and mutual funds with prudent portfolio guidelines for diversification and limits to related-party investments.	Create more flexible system of risk classification for securities to stimulate capital markets.
SOCIAL SECTORS *Social Security System:* Protection and security of pension funds.	Pension system reform of 1981.	Modify social security law to permit greater investments in equity markets (noted above) and affirm principles of portfolio management.	
Reduce costs and increase competitiveness of AFPs.		Increase competition among pension funds by lowering capital requirements for entry and encouraging new firm-based funds.	Introduce administrative and collection procedures to increase efficiency of private pension funds.

Structural issues	Measures taken by government	Conditions of Board presentation	Prior to second tranche disbursement
Increase long-term coverage of system.	Increase the coverage by extending automatic disability and survival benefits to temporarily unemployed workers.	Complete a study of the coverage of self-employed.	
Encourage widespread knowledge of new system and enhance workers' identification with their funds.		Improve presentation of information on AFP yields, commissions and benefits in quarterly report to affiliates; permit voluntary savings accounts.	Complete study of ways to cut operating costs so as to reduce fixed commissions.
Health System: Consolidate gains of past health invest-ments, especially in primary and preventive health care.	Focusing programme on lowest income groups.		Improve preventive health care and broaden preventive action to include chronic diseases of adults, including cancer, cardio-vascular and other diseases.
Improve efficiency in use of resources allocated to SNSS.	Partial decentralisation and municipalisation of health system beginning in 1981.		Implement administrative systems to improve cost containment, accounting, user fee collection, and hospital management.
Improve efficiency of the private health care system.			Strengthen regulation of private health care industry (e.g.: cancellation of policies) and clarify contracting relations with public sector.

Structural issues	Measures taken by government	Conditions of Board presentation	Prior to second tranche disbursement
Improve efficiency of investment in health.			Undertake two-year programme to rehabilitate machinery & hospitals.

NOTES

1 Another reason for arguing that the fungibility problem was not serious in sub-Saharan Africa in the 1970s is the following. When a developing country government is following 'bad' policies according to the donors' perceptions, it is much more likely that project aid will in fact be financing the project to which it is nominally related – i.e. the top priority project of the donor will be different from that of the recipient. So it would *not* have been undertaken *in any case*, contrary to the necessary pre-condition for fungibility. On this, see Singer (1965: 541–2). In sub-Saharan Africa in the 1970s, most donors would have criticised or disagreed with the dominant priorities and policies.

2 The Executive Board of the World Bank is a subordinate body to the Bank's Board of Governors, which consists of one Governor for each member country, usually the Minister of Finance or equivalent. The Governors delegate most of their powers to a Board of Executive Directors, which performs its duties on a full-time basis at the Bank's Washington headquarters. Although in 1970–80 there were 121 member countries, there are only twenty-two Executive Directors, so some Directors – especially from developing countries – speak for many countries and not just one, like the Executive Directors for the United States and the UK, for example. The Executive Directors decide on Bank policy within the framework of the Articles of Agreement and also decide on all loan and credit proposals. But, compared with the Board of the IMF, the Executive Directors of the Bank have notably less power in relation to their senior management team, on whom they tend to rely rather heavily for expert guidance.

3 The Pearson Report resulted from the initiative of a previous President of the World Bank, George Woods, who towards the end of his period of office in 1967, appointed three ex-ministers of Western governments, economists and one banker to act as a Commission on International Development and conduct a 'grand assize' on the question of aid and economic development. This was the origin of the aid target of 1 per cent of GNP, as well as the idea of more long- term programme lending. The Indian Executive Director of the Bank frequently pressed the latter idea on his colleagues during the 1970s.

4 In many ways, the Argentina loan of October 1988 was an aberration, and one must be careful not to draw conclusions about the normal character of Bank lending from this case. The one conclusion (and it is a very important one) that can be drawn is that the Bank occasionally capitulates to political pressure from a major shareholder (usually, as in this case, the United States) to make or withold loans for essentially political reasons. The basic structure of the Bank with highly unequal 'shareholdings' creates the circumstances in which this can happen. In the Argentinian case, pressure was exerted by US Treasury Secretary Baker with a view to preventing turbulence in the Southern Cone during the period of the US Presidential Election. Baker himself then swiftly departed to join George Bush's successful election campaign. The Bank has since tried to recover some ground

after its humiliating submission to US pressure. As of November 1989, only $125 million had been released to Argentina, and no request had been received by the Bank for release of the second tranche. The Bank's view is that Argentina's reform programme is well off track, and that fresh negotiations for a fresh loan would be needed if it gets back on track and Bank assistance is sought. Clearly, a damage limitation operation is in place.

5 It is sometimes argued that once lending targets are set, all the Bank's institutional incentives to its staff are harnessed to ensure that the lending target is fulfilled. It is certainly true that staff see lending as their major job function, and that successful lending operations raise staff morale and attract institutional rewards. But there is also another side to this story. The Bank, like other bureaucracies, tends to place its high-flying staff in countries where the Bank's operations are most complex and embattled, e.g. recently in Brazil and Nigeria. It is therefore not at all uncommon to find promotions being given to staff who have *failed* to hit the country lending target.

6 Nigeria managed to borrow from the Bank once it had agreed with the Fund the terms of a Letter of Credit, although because of domestic political considerations it did not draw down at that time any of the IMF credit. This showed great ingenuity on the part of General Babangida, but it is another exceptional case. Informal cross-conditionality remains the norm.

Part II

THE DYNAMICS OF
POLICY REFORM

3

CONDITIONALITY AS
BARGAINING PROCESS

3.1 THE CHARACTER OF WORLD BANK
CONDITIONALITY

As described in Chapters 1 and 2, both the world economy and the Bank's diagnosis of its problems had by the beginning of the 1980s changed in ways which made its principal operational instrument – the loan to finance a particular development project – appear inadequate as an approach to the major problems which faced it at the time: unprecedented levels of balance-of-payments deficit and debt service all over the developing world, stagnation in most of Latin America, and long-term decline in sub-Saharan Africa. Projects manifestly provided too small and slow-disbursing a financial flow to deal with the debt and balance-of-payments problems, and the conditions attached to them did not touch those levers of economic control – exchange rates and agricultural prices, interest rates and trade policies – which, at least within the Bank, were widely seen as providing the key to project success and the relief of underdevelopment more generally.[1] By providing quick-disbursing finance linked to understandings concerning the manner in which those levers of control were to be managed, the new instrument of policy-based lending held out the hope of killing two birds with one stone; more generous financial flows and more effective economic policy combined in the same package. The question breaks down into two parts: under what circumstances did the Bank succeed in changing economic policy within recipient countries, and did such changes as were made have the desired effect? Part II of this book is directed at the first of these questions, and Part III at the second.

The vehicle which the Bank chose as a means of changing the economic policies of LDC governments – conditionality – is new neither in international finance, nor in human relations more generally. Conditionality is simply a side condition designed to ensure the execution of a *contract*. A contract is a promise by one party to do something now in exchange for a promise by the other party to do something else in the future. Since the borrower, in a loan contract, fulfils his side of the bargain later than the lender, he may be tempted to default on repayments; the lender needs a threat to discourage this. The threat normally employed by commercial banks is to require the borrower, as a condition of the loan being given, to pledge a capital asset such as a house or a piece of land, known as *collateral*, to the lender: if repayments fall into arrears, the borrower has a legal obligation to hand the asset over to the lender.

In international finance, the problem of discouraging default remains, but the lender does not have the same range of threats available to him. A commercial bank, government, or international agency such as the IMF cannot sue the government of Peru in an international court of law if a Peruvian company, or indeed the government of Peru itself, fails to repay a loan.[2] Nor can it demand collateral in the form of physical assets. What substitutes for collateral are available in such a situation? There are three possibilities. The lender can refuse follow-on finance to all borrowers whose loans go into arrears; but the more hopeless a debtor's repayment possibilities become, the less potent a threat this is as a means of extracting repayments on current debt.[3] He can demand a government guarantee; but government guarantees are not always honoured. The final possibility is that if there exist government policies which can reliably be expected to increase the likelihood of repayment of the loan, the lender may insist on the implementation of these policies, and suspend disbursement of the loan if the policies are not implemented. This is of course precisely the threat strategy employed by the IMF, which lends to governments for balance-of-payments support, and which as a general rule requires borrowing governments to implement a package of macroeconomic policy conditions which it believes will improve the balance of payments. These 'policy conditions' vary from country to country but generally include restrictions on monetary growth and public expenditure, and often include devaluation, increases in taxes or public utility prices or wage controls (Killick *et al.*, 1984: chapter 6). The effectiveness of these conditions, and their political and social consequences, remain of course the subject of strenuous controversy, but in the midst of all this, three things remain clear and undisputed: the purpose of IMF conditions is to serve as a substitute for collateral, by increasing the likelihood of loan repayment and giving the lender an early warning of potential repayment difficulties; the conditions are defined in terms of unambiguous, and monitorable, performance indicators, such as the rate of expansion of central bank credit to the public sector or the official exchange rate against the US dollar; and if conditions are broken by the borrower, the lender always enforces his threat to interrupt disbursement of the loan, unless a specified 'waiver' or 'modification' is negotiated (Killick, *et al.*, 1984: chapter 4).

It is otherwise with the forms of conditionality which the World Bank has introduced in the 1980s. In the first place, the purpose of conditionality is no longer primarily to maximise the probability of repayment of the loan, but rather as we have seen to enable the borrower to remove what the lender sees as fundamental policy-induced obstacles to economic growth. Some measures introduced as side conditions for the grant of a SAL or a SECAL – notably cuts in tariff rates and increases in the prices paid to farmers by statutory boards – may actually increase the short-term public sector deficit and to that extent aggravate the problem of debt service; indeed, the case studies of Volume 2 record a number of instances in which conditions on Bank policy-based loans were *relaxed* (or new finance provided) in order to facilitate the repayment of international debt.[4] The achieving of influence over the levers of government policy, instead of being a means to the end of more certain repayment, thus becomes an end in itself.[5] Second, some conditions attached to World Bank policy-based loans, unlike IMF stand-bys, either take a long time to monitor (e.g. 'Raise the tax/GNP ratio to 16 per cent over the next five years', Thailand: SAL I) or else because of their institutional nature are not framed in precise quantitative terms; there must always be room for honest disagreement over whether a condition such as 'Establish an action programme for the promotion of exports' (Jamaica: SAL I) or even 'Substantial reductions in support prices for rice, corn and sorghum to be announced by March 1985' (Panama: SAL I) has in fact been implemented. Finally, not all of the conditions attached to World Bank policy-based loans are in fact enforced in the sense that their breach leads to withdrawal of financial support. On the Bank's assessment '[Only] about 60 per cent of agreed conditions [our own assessment in Chapter 5 points to a substantially lower figure] were fully implemented during the loan period' but, as the Bank concedes in the same paragraph, 'in almost every case release [of the second tranche of the loan] has eventually been made, even though the original conditions were substantially less than 100 per cent satisfied' (World Bank, 1988: 15). A number of recipient countries which have been most remiss in complying with conditions, including Kenya, Ecuador and the Philippines prior to 1985, have had little difficulty in obtaining follow-up programme finance from the Bank, a fact of which other borrowers from the Bank are well aware. All in all it seems inappropriate to think of World Bank conditionality as constituting a substitute for collateral; rather, we shall argue, it is a bargaining counter in a game in which the donor (the Bank) seeks to influence economic policy in the manner desired by it, whereas the recipient resists all such attempts at influence which do not harmonise with its own political priorities. Table 3.1 sets out the relationship between the commercial-bank, IMF and World Bank varieties of conditionality.

3.2 THE THREE STAGES OF THE CONDITIONALITY GAME

Our point of departure, then, is that conditionality as practised by the World Bank is a *game* in the sense of being a relationship in which the two

Table 3.1   Three types of conditionality in financial transfers

	Type of loan		
	1 By commercial bank to private individual or company	*2* By IMF to sovereign government (eg stand-by agreement)	*3* By World Bank to sovereign government (eg SAL or SECAL)
Instrument (condition)	Collateral must be transferred to bank in event of loan default	Various, usually including ceilings on central-bank credit and public spending	Various, usually including increases in agricultural prices and trade liberalisation
Target (purpose of condition)	Maximise probability of repayment	Maximise probability of repayment through reductions in aggregate demand	Increase aggregate supply by increasing economic efficiency (usually involving reductions in state control over specific markets)
Link between instrument and target	Very tight	Fairly tight	Rather loose
Can compliance with condition be monitored?	Instantly	Yes, after short delays	Often not for a number of years
Is condition legally enforceable?	Yes	No	No

parties have (at least partly) opposed interests which they pursue by taking note of each other's likely behaviour, and in which the outcome depends on the strategies pursued by each party. This premiss needs to be defended, since not all writers on the Bank accept it. Hayter (1971) for example espouses the view that Bank conditionality is necessarily coercive, in the the sense that it is always implemented and always damaging to the recipient country;[6] on this view, there is no contest worth discussing, since the Bank always wins on its own terms. By contrast, a number of apologists for the Bank have depicted the implementation of its conditionality as being in the mutual interest of donor and recipient,[7] and if this is accepted then by definition no game is involved. But both these interpretations conflict with readily available evidence. If Bank conditionality is truly coercive, it is impossible to explain the fact, noted above, that around half the Bank's conditions to date have not been complied with. And if it is truly in the mutual interests of both donor and recipient, it is impossible to explain the fact that the governments of developing countries have not spontaneously implemented the policy changes desired by the Bank without any prodding from that institution. There is *prima facie* evidence, therefore, both of an inherent conflict of interest between the borrower and the lender of conditional aid, and also of the outcome of that conflict being not predetermined, but the outcome of strategy and external circumstance.

If it is accepted that conditionality is a game, the next step is to examine what its rules are, and what each player is seeking to achieve by playing the game.

For logical simplicity, the conditionality game can be divided into three periods or 'acts':

1 An initial negotiating process (Act 1) in which donor and recipient try to agree on the conditions that are to be attached to a development loan. If successful, this process culminates in agreement on a 'set of specific actions, to be taken by a government and monitored by the Bank' (Stern 1983:93), some of which may have to be undertaken before the first disbursement is made.

2 An implementation process in which the recipient government decides how far to honour the promises it has made during Act 1.

3 A response by the donor in the following period consisting of a decision to grant or refuse further finance to the recipient in the light of the recipient's performance during Act 2.

If the response is positive, there will be subsequent acts to the play – i.e. follow-up loans – but they will have the same logical structure as Acts 2 and 3.

Acts 1 and 3 are bargaining processes – i.e. interactions between the donor and recipient – whereas Act 2 consists of a unilateral action by the recipient. During a bargaining process, either donor or recipient may lay down an *ultimatum*, and if this is not accepted by the other party, negotiations fail at once. If negotiations are able to proceed, they focus around two major issues: the amount of money that the loan will provide, and the policy conditions that will be attached to it.

We now consider the objectives of donor and recipient. The recipient government has a financial motive to maximise the inflow of finance in support of its balance of payments, and a political motive to resist at least some elements of conditionality. The first proposition needs little development, but the identity of the losers from conditionality needs to be made clear. As will be elaborated in the next chapter, the conditions attached to the Bank's SALs and SECALs consist essentially of measures to remove what it sees as harmful state interventions in particular markets, in particular the markets for agricultural produce, energy, credit and foreign exchange. These measures provide specific groups, thought to have political leverage, with a shield against market forces: cheap electricity, petrol and food for urban consumers; access to rationed foreign exchange for selected importers; access to subsidised fertiliser and credit for privileged farmers. The opposition to reform, then, comes from these groups. There are of course gainers from reform, as well as losers – if there were not, the argument for conditionality would fall at the first fence – but it is our contention that these gains, first of all, accrue to the politically weak rather than the strong – for example, small farmers, importers who lack licences – and second, accrue over the long period rather than the short. Even if a recipient government accepts the long-period economic argument in favour of liberalisation, therefore, it will be subject to short-term political pressures to resist it. And it is by no means certain to accept that argument anyway, since its policy priorities and its economic analysis may differ from the donor's. As it enters the negotiations of Act 1, therefore, the recipient will be seeking to obtain as much finance as it can in return for as small as possible a burden of disadvantageous conditions. Its utility function is therefore as set out in Figure 3.1; the greater the political cost of the conditions with which it expects to have to comply, the steeper the trade-off.

We now consider the motivation of the donor. As a first approximation

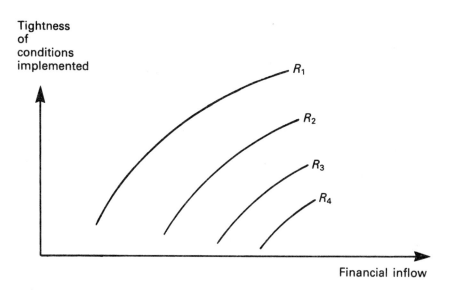

Figure 3.1 The recipient government's utility function

Note: Subscripts 1 to 4 represent increasing levels of recipient utility.

we may suppose that he will try and extract as much policy reform as he can from a given recipient over a given time period. There are various reasons for supposing this: at the technical level, if government-imposed price distortions are thought to be the major barrier to growth in developing countries, then the more distortions the Bank is able to buy out in a given operation, the more successful the operation; and at the level of staff motivation, the more policy-reform conditions a country loan officer is able to negotiate as part of a particular loan agreement, the more impressed his superiors in the operational departments of the Bank (and for that matter the shareholders in the Executive Board) are likely to be. As we shall argue in Chapter 5, there are so many potential excuses for slippage that do not reflect on the competence of the Bank (deterioration in the external environment; political change in the recipient country; overestimation of administrative resources by the recipient government) that there is little to deter the Bank negotiating team from going for as much policy reform as it can get. Advice has been given by the Bank's recent review of policy-based lending (World Bank, 1988: 15–16) to confine conditionality to a few 'key conditions', but there is little evidence that this advice has so far found its way through into the design of policy packages.

There does exist a constraint on the enforcement of conditionality: which is simply that the Bank, as a bank, needs to lend if it is to maintain its profitability. The major vehicle for its lending has historically been the development project, which still accounts for some 75 per cent of disbursements; but even in the 1970s the Bank was experiencing serious difficulties, which the subsequent world-wide recession aggravated, in spending its project budget. In 1987, indeed, net transfers from the Bank to developing countries turned negative for the first time.[8] In this environment, the newly-invented instrument of policy-based lending carried a triple burden: first, to bridge the gap between desired spending and the value of viable projects; second, to improve the policy environment in which those projects operated; third and least publicised, to protect the Bank's own financial position in those highly indebted countries which were left dangerously exposed by the exit of the commercial banks after the completion of a Fund stabilisation programme. The value of the Bank's bad debts has recently been increasing, and at the end of fiscal year 1993 the value of loans 'in nonaccrual status' – i.e. more than six months late – amounted to $3 billion, around 3 per cent of its portfolio. At present the bad debtors are small countries such as Guyana, Liberia, Peru, Nicaragua, Haiti and Syria; the Bank's great fear is that they will shortly be joined by one of its larger debtors. It has been calculated (by Robert Wade, 1989) that the value of overdue loans would only have to rise to $10 billion for the consequent loss provision to wipe out the Bank's net income, and force it to eat into its equity subscriptions; in this event, the Bank's credit rating on the international financial markets could well fall, the cost to it of borrowing money would consequently increase, and the small margin which it could earn on its good loans would be further eroded, thus putting its entire financial stability at risk. The Bank is not at that point yet, but the default of any one or two of its major debtors (Brazil $12 billion, Indonesia $16 billion, Mexico $16 billion, Turkey $9 billion, India $15 billion, China $9 billion, Philippines $6 billion)[9] could take it there very quickly. Within a number of these countries, the financial state of public corporations and the banking system is such as to make the threat a serious one; the Bank's own *World Development Report* for 1989 described the scale of the resulting insolvency problem as 'without' precedent'.[10] The Bank's major defence against such a threat is to pump out programme finance on demand.

It will readily be seen that such a strategy will in many cases be inconsistent with the principle of disbursing programme loans only when the conditionality is completely agreed, and of withholding second tranches and follow-up finance until the agreed conditionality has been complied with. The Bank's country loan officers, in other words, are under intense pressure to meet country commitment targets whatever the negotiating posture adopted by the recipient government, and to meet country disbursement targets however unpromising that government's subsequent implementation performance. The following quotations (from Wade, 1989) will give the flavour of the pressure:

> When I worked on Bangladesh we decided at a country program division meeting that the lending program for the next year should be slowed, because Bangladesh could not absorb any more money. Everyone agreed. Then the division chief spoke. He said he also completely agreed. But if he went to his director and told him the lending should be slowed down, 'tomorrow you will have a new division chief'.

> Will people ever be rewarded for saying no? It depends on how you say it. If you say: let us delay now because then we will save appraisal time later on, or let us delay appraisal and save time at negotiation so that we can do better preparation and save supervision time . . . then it is alright to say no. But you have to show that saying no now will save resources and facilitate the loan later. If you join a division as lead economist and try to delay something that is already nearly ready for the [Executive] Board . . . well, you wouldn't.[11]

In principle, there exist a number of screening devices within the Bank to counteract any pressure towards irresponsible lending. In chronological sequence within the project cycle these are: technical advice from economists in the early stages of loan preparation; the formal discipline of project appraisal; feedback from the Bank's Operations Evaluation

Department; the Operations Committee (formerly the Loan Committee) of senior Bank officials which scrutinises all loan proposals before submission to the Board; and the Executive Board itself. But each one of these disciplines is weaker for programme than for project lending as a consequence of organisational change within the Bank and the absence of any decent methodology for establishing what programme loans achieve. The Bank's economists, who in relation to a project loan would need to establish the existence of a satisfactory rate of return, would for a programme loan only need to establish that the conditions *if implemented* would remove constraints to supply expansion; these economists, and other technical specialists, in relation to loan administrators, have become weaker in terms of both numbers and power since the 1970s;[12] the Operations Evaluation Department (see Figure 2.1) has become noticeably feebler since the MacNamara years, and in particular has worked out no methodology for assessing the impact of programme lending;[13] the Operations Committee, which formerly contained no regional vice-presidents except the one whose proposal was under examination, now contains all the regional vice-presidents, who in consequence have a strong motive to take a lenient view of each other's loan proposals in the hope that their own submissions will be treated with similar charity; and the Executive Board, finally, is not a body which votes on or vetoes loan proposals (it does not even pass an opinion on second-tranche releases) but which confines itself, rather, to interrogation, expressions of anxiety, and on occasion, praise. In short, there are powerful internal pressures to lend, which the Bank's sophisticated quality filters are less well able to resist in the case of injudicious programme loans than in the case of injudicious project loans. These pressures, of course, act as a counterpoise to the more overt pressure to impose, and then to enforce, as many conditions as possible.

Figure 3.2 summarises the argument in terms of motivation up to the point so far reached. The recipient is torn between a desire to maximise his financial inflow and a desire to minimise the political cost imposed by implementing the associated conditionality; the donor must trade off a desire to *maximise* conditionality (and hence what he sees as beneficial reform) against a desire to spend his budget. The donor and recipient, therefore, have conflicting interests concerning the implementation of conditions and a common interest in spending the donor's budget. The bargaining range within Act 1 – the first stage of the lending cycle – is defined by those possible outcomes which are 'Pareto-optimal', in other words, cannot make the donor happier without hurting the recipient, or vice versa. If for the moment we work on the simplifying assumption that the Bank begins with a fixed and unalterable planning allocation for programme lending to each developing country, the possible outcomes all lie between points T_i and T_j on Figure 3.2; that is, the level of programme lending to each country is predetermined by the budget ceiling, and all

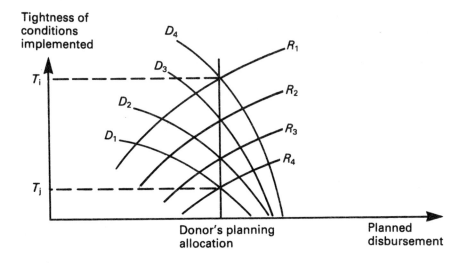

Figure 3.2 Donor and recipient objectives and the bargaining range for Act 1

Note: Subscripts 1 to 4 on R and D curves represent increasing levels of recipient and donor utility respectively.

that is left to argue about is the political price – in terms of conditions implemented – which the recipient must pay.

It will be the major task of Chapter 4 to explain the outcomes to be observed in Act 1 (that is, at the design stage) and of Chapter 5 to explain what happens in Acts 2 and 3 during the stages of implementation and follow-up. As we shall there argue, the less the donor needs the recipient – either as outlet for funds or as political ally – and the more the recipient needs the donor – because of the gravity of its debt or foreign exchange position, or because it does not believe that it can borrow from any other source – the greater the loss for the recipient if there is a breakdown of negotiations, and the less room for manoeuvre the recipient has in those negotiations. However, the extent of room for manoeuvre does not, on its own, determine the outcome of the game. For if a weak recipient is willing to gamble that the donor will not penalise him for any slippage that he perpetrates in Act 2, he *may* – if his guess is right – be able to walk on both sides of the street, taking the money and dodging such conditionality as was imposed on him in Act 1. The less he expects to need the donor in Act 3, the less he can expect to lose by applying this strategy; but the discussion of Chapter 5 will reveal a number of cases of Davids who managed to outpoint Goliath even though their dependence on him extended forward into a fourth and fifth act.

74

What is becoming obvious is that each party's *expectation* of the other's future behaviour is of fundamental importance to the strategy chosen and hence to the outcome of the game. In determining its bargaining strategy for Act 1, the recipient will be aware that any deal which is struck is an obsolescing bargain, on which he is at liberty to renege in Act 2; but that he may need more money from the same donor in Act 3, the likelihood of which may depend on the extent of his slippage in Act 2. For his part, the donor knows that it is rational for the recipient to comply with externally imposed conditions only for as long as he expects to need such finance, and then to abandon compliance in the last act of the game, and needs a strategy to discourage such behaviour; but the only foolproof one is not to lend at all.[14] And this is only rational if the donor sets store only by the enforcement of conditions and not at all by disbursement, which by our discussion above appears to be a less than plausible description of the Bank in the late 1980s.

Figure 3.3 takes the discussion a little further by setting out the possible moves in the game in the form of a 'game tree', that is, a chart of the possible moves which each player can make at each stage.

The bargaining process begins with a developing country in a state of balance-of-payments deficit making a request for programme finance from the Bank, which responds by inviting the potential recipient to prepare a reform package, without at this stage discussing money at all. The recipient government responds by offering a reform package of tightness T_j: as in Figure 3.2, the subscript j is used to stand for the recipient, and the subscript i for the donor.

It is for the recipient now to decide whether to treat this offer as an *ultimatum*. If he does, the donor either declines, in which event negotiations are at an end, or else accepts, in which event he agrees to lend a sum of money X in return for reforms of tightness T_j. If the recipient does not impose an ultimatum, the donor responds by proposing a reform package which we may assume (recalling Figure 3.2) to be tighter than T_j; call this T_i. To this he attaches a sum of money X. If he treats this offer as an ultimatum, the recipient either declines, in which event negotiations are once again at an end, or else accepts. If he does not treat it as an ultimatum, negotiations begin. If they are successful, they result in a deal being struck by which the Bank agrees to lend X (for the moment, we shall treat the size of the loan as being non-negotiable) in return for a reform programme of tightness T_j, intermediate between the lender's and the borrower's opening bids. The tightness of any deal reached at this stage is likely to depend on various determinants of donor's and recipient's 'bargaining strength', including the size of the donor's lending programme in the borrower country, the extent of his geopolitical interest in that country, and the borrower's economic vulnerability. These hypotheses are formally investigated in Chapter 4. If negotiations are unsuccessful – that is

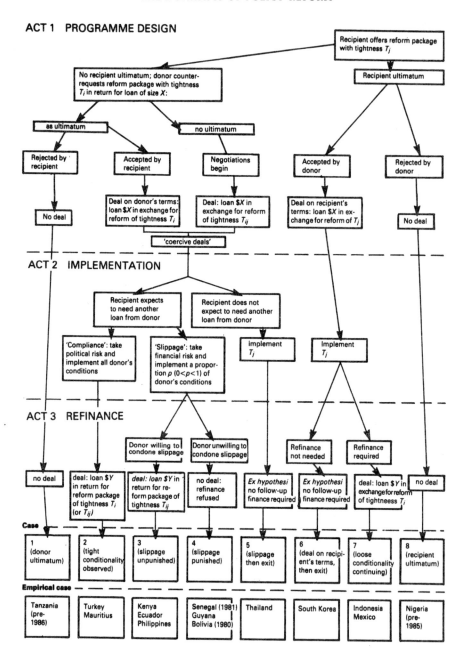

Figure 3.3 The 'tree' of the conditionality 'game'

to say, one party refuses to give ground – then we are back with a donor or recipient ultimatum, as the case may be.

By the end of Act 1, therefore, we have four possible outcomes: breakdown of talks as a result of an unsuccessful ultimatum by either party, settlement on the donor's terms, settlement on the recipient's terms, or something intermediate between the last two possibilities. The last case, of course, covers a multitude of possible outcomes, which will be considered in the next chapter and the appendix to this one.

We now move forward to Act 2, the implementation stage, during which the ball is in the recipient's court. Let us at this point make a distinction between those outcomes of Act 1 which are *coercive* for the recipient (that is, require him to implement policy changes against his will, i.e. anything tighter than T_j) and those outcomes which are not coercive (i.e. T_j only). In the latter case, the recipient has no motive to implement anything other than the agreed package. In the former case, he must balance the expected political costs of complying with coercive policy changes against the expected financial costs of failing to do so. If he does not expect to need another loan from that donor, the expected financial costs are zero, and he can renege on the Act 1 deal with impunity. But if he does expect to need another loan, he must make a gamble: either the political gamble of going the whole way with the Bank and Fund's draconian measures and running the risk of losing office, or the financial gamble of defying the Bank, implementing T_j against a promise of implementing T_i or T_{ij}, and running the risk of being punished by a withdrawal of future Bank finance.

The scope for real conflict has now narrowed down a great deal; for if the recipient has complied with the agreed Act 1 conditionality, whether tight or loose, and wants follow-up finance, the donor has no motive to refuse it to him. It is only in the alternative case – which, however, is extremely common – where a recipient who needs follow-up finance none the less calls the Bank's bluff by perpetrating severe slippage on agreed conditions, that the Bank needs to decide what to do next. Broadly, it has four options open to it. It can either:

1 give priority to the need to discourage slippage, and refuse refinance in all such cases; or
2 give priority to the pressure to lend, and offer refinance in all cases; or
3 punish in proportion to the crime, and offer refinance only if slippage falls below a certain level; or
4 impose a random punishment, and punish (by refusing refinance) an arbitrary proportion $(1 - \gamma)$ of those borrowers perpetrating slippage of any kind. If this strategy is followed, 'delinquent' borrowers cannot foresee whether or not they will be punished.

From Figure 3.3 the following implications will be apparent, without going into any calculations of the donor's and recipient's profit and loss from different strategies:

First, if the recipient expects to need only one loan from the donor (that is, Act 3 is the last round of negotiations that he can foresee) it is *always* rational for him to accept whatever conditions the donor proposes, since if he adopts this strategy he will, at worst, secure a loan X which is implemented at tightness T_j, that is, on his own terms, whereas if he adopts a tougher bargaining strategy he runs the risk of encountering a donor ultimatum which could lead to his receiving nothing. Unless, therefore, the political costs of *his own chosen* policy reforms outweigh the financial benefit of the loan – which would appear implausible – it always pays for the recipient who anticipates a quick exit from the policy-based lending process to give ground at the negotiation stage, and accept any conditions which the donor proposes, a strategy effectively deployed by South Korea and Thailand to give themselves a financial breathing space during the recession of the early 1980s until they grew independent of the need for Bank SAL finance.

Second, that ultimatums by either donor or recipient are irrational unless they are motivated, respectively, purely by the desire to impose or to escape conditions. If donor and recipient abstain from ultimatums they get out of the deal, at least, a loan on their adversary's terms; if they impose ultimatums they get simply the rather small probability of a loan on their own terms. Unless, therefore, the utility cost of possibly having to settle on the other party's terms rather than one's own exceeds the satisfaction of doing a deal of some kind, then an ultimatum will be hurtful to the party imposing it. And ultimatums are indeed rare in the history of policy-based lending, strong though the interest of each party may be in bolstering its negotiating position by giving the outside world the impression that an ultimatum is being delivered. Where they are apparent, they are more often implicit than explicit: for example, there is no macroeconomic conditionality on Bank loans to China, and sparse conditionality on programme lending to Mexico and Indonesia, not because of any explicit ultimatum by those recipients, but because of an unspoken understanding that their governments will not welcome detailed programmes of policy reform being imposed on them, coupled with a strong awareness in the Bank of the importance of maintaining the lending programme in those countries.

Third, it is possible – and has happened quite frequently in real life, for example the Ecuador and Kenya case studies in Volume II – that a recipient whose bargaining position is weak in the sense of a very poor financial position which obligates it to ask for follow-up finance will none the less emerge 'victorious' from the game in the sense of implementing conditionality on its own terms and yet still obtaining follow-up finance. This is the situation described in Figure 3.3 as Case 3 – 'slippage unpunished'. It arises simply because the most obvious punishment for such behaviour, namely refusal of further credit, (strategy (i)) *if imposed universally*, puts the Bank's financial standing and its cash flow at risk. But to condone all breaches of conditionality (strategy (ii)) will expose that conditionality as a paper tiger. This leaves the options described as (iii) and (iv) above – random punishment, or predictable forgiveness for slippage below a certain threshold. It will be demonstrated in Morley (1992) that random punishment in Act 3 is a more effective deterrent, given the desired level of disbursement, than a punishment geared to the level of slippage, essentially because it prevents recipients being able to build into their expectations a presumption that a certain level of slippage on agreed conditions will always be tolerated. This 'optimal solution' from the point of view of balancing the Bank's need to lend and to discourage slippage is, however, not equitable in the sense of ensuring equal treatment of equal slippage.

3.3 EXTENSIONS OF THE GAME FRAMEWORK

The discussion so far has represented the relationship between donor and recipient as a game between two parties each of which is united in its objectives, able to deliver what it promises, and restricted to the strategy of being able to offer or refuse, respectively, a loan of fixed size with fixed conditions attached. Each of these assumptions is suspect; this will become fully apparent only in the next two chapters. The importance of the point at this stage rests in the possibility that 'a sensible strategy' for either party may consist rather in trying to change the rules of the game, rather than in playing it as cleverly as possible according to the rules set out in the previous section.

Extent of common interest within donor and recipient

We have so far pictured the government of each developing country (e.g. Figure 3.1) as a homogeneous entity with a common interest in raising external finance and in evading externally imposed conditions. However, within each government the group which has the principal interest in raising external finance – essentially the ministry of finance and central bank – will not, as the case studies of Volume 2 amply demonstrate, be the group which has the principal interest in resisting conditionality; the former group, indeed, may share the analytical premises of the Fund and the Bank, may indeed contain staff who have worked for the Fund and Bank, whereas the latter group, usually well represented in the ministries of agriculture, commerce, industry and labour, will be subjected to persistent lobbying from producers and traders currently protected from the market by the shield of restrictions which the Bank is trying to dismantle. The division of interest between the two groups is amplified because the financial proceeds of structural *and sectoral* adjustment loans generally accrue to the ministry of finance, whereas the costs of implementing the conditionality generally fall on the line ministries above named.[15] In such an environment the donor's strategy for getting policy reform implemented may be well advised to stretch beyond simple threats and inducements directed at the ministry of finance, in relation to whom they may in any case be redundant if that ministry is as keen on the Bank's proposed reforms as the Bank itself, into the realm of inducements directed at those parts of government which bear the political costs of implementation. In the Bank's language, such an approach may be necessary if the recipient government is to effectively 'own' the programme, and the question of how such 'ownership' may be brought about is currently a central preoccupation in the Bank (World Bank, 1988: 93–4).

Nor can the World Bank – as already amply documented – be reasonably treated as a body with one mind, one voice and one view of the right negotiating position to be taken in a particular developing country. As a broad proposition, the further down the office one descends, the less conditionality comes to appear in High Noon terms as a two-person confrontation. The Senior Vice-President, Operations, is far more likely to see conditionality as a two-person game than members of the (World Bank) resident mission in a recipient country, and there is indeed no doubt that both country-desk officers and – even more – Bank representatives within developing countries have found themselves frequently involved in mediating between the tightest package that is acceptable to the recipient government and the loosest package that is acceptable to the Senior Vice-President.[16] But positions taken by different levels of authority within the Bank may themselves change over time in the course of the project cycle, as Robert Wade relates:

> Staff speak of a common cycle to be seen in negotiations about conditions. In the early stages, division chiefs and country directors urge their staff to be very tough in insisting upon big changes: big reductions in tariffs sooner rather than later, for example. A mission may negotiate agreements, only to be told on its return that the agreements are not tough enough and should be re-opened. But if the government resists and continues to resist, the country director will in the end 'give away the store' rather than hold up the loan beyond the planned fiscal year. For managers are very concerned to meet their lending targets. And beyond this, they are concerned about 'good relations' between the Bank and the country. Building up or maintaining good relations may dictate loosening of resisted

80

conditions. Hence the cycle of intervention; in the early stages managers intervene to stiffen the negotiating position of their staff; in the later stages they intervene to soften them.

(Wade, 1989: 50–1)

If Bank priorities between tightness and disbursement, then, vary between staff and over time, it may be a more effective strategy for the recipient government's negotiators to take advantage of these variations to build up alliances with targeted Bank staff over regular lunch engagements, than to deploy formal bargaining power against those staff within the committee room. Such an approach may be able to build ambiguity, alternative reform strategies and additional time for implementation into loan agreements before the government's alternative view of what is feasible manifests itself as formal slippage.

Feasibility of implementation

According to the model so far developed, all slippage is *willed* by the government as part of a conscious strategy; but in real life, not so. In principle, a sharp distinction exists between slippage due to lack of government desire, and slippage due to lack of government capacity; and the latter should be precluded by a choice of conditions which takes realistic account of what the government can deliver. But what the government can deliver, in terms of money and manpower, will depend on the state of the budget and the balance of payments, and the budget and the balance of payments will change with each change in the weather and the price of the country's principal export crop. Whether the increases in quantitative restrictions and in tariff levels implemented by the governments of the Philippines and Thailand in 1983, for example, – both of them formally cases of 'increased slippage' – should be seen as deliberate acts of defiance or reflections of a change in what was financially feasible, is a question which is very difficult to measure with any precision. Nevertheless, sometimes it is possible to make informed judgements on whether slippage is culpable or not, which we do in the case studies of Volume 2.

Additional options available to the donor and recipient

Also excluded from the schema of Figure 3.3 is the possibility that both donor and recipient may add leverage to their position by making common cause with others in the same position. On the recipient side, as in the case of debt negotiations, there is no sign of the appearance of a cartel, and collaboration has taken the form of informal exchanges of information between recipients, enabling them to take advantage of one another's strategies. Collaboration between donors, on the other hand, is quite overt. Not only is there explicit harmonisation of conditions, and indeed cross-conditionality, between Bank and Fund as discussed in the previous chapter, but in addition the Bank has made no secret of its wish that other donors of bilateral programme aid, and indeed private banks as well, should tie the disbursement of their own lending to the prior agreement of a policy reform package approved by Bank and Fund. The Bank's ability to orchestrate the donors has varied from strong (Kenya 1983: see Volume 2, page 289) to spectacularly unsuccessful (Ecuador 1987; see Volume 2, page 427). But it is clear from the available evidence that in a number of cases the Bank has possessed the ability, contrary to our working assumption so far, to tailor the amount of money attached to a particular policy-reform package to the amount of reform that country is offering to implement. This can also of course be done through virement within the internal Bank planning framework: for example, if a $75 million credit for Malawi falls through, it may be possible to raise the value of a planned $100 million credit for Zambia to $175 million in the hope of extracting a more far-reaching reform programme. In other words, the Bank may, and to some extent openly does, use variations in the budget for each programme-lending operation to buy additional policy reform. The implications of this possibility will be considered in detail in Chapter 4.

APPENDIX. A POSSIBLE SOLUTION: POTENTIAL STRATEGIES FOR DONOR AND RECIPIENT IN ACTS 2 AND 3

Of the eight possible outcomes of the bargaining process depicted in the game tree of Figure 3.3, five offer little or no scope for the exercise of strategy by donor or recipient. In cases 1 and 8 a donor or recipient ultimatum, respectively, is rejected by the other party and negotiations break down. However, this will be irrational unless they are motivated, respectively, purely by the desire to impose or escape conditions – in other words, if loan disbursement has no weight in the utility function. In cases 6 and 7, the donor agrees to disburse a loan on the recipient's terms because his desire to lend overrides his desire to enforce conditionality. In case 5, there is a negotiating process surrounding the determination of conditionality in Act 1, but no mystery surrounding the ultimate outcome since the recipient, by hypothesis, does not expect to need a loan in Act 3 and therefore has no motive to comply with any externally imposed conditions (i.e. conditions in excess of T_j) in Act 2, since to do so imposes political costs which offset the benefit of the loan, and not to do so does not. His optimal strategy is therefore to accept whatever conditions the donor proposes in Act 1, and then in Act 2 to comply only with those conditions which formed part of his original intention, i.e. T_j. This leaves us with cases 2, 3 and 4, in which the donor attempts to exert 'leverage' by extracting from the recipient a set of reforms in excess of those which he would have spontaneously carried out. If such leverage is attempted, the recipient must decide in Act 2 how much of it to accept and, if this is less than the amount agreed, the donor must subsequently decide in Act 3 whether and how to punish such 'slippage' by restricting the supply of further finance. Let us now consider the strategies which it may be sensible for each party to pursue in this context. We shall assume for simplicity that the utility functions of both donor and recipient can be represented as linear.

The notation to be adopted is set out in Table 3.2.

Table 3.2 Notation

α	=	subjective utility attached by donor to one extra unit of tightness negotiated with recipient (i.e. if $\alpha = 1$, one extra condition imposed on the recipient adds one unit to the donor's utility)
β	=	subjective (dis)utility attached by recipient to one extra unit of tightness negotiated by donor (i.e. if $\beta = -2$, one extra condition imposed on the recipient subtracts two units from the recipient's utility)
γ	=	probability of escaping punishment, i.e. likelihood that donor will grant follow-on finance during Act 3; hence $(1 - \gamma)$ = a measure of the donor's punishment
p	=	percentage of agreed Act 1 conditions implemented by recipient in Act 2; hence $(1 - p)$ = a measure of slippage on agreed conditions
q	=	probability of loan repayment
L	=	value of entire loan portfolio lent by creditor i to debtor j
r	=	discount rate prevailing between Act 2 and Act 3
X	=	value of finance granted in Act 1
Y	=	value of finance (if any) granted in Act 3
i	=	donor subscript
j	=	recipient subscript
t	=	'tightness' of package of conditions agreed at end of Act 1. (An index of *number* and *severity* of policy reform conditions imposed.)
OSR	=	debt services ratio (debt service payments due as a percentage of exports)

Using this notation, the payoffs to be expected by donor and recipient in Acts 2 and 3, depending on the recipient's compliance in Act 2 and the donor's response in Act 3, are as set out in Table 3.3. The recipient's utility, following Figure 3.2, is positive in lending x but negative in tightness t:

$$U_j = f(t, x); f_t < 0, f_x > 0 \tag{1}$$

whereas the donor's utility is positive in tightness actually enforced (tp) lending (x) and repayment (q)

$$U_j = g(tp, x, q) \, g_t > 0, g_x > 0, g_p > 0, g_q > 0 \tag{2}$$

We assume for simplicity, at this stage, that the donor's decision to grant refinance or not (γ) is an all-or-nothing decision, i.e. γ = either 1 or 0 and that the probability of loan repayment (q) is unaffected by the strategies deployed by donor and recipient.

Table 3.3 Cases 2, 3 and 4 of the game tree: donor and recipient payoffs

Recipient strategies	Donor strategies			
	Offer refinance in Act 3 ($\gamma = 1$)		*Do not offer refinance in Act 3* ($\gamma = 0$)	
Satisfactory compliance in Act 2	Donor $\quad X + \alpha T$	(Act 2)	Donor $\quad X + \alpha T$	(Act 2)
	$\dfrac{Y + \alpha T}{(1 + r)}$	(Act 3)	0	
	Recipient $X - \beta T$	(Act 2)	Recipient $X - \beta T$	(Act 2)
	$\dfrac{Y + \beta T}{(1 + r)}$	(Act 3)	0	(Act 3)
	——— Outcome 2 ———			
Unsatisfactory compliance in Act 2	Donor $\quad X + \alpha p T$	(Act 2)	Donor $\quad X + \alpha p T$	(Act 2)
	$\dfrac{Y + \alpha p T}{(1 + r)}$	(Act 3)	0	
	Recipient $X - \beta p T$	(Act 2)	Recipient $X - \beta p T$	(Act 2)
	$\dfrac{Y + \beta p T}{(1 + r)}$	(Act 3)	0	(Act 3)
	——— Outcome 3 ———		——— Outcome 4 ———	

On the assumptions set out in Table 3.3 the game has a dominant strategy equilibrium in the bottom left-hand cell of the table, in which the donor always refinances and the recipient always evades conditionality: the exploitative outcome 3, 'slippage unpunished' of Figure 3.3. It is optimal for the recipient because, whether he gets refinance or not, some slippage is politically better for him than no slippage; it is optimal for the donor because, whether the recipient's compliance is satisfactory or not, it is better to lend than not to lend, always supposing that $(Y + \alpha p T) > 0$, i.e. that the donor's utility loss from the recipient's slippage does not counterbalance his utility gain from lending[17]. If this supposition is true, the donor's threat to refuse refinance in the event of poor compliance will not be a credible one, and conditionality will be a paper tiger.

There are various reasons for feeling uneasy with this solution to the game. Empirically, Figure 3.3 has already suggested (and Chapter 5 below will further document) that there are other possible outcomes to the game than 'slippage unpunished': punishment does sometimes occur. And in terms of the structure of our model, the linkage between conditionality, repayment and the donor's utility – the creditor's dilemma – has not yet been satisfactorily incorporated. We now modify the model to take account of these difficulties.

In the Appendix to Mosley (1992), we present a very simple model in which recipients become more likely to comply with conditions, but less likely to be able to repay debt, as the severity of punishment is increased. After a certain point, punishment becomes counter-productive for the donor in the sense that it subtracts more from the donor's utility by prejudicing future repayment of debt than it adds to it by motivating compliance with conditions. Where that point will lie depends on the likelihood that a given act of 'punishment' (refusal of refinance) will push the recipient over the line where he cannot service his current debts, which in turn will depend, other things being equal, on his ratio of debt service to income. In other words, the 'effectiveness' of punishment will gradually deteriorate as the recipient's debt service ratio increases, and become negative once a 'critical' debt service level – which is 40 per cent in the arithmetical examples of Mosley (1992) – is reached, as in Figure 3.4.

If we incorporate this idea into Table 3.3, the donor's Act 3 payoff in the event of 'unsatisfactory compliance, no refinance' ($\gamma = 0$) is no longer simply 0; it will depend on the recipient's ability to service debt, as in Figure 3.4. If his debt position is such that 'effectiveness of punishment' is negative, the Act 3 payoff will become negative, and the 'exploitative strategy equilibrium' (outcome 3) under which the donor continues to finance and the recipient continues not to comply with conditions will still hold *a fortiori*. If, on the other hand, his debt service ratio is 'sub-critical' such that punishment looks likely to be 'effective' (i.e. increase the repayment probability of this and other debtors, and increase the donor's utility by more than the $Y + \alpha pT/(1 + r)$ which the donor derives from condoning non-compliance), the game's dominant strategy equilibrium will shift to 'deadlock' – the bottom right-hand

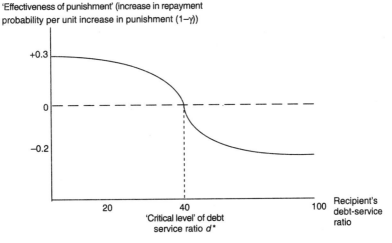

Figure 3.4 'Effectiveness of punishment' in relation to
recipient's debt service ratio
Source: Appendix to Mosley (1992), Equation [10']

85

cell of Table 3,3, or outcome 4 in Figure 3.3. The recipient continues to prefer unsatisfactory compliance; the donor, by hypothesis, now prefers not to offer refinance; hence we have the orthodox prisoner's dilemma outcome. It therefore follows as a testable prediction that:

Donors of conditional assistance will refuse follow-on finance only to recipients whose debt-service ratio is below the critical level d*. *For such recipients, the level of 'refinance' will be proportionate to the level of slippage* p; *for those whose debt service ratio is above the critical level, the level of refinance will be unconnected with the level of slippage. In any event (since there will be empirical difficulties in specifying a proxy for* d*) *refinance* γ *should be negatively related to slippage* (1 − p).

In the final part of this appendix we shall work with an empirical punishment function of the simplest possible type:

$$\gamma = \gamma_0 + \gamma_1(1 - p) + \gamma_2 DSR \qquad (3)$$

expected
sign of
regression
coefficient   −   +

All this, of course, will be foreseen by a rational donor during Act 1 when the conditions attached to the loan are being negotiated, and by a rational recipient when calculating slippage during Act 2. If the donor, at the beginning of negotiations, would prefer by the end of Act 3 to be in a continuing financial relationship with the recipient than not to be − for whatever reason − it makes sense for him to follow a strategy which minimises the likelihood of deadlock and maximises the likelihood of lending being able to continue. The best way of doing this is likely to be to tailor the level of tightness t to some prior estimate of the recipient's expected (administrative and political) ability and willingness to implement conditions − which, of course, will itself be partly determined by expectations of the donor's behaviour. To incorporate these ideas, let us write out the game in extensive form (see Figure 3.5).

First let us note that if the recipient's debt-service ratio is *above* the 'critical' level, then by hypothesis (Figure 3.5) it is not rational for the donor to punish, and by the same token, the recipient, knowing this, is not constrained in his choice of reform programme: his optimal strategy is simply to implement those conditions which, in terms of domestic political considerations, he wishes to implement, (t_j) and to ignore all others.

The recipient whose debt service level is *below* the critical level will, as Figure 3.5 shows, receive the payoff:

$$R = \Pi(p)\left[X - \beta t + \frac{Y - \beta t}{(1 + r)}\right] + (1 - \Pi(p))[X - \beta pt] \qquad (4)$$

86

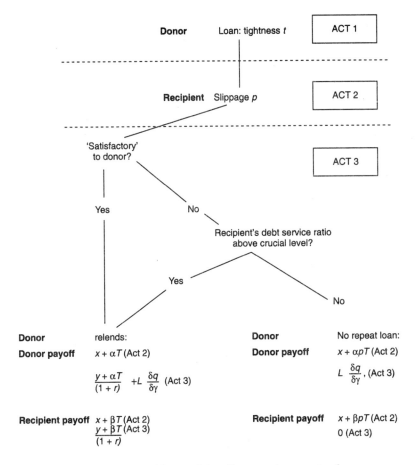

Figure 3.5 The conditionality game in extensive form

where $\Pi(p)$ is the probability that the donor will define a specific level of slippage p as 'unsatisfactory' and grant follow-on finance ($\gamma = 1$). By hypothesis, the recipient cannot foresee this probability. Differentiate (4) with respect to p and set this function equal to zero to determine the recipient's optimal reaction function, p^*:

$$\frac{\partial R}{\partial p} = -\Pi'(p)\left[X - \beta t + \frac{Y - \beta t}{(1 + r)}\right] + p(1 - \Pi(p)) + \Pi'(p)\{X - \beta pt\} = 0 \qquad (4')$$

whence:

$$p^* = \frac{\Pi'(p)\left[\dfrac{Y - \beta t}{(1 + r)} - \beta t\right]}{1 - \Pi(p) - \beta t \Pi'(p)} \qquad (2')$$

where $\Pi'(p)$ is the recipient's *ex ante* subjective expectation of the likelihood that a given change in slippage (dp) will cause a change in the donor's evaluation of his performance, and hence in the likelihood of punishment. If we differentiate [4''] with respect to tightness t, we get

$$\frac{\partial p*}{\partial t} = \frac{(1 - \Pi(p) - \beta t \Pi'(p))(-\dfrac{1}{1 + r} - 1) - \beta(\Pi'(p))^2\,(\dfrac{Y - \beta t}{1 + r} - \beta t)}{(1 - \Pi(p) - \beta t \Pi'(p))^2} \qquad (4''')$$

of which the overall sign is ambiguous. If a plausible range of values, however, is applied to each of the coefficients in (4''') ($\Pi = 0.5$–1, $\beta = 0.5$, $T = 10$–20, $r = 0.05 - 0.10$, $Y = 10$) the absolute value of (4''') always turns out negative: in other words, it appears *a priori* that high levels of tightness may prejudice implementation performance. It is notable that as the recipient's distaste for reform β increases, so his propensity for implementation $\partial p*/\partial T$ goes towards minus infinity; whereas that propensity increases, and ultimately becomes positive, as the size of the expected Act 3 loan Y is stepped up.

The reaction function (4'') then becomes a constraint within the donor's utility function:

$$U_i = g(tp, x, q) \qquad (2)$$

Substituting the recipient's 'optimum slippage reaction function' $p*$, as derived in (4'') for p in (2) we have the following expanded utility function which the donor must maximise in order to determine the tightness of its conditionality in Act 1:

$$U_i = g\left(t\left[\frac{\Pi'(p)\dfrac{Y - \beta t}{(1 + r)} - \beta t}{1 - \Pi(p) - \beta t \Pi'(p)}\right], x, q\right) \qquad (2')$$

Since the volume of lending x and the probability of loan repayment q do not relate directly to tightness, we may immediately differentiate [2'] with respect to tightness, t, in order to solve for its optimal level $t*$:

$$\frac{\partial U_i}{\partial t} = g'(\Omega) + \frac{g}{1 - \Pi(p) - \beta t \Pi'(p)^2} \cdot -\beta[\Pi'(p)]^2\left[\frac{Y - \beta t}{(1 + r)} - \beta t\right]$$

$$+ \left[\beta + \frac{\beta}{1 + r}\right](1 - \Pi(\beta) - \beta t(\Pi'(p))^2 = 0$$

where

$$\Omega = \left[\frac{\Pi'(p)\left[\dfrac{Y - \beta t}{(1 + r)} - \beta t \right]}{1 - \Pi(p) - \beta t \Pi(p)} \right]$$

whence

$$t^* = \left[\frac{1}{\beta}\right]\left[\frac{\beta + g + \beta(1+r)^{-1} + g'(\Omega)}{1 + \Pi(p) - \beta^2\Pi(p)r - \beta\Pi'(p)Y - r\beta\Pi'(p)^2 + \beta^2\Pi(p)^2 + 2r\beta\Pi'(p) + 2\beta\Pi(p) + 2\beta r\Pi^2(p)}\right] \quad (5)$$

By differentiation of (5) it will be clear that $\partial t^*/\partial\beta$ is negative: as the recipient's subjective distaste for conditionality β increases, the entire denominator of (5) increases, and hence optimum tightness diminishes. The sign of $\partial t^*/\partial\Pi$, the response of optimum tightness to the recipient's expectation of punishment, is ambiguous, but commonsense suggests that it should be positive.

Let us recapitulate our results in reverse order. We have analysed conditionality as a two-person, three-stage, non-cooperative game. At first glance it appears that the game will have a stable equilibrium in which the recipient exploits the donor, but further analysis of the donor's final-stage payoff suggests that this possibility is confined to cases in which the donor confronts the 'creditor's dilemma' of conditionality enforcement versus debt enforcement. Proxying 'difficulty of repayment' by the recipient's debt-service ratio we have the following prediction for 'Act 3' of the game:

Enforcement of conditionality (3) *The donor's punishment (1-γ) will be insignificantly different from zero for recipients with a debt-service ratio in excess of the critical value* d* *but positive (and related to slippage* (1 − p)) *for recipients with a debt-service ratio below this critical value. Across any sample of recipients refinance* γ *should therefore be positively related to the recipient's debt-service ratio, and related to slippage.*

Moving back to Act 2 of the game and examining the motivation of recipients whose debt-service ratio is below the critical level, we expect that:

Slippage (4‴) *Implementation* (p) *is probably positively related to the level of tightness* (T) *on the Act 1 deal, hence actual slippage* (1 − p) *will probably be negatively correlated with the tightness of the preceding agreement.*

Moving back, finally, to Act 1 and incorporating the recipient's expected slippage as a constraint into the donor's calculation of optimal tightness, our prediction is:

Tightness (5) *As the recipient's subjective distaste for conditionality increases, optimum tightness, and therefore actual tightness, will diminish.*

The last of these predictions is difficult to test because it relates to a subjective expectation rather than to objectively measurable data. The first two predictions, on the other hand, do relate to measurable data and in the following section we examine the fit between the two.

Slippage (equation 4‴) It is apparent by visual inspection of Table 5.6 (p. 174) that slippage p on agreed conditions was positive in respect of nearly all of the sample of loan agreements examined. Indeed, it averaged over 50 per cent across the sample as a whole. Ordinary least-squares regression analysis applied to the World Bank data in Table 5.6 gave the following relationship between tightness and slippage:

Slippage = 13.9 + 2.82* (tightness of loan conditions),
         (1.09) (2.43)

Number of observations = 28, $\bar{r}^2$ = 0.15, s.e.e. = 20.36, Student's t-statistics in brackets below coefficients.

Slippage, in other words, appears to have a positive and significant relationship (at the 95 per cent level) with tightness on the previous loan. The r^2, at 15 per cent is, however, quite low, and the likelihood that the level of slippage can also be partly explained by the recipient's 'innate distaste' for conditions β (see equation 4‴) cannot be discounted.

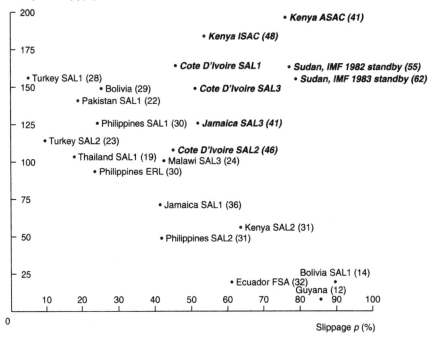

Figure 3.6 World Bank and IMF operations: donor's 'punishment' in relation to recipient's slippage and debt service ratio, 1980–90
Source: for all data Table 5.6

Figures in brackets following data points are the country's debt-service ratio for the two years following the grant of a programme loan. Countries named in **bold italics** have debt service ratios for this period exceeding the critical 40% level, (see text, p85).

'Punishment' (equation (3)) It is also readily apparent from Table 5.6 that heavy punishment of slippage, in the sense of a coefficient of repeat finance γ at or close to zero, is rare, being confined to three cases out of 26 (Bolivia I, Guyana, Ecuador II). A graph of the relationship between slippage $(1 - p)$ and refinance γ (Figure 3.6) suggests that a relationship between the two may

Table 3.4 Results of regression analysis relating slippage, refinance and indicators of 'donor dependence'

Ordinary least squares analysis applied to equation 3 above. Dependent variable: level of refinance during two years following implementation of loan agreement as percentage of finance during two years preceding loan agreement (γ).

Data set	No. of observations	Constant	Slippage	Debt service ratio	Value of World Bank loans outstanding	$\bar{r}^2$	s.e.e.
			Regression coefficients on independent variables: (Students' t-statistics in brackets)				
$\bar{r}^2$	s.e.e.						
[3a] All observations	36	0.84** [2.92]	−0.0077* [1.98]	0.0202** [2.61]		0.17	0.459
[3b] All observations	36	0.78** [2.36]	−0.0071* [1.66]	0.0202** [2.58]	0.00002 [0.35]	0.15	0.5040
[3c] Observations 1–10, 13–15, 17–25, (debt service ratio below 40%)	22	1.53** [2.87]	−0.0131** [2.69]	0.0024 [0.14]		0.21	0.5308
[3d] Observations 11–12, 16, 26–36 (debt service ratio above 40%)	14	0.28 [0.57]	−0.0066 [0.95]	0.0163 [1.22]		0.19	0.3731

Source: for all data Table 5.6 below
Notes: ** denotes significance of a coefficient at the 1% level
 * denotes significant of a coefficient at the 5% level
Diagnostic tests:

	Whole sample (e.g. 3a)	'Low debt' sample (e.g. 3c)
Serial correlation	$F(1,32) = 0.0093$	$F(1,20) = 0.2823$
Functional form	$F(1,32) = 1.0246$	$F(1,20) = 0.7305$
Heteroscedasticity	$F(1,34) = 1.5493)$	$F(1,20) = 2.5484$
Predictive failure		$F(14,19) = 0.7113$
Chow test for structural stability		$F(3,30) = 1.8517$

indeed exist. But the scatter of observations in Figure 3.6 has a striking visual similarity with the theoretical picture presented in Table 3.3. First, the relationship between slippage and punishment is asymmetric, in the sense that there is often slippage with no punishment, but never punishment with no slippage. Second, the asymmetries, as our theory predicts, are strongly correlated with the recipient's debt-service ratio.

Regression analysis of the data in Table 5.6 yields the relationships set out in Table 3.4. This shows that the coefficients of 'refinance' (γ) on slippage $(1 - p)$ and the recipient's debt-service ratio were significant, with the expected sign (equation [3a]); the variable 'value of World Bank loans outstanding', an additional potential indicator of the donor's vulnerability, is, however, insignificant and adds nothing to the predictive power of the relationship (equation 3b). If, however, the sample is divided into those countries above and those countries below a debt-service ratio of 40 per cent (the 'critical value' used in the arithmetic example portrayed in Figure 3.4), the estimated regression equations diverge. *Below* that critical level of the debt-service ratio (equation 3c), the regression coefficient of slippage on refinance remains strongly significant; above that level (equation 3d), it loses significance, and the relationship falls apart. The hypothesis that the donor's punishment (coefficient on refinance) is zero can be rejected in respect of recipients whose debt service ratio was below 40 per cent but cannot be rejected in respect of recipients whose debt service ratio was over 40 per cent. It is therefore reasonable to infer that the authorities' actual reaction function during the 1980s was something reasonably close to the punishment rule (3) which we suggested it would be rational for them to adopt, with punishment behaviour being heavily constrained by an assessment of the borrower's repayment prospects, and losing all connection with 'crime' (slippage), as our theory predicts, in those cases where the delinquent was debt-distressed.

NOTES

1   For an exposition of the prevailing Bank view see Please (1984): 27. This view is contested by Oppenheimer (1987) who argues that conditions relating to prices and fiscal policy were commonly attached to project loans as far back as the 1960s, and indeed acquired more leverage from the fact that country lending targets, at that time, did not exist.

2   In particular, as a multilateral lender the World Bank is unable to freeze assets owned by citizens of the debtor country in the creditor country, as suggested by Bulow and Rogoff (1989).

3   This is because once a debtor becomes insolvent, he will fear that to repay a given loan (say to the IMF) will make little difference to his credit rating, and hence to his ability to borrow on the international money markets. In such a situation he has little incentive to repay the IMF: for extension of this argument, see ECLA (1987), Griffith-Jones (1988a) and Krugman (1988).

4   See for example the case studies of Jamaica by Jane Harrigan and of the Philippines

by Paul Mosley in Volume 2 of this book: both medium-scale debtors of great geopolitical importance and a highly vulnerable debt-service position. The great fear is that a major debtor may be next in line – such as Argentina, with outstanding loans to the Bank of $2.1 billion (as at end of June 1988). Hence the huge composite loan of $1.25 billion in Argentina in October 1988, approved in double-quick time, without any IMF stand-by being in position, and in face of Argentina's reputation as amongst the least compliant with Bank conditionality. Disbursement of this loan was however interrupted in early 1989 (see Chapter 2, note 4).

5   On this matter we may quote two of the people most closely associated with the implementation of the development counter-revolution within the Bank. First Ernest Stern, until recently Senior Vice-President in charge of the entire policy-based lending operation:

In contrast (to conditionality on project loans) SAL conditionality is related entirely to issues of macroeconomic and sectoral policies. It raises the level of dialogue to the highest ranks of government and provides a single focus that helps ensure that adequate attention is given to the programme's prompt implementation. Whereas in project lending, the Bank will typically be dealing with agencies or sectoral ministries, SALs are always the concern of the key government decision-makers.

(Stern, 1983: 104).

The senior author of the 'Berg Report' goes further still:

Structural Adjustment Loans are not intended as relief for the balance of payments of the (recipient) country. Instead the money is mainly intended to help bring Bank representatives to the borrower's policy-making high table, where basic policy issues are decided by policy-makers, not merely explored by technical analysts.

(Berg and Batchelder, 1984: 10)

6   Hayter states her position thus in her first book on conditionality:

The involvement of the international agencies in general economic policies is not, as is sometimes supposed, a process in which officials of the agencies and of the government concerned sit down together and discuss, with open minds, the best solutions to the government's particular problems ... The process is rather one in which the international agencies attempt to ensure that policies on which they themselves have decided are adopted by the governments hoping to receive aid.... [These policies] distract attention from, and frequently conflict with, action to improve the conditions of life of the majority of Latin Americans ... With few exceptions, stabilisation programmes supported by the international agencies have resulted in low or zero rates of growth, and low or negative rates of *per capita* growth (*sc.* of GDP) during the period when stabilisation was attempted.

The quotation is from Hayter (1971: 154–8); for an update of her views, see Hayter and Watson (1985). In relation to Africa, a similar position is taken by the Institute for African Alternatives pamphlet *The IMF, the World Bank and Africa* (London, 1987) which argues that the Fund and Bank can be regarded as having common objectives and that 'between them they now manage each [poor] country entirely' (p. 9).

7   Stern (1983) for example writes that

Distortions in the policy and allocation framework [of LDCs] that were undesirable in the 1960s have become unsustainable in the much more difficult economic environment of the 1980s ... Structural adjustment is the central problem of development at present, and experience has shown that SALs are an important means of assisting a country – intellectually and financially – in reorienting its development strategies.

This theme is echoed by Stanley Please:

Domestic policy reform for most developing countries has now become essential and urgent if these countries are to be able to maintain a reasonable rate of growth of incomes and to achieve their other development objectives of human resources development and the provision of basic needs, it is for these reasons ... i.e. the urgency of policy reform and the limited effectiveness of project lending ... that the Bank introduced Structural Adjustment Lending (SAL) into its operations in 1980.

(Please, 1984: 26–8).

8 See Table 2.3 above.
9 Data for end of fiscal year 1993, from World Bank *Annual Report 1993*, pp. 205 and 225.
10 World Bank, *World Development Report 1989*, p. 3.
11 Interviews of World Bank loan officers with Robert Wade, November 1988.
12 Wade (1989: 45).
13 Until 1984 the Operations Evaluation Department carried out an independent audit of every completed project financed by the World Bank; it now no longer does so, and confines its attention to a sample. It has carried out a number of *ex post* evaluations of policy-based operations, none of which attempt any statistical or model-based assessment of the project's impact; and also the first general review of structural adjustment lending (World Bank, 1986). This went through a number of drafts, of which the penultimate one made allegations concerning lack of co-ordination between Bank and Fund, and concerning the negative distributional impact of SALs, which were struck out from the final version. Again there was no attempt to measure the ultimate impact of SALs, and such statistical assessment as did take place was confined to comparisons of the value of intermediate targets (public sector deficit, balance of payments, implementation of policy reform) in the period before and after the grant of the SAL. There have been reviews of the policy-based lending process since this one (notably World Bank, 1988, 1990, 1992c; Nicholas, 1988), but these reports, which represent a notable technical step forward, were carried out in the Country Economics Department of the Bank's Policy, Planning and Research complex, not in the Operations Evaluation Department.
14 If (by arbitrary choice of period) Act 3 is the last round of conditionality negotiations that the recipient can foresee, it has no reason to comply with any externally imposed policy conditions at this stage, since it does not expect, *ex hypothesi*, to make any further borrowings from the donor, and hence is invulnerable to any punishment he may impose by refusing further credit. Having a rational expectation of this behaviour, the donor will not lend, if the enforcement of conditionality is important to him. Having a rational expectation of this behaviour, the recipient, moving back to Act 2, will have no incentive to abide by the conditions set in Act 1, since doing so will avail him nothing, and that in turn will eliminate the donor's incentive to lend in Act 1. Under perfect foresight, therefore, the market for policy-based lending fails completely! The missing element from this story, apart from the implausibility of donor and recipient being able to predict each other's behaviour accurately, is of course the pressure on the donor to lend regardless of implementation performance.
15 See the Kenyan and Ecuador case studies (Chapters 16 and 19 in Volume 2). It has

been suggested that sectoral loans might be disbursed in kind (e.g. agricultural-sector loans in the form of fertiliser), so that their proceeds accrue only to the sector in which the planned programme of policy reform is to take place. This appears a promising strategy for increasing commitment at the sectoral ministry level, but has not yet been tried. It is taken up further in Chapter 9.

16 It is notable that in countries where such Bank local representatives do not exist (e.g. Ecuador, see the case study at Chapter 19 in Volume 2) there has been a much greater tendency to impose unrealistically tight conditionality, because there existed no go-between to give Washington staff informed advice about what might be politically feasible.

17 The game set out in Table 3.3 has a superficial resemblance to the 'one-sided' or 'asymmetric' prisoner's dilemma (e.g. Rasmusen, 1989, p. 97) which, however, always solves according to the deadlock outcome (outcome 4 in Table 3.3). The reason why the outcome may be different in the game of Table 3.3 is that the game has two stages after the initial conditionality deal is done, and for the donor the possibility of making a profitable loan in Act 3 is assumed at this stage to dominate the elimination of that possibility, whatever the recipient's slippage behaviour in Act 3. This assumes no impact of slippage on repayment: this possibility is examined later.

4

PROGRAMME DESIGN

4.1 INTRODUCTION

In this chapter we consider in detail the manner in which the policy reform conditions attached to World Bank programme loans are designed and negotiated, that is, the cluster of actions represented as Act 1 in Figure 3.3. The questions to be tackled, in sequence, are: what is the condition which the Bank saw itself as trying to remedy by means of conditional programme finance? How did it derive its diagnosis of what was wrong, and its prescription of what had to be done to make things better? How was the division of labour between the different agencies offering development finance – notably the Bank, the Fund, the bilateral agencies, and the commercial banks – arrived at? How did the Bank determine the order in which its own prescriptions were to be offered to developing countries? Bearing in mind the likelihood that the recipient might expect the dose to taste nasty, what strategies did the Bank use to sugar the pill? What strategies did the patient employ to get the best out of his doctor, and what was the shape of the deals that resulted? Can the shape of these deals be related to indicators of the nature of the disease, or alternatively to the degree of the donor and recipient's bargaining power? What has the Bank learned from fifteen years of experience, and what else could it usefully learn?

Even the analysis so far presented is sufficient to expose the limits of the hackneyed medical analogy which provides our point of departure. For whereas it is relatively unusual for patients to bargain with their doctors, bargaining, as we argued in the previous chapter, lies at the heart of the relationship between the Bank as lender and the government which borrows from it. We shall be arguing that it is the power-relationship between donor and recipient, rather than the severity of the economic 'disease' from which a country is suffering, which principally determines the nature of the prescription offered as part of a conditionality package. And the fact that the doctor, in this case, has to pay the patient to accept the prescription

96

instead of being paid by him points to a bargaining relationship somewhat different from that which normally pertains between doctors and their clients. The process of treatment, and the patient's response to it, lie outside the scope of this chapter; but as demonstrated in Chapter 3, the donor's and the recipient's expectations about the manner in which the prescribed course of treatment will be self-administered by the recipient play a crucial part in determining the design of conditionality packages. Much of what has to be designed even at this stage, we shall be arguing, consists not of lists of remedies to be taken in a specific order, but of strategies to persuade the recipient to continue to take them.

4.2 DIAGNOSIS

In one sentence, the condition which the Bank saw itself as having to treat in the early 1980s, in every developing country with a balance-of-payments deficit, was excessive government intervention in particular markets, leading to an anti-trade bias and levels of output below those which could be achieved with a more efficient allocation of resources. Not 'getting the prices right', in the famous phrase, was costing developing countries, in the Bank's opinion, 2 or 3 per cent per annum on their current growth rates by depressing supply in individual markets.[1] These beliefs were backed up by statistical exercises (most memorably in Chapter 4 of the Bank's 1983 *World Development Report*) suggesting a negative correlation between the number of price distortions in individual developing countries and the rate of economic growth. Failure to get the prices right was also, of course, in the Bank's opinion causing a number of its own projects, particularly in Africa, to fail which in 'the right policy environment' might be expected to succeed. As the Bank's Senior Vice-President (Operations) of the time relates, many of the interventions which caused the Bank most worry were seen by it as unsuccessful attempts to shield the economy against the consequences of excessive macroeconomic expansion in the depressed economic environment of the late 1970s and early 1980s:

Some developing countries postponed domestic policy reforms, or introduced them only slowly, and relied instead on increased external borrowing. In others, government sought to offset constraints imposed by external factors or uncertainty on the part of private investors through increased deficit financing to expand public sector investment programs. But as economic activity slowed down and external capital flows, both commercial and concessional, became less buoyant, the costs of such partial adjustments became increasingly severe. This was reflected in growing expenditures on subsidies and in unsustainable budget deficits. To limit inflation and control the balance of payments deficit, some of the countries then resorted to

97

price controls and import restrictions, which led to a misallocation of resources and to an incentive system biased against exporters . . . Export growth has been handicapped by overvalued exchange rates, inadequate price incentives for producers, and the mismanagement of agencies handling credit, marketing, and export promotion. Mobilisation of domestic resources has been undermined by negative real interest rates.

(Stern, 1983: 88)

The implication of this passage is that the Bank of the time saw the disease as consisting not only of harmful government interventions in specific markets, but also of the excessive macroeconomic expansion which gave rise to them and the 'mismanagement of agencies' to which they in turn led. If this position is accepted, the Bank needs to decide how much of its effort to invest in 'getting prices right' strictly defined and how much in interventions which lie both upstream of that objective (i.e. getting the macroeconomic balances right) and downstream (i.e. reforming institutions which may hold the key to an adequate supply response to such prices as can be 'got right'). This will emerge as one of the key dilemmas of adjustment lending, and the next two sections will relate how the Bank attempted to resolve it: broadly, the argument will be that the Bank chose to hedge its bets by operating at all three levels, but this may not have been wise.

Interlinked with the question of the level at which the Bank should operate is the question of the organ on which it should operate, that is, the market in which it should intervene. On this matter, the theory of welfare economics offers little guidance. It is able to say that, under specified conditions, an economy without state controls (a 'competitive equilibrium') yields the maximum output that can be extracted from the resources at hand; and hence, by implication, that if the specified conditions are satisfied, a removal of all state controls will increase output. But, first, the specified conditions (perfect information, absence of externalities, and constant or decreasing returns to scale) are seldom satisfied, least of all in less developed countries; and second, even if they were, the theory is only able to say that a *total removal* of all controls will increase output; not a partial removal, which is all that lies within the realms of political possibility. On the question of whether the removal of some controls within an economy characterised by multiple imperfections will be of any help, the relevant economic theory (the 'theory of the second best') is silent.[2] Common sense and medical analogy might suggest that if a patient is suffering from multiple injuries, treating some of them would be better than doing nothing; but the application of the analogy requires that a harmful market intervention be clearly recognisable as such, and it is easy to cite cases (such as the reduction of tariff levels in an economy characterised by

98

serious budget and balance-of-payments deficits or the removal of import subsidies in an economy characterised by capital market failure where the removal of one market intervention on its own will manifestly make things worse.

It has to be faced, therefore, that the Bank's policy recommendations in the area of stimulation of aggregate supply, by contrast with the Fund's policy recommendations in the area of deflation of aggregate demand,[3] lack a theoretical basis (Helleiner, 1990: 9); they do have the backing of an empirical argument, but this is confined to a set of observations on the relationship between price liberalisation and aggregate supply whose import, particularly at the aggregate level, is somewhat ambiguous.[4] In particular, these observations offer no answer to the question 'which government interventions represent major distortions, and which do no harm?' or to the still more practical question 'which distortions should be removed first?' In attempting to distinguish cancers from pimples, the Bank has for the most part had to depend on a blend of country experience and intuition. There is one rule of thumb which it can use, however: the more deeply embedded in a country's productive structure a particular good or service is (i.e. the greater the value of potential productive activities to which it provides an input), the greater the likelihood that a distortion in its price will do damage. And as a look back at Table 2.3 will confirm, most of the prices on which the Bank has concentrated its conditionality (at least in SALs) are prices of inputs, such as agricultural products, energy, and credit.

Table 2.3, however, is Hamlet without the Prince. For the Bank has made no secret of the fact that it regards the most important price of all (particularly in economies which are very open to international trade, such as those of sub-Saharan Africa) as the exchange rate, which determines the cost of all inputs which have an import component, and the competitiveness of all exports;[5] yet the exchange rate is absent from the table, since by the agreed division of labour between Bank and Fund the Fund takes the lead in giving advice on the exchange rate to developing countries. If the Bank wishes to exercise influence on trade policy, therefore, it is limited to either trying to persuade Fund staff, or alternatively attaching its conditionality to components of trade policy other than the exchange rate, such as export promotion or the removal of import quotas. The Bank's pressures towards trade liberalisation have been reinforced by more than two decades of research (e.g. Little, Scitovsky and Scott, 1970; Krueger, 1983) purporting to show that 'import substitution' industrialisation strategies have been less effective than strategies of 'export promotion'. There is no doubt that high levels of long-term protection on imports of raw materials or intermediates do push up the cost structure of industry and reduce the competitiveness of exporting industries, nor that the Far East represents a more successful model of industrialisation, in terms of both efficiency and equity, than Latin America; on the other hand, the work of

Krueger and her associates, and more recently the *East Asia Miracle* team (World Bank, 1993), has neither invalidated the infant industry argument for protection nor established countries such as Taiwan and South Korea as plausible examples of *laissez-faire*. The Bank's efforts at trade policy reform constitute for this reason one of the most controversial elements of its proposed reform programme.

There remains a third issue to be resolved before it is possible to pass to the prescription stage. For if the diagnosis is 'deficiency of aggregate supply, caused by imperfection of markets', there are two potential approaches to the problem, within each market: (1) remove restrictions so that prices can be allowed to rise and fall freely, and (2) attempt to flatten out the supply curve so that if they do rise, the output response will be greater. The key unresolved issue between radicals and conservatives within the Bank is what blend of these two approaches should be adopted. At one end of the spectrum is the view that the Bank's adjustment programmes should concern themselves purely with the removal of restrictions, leaving the business of 'easing the basic constraints to growth: provision of infrastructure, technological changes, education, health, population, and so on' (Please, 1984: 18) to the Bank's project divisions. At the opposite end is the view that a true programme of supply-oriented structural adjustment should have as its objective 'to raise the elasticity of export supply from near zero to at least 0.5, in order to enable the Marshall-Lerner conditions to operate'.[6] The second view comes close to the aspirations of the Latin American structuralists of the 1950s, who likewise saw the roots of chronic economic debility as lying in an inadequate supply response, particularly in the markets for labour and agricultural produce.[7] But once the focus is shifted to measures which will flatten the supply curve, it becomes necessary to recognise that not all market distortions are caused by government intervention, and that the correct prescription may be, not liberalisation to deal with government failure, but rather, *expanded* government intervention to deal with market failure – for example, land reform, credit for small producers out of reach of commercial banks, agricultural research and extension, rural electrification, investment in feeder roads and port facilities. Such interventions, if this argument is accepted, need to become part of supply-orientated conditionality alongside measures to liberalise prices.

This argument has added force in any country where the infrastructure is particularly weak and the ability of the price mechanism to allocate resources efficiently correspondingly bad – Cambodia, Bolivia, Guyana, Vietnam, Nepal, Bangladesh. But as may be expected, the argument between the two wings of the Bank is at its most intense in relation to the poorest region of all, sub-Saharan Africa. On one side of the argument, macroeconomic fundamentalism is expressed by the authors of the Bank's 1994 report, *Adjustment in Africa*:

Better macroeconomic policies have already turned growth around in Africa. Avoiding overvalued exchange rates and keeping inflation and budget deficits low might sound like a boring recipe, but it works. It has worked in East Asia and it will work in Africa. . . . In promoting exports, governments should not try to pick 'winners'. Government can best help entrepreneurs discover and develop competitiveness exports by getting out of the way.

(World Bank 1994c: 184 and 192)

Against this, a recent Bank study of the management of agricultural development in Africa has castigated the recent shift in development philosophy 'away from integrated rural development and in favour of adjustment lending and private sector initiatives' as being:

flawed by its inadequate recognition of the variety of causal factors underlying past growth (or decline), of the likely effects of price-based policy reforms on aggregate supply responses, and of the complementary, nonprice micro-economic actions needed to ensure that the policy reform process was sustainable beyond the short term, and that it was harmonised with underlying developmental realities and long-term goals.

(Lele, 1989: 8)

Kevin Cleaver, of the Bank's projects staff, is likewise emphatic about the major role of state agricultural services, and the relatively minor role of prices, in African agricultural development:

'Appropriate' price policy would have a relatively small impact on agricultural growth. The analysis suggests that these policies are not the most important factors affecting agricultural growth. Indeed, [they] have a relatively small impact compared to other factors such as Government involvement in farm input supply, population growth, and government's ability to operate and maintain its agricultural investment.

(Cleaver, 1985: abstract on opening page)[8].

The monetarist-structuralist controversy of the 1950s, then, has been replaced by a pricist-structuralist controversy of the 1980s *within* the Bank. At issue are three questions: do the limits on the operation of the system in developing countries have macroeconomic roots which need to be tackled by the Bank? does price liberalisation have to be complemented by policy measures to expand output directly? and finally, which markets should the Bank concern itself with as a matter of priority? These questions remain unresolved, and the absence of a clear dogma on these issues, as we shall see, was to result in enormous variations of conditionality as between programmes, even those prescribed for countries in a similar economic predicament.

4.3 PRESCRIPTION I: BANK-FUND RELATIONS

In making the transition to medium-term programme lending the Bank was, as noted in Chapter 2, colonising new ground; it was even exceeding the authority of its own Articles of Agreement, which stipulate that 'Loans made or guaranteed by the Bank shall, except in special circumstances, be for the purpose of specific projects of reconstruction or development'.[9]

Until the middle 1970s this territory was not contested; but in 1975 the IMF introduced its Extended Facility, allowing for disbursement of loans over three years and repayment over a period of up to ten,[10] which began to be heavily used from the onset of the recession of the 1980s. The introduction of structural adjustment lending in 1980 was resisted by the Bank's Executive Board as described in Chapter 2, and indeed by the early 1980s, as Feinberg writes,

> [both] the fund and the Bank were now providing balance of payments loans, tranched over one to three years, with medium-term amortisation periods. Both programmes supported macro-economic and micro-economic adjustments, and focused on improving both external and internal accounts. The degree of overlap between the two institutions had greatly increased.
>
> (Feinberg, 1986: 7)

The first and simplest route towards reconciliation was simply to separate Bank and Fund operations in time, thereby enabling each institution to lead in successive phases of the economic cycle. Indeed, the convention soon became established that any developing country in balance-of-payments difficulties should approach the Fund first for a stand-by credit, and that requests for Bank programme finance would be considered only after agreement had been reached with the Fund. The application of this convention, in principle, would require governments to put their macroeconomic house in order, by means of a programme of fiscal and monetary stabilisation under the tutelage of the Fund, before embarking on programmes of supply expansion under the guidance of the Bank. There would be a token Bank staff member on each Fund mission, and vice versa, to ensure consistency of recommendations, but it would be accepted by all parties that the needs of balancing the external account would prevail in the case of Fund missions, and the needs of allocative efficiency would prevail in the case of Bank missions. In the early 1980s, the convention was strictly applied, and not one of the Bank's *Structural* Adjustment Loans, to early 1989, was agreed without an IMF stand-by agreement already being in place (Nicholas, 1988: 4). However, as the focus of the Bank's adjustment lending shifted from whole-economy to sector-based operations, it became commoner for the Bank, if anxious to sustain its lending programme in a particular country, to grant sector loans in the absence of any IMF stabilisation agreement. To date this has happened in Hungary, Brazil, Colombia, Indonesia, Pakistan, Turkey and, as previously described, Argentina in October 1988. Significantly, all of the countries named except for Hungary are countries where the Bank's concern to sustain its large and profitable lending programme places it, as earlier discussed, in a weak position to enforce its conditionality.

For 'division of labour through sequencing' to be effective it is in any case vital that the Fund's initial intervention should be an effective one, in the sense of dealing sufficiently well with the initial balance of payments emergency to enable the Fund to be off-stage once the Bank appeared with its package of supply-side reforms. In the event, as Table 4.1 demonstrates for our case-study countries, this has generally not happened.

Of all these case studies, only Thailand, and to a lesser extent Turkey, approximate to the intended sequence of IMF stabilisation programme, followed by Bank structural adjustment programme, followed by steady growth under the impetus of private foreign capital inflows. In all the other cases, except for the aborted programme in Guyana, the Fund was forced to return with a stabilisation programme shortly after the beginning of the Bank's policy dialogue, with the consequence that the recipient government found itself implementing structural adjustment, not on a firm base of financial stability, but in the midst of stabilisation.[11] Compliance with Bank-inspired measures which required an improving fiscal or balance

Table 4.1 Nine case-study countries; sequencing of Fund and Bank operations

Country	1980	1981	1982	1983	1984	1985	1986	1987	1988
Turkey	F/B1	B1	F/B1	F/B1	B1	B2	B2	B2	
Philippines	F/B1	F		F/B1	F	B2	F	B2	B2
Thailand		F	B1	B1					
Kenya	F/B1		F/B1	F		F	B2		F/B2
Ghana				F/B2	F/B2	F/B2	B2	F/B1	F/B2
Malawi	F	B1		F/B1		B1	F	F/B2	B2
Guyana	F	B1							
Jamaica		F	B1	F/B1	B1			F/B2	
Ecuador					F	B2	F		B2

Key: F   = IMF stand-by or Extended Facility credit
     B1 = World Bank Structural Adjustment Loan
     B2 = Other World Bank policy-based loan
Source: Country case studies (see Volume 2 for details).

of payments environment for their implementation (such as tariff reduction and investment in export promotion measures) was in such circumstances made unwise, if not precluded, by the need to satisfy the IMF's performance criteria. The presence of both Fund and Bank on stage at the same time, in addition, forced both institutions to confront the fact of overlapping areas of responsibility for policy advice.

By its Articles of Agreement, paragraph 8(b), the Bank is obligated 'in making decisions on applications for loans or guarantees relating to matters directly within the competence of any international organisation . . . to give consideration to the views and recommendations of such organisation'; there is no comparable obligation for the IMF under its own Articles. Stanley Please has argued (personal communication) that this points to a fundamental asymmetry in the relationship between Bank and Fund: 'whereas the Bank has always accepted the Fund's leadership in situations of financial emergency, the Fund has not done likewise at times when longer term structural supply-side issues become of paramount concern'. The difficulty is, of course, that for the Fund to be called in in the first place, the situation must by definition be one of financial emergency; no borrower undergoes the privations associated with an IMF stand-by if that discipline can possibly be avoided. If the Fund is on stage at all, therefore, any advice which the Bank may give is subject to the constraints imposed by a deficit reduction plan agreed with the Fund, nearly always involving stipulations on the level of government borrowing, tax rates, interest rates and exchange rates. Subject to these stipulations the Fund has been happy to devolve to the Bank, within the areas of overlap defined above, work of a clearly microeconomic, or alternatively of an institutional reform, nature. Examples are given in Table 4.2.

Until 1986, this division of labour was worked out informally between Bank and Fund: within the 'grey areas', any disagreement which arose could only be resolved by a concession from one or other side, which could often be achieved by a simple change of label.[12] Beginning in that year, however, the Fund began to make highly concessional disbursements from what became known as its Structural Adjustment Facility (SAF – subsequently Enhanced Structural Adjustment Facility or ESAF) in low income countries, each of which was conditional on the agreement of a programme of policy reform jointly agreed between Bank, Fund and recipient government. (Within our group of case-study countries, SAFs or ESAFs have so far been made available to Malawi, Ghana and Kenya). The Fund, as the lender of ESAF money, takes the lead in defining the character of the programme, and simply photocopies out of current Bank agreements such conditions as it wishes to add to its own policy recommendations. With the advent of the ESAF, cross-conditionality between Bank and Fund, already implicit in the linkage between Fund stand-bys and Bank

Table 4.2   Division of labour between Fund and Bank in trade and financial policy in
certain case-study countries, 1983–8

	Agreed Fund responsibility	*Agreed Bank responsibility*	*Grey area or area of changing responsibility*

Ghana	Exchange rate
	Public expenditure
	Tax revenue
	Credit ceilings
		Public utility
		  prices
		Tax structure
		Public investment
		  budget
		Interest rates
			Cocoa prices
			Price controls

Kenya	Exchange rate
	Public expenditure
	Credit ceilings
		Tariff structure
		Public investment
		  budget
		Agricultural prices
		Financial market
		  reform
			Import controls
			User charges

Ecuador	Growth of monetary
	  aggregates
	Exchange rate
		Real interest rates
		Development bank
		  reform	

Jamaica	Growth of monetary
	  aggregates
		Import controls
		Public enterprise
		  reform, including
		  price structure
		Tax structure
		Incentives to exporters
			Exchange rate

Source: Country case studies in Volume 2.

policy-based operations, became explicit.

Can the division of labour between Fund and Bank set out in Table 4.3, together with the invention of the ESAF, be seen as a satisfactory solution to the problem of overlap between Bank and Fund responsibilities? Of the three parties involved, the Fund would probably be most inclined to say yes. The Bank must face the fact that of the key prices which it is the objective of structural adjustment programmes to set right, the exchange rate – the most important of all – remains formally outside its jurisdiction, and a second, namely the real interest rate, is impossible to control if the quantity of domestic credit, of which it represents the price, has already been predetermined by a prior agreement between the government and the Fund.

The Jamaica and Philippines case studies provide ample illustration of the frustration which this caused for the Bank. In Jamaica between 1980 and 1983, a two-tier exchange rate was maintained, the official exchange

Table 4.3 Nine case-study countries: trends in different components
of public expenditure, 1980–8
(Real levels of government expenditure in category mentioned, 1980 = 100)

	1980	1981	1982	1983	1984	1985	1986	1987	1988	Percentage change 1988 over 1980
Turkey										
Overall total	100	99	. .	111	123	129	111	132	133	+33
Recurrent:	100	95	. .	111	132	147	132	151	154	+54
Development:	100		. .	123	101	86	76	86	79	−21
Philippines										
Overall total	100	107	105	102	80	91	104	129	139	+39
Recurrent:	100	99	107	107	89	106	122	154	. .	+54*
Development:	100	136	100	91	58	48	58	59	. .	−42*
Thailand										
Overall total	100	105	118	122	126	140	139	142	139	+39
Recurrent:	100	107	120	128	137	149	150	161	158	+58
Development:	100	101	115	107	96	116	109	103	93	−7
Kenya										
Overall total	100	111	103	96	90	103	101	125	. .	+25*
Recurrent:	100	110	127	120	121	125	129	147	. .	+47*
Development:	100	111	78	71	58	84	62	108	. .	+8*
Malawi										
Overall total	100	99	81	84	85	100	106	99	. .	−1*
Recurrent:	100	127	112	114	110	132	147	150	. .	+50*
Development:	100	67	49	52	57	63	62	42	. .	−58*
Ghana										
Overall total	100	103	85	55	70	101	107	111	135	+35
Recurrent:	100	94	77	37	68	94	103	98	116	+16
Development:	100	165	79	49	83	153	142	229	295	+195
Morocco										
Overall total	100	114	116	104	100	107	104	101	. .	+1*
Recurrent:	100	111	110	114	114	118	116	114	. .	+14*
Development:	100	117	127	82	69	61	79	70	. .	−30*
Ecuador										
Overall total	100	118	114	94	98	116	126	. .	. .	+26†
Recurrent:	100	109	105	.	.	.	.	.	.	. .
Development:	100	216	164	.	.	.	.	.	.	. .

Source: *IMF Government Finance Statistics Yearbook* 1989. Summary table rows 7 and 9. GDP
deflator is used to convert current price to constant price values.
* Figure relates to 1980–7 period only.
† Figure relates to 1980–6 period only.

rate appreciated in real terms and the central government budgetary deficit deteriorated from 7.7 to 10 per cent of GDP. The Bank felt that its own programme as designed 'was broadly appropriate', was complied with 'on a strictly legal basis' and 'would have achieved most of its expected benefits if the stabilisation programme had been successful' (Harrigan, Volume 2, Chapter 17). But the stabilisation programme, including in particular the management of the exchange rate, was under the supervision of the Fund; and because it was not implemented, many of the measures which the Bank persuaded the Jamaica government to bring in to give an incentive to agricultural and manufacturing exporters were not able to have their planned effect. By 1984, the growth rate of GDP had turned negative, reserves had declined alarmingly and inflation had doubled to over 30 per cent. When the Jamaica government turned to the Fund for a stand-by, the Fund's response was conditioned both by the severity of the current economic predicament and by the failure of the previous stabilisation attempt; it amounted to a quick and savage monetary deflation, which pushed the nominal interest rate up by 7 percentage points between 1984 and 1985 (Harrigan, Volume 2, 17: 338–9). These measures not only failed to attract the hoped-for inflows of foreign capital into Jamaica; they also created a situation in which the private sector was too far handicapped by high interest rates (which the Bank, in spite of its nominal responsibilities, had little power to influence) to be able to take advantage of the changes which the Bank had wrought in the incentive structure. The Philippines, prior to 1984, represents a broadly similar case. Again the Fund condoned an appreciation in the real exchange rate through a series of stand-bys (Mosley, Volume 2, Chapter 12); again, once the full consequences of letting the macroeconomy ride had been borne in on the Fund, their response in 1984 was a ruthless monetary deflation, which pushed interest rates up to 40 per cent (and caused real GDP to fall by 10 per cent between 1983 and 1985); again the Bank found that its painstaking efforts to provide microeconomic incentive (in the areas of import control removal and rationalisation of the public investment programme) had been blown off course first by the Fund's leniency on exchange rates and then by its macroeconomic overkill. The reaction of one Bank economist to its experiences in the Marcos years was simple: 'The Fund let us down'.[13]

The problem goes deeper; for under the agreed division of labour the Fund takes responsibility not only for exchange rates and the money supply, but also for public expenditure totals and overall budgetary balance. All Fund stand-by agreements contain a provision for central bank credit to the public sector (and sometimes, explicitly, public expenditure) to be restrained; but the Fund, in keeping with the macro nature of its conditionality, does not give guidance as to where the cuts should fall. In

107

practice, however, as Table 4.3 illustrates, the cuts nearly always fall on the development rather than the recurrent part of the budget, for good political reasons: the recurrent budget finances people's jobs, whereas the development budget only finances structures as yet unbuilt; and the recurrent budget, if cut, cannot be topped up by an appeal to the international aid agencies, whereas the development budget can. For the same political reasons, the cuts in the development budget are themselves not spread evenly; they fall relatively lightly on areas such as defence and public administration, and relatively heavily on sectors which lack political leverage (and which, again, there is hope of persuading the international agencies to rescue) such as health, education, and agriculture. The social consequences of this response have been vividly illustrated by Cornia, Jolly and Stewart (1987). For now, our concern is with the productive consequences, which are that by the time that the Bank gets down to its job of stimulating the supply side – particularly those parts of the supply side that are heavily dependent on government services such as smallholder agriculture – there may be relatively little left to stimulate. In some countries, therefore, a stabilisation programme should not be seen as a necessary precondition for a programme to stimulate supply. The problem is clearly worst in sub-Saharan Africa, where the share of smallholder agriculture in the economy is greatest and its dependence on government services such as research, extension, road-building and credit most intense; and preliminary statistical investigations suggest the presence of a link between the level of government development expenditure and marketed output in agriculture (Mosley and Smith, 1989: Figure 2). But in all developing countries the same general problem arises: given that Bank-inspired structural adjustment measures are normally preceded by Fund-inspired stabilisation measures, is the effectiveness of the Bank's adjustment programmes impaired by the manner in which LDC governments have chosen to respond to the Fund's macro-level conditionality?

It will by now be clear that the Bank, in attempting to control the apparatus of economic policy-making in developing countries, has been thwarted not only by the governments of those countries, but also by the territorial ambitions of the Fund. For the Bank to invoke, at the time of its own supervision missions, prior Fund conditions which were not mentioned at the time of the Bank's loan appraisal (page 57 above), is neither in moral nor practical terms a satisfactory solution to the problem. Logically, what are the alternatives? If one discounts the possibility of a merger between Bank and Fund, the options are four: retreat by the Fund; retreat by the Bank; some combination of the above; and a continuance of the status quo. Not surprisingly, preferences between these options are heavily coloured by which side of 19th Street the speaker happens to be standing on,[14] and since this is essentially a book about the Bank, it becomes the more important to give proper weight to Fund views of how the dilemma should be resolved.

To recapitulate: the dilemma arises because it is not possible to divide the set of available policy instruments into macro (or demand side or short term) and micro (supply side or medium term), and to allocate them to Fund and Bank respectively. Many of the aggregate expenditure flows which the Fund seeks to regulate have micro implications for the pattern of output, and some of the prices which the Bank tries to 'get right', notoriously the exchange rate, have macro implications for the balance of payments. Given the problems associated with drawing a firm dividing line between Bank and Fund policy *instruments*, Stanley Please, one of the architects of Structural Adjustment Lending within the Bank, has argued (1984: 72) for a dividing line to be drawn between *countries*: in those 'facing an emergency financial crisis' the Fund would lead, and in those 'for which the immediate issues of macro balance are not of concern . . . but for which structural problems need to be given urgent and continuous attention', the Bank would lead. But quite apart from the political difficulties involved in persuading the Fund to abdicate the role of lead institution in specific countries, it is not at all easy to identify the countries where such a renunciation might logically take place. In all of the countries of Table 4.1 except Thailand, and indeed through most of Africa and Latin America, a state of 'emergency financial crisis' persists, little though it was predicted at the beginning of the 1980s, and in consequence the Fund remains heavily committed. Elsewhere (Thailand being a good case in point) little need for Bank programme finance, or policy advice, is evinced by the government. It also seems that the Bank's persisting suspicion of the Fund as being 'soft on exchange rates' may be overdone: the shift to market-determined interest rates constitutes the major change in the economic policy-making environment in Africa in the 1980s, and is almost entirely to the credit of the Fund.[15] Our own proposal would therefore be the obverse of Please's, namely that the Bank should withdraw from its informal role of second-guessing the Fund's advice on exchange rate policy, and trust it to be an eloquent advocate of the principle of market-determined exchange rates; but that, in return, Bank staff should accompany all missions dispatched to negotiate stand-by agreements in Bank borrower countries, with a view to advising on the micro implications and apportionment of any stabilisation measures which the mission may recommend. In particular, Bank staff might be expected to advise on stabilisation options which avoid cuts in development spending, at the cost of some increases in taxes and user charges. In this way they might be able to avoid the supply-inhibiting consequences of stabilisation which are only too apparent from Table 4.3. Under this proposal, both parties would retreat from their existing positions a little in relation for a concession by the other party; there is, importantly, no prima facie net loss in influence for either Fund or Bank.

109

4.4 PRESCRIPTION II: THE SIZE AND SEQUENCING OF THE DOSE

The Bank, then, approaches the negotiating table already tightly constrained concerning what it may prescribe; if an area of policy has balance-of-payments implications, then the Fund will see it as its own territory. On the other hand, if it has implications for the growth of the supply side, then the Bank will also see it as its own territory, and as Table 2.3 illustrated, the range of Bank conditionality on structural adjustment loans has embraced all markets in which distortion is perceived to exist and all areas of public sector activity which are believed to have a bearing on the rate of economic growth. The question which now has to be addressed is how this prescription was arrived at.

Formally, the prescription has four elements: a designation of areas in which policy action is needed; a specification of what action is needed in each of those areas; a specification of the sequence in which those actions should be taken; and a sum of money to be attached to the package. In principle the first and last of these elements are linked, and the value of a loan can be increased to 'buy' more policy reform, but as earlier related, planning allocations for policy-based loans are determined several years in advance, and the Bank's ability to vary them in response to need will depend on circumstantial events, such as underspends in other country programmes.

In principle, the designation of potential areas for action will derive from a proposal by the recipient government, to which the Bank will make a response based on its own diagnosis. As earlier related, the fundamental diagnosis underlying the Bank's decision to become involved in policy-based lending is misdirected intervention by LDC governments in specific markets. The severity of those interventions, as measured at the end of the 1970s, is conveniently summarised by the Bank in its 1983 *World Development Report*, and we may conveniently begin by examining the relationship between that diagnosis and the policy action prescribed by the Bank at the time. This is set out, for those seven countries which also form the subject of our country case studies, in Table 4.4; the measurement of distortion in each market is on the three-point scale 'mild', 'moderate', 'severe' and the countries within the table are presented in increasing order of aggregate price distortion. The analysis is confined to those markets which appear in the analysis of the *Report*.

On the evidence of Table 4.4, the Bank did indeed attempt to reform all markets where distortions were diagnosed as being 'severe', although there are cases outside of the table where it diagnosed a particular distortion as being fundamental, such as the underpricing of petroleum products in Ecuador (Volume 2, Chapter 19), and then proceeded to leave it out of the conditionality negotiations on account of what were believed to be

110

overriding political barriers to reform. On the other hand, the Bank also tilted at a number of windmills, including the foreign exchange regime in Turkey, fertiliser subsidies in Malawi, sugar and banana marketing in Jamaica, and food crop marketing in Kenya, Thailand and Malawi:[16] that is, sectors in which state distortion of the market was, *by its own analysis*, 'mild'. Indeed, statistical analysis suggests that there is little correlation between the severity of price distortions and the tightness of policy packages prescribed by the Bank: across the range of developing countries for which the Bank published data, the average number of conditions negotiated with low-distortion countries (just over ten) is insignificantly different from the number negotiated with high-distortion countries.[17] In other words, it is likely that factors other than strict economic analysis influence the Bank's decision concerning the number of areas in which to intervene. Which are they?

Most obviously, the content of conditionality packages was influenced by the bargaining relationship between the Bank and the recipient government. In recipient countries whose debt or balance-of-payments position was particularly dire, as will be formally demonstrated in section 4.7 of this chapter, the conditionality was abnormally tight; and if the recipient was heavily dependent on the Bank for finance, its bargaining position was further prejudiced. On the donor side, the major force weakening the Bank's own position, as we saw in Chapter 3, is pressure to spend the budget; and the larger the country budget, the greater the pressure to spend it. Thus, broadly speaking, the tightest conditions are those imposed on small countries in sub-Saharan Africa, which lack the economic strength, the alternative borrowing sources or the importance within the Bank's own portfolio which would enable them to dictate terms to the Bank, even if, as in Malawi, the need for policy reform on efficiency criteria is not revealed by the Bank's analyses as being serious. By the same token, the loosest conditions are those imposed on large countries with a great deal of scope to borrow elsewhere, such as Brazil, the Philippines and South Korea; in the limit, countries in this position have been completely exempted from conditionality, such as Indonesia, whose enormous ($300 million) Trade Adjustment Loan of March 1987, in the Bank's phrase, was 'entirely tied to policy actions previously performed'. All that is negotiated at this stage, of course, is a *promise* to carry out certain policy reforms which, as we shall see in the next chapter, is not always kept; hence the machiavellian recipient who expects his financial dependence on the Bank to diminish soon can happily agree to a very tight list of conditions, however little he feels they are needed, if he does not expect to need to implement them anyway. Considerations of this kind may explain the acceptance of a puzzlingly tight list of conditions by Thailand (Volume 2, Chapter 13) and Pakistan.

Obvious though it may be why recipient governments accept the

Table 4.4 Seven cast-study countries: adjustment-loan conditionality in relation to diagnosis of 1983 *World Development Report*

Elements of intervention	Exchange rate	Protection of manufacturing	Protection or taxation of agriculture	Capital market	Labour market	Energy pricing
Malawi (composite distortion index = 1.14)						
Distortion index	mild	mild	mild	moderate	mild	mild
Bank prescription (SAL's I, II and III, 1981–5)	none	none	changes in agricultural prices; elimination of fertiliser subsidies	none	none	increases in electricity prices
Thailand (composite distortion index: 1.43)						
Distortion index	mild	moderate	mild	mild	mild	severe
Bank prescription (SAL's I and II, 1982 and 1983)	none	reform tariff structures; eliminate export taxes	land reforms; review marketing system	none	none	raise price of electricity and gasoline
Philippines (composite distortion index: 1.57)						
Distortion index	mild	moderate	moderate	moderate	mild	moderate
Bank prescription (SAL's I and II, also ERL, 1980–7)	none	remove import quotas	none	reform development banks	none	none

Kenya (composite distortion index: 1.71)						
Distortion index	mild	severe	mild	moderate	moderate	mild
Bank prescription (SAL's I and II, ISAC and ASAC 1, 1980–8)	no direct action, but various export promotion measures	abolition of import licensing system	reform of marketing for maize, other food crops and fertiliser	reconstruction of three development banks	none	none
Turkey (composite distortion index: 2.14)						
Distortion index	mild	moderate	moderate	severe	moderate	moderate
Bank prescription (SAL's I to V, 1980–5)	multiple export promotion measures	abolition of import quotas; cuts in tariffs	none	increase deposit rates; reform investment banks	none	raise energy prices to world levels
Jamaica (composite distortion index: 2.29)						
Distortion index	moderate	moderate	mild	severe	severe	moderate
Bank prescription (SAL's I to III, 1982–5)	amend allocation system for foreign exchange	remove import quotas	reform external marketing organisations; restructure sugar and banana industries	interest rate and equity market reforms	none	raise electricity prices
Ghana (composite distortion index: 2.86)						
Distortion index	severe	severe	moderate	severe	moderate	severe
Bank prescription (SAL and various programme credits 1983–7)	introduce auction system for foreign exchange	liberalise import controls	raise cocoa price and reform cocoa Marketing Board	new banking regulations	none	decontrol petrol price

Source: Case studies in Volume 2.

attachment of so many side conditions to their loans, it is less clear why, in markets where distortion is low (Table 4.4) and the probability of implementation remote, the Bank imposes them. The Bank is well aware of the problem, and its 1988 review of policy-based lending warns that:

> any improvement in implementation is likely to depend on greater selectivity in setting conditions and on greater care in monitoring progress. This would involve increased reliance on tranche conditions – limiting conditions to a reasonable number of key concerns [and] setting realistic schedules for implementation . . . Limiting conditionality to a small number of agreed concerns also seems essential if the Bank is to take a stricter position on fulfilment. The gains from being strict should outweigh by a large margin any losses from shortening the list of conditions.
>
> (World Bank, 1988: 93)

Strong though the logical arguments are in favour of 'a reasonable number of key conditions', there is evidence to suggest that the internal momentum within the Bank towards over-prescription is deeply rooted, and may be difficult to arrest. The numbers of conditions attached to SALs and SECALs show little sign of declining over time,[18] and there are a number of cases where an over-ambitious Bank operation on which compliance was low (such as the second SAL in Kenya, in 1983) was followed by another over-ambitious operation on which compliance was again low (such as the first Agricultural Sector Loan in the same country, in 1986). What are the sources of this momentum? In the first place, an individual professional officer within the Bank has everything to gain from designing a comprehensive programme of reform, which appears to get to grips with all the major supply-side constraints, rather than a timid-looking programme which appears as a surrender to vested interests within the recipient country; if he can square the programme with the recipient government, he will win plaudits from the Executive Board, and because of this he will also win plaudits from his seniors within the Bank. In the second place, the format of the SAL, in particular, invites competitive attempts by all the sectoral departments of the Bank (agriculture, transport, power, etc.) to score a policy success for their own department, and by the diverse members of the Executive Board to achieve their own pet reforms, in the country which is currently negotiating with the Bank. The result, as described in Chapter 2, is an all-embracing 'Christmas Tree' project which the most committed administration cannot hope to implement. Third, if an over-ambitious programme does go wrong, there is little for any individual within the Bank to lose: success or failure is always difficult to establish with a programme operation, and cannot be embodied in an *ex post* rate of return, as it can with project assistance; if failure is alleged, it can always be blamed on the recipient country or on extraneous events, rather than on programme design at the Bank end; fourth, by the time that judgement on the design is made, the designer will very probably have moved to a different desk with responsibility for a country on the opposite side of the world.[19] Finally, if the design of a proposed conditionality package appears over-ambitious to the prospective recipients, they have a strong incentive not to press the point. To do so may put the negotiations, and the much needed loan, at risk; even more to the point, the people who are doing the negotiating may well be representatives of the ministry of finance and the central bank who have much to gain from the implementation of the Bank's conditionality. The losers from Bank conditionality, though they have the power to prevent or delay implementation, may well not have a strong enough voice in the initial negotiations to prevent infeasible policy reforms from being written into the Letter of Development Policy.[20] To sum up the argument to this point: the number of reforms that the Bank believes to be economically optimal within a certain period exceeds the number which are politically feasible, which in turn exceeds the number which are administratively feasible. But Bank staff on the operations side are under strong internal pressure to underestimate the size of the gap between what is feasible and what is optimal,[21] and their counterparts in LDC ministries of finance will have a strong incentive to conspire with them in overestimating what is feasible within a given time period. Overlong prescriptions are therefore, we fear, by no means a thing of the past.

The next design problem to be resolved is the nature of the policy reform that is to be recommended. If the disease is indeed that the prices are wrong, then the solution, trivially, is to get them right; but even supposing that the right price is known, there may be many different ways of getting them right. In particular, if what is desired is to simulate the price that would prevail in free-market equilibrium, this can be done either by *creating* a free market (i.e. privatisation) or by *simulating* a free market (i.e. amending the policies which the relevant government authority is to pursue). And whichever option is chosen, there are various ways of providing institutional support (e.g. technical and marketing information) to the industry in question. Finally, in some areas such as trade protection, the question of total *laissez-faire* does not arise, but there are a multitude of different ways of departing from it.

One way of illustrating the range of design options is to examine the different measures initially suggested by the Bank and the recipient, and then the compromise between them and what was eventually adopted. This is done in Table 4.5 for four measures: maize marketing reform in Kenya; the fertiliser subsidy in Malawi; reform of the development banks in the Philippines; and food-crop marketing in Ecuador.

Table 4.5 suggests that when Bank and government together faced the

Table 4.5 Design options for specific structural adjustment measures

	Initial Bank proposal	Initial government proposal	Measure finally agreed
Philippines: Reform of government financial institutions (Economic Recovery Loan 1986)	Privatise: confine lending to agriculture and small industry	Merge institutions; no restrictions on lending portfolio	Rationalise institutions separately and dispose of non-performing assets; no restrictions on lending portfolio
Ecuador: Agricultural marketing and trade policy (Agriculture Sector Loan, 1985)	Eliminate public purchases of maize and rice and replace all QRs by tariffs	Prepare statement of agricultural development policy and long-term marketing programme	Eliminate public purchases of maize and rice and replace QRs by tariffs
Kenya: Maize marketing (SAL 2 and Agriculture Sector Credit, 1982–7)	Maize marketing board to retreat to position of buyer of last resort	Maize board to raise buying price for maize	Private traders to be admitted to maize market
Malawi: Fertiliser subsidies (SAL 3, 1985)	Subsidy to be phased out over three years	Subsidy to be keyed to level of import prices	Subsidy to be phased out over five years

Source: Country case studies in Volume 2.

problem of an inefficient government intervention in the market, the Bank's preferred strategy was to reform the delinquent institution, often implying a *decrease* in government control over that institution.[22] This, again, was uncharted water for theoreticians: as the Bank had conceded in its 1983 *World Development Report* (p. 50) 'the key factor determining the efficiency of an enterprise is not whether it is publicly or privately owned, but how it is managed', and once barriers to entry into an industry have been removed there is no *a priori* presumption as to whether better management will be found in the public or private sector. Also unclear, at the beginning of the reform process, were the administrative costs associated with different reform methods, but it has emerged over time that some of the Bank's recommendations, such as 'introduce an auction system for foreign exchange' (Ghana: SAL I), 'privatise the marketing of maize' (Kenya: SAL II) and 'rationalise the structure of protection' (*passim*) have involved tasks of a complexity which lay beyond the capacity of the civil service to which the proposals were being put. The irony has thus arisen that aid donors, who have been accused of imposing excessive demands on a recipient country's administration by planning too many projects (e.g. Morss, 1984) now court the accusation of overloading the same administrators by asking for an infeasible agenda of policy reforms to be carried out as conditions on that programme aid. To some extent, where all that is required is a simple advance in office procedure (such as the computerisation of budget data to enable a recipient to comply with a condition on budget control) technical assistance can fill the administrative gap; but there are limits on the volume of new expatriate manpower which most LDC governments are willing to accommodate. In short, there is uncertainty both about the potential benefits of different 'technologies' of market liberalisation, and also about their associated administrative costs. In making recommendations at this level, the Bank therefore had to resort to improvisation, informed by advice as to what was politically possible. Frequently, in the event of disagreement between Bank and recipient government, a compromise was found by delegating the final recommendation as to how reform should be carried out to a consultant acceptable to both parties.

The third dimension of design is the *sequence* in which reforms should be recommended for implementation. This is an area in which the Bank has clearly learned from its experience over the 1980s. At the beginning of the decade the conventional wisdom was that stabilisation should precede structural reform, but that once structural reform was initiated, the necessary elements in the programme might as well be done as quickly as possible, in no particular order: the faster you got to the production possibility curve, the better. The experience of the 1980s has exposed a number of practical difficulties with this approach: trade liberalisation in the midst of stabilisation, if it turns out to be politically possible, may perpetuate a government fiscal crisis; removing controls on the international movement of capital will lead to capital flight if controls on domestic interest rates remain in place; measures to terminate public provision of a particular service may be premature if there is no private sector to encourage. Early attempts to stabilise, liberalise external trade and stimulate the supply-side in one glorious burst tended to lead quickly, as in Chile in the early 1980s, to capital flight, rising unemployment and consequent interruption of the structural adjustment programme (Foxley, 1983). These observations merely reflect the general principle of second-best theory that, if one distortion is removed in an economy with many distortions, the result may be to reduce rather than increase welfare. In response to this problem, there has been substantial research effort on the optimal sequence of liberalisation through the middle and late 1980s, much of it sponsored by the Bank, but its results have been of a satisficing, rather than an optimising, nature. The principal conclusion of Edwards' hundred-page theoretical paper on this subject (1986: 96) is that it is *'probably sensible* (our emphasis) to allow reform of the internal capital market to precede any liberalisation of international capital movements', and Williamson cautiously describes 'the right model, as I see it' as being:

117

First, liberalise imports of critical inputs, especially of inputs needed for tradable production. Second, devalue to the point needed to gain (and maintain) a competitive exchange rate. Third, borrow anything that may be needed to restore (and maintain) full capacity operation of the economy as soon as possible. Fourth, advertise your intention to liberalise imports as soon as circumstances permit . . . Fifth, once the economy is operating at full capacity, use payments improvements to liberalise imports across the board. When you have finished liberalising imports, start thinking of liberalising the capital account or appreciating the currency.

(in Corbo *et al.*, 1987: 103)

But there is not even agreement up to this point. For example Michalopoulos of the World Bank insists that:

Experience . . . suggests that future reforms ensure that export expansion programmes be accompanied by import liberalisation . . . Experience does *not* in our view suggest that import liberalisation should be undertaken only after export reforms have increased the supply of foreign exchange. This kind of sequencing is likely to be self-defeating, since it is extremely difficult to reorient producers toward export markets as long as heavily sheltered domestic markets offer them assured profits.

(in Corbo *et al.* (1987): 45)

As Williamson has observed, this argument appears to assume the absence of excess capacity in the economy which can meet incremental demand for exports; one may add that nearly all the successful NICs – in particular Taiwan, South Korea, Thailand, Malaysia and Brazil – have adopted precisely the sequence which Michalopoulos describes as 'self-defeating'. But even if Williamson's rule of thumb is accepted, a number of gaps remain. Where, in particular, do those micro-measures which remain squarely within the Bank's territory – rationalisation of public investment, removal of price controls, agricultural marketing reforms – fit in to the sequence? These questions are by no means sorted out, but an exploratory survey (Smith and Spooner 1989) suggests the following additional principles:

1 Measures to promote the private sector and to move to market prices should precede reductions in the role of government. The effectiveness of privatisation efforts in agricultural marketing, for example, is reduced if insufficient effort has been made to stimulate the private sector, in particular by the elimination of subsidies which reduce the profitability of private trade.

2 Domestic financial markets must be liberalised before produce markets, otherwise limited access to finance will reduce the effectiveness of

118

privatisation programmes. For example, the ceilings imposed on the Bank of Sudan on individual commercial bank lending to the private sector, together with legal restrictions on the type of commodities which can be financed with bank credit, have constrained the ability of the private sector to respond to measures of market liberalisation which the government had previously introduced.

and from section 4.3:

3 If a stabilisation programme is achieved through public expenditure reduction, such reduction should cause the development budget for productive sectors not to be reduced, otherwise the structure of services on which small farmers and businessmen depend may be undercut.

If these three principles are interpolated into Williamson's recommendations concerning the relationship of stabilisation and the liberalisation of the external account, we reach the following sketch (Figure 4.1) of a

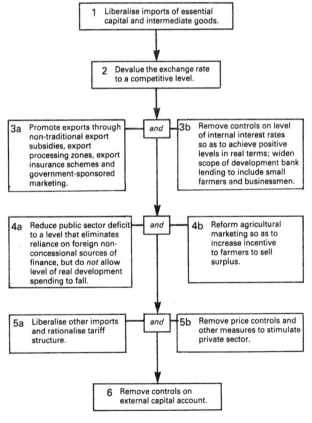

Figure 4.1 A possible sequence for a liberalisation programme

119

liberalisation sequence which, if not economically optimal, is at least a sensible path towards expansion of the supply side:

By now it will not astonish the reader to learn that neither the liberalisation sequence *recommended* to the countries within our sample, nor the sequence *actually implemented*, bore much relationship to the sequence set out in Figure 4.1. The actual sequences followed in a group of those countries were as follows:

	As recommended	As implemented
Kenya	(1+3a+5a),2,3b,4a,4b,5b	2,3b,5b
Philippines	(1+5a), 4a,2,3b	5a*,4a,2,3b
Turkey	2,(3a+4a),1,3b,5a	2,(3a+1),3b,5a
Thailand	2,(1+5a),(3a+4a+4b),5b	2,(1+5a*),(3a+4b)
Jamaica	2,(1+5a),(3a+4b),5b	(1+5a),(3a+4b),2,5b
Malawi	(2+4a),4b,5b	2,4b
Ghana	1,2,3a,(4a+4b),3b,(5a+5b)	1,2,3a,4a,(5a+5b)

* subsequently rescinded.

In all countries of this sample except Turkey and Malawi, it appears, the Bank's first move was to ask for a hefty dose of trade liberalisation, without prescribing which part of the import bill it should be applied to; country sequences thereafter were diverse, but recommendations to stimulate the private sector, rightly, came towards the end of the programme. Removal of restrictions on the external capital account, so much an issue in the Southern Cone of Latin America, did not figure in these programmes. As the lessons of the early 1980s became apparent, the Bank became more seized of the need for a gradualist approach, and the set of recommendations for Ghana, the latest of the programmes listed, corresponds more closely than any other to the sequence suggested earlier as 'sensible'. At the level of implementation, the Fund achieved an early real devaluation in all the countries in the table above except for the Philippines and Jamaica, and also sharp cuts in government development spending (Table 4.3). But in part because of these cuts, and in part because of the political opposition which could be mobilised against them, implementation of the supply-increasing policy changes recommended by the Bank (in particular trade liberalisation, export expansion measures, and the reform of agricultural pricing and marketing) has been very incompletely carried out. In other words, the Fund's demand-deflationary part of the programme has been implemented much more effectively than the Bank's supply-stimulating part, imparting a deflationary bias to the entire adjustment process. Although the full development of this point waits on our discussion of implementation in Chapter 5, we raise it here because it has two major implications for programme design. First, as earlier stressed, any budgetary cuts carried out at the beginning of the programme must be of such a type as not to prejudice the services and infrastructure on which the government will depend in order to stimulate export supply later on in the programme. Second, if there are obvious political obstacles to the implementation of the early elements in the programme, then any effective design must embrace a strategy for overcoming those obstacles as well as a set of economically efficient policy changes. One of the first measures in the Bank's package that is likely to attract such opposition is the liberalisation of imports of key capital goods and intermediates, and an indication of a possible way round the problem is provided by our Philippines case study; users of imported artificial fibres were offered an increase in the drawback which they were able to claim on customs duties attached to their exports (Volume 2, Chapter 12 page 70). This points the way to a more general principle, which is that if a measure required by a structural adjustment programme is frustrated by the political opposition of those who lose from it, the right approach is to compensate those losers, obviously in a way which does not restore the original distortion. Detailed examples of how this may be done are given in the next section.

The final element of programme design to be decided is how much money to offer in return for the agreed conditionality package. On this matter the Bank has only limited room for manoeuvre, since a planning allocation for programme lending for each country is decided, in terms of a range, five years in advance, and this can only be adjusted in response to need by altering the planning allocation for other countries. These allocations broadly reflect the size of the Bank's country programmes (Table 6.1): $50 million or less per loan for small African countries; $100 to $200 million for medium-sized economies such as Thailand, Morocco, Ecuador; $300 million plus for giants such as Brazil, Indonesia, Nigeria. Within the range, adjustments can be made in response to the size of the recipient's balance-of-payments deficit at the time of negotiation. When the Bank's negotiators sit down to do business, moreover, they have little scope to make progress by beginning, in bazaar fashion, from a low opening figure and then 'buying' additional reforms by means of additional injections of cash, since the planning allocation for the loan under negotiation has already been made known in terms of a range, under prevailing Bank operating procedures, to people at the higher levels in the recipient country's government, such as the permanent secretary for finance. But the need for flexibility remains, since the political discomfort that is likely to result from the acceptance of a Bank package is an experience which negotiators for the recipient country will be determined only to undergo in return for the payment of the appropriate price. 'You cannot make a revolution with $100 million', Ecuador's Minister for Finance declared on being invited to carry out fundamental agricultural reforms in 1985 in return for the sum mentioned, and the characteristic second move of negotiators for the recipient government, after they have offered their own proposed package and the Bank has added its own suggestions, has been to invite the Bank to name its price for the implementation of those suggestions.[23]

How generously the Bank is able to respond to such an invitation will depend on circumstances. If other countries within the department have also been spending to the limit of their budgets, the departmental director may have to refuse the request, with the consequence that an embarrassingly bare reform package is presented to the Executive Board. But if some countries have been underspending (for example, because large civil engineering projects are running behind schedule) then the task manager for the loan under negotiation will certainly have the freedom to buy the promise of additional reforms, and in the limit, if there is a serious underspending problem, operations staff negotiating a particular loan may find that its value has been unilaterally increased on instructions from Washington.[24] The Bank's ability to attach the right price-tag to a particular reform package – i.e. the loan size which will elicit the amount of reform which they believe to be economically and politically appropriate – therefore depends on the ability of other divisions within the Bank to stick to their budgets. But if it finds itself boxed in in relation to loan size, it has other instruments of persuasion which it can deploy. These we now consider.

4.5 BANK NEGOTIATION STRATEGIES

If the Bank's objective is taken as being to disburse a loan of given size on the conditions which it believes to be most appropriate, the Bank has on the surface two strategies available to it: it can threaten, or it can promise. The main *threat* at its disposal is to refuse to disburse, and to persuade other donors not to offer programme finance, if its own list of conditions is not accepted; but as explained in Chapter 3 this will be a paper tiger unless the recipient country actually expects to have to implement the conditions, i.e. to need the Bank's help on a long-term basis. Where the recipient's plight has been sufficiently desperate to make this the position (e.g. Ghana in 1983, Tanzania in 1985) the Bank's strategy has bordered on ultimatum. But this is not the normal case. More usually the Bank has been in sufficient internal need of a deal to need to offer *inducements*, and of these the most obvious is more money in compensation for the acceptance of those conditions which the recipient finds unpalatable. But, as we saw, the Bank's ability to make discretionary additions to its planning allocation depends on chance; and if its own scope for varying the cash element in the deal is restricted, it may have to appeal to its colleagues in other multilateral or bilateral agencies to sugar the pill for it by offering co-financing. Collaborative packages of this kind have been common (e.g. US and UK support for the first Turkish Structural Adjustment Loan of 1980; US and Japanese support for the Philippines Economic Recovery Loan of 1986; Japanese support for the Kenya Industrial Sector Loan of 1988, etc.) and have frequently enabled the Bank to surmount a difficult negotiating hurdle, more particularly since it is known that the conditionality imposed by bilateral donors is even softer than the Bank's. Only in the case of the Kenya Second and the Malawi Third SALs has a co-financing donor (USAID in each case, plus the UK Overseas Development Administration in Kenya) held up disbursement of its own programme loans pending evidence of compliance with the Bank's conditions. As an additional inducement, the Bank also on occasion makes model-based forecasts of the impact of programme loans, such as shown in Table 4.6.

These predictions – over-optimistic, as is common – have in practice been aimed more at the Executive Board than at the governments of recipient countries, and have constituted only a minor instrument in the Bank's apparatus of persuasion. In our view, this is unfortunate, since the logical way of persuading anyone to undertake a sacrifice is to give them some measure of the benefit they can expect in return for it. But to be used effectively in this way, the forecasts would have to be broken down by condition; that is, the recipient would need to know exactly what gain could be expected from raising electricity prices, from decontrolling agricultural marketing, and so on. Once presented with these micro-forecasts, it would then be possible for the recipient to develop the policy dialogue by modifying the assumptions underlying the model or by using it to derive forecasts of the impact of his own favoured policy reforms. An indication of how the Bank's own models could be used for policy dialogue using a micro-computer is provided in Chapter 8.

Simply to get the recipient to agree to a specific list of conditions, however, constitutes only a small part of the objectives of a forward-looking donor. Also needed is a strategy for persuading him to comply with the conditions. In principle, this function is fulfilled by the Bank's implicit threat not to offer repeat finance, or even disburse the second tranche of a loan, unless all the conditions are complied with; but this is not a very credible threat, since as a consequence of pressure to disburse second tranches are (with the exception of the Argentinian case) always handed over (Nicholas, 1988: 22) and repeat finance very often provided, in spite of a rate of slippage which averages, we shall argue in the next chapter, at least 50 per cent. What are the alternatives? The simplest is to ask for more – in the limit, all – the desired conditions to be performed in advance of the loan's being handed over, or 'front-loading' as it is known; this has been recommended (e.g. World Bank, 1988: 8), but is only practicable in the case of reforms which can be carried out by pushing a button, such as

Table 4.6 Output changes predicted by the World Bank in the event of conditions being met

	Ecuador Ag. sect. Loan (1985)	Ivory Coast SAL I (1981)	Ivory Coast SAL II (1983)	Jamaica SAL II (1983)	Kenya SAL II (1982)	Malawi SAL II (1983)	Philippines SAL I (1980)	Philippines SAL II (1983)	Thailand SAL II (1983)
Total output growth rates:									
With structural adjustment	—	6.8	6.5	4.0	4.3	3.4	6.4	6.5	5.4
Without structural adjustment	—	4.9	4.5	-0.2	3.8	2.4	5.5	4.0	4.8
Agricultural output growth rates:									
With structural adjustment	8.0	4.2	6.0	—	3.9	3.4	5.0	—	4.0
Without structural adjustment	3.0	1.9	4.2	—	2.7	2.4	4.7	—	3.1
Export growth rates:									
With structural adjustment	—	7.6	5.1	6.8	4.7	5.5	10.7	8.5	6.8
Without structural adjustment	—	5.5	2.5	5.5	4.0	4.0	9.3	6.5	4.5

Note Predictions are for following periods: Ivory Coast I and Philippines: 1980–5; Jamaica, Kenya: 1981–6; Thailand: 1982–90; Malawi: 1983–7; Ecuador, Ivory Coast II: 1985–90.

changes in agricultural or energy prices, and not in the case of those institutional reforms which are the Bank's forte. Much better in any case, from the point of view of sustaining the reform process, is a strategy which will make the implementation of the Bank's preferred programme appear attractive to the government, or in current Bank language (e.g. World Bank, 1988: 93) enable it to 'own' the programme. There are three potential ways in which this can be done, which we shall characterise as *facilitation*, *stiffening* and *bribery*. All three may be appropriate in different cases.

Facilitation, the simplest technique, consists simply of removing those obstacles to government performance of a condition which can be removed by external agency. The obstacle can be purely technical, as when a request by the Bank in 1981 that the Kenya government control public expenditure more effectively was made easier of attainment by financing the installation of micro-computers, and associated technical assistance, which enabled the Treasury to know for the first time the up-to-date budgetary position in each ministry. However, it may consist of a lack of co-ordination between executive agencies, which the Bank may offer to reduce by acting as an external chairman. In Thailand the Bank, in the view of one policy-maker, 'indirectly helped the Thai government to set the priority of measures . . . [and] helped point out which government agencies should be responsible for which measures' (Volume 2, Chapter 13, Appendix Table C3, interviewee C). By the mere fact of forcing an interministerial exchange of views on specific policies which it has proposed as subjects for conditionality, in other words, the Bank may be able to bring about co-ordination which might not otherwise take place.

Stiffening consists of measures to reinforce the position of those within government who are fully committed to the reform programme in relation to those who are less fully committed. Characteristically, we have argued, the former will be in the ministry of finance and central bank, and the latter in spending ministries such as agriculture and industry. At the simplest level, the Bank may simply furnish the former with data and intellectual arguments with which to confront the latter, as when the Bank's representative in the Philippines drew attention to the problem of public enterprise performance by demonstrating that the owings of public enterprises accounted for almost the entire external debt. More deviously, the Bank may work with the ministry of finance to devise reform measures, as in Ecuador, which do not have to go through the legislature and hence run no risk of being thrown out as a result of populist pressure (Volume 2, Chapter 19, page 432). It may try to impose a precise schedule on a sequence of measures which the government has expressed an intention of doing at an undefined time in the future, as when a Kenya government statement of intention to rationalise the structure of protection against imports was converted, in the conditionality for the Industrial Sector Adjustment Credit of 1988, into an undertaking to remove all quantitative restrictions on imports by 1990; but this strategy may backfire, as it deprives the recipient ministry of finance of the freedom to initiate the reform in question at the time which they consider auspicious for broaching the matter with the President.[25] Finally, it may give overt or veiled promises of future finance if certain key conditions are met. In Thailand such promises have specifically been described as 'creating a commitment among Thai policymakers, which helped speed the decision process' (Volume 2, Chapter 13, Table C.3, interviewee D), but this again is a high-risk strategy since both the present availability of finance and future promises of it may take away the pressure which would otherwise exist on policy-makers to adjust. Once external finance is available, for example, it may become possible to fund the deficits of public corporations rather than raise their charges and reduce their personnel: money opens up alternative options, which may either increase or reduce commitment.[26] It is at least debatable that 'government commitment', in particular to the conditions of sectoral loans, may be easier to achieve by allocating resources to the spending ministries who are traditionally the opponents of reform than to their adversaries in the ministry of finance. But this implies the alternative and more conciliatory strategy of *bribery*, that is, buying out opposition to reform. Examples of the use of this strategy as a means of co-opting opposition to reform were given in the previous section. To take the argument a step further, let us consider systematically where the opposition may come from. Table 4.7 gives a simple schematic picture of the groups which may be expected to lose from different types of structural adjustment measure.

From this table it is easily possible to visualise ways in which the opposition of particular groups (and their sponsors within government) to an adjustment programme may be co-opted by non-distortive compensatory measures. For example, local manufacturers who lose the benefit of quota restrictions against imports can be compensated by temporary import surcharges (as was explicitly provided for in the case of the Bank's Trade Policy Loan to Mexico in 1985, and done anyhow without the Bank's permission in Thailand, the Philippines and Ghana, as recorded in our case studies). Farmers who lose a fertiliser subsidy can be compensated by expansion of agricultural credit or selective investment in rural road-building; holders of licences to import or move grain can be offered *ex gratia* lump-sum payments at the point of transition to a free market; urban wage-workers who lose the benefit of government food subsidies can be compensated by reductions in import duties on food. If this is properly done, the conflict which lies at the heart of policy-based lending collapses, since the recipient government loses the motivation to delay implementation of policies which offend vested interests; and in those cases, such as the last mentioned above, where the losers from the implementation of

126

Table 4.7 Possible effect of adjustment measures on different occupational groups

Income groups	Industrialists	Capitalist farmers	Urban wage-workers	Subsistence farmers
Policy measures:				
Exchange-rate devaluation	+[1]	+[1]	−	−[2]
Increases in agricultural prices	−	+	−	+[3]
Removal of import restrictions	−[4]	+	+	0
Removal of food subsidies	−	+	−	0
Removal of agricultural input subsidies	0	−	0	0
Positive real interest rates	−[5]	−[5]	+[6]	0

Symbols: +, positive effect on occupational group named;
−, negative effect; 0, neutral effect.
Notes: 1 If net exporters.
    2 If purchasers of consumption goods.
    3 If applied to food crops.
    4 If manufacturing for the home market.
    5 If net borrowers.
    6 If net lenders.

conditionality are in the lower income groups, the application of the compensation principle will kill two birds with one stone, as it will also lower the social costs of adjustment. At the practical level, there is evidence of the Bank having learned from experience, and the Ghana programme, the latest of those reviewed to get under way, is the only one to contain an explicit compensatory component (PAMSCAD, reviewed in Volume 2, Chapter 14). But although every Bank publication about adjustment lending routinely contains a section about the importance of government commitment to adjustment programmes, none of them has so far been willing to accept that large parts of government, in the absence of compensatory measures, will be committed to obstruct and not to speed the implementation of any measures which threaten economic harm to their clients.[27]

4.6 RECIPIENT NEGOTIATION STRATEGIES

The recipient government, we may suppose, is concerned to achieve a transfer of money on terms which approximate as closely as possible to the actions which it would spontaneously have carried out in the absence of any external pressure. Two possible routes towards this objective have already been indicated: the 'recipient ultimatum', or blank refusal to go beyond the list of policy reforms put forward at the beginnning of Act 1, and the 'machiavellian response', or total submission to the lender's request with a view to subsequently wriggling out of any conditions which are felt to be coercive. But these should be seen as limiting cases: the first is risky for any recipient who is dependent on Bank finance, and the second is rash for any recipient who is uncertain whether his dependence will continue into a second round of negotiations. There are, however, a number of intermediate options.

The first and most obvious may be described as *preference concealment*: this involves the recipient government offering a deliberately smaller adjust-ment package than it knows to be required, leaving measures which it always intended to implement to be offered to the Bank at later stages of the negotiation process under the guise of concessions. This 'false-naïve' strategy was very well deployed by the government of Ecuador, which in February 1985 offered, with a great flourish, to remove the maximum consumer price on wheat flour at a time when a record harvest made this no real concession, and the government of Turkey, which in 1984 presented a programme of financial-sector reforms at a late stage of the negotiations for SAL 5 which had been part of its 1982 general election manifesto. If this strategy can be made to work, then the conditions attached to the agreement are, in effect, fungible, and any policy leverage which the donor believes he is exerting will be imaginary.

The second strategy which a borrower may deploy takes place outside the negotiating chamber: it is to seek out *alternative sources of finance*, if possible without any conditionality attached but failing that with conditions which will in some sense be more comfortable than what the Bank is asking for. Zero-conditionality money is in practice only attainable from commercial banks, who have of course been reducing their Third World exposure in recent years; but in 1984 it was possible for the government of Thailand, which was beginning to get into difficulties in its policy dialogue with the Bank over the matter of energy prices and industrial protection, to break off negotiations over a proposed Third Structural Adjustment Loan on discovering that it could raise the money it needed, at an interest rate fractionally above that charged by the Bank but without conditionality, on the Tokyo market. Such borrowing possibilities are of course not open to all, but the case of Kenya illustrates what is possible for the government of a much poorer country. Faced with pressure since 1982 from the Bank to privatise the marketing of maize, its main food crop, it has been able (a) to obtain Japanese bilateral assistance in 1983 for the construction of bulk storage facilities for maize (a policy which had been advised against by the Bank, as in the event of privatisation they would become irrelevant), (b) on the specific matter of maize marketing, to enter into a $100 million technical assistance agreement with the EEC on which the conditionality is noticeably weaker and the emphasis on food security noticeably greater than that which the Bank was seeking to impose,[28] (c) to obtain large increases in bilateral *project* aid commitments, noticeably from donors which impose little policy conditionality such as Finland, Denmark, China and South Korea, which individually are of small size but collectively reduce the leverage which the Bank, acting on its own, is able to exert. To date, as related in Chapter 16 of Volume 2, reform of maize marketing in Kenya has been trifling. The strategy involved has been described as 'policy arbitrage': loan conditions, like any other good or service, are a commodity which the wise buyer will purchase in the cheapest market, and it is only LDCs with very poor credit ratings who will be unable to find alternative sources to the finance which the Bank is seeking to supply.

The third option is to negotiate *ambiguity* into the conditions, so that at the time when judgement is made by the lender he is forced to give the borrower the benefit of any doubt. Consider the following list of conditions:

'Prepare a satisfactory programme of action for the sugar sector'
  (Mauritius: SAL II)
'Reduce the domestic price of cement by July 1984'
  (Panama: SAL I)
'Review the level of motor fuel excise taxation'
  (South Korea: SAL II).

It could reasonably be considered that any action whatsoever by the government in the areas mentioned could be interpreted as compliance with these conditions. Loosely-written conditions obviously create room for manoeuvre for the recipient. Less obviously, it may be in the interest of the donor to write conditions which help to build a climate of trust in policy dialogue, and which certainly will not stand in the way of timely disbursement of the loan. On a casual assessment, about one-third of all conditions attached to Bank adjustment are of this type; but this fact inevitably makes assessments of implementation (of the type which will be attempted in the next chapter) a little arbitrary.

Finally, but again a common strategy in the early stages of negotiation, the recipient can play for time by asking for a problem to be *studied* rather than acted upon. Naturally the strategy has to be employed selectively, and it can only be employed once, since once a study is available there is nothing to do but to act on it. But, as one battle-weary Bank negotiator put it, 'after three days of negotiations people are tired, so in order to reach a compromise people say "Oh, let's stick in a study" as a tool to build consensus. This is always a waste of time'. (Interview, World Bank Operations Evaluation Department, 11 September 1986).

The strategies mentioned above, and in the previous section, should not be thought of as a menu which is permanently available to all donors and recipients. The negotiating teams on each side now have up to nine years' experience of one another's opening gambits, and have worked out appropriate neutralising responses. The Kenyan Defence ('Condition A seems a little risky, perhaps we should commission an independent study of that one'), the Pakistani Sacrifice ('We would be willing to accept the political cost of Condition B if you would add an additional $50 million to the loan amount') and the Thai Variation ('We cannot forecast the price of oil, so please substitute "substantial increases in energy prices" for "35 per cent increases in the price of diesel"'), among many others, are now well-known moves, and because they are well known, they can usually be anticipated, and will only be effective when a window of opportunity suddenly opens. This may occur because of adventitious reasons, e.g. one side or the other is forced to field an inexperienced negotiator. But more usually it will happen because of changes in the fundamental bargaining environment in which the two parties operate. Let us now examine the determinants of this environment, and whether it is possible to interpret the nature of the deals which are struck between the two parties in terms of their relative bargaining strength.

4.7 OUTCOMES: SOME HYPOTHESES TESTED

It will be useful to sum up the general argument to this point. In terms of economic efficiency, it would be logical for the Bank to attach conditions to its programme loans which remove what it feels to be gravely distortive policies, in an appropriate sequence in which each step makes easier the achievement of the succeeding ones. But this is by no means what we always see, for two reasons. The first is that the Bank has little influence over the level of distortion in those markets which by mutual agreement are the preserve of the IMF. The second is that the Bank is under powerful pressure to disburse its programme lending in a reasonably regular and predictable manner, which will imply that the number and type of conditions which the Bank is able to extract from a given recipient over a given time period will reflect the nature of its bargaining relationship with that recipient, rather than its objective diagnosis of the recipient's economy.

What will determine the nature of that bargaining relationship? Our point of departure is the proposition set out in Chapter 3, that bargaining strength will depend on the *risk limit* of each party, or the cost to it of settling on its adversary's terms, by comparison with the cost of doing no deal at all; the weaker each party's bargaining position, the greater the cost of doing no deal at all, and the smaller the risk limit. The cost of doing no deal will be more serious for the recipient, we may suppose, the graver its economic predicament and the smaller its capacity for raising development finance from other sources than the Bank. And they will be more serious for the Bank, the larger its lending programme in that country, and the greater the pressure to which it is subjected by its Executive Board to maintain a lending programme for geopolitical reasons. In all of this it must be borne in mind that what is here being negotiated is the opening contract in a multi-stage relationship, and that the negotiating behaviour of both parties is conditioned by anticipations of what will come later. In particular, the recipient will be mindful that he can get away with violating conditions if he expects the relationship to be a transient one, and the Bank will be concerned, either by emboldening its friends within the recipient government or by buying off its opponents, to discourage such violations.

How well do the nature of the deals struck in Bank policy-based lending agreements reflect such bargaining realities? To answer this question, we proceed in two steps. In the first stage we use simple tabular methods to examine factors operating purely on the recipient's side of the bargaining table, and in the second stage we use regression methods to take into account the Bank's bargaining position as well.

Table 4.8, then, sets out data on the 'tightness' of deals struck by the Bank in its negotiations with the first eleven countries to receive Structural Adjustment Loans in relation to the putative determinants of recipient bargaining strength mentioned earlier: current-account balance in the years prior to the award of the SAL, and the share of Bank finance in the recipient's external capital flow as an indicator of its dependence on the Bank for money. The measure of tightness used is simply the *number* of conditions imposed on each country and, as such, does not capture tightness perfectly; most people would agree, for example, that for a recipient government eliminating quotas is 'tougher' than reducing subsidies, eliminating quotas is tougher than reducing tariffs, and privatising agricultural marketing is tougher than adjusting agricultural prices. However, a reading of the record suggests that the countries on which the largest number of separate conditions were imposed were also those for which the individual conditions were politically and administratively most demanding.[29] Table 4.8 shows that significantly tighter conditions were negotiated with the poorer countries in the sample, those with the worst balance-of-payments problems, and those most dependent on SAL finance for official capital flows from abroad. The poorer the recipient's initial *political* bargaining position, in other words, the more stringent the conditions imposed on it, regardless of the severity of the level of *economic* mismanagement as measured by the severity of distortions in individual markets.

Table 4.8. Tightness of SAL conditions and possible determinants

Country	Year first SAL disbursed	Tightness score	Possible determinants of tightness:		
			Per capita GDP 1980 ($)	Current account balance [1]	Financial dependence on Bank [2]
Five tightest countries					
Guyana	1981	13	660	−15.8	22.9
Kenya	1980	12	350	−11.4	20.3
Malawi	1981	11	190	−20.1	38.4
Pakistan	1982	12	310	− 4.3	20.8
Turkey	1980	13	1,130	− 3.8	14.6
Sub-group average ($\bar{x}_1$)		12	528	−11.1	23.4
Six loosest countries					
Bolivia	1980	6	580	− 5.9	11.3
Ivory Coast	1981	10	1,050	−14.5	12.8
Jamaica	1982	10	1,140	− 5.5	16.6
Philippines	1980	6	700	− 5.2	17.0
South Korea	1981	11	1,400	− 6.2	4.5
Thailand	1982	11	660	− 6.3	11.1
Subgroup average ($\bar{x}_2$)		9	920	− 7.2	12.2
t-statistic			3.15**	1.86*	3.75**

Source: IMF, *International Financial Statistics*, various issues, except for tightness score, which is a simple arithmetic mean of the number of areas (from Table 2.3) in which conditions were imposed in successive SALs between 1980 and 1986.

Notes: 1 Average for 1978–80 as percentage of GNP.
  2 Dollar value of SALs as a percentage of borrower's gross public external capital flow for years 1982–6.
  * Difference between sample means significant at 10% level.
  ** Difference between sample means significant at 5% level.

We now extend the analysis in three ways. We introduce into the sample countries which received sector loans from the Bank, in addition to the SAL recipients listed in Table 4.8; we consider determinants of the Bank's bargaining position, as well as the recipient's; and we use regression methods to attempt to capture the precise quantitative influence of individual determinants of bargaining power. The results of this analysis are set out in Table 4.9. The determinants of donor bargaining power considered in the table are, first, the size of the donor's lending programme in the country under examination (on the presumption that the larger the Bank's lending programme in a particular country, the greater its potential financial loss if programme lending is interrupted) and second, a binary dummy variable to indicate whether the borrower has a significant geopolitical relationship with the United States, on the hypothesis that if it has, the United States government will lean on the Bank in case of need to discourage any interruption of programme lending on purely technical economic grounds.

Table 4.9 Relationship of tightness to determinants of donor and recipient bargaining position: results of regression analysis

Ordinary least-squares analysis. Dependent variable: average 'tightness' (number of conditions imposed)[1] on World Bank policy-based loans from 1980–8.

Sample	Number of observations	Constant	Regression coefficients on independent variables			
			Indicators of recipient bargaining power		Indicators of Bank bargaining power	
			Balance-of-payments deficit[2]	Dependence on Bank for finance[3]	Size of country lending programme[4]	Geopolitical dummy[5]
All countries in sample[6] ($r^2 = 0.49$)	23	5.57** (2.71)	0.21 (1.18)	0.098 (1.05)	−0.00036* (1.72)	2.44* (1.69)
Countries principally receiving SALs[6] ($r^2 = 0.25$)	15	5.89* (2.27)	0.35* (1.62)	−0.36 (0.31)	−0.00021 (0.46)	2.42 (1.12)
Countries principally receiving SECALs[6] ($r^2 = 0.61$)	8	3.37 (0.83)	0.27 (0.65)	0.19 (0.77)	−0.00023 (0.78)	−0.12 (0.049)

* Significant at 10 per cent level.
** Significant at 1 per cent level.

Sources and definitions

1 'Tightness' is the average number of policy areas (out of the 20 listed in Table 2.3) in which conditions were imposed on World Bank policy-based lending agreements in the years 1980–8. It is a number constrained to be between 0 and 20, as in Table 4.8 above.

2 'Balance-of-payments deficit' is the average deficit on current account, as a percentage of GDP, during the two years preceding the first SAL or SECAL agreement between the country in question and the Bank. It is measured as a *positive* figure: thus, a positive coefficient in the table indicates that as the balance-of-payments deficit increased, tightness also tended to increase. *Source*: IMF *International Financial Statistics*.

3 'Dependence on Bank for finance' is the value of Bank policy-based lending (SALs plus SECALs plus miscellaneous policy-based operations such as trade policy loans) as a percentage of total external capital flow (public, publicly guaranteed, and private non-guaranteed) over the years 1980–8. Source for Bank policy-based lending, Nicholas (1988), updated with material kindly supplied by World Bank Country Economics Department; for external capital flow, successive issues of World Bank *World Development Reports* (Table 22 in 1989 edition).

4 'Size of World Bank lending programme' is the combined figure for IBRD loans and IDA credits outstanding at 30 June 1989, as derived respectively from pages 186–9 ('Summary Statement of Loans') and pages 210–11) ('Summary Statement of Development Credits') of World Bank, *Annual Report* 1989.

5 'Geopolitical dummy' is a variable taking the value 1 for sample countries with which the United States has a significant political or strategic relationship (judged to be Kenya, Pakistan, Turkey, Jamaica, Philippines, South Korea and Mexico) and 0 for other sample countries.

6 The sample consists of 23 developing countries which received policy-based loans from the Bank between 1980 and 1988. The subgroup 'Countries principally receiving SALs' consists of Guyana, Kenya, Malawi, Pakistan, Turkey, Mauritius, Bolivia, Ivory Coast, Jamaica, Philippines, South Korea, Thailand, Zaire, Panama and Chile ($n = 15$). The subgroup 'Countries principally receiving SECALs' consists of Mexico, Ecuador, Ghana, Colombia, Indonesia, Brazil, Niger and Nigeria ($n = 8$).

If our initial hypothesis is correct, the regression coefficients should be significantly positive in respect of the two indicators of recipient bargaining power (i.e. tightness should be greater in countries where the recipient's bargaining position is weak) and significantly negative in respect of the last two (i.e. tightness should be less in countries where the donor's bargaining power is weak). The aggregate data of Table 4.9 broadly support the first half of this proposition (i.e. tightness is indeed positively associated with the level of balance of payments deficit and of dependence on the Bank) but only part of the second half. Conditionality is indeed significantly looser in countries where the Bank has a large lending programme, but it is actually significantly *tighter* in countries where the US has a substantial geopolitical interest. These results do not change significantly when the sample is split up into two groups consisting of 'mainly SAL' and 'mainly sector-lending' countries, except that the coefficient on financial dependence on the Bank becomes (insignificantly) *negative* in the 'mainly SAL' group. Taking the results of this exercise together with the information in Table 4.8, we draw the provisional conclusion that gravity of economic crisis, dependence on the Bank and absence of a large Bank lending programme did act together to weaken the borrower's negotiating position and cause tougher conditionalities to be imposed. Alliance with the United States does not, on the evidence of Table 4.9, earn the recipient a gentler prescription *at this stage*; as we shall see in the next chapter, what it did yield was a more forgiving treatment of slippage on conditions in Act 3.

4.8 CONCLUSIONS: WHAT HAS THE BANK LEARNED FROM EXPERIENCE? WHAT ELSE COULD BE DONE?

It has been the major theme of this chapter that the design of loan conditions, conceived as a means of overcoming distortions imposed by the state on the economy, has itself been heavily distorted by political pressures operating both within and outside the Bank. The strength of conditionality has been related to the strength of the Bank's bargaining power rather than to the severity of the problems diagnosed in the recipient's economy, and under the stress of internal pressures has usually exceeded what the governments of recipient countries have been able to deliver.

Much of this has been understood by the Bank. Their latest assessments of policy-based lending, as we have seen, stress the need for shorter lists of conditions, more tightly policed, with 'key conditions' identified and a higher down-payment, and it is only necessary to compare the Ghana series of operations from 1985 on with the Kenya series from 1980 on to appreciate the progress which has been made in the art of sequencing. The shift from the SAL to the SECAL mode of financing is itself a response to the problem of overload. However, of the recommendations mentioned only the higher down-payment has made its way through into current Bank practice. There is no sign of lists of conditions shrinking or the level of implementation improving, and the idea of identifying 'key conditions' remains at present purely an abstraction.[30]

There are two other design lessons which, in our view, have not yet been accepted by the Bank. The first is that since the roots of resistance to policy reform are in essence political the Bank requires a strategy to pre-empt that resistance. The resistance comes both from vested interests who expect to lose from reform and from those who represent them within the recipient government, and in our view needs to be bought out by a two-pronged strategy: non-distortive compensation payments to potential losers, and disbursement of policy-based loans direct to the implementing ministry (possibly in kind) rather than, as at present, direct to the ministry of finance. It may also help if implementation is explicitly planned to begin on an experimental basis – for example, a proposal for liberalisation of food-crop trading could be implemented in one province only to begin with, so that the recipient may see, and be convinced by, the results – rather than on a comprehensive basis. The second general lesson, though, is that obstacles to aggregate supply – whose removal constitutes the major objective of structural adjustment programmes – arise from market failure as well as from government failure, and that future policy-based operations would be well advised to incorporate measures to fill gaps in the market – such as land reforms and credit institutions for the support of small farmers and informal-sector businessmen – in addition to measures which eliminate unwise intrusion into that market by government. Such measures might render policy-based lending more effective as an instrument for assisting lower income groups as well as for boosting competitiveness and growth.

NOTES

1 In its early 1980s projections for the economies of Ivory Coast, Jamaica, Kenya, Malawi, Philippines and Thailand, the Bank estimated that the growth of GDP 'with structural adjustment' over the following five years would be between 1 and 4 per cent in excess of that which would be achieved 'without structural adjustment' (see Table 4.6). See also Mosley (1987, table 4). The particular appeal of 'getting prices right' from an economic planner's point of view is that it offers the prospect of increases in the level of output that can be obtained with *given resources*, i.e. increases that are costless in an economic sense. They may well have political costs; but these lie outside the frame of reference of an economist who sticks to his last.
2 For a development of this argument with particular reference to the writings of Deepak

Lal (a key figure in the Bank's research department in the early 1980s) see Toye (1987: 72–4).

3 The intellectual basis for Fund policy recommendations is supplied by the 'Polak model', whose original incarnation goes back to 1943, which simulates the link between domestic credit expansion, foreign exchange reserves, and the balance of payments, and gives the Fund an indication of the extent to which the growth of money supply (or other measure of aggregate demand) must be reduced in order to improve the balance of payments by a given amount; for an exposition of the Polak model see Killick *et al.*, (1984: 74–6) or, for more detail, Bolnick (1975). The Bank has no equivalent of the Polak model, although it does have both computable general-equilibrium models and sectoral models of the linkage between targets and instruments for particular sectors in specific countries. Both of these approaches are used in Chapter 8 below for the purpose of estimating the *ex post* impact of Bank conditionality.

4 At the level of individual markets, there exist many studies which demonstrate, particularly for agricultural products, that the relationship between price and supply is significantly upward-sloping (for a summary see Bond (1983). But the statistical validity of the Bank's claim in the 1983 *World Development Report* that the *overall* level of price distortions is negatively associated with economic growth is more questionable. For a critique, see Evans and Alizadeh (1984).

5 Agarwala (1983: 19), the principal contributor to the price distortions analysis of the 1983 *World Development Report*, argues that (distortions in) the exchange rate have a stronger association with output growth than any of the other price distortions considered in that report (agricultural prices, wages, interest rates, agricultural inputs, electric power, petroleum).

6 Interview with World Bank senior economist, 25 February 1985. The Marshall-Lerner conditions require a country's elasticity of export supply and import demand to sum to at least one if a devaluation is to improve the balance of payments.

7 See for example the essay by Furtado in G. M. Meier (ed.) (1987) *Pioneers of Development Economics*, vol. 2, World Bank.

8 For an excellent analysis of the Bank's two alternative perspectives see the essay by Lipton (1987) which is a comparative review of the Bank's 1986 *World Development Report* and its report *Poverty and Hunger*.

9 World Bank, *Articles of Agreement* (as amended effective 17 December 1965): Article 3, section 4 (vii).

10 A stand-by is normally disbursed over one year and repaid over three.

11 This may, in part, be the result of over-optimistic forecasts of economic recovery, and in particular of export prices (see Volume 2, Chapters 14 and 17).

12 An example in which the Fund voluntarily handed over control of a grey area is the cocoa price in Ghana, as described by Toye in Volume 2, Chapter 14: 161–3. Also in Ghana, one of us has experience, as a consultant for the Bank in 1985, of recommending a subsidy on non-traditional exports, which was vetoed by the Fund on the grounds that it was not Fund policy to support the introduction of new subsidies, but then reinstated into the recommendations to the Ghana government after it had been retitled as an export bonus.

13 Interview with World Bank economist, Washington DC, 9 September 1986. (Relations between the Philippines desks of the Fund and Bank have improved since the Aquino government took over in 1986). For a detailed account of macroeconomic policy in the Philippines between 1983 and 1985 see Volume 2, Chapter 12; also Taylor (1988: 103–7).

14 The main World Bank building is on the east side, and the main Fund building on the west side, of 19th Street in Washington DC.

15 For evidence of continuing Bank anxieties about the Fund position on devaluation, see World Bank (1988: box 3.1: 57). The Bank's most recent report on sub-Saharan Africa

(World Bank 1989c), however, at page 3, shows that for sub-Saharan Africa as a whole real exchange rates have declined, between 1983 and 1988, from 120 to 92 (1971–2 = 100), suggesting that the principle of freely-floating and competitive exchange rates has now taken root.

16 The attempted reform of state food-crop marketing agencies was possibly the area in which the Bank expended most staff time per unit of reform achieved: see not only the country case studies mentioned, but also the unsuccessful attempt to reform ENAC, the National Food Storage and Marketing Organisation in Ecuador (Volume 2, Chapter 19). That governments should be reluctant to abdicate their responsibility for food security is not surprising: less clear is why the Bank, whose professed objective was to boost exporting sectors, chose to use up so much of its energy in an area where reform was neither politically probable nor relevant to this objective.

17 In Mosley (1987: Table 8), we show that the average number of conditions negotiated on each SAL with 'low-distortion' countries, for agreements negotiated up to 1986, was 10.2, whereas the average number of conditions negotiated with 'high-distortion' countries was 10.3. The position has since been complicated by the increasing proportion of conditional finance agreements which attach to specific sectors rather than to the entire economy.

18 Average tightness on SALs and SECALs negotiated in 1989 and 1990 was 11, on the measure used in Tables 4.8 and 4.9; insignificantly changed from the 10.4 for the period 1980–6 which emerged from Table 4.8.

19 As one of Wade's interviewees declared (1989: 40) 'The Bank always blames the country for poor performance. This is an axiom'. In the cases discussed in Volume 2 where the conditionality package was manifestly over-ambitious, and not implemented (Ecuador; Kenya SAL II; Philippines SAL II) there is little evidence that the failure to implement has had any adverse effect on the designers' careers.

20 The opponents of reform are usually to be found in the down-line ministries of agriculture, industry, trade, etc: for further discussion see Chapter 5. In recent years the Bank has devoted strenuous effort to trying to reduce the opposition of the agencies, or in Bank language to increasing their 'ownership' of the reform programme; see for example World Bank (1988: Chapter 4).

21 A classic case of this 'conspiracy towards overreach' is provided by the case of the Second Structural Adjustment Loan in Kenya. This included a massive number of conditions, many of which were not implemented, but a number of which (including the most controversial, the privatisation of maize marketing) were put there at the instance of the Permanent Secretary to the Kenya Treasury, who found it politically convenient to be able to invoke Bank pressure in support of unpopular reforms which he had long wanted to implement, and who therefore had a strong motive to tell the Bank that the proposed reforms were feasible. (For more detail see Volume 2, Chapter 16).

22 There were exceptions to this principle, including the reform of State Economic Enterprises in Turkey, where the Bank from the start adopted a strategy of reform of state enterprises, with removal of price controls, rather than outright privatisation. See the study of Turkey by Kirkpatrick and Onis (Volume 2, Chapter 11), also the essay by Saracoglu (Deputy Governor of the Central Bank of Turkey) in Corbo et al. (1987).

23 For further detail see Volume 2, 420. In similar vein the Finance Minister of Pakistan, negotiating his country's Structural Adjustment Loan with the Bank in 1982, described the Bank's draft list of reforms as 'worth at least a billion dollars'; in the event he was only able to get the value of the SAL increased from $100 million to $140 million, but many of the Bank's more contentious draft proposals were dropped.

24 As Wade puts the point:

> The amount of the loan can change wildly during the process of preparation, as directors juggle their portfolio of loans against their lending targets. There are, for example, no clear grounds for deciding whether an education sector adjustment loan to India should be $100 or $200 million. The task manager for that loan may suddenly be told by his director that the loan amount is going up from $100 to $175 million, because a loan of $75 million for Bangladesh has fallen through. That is why SALs came to be called (pre-reorganisation) 'Stern's Arbitrary Loans'.
>
> (Wade, 1989: 51)

25 One of us relates that in Ghana the Bank actually moved away from time-bound conditionality over the 1983–8 period:

> The initial conception it relied on was too simple, too rigid and too ambitious, the fundamental idea being that should the government fail to perform agreed dated actions it would forthwith be financially penalised. Something much more flexible than this soon turned out to be necessary. Interestingly, the very term 'condition' drops out of the Bank's vocabulary in dealing with Ghana just after the time when the Structural Adjustment Credit (SAC) was negotiated in March 1987. A new format is adopted in which 'agreed actions' are recited, accompanied by an explanation of the thrust of government policy on the issues with which the credit is concerned.
>
> (Toye, in Volume 2, Chapter 14: 39).

This policy of relaxing the linkage between the agreed policy framework and specific dated actions actually appears to have strengthened the Ghana government's commitment to that framework.

26 The regression findings in Chapter 7, which show a positive lagged relationship across a sample of countries between growth and SAL *conditions*, but a negative unlagged relationship between growth and SAL *money*, suggest that this potential mechanism, by which SAL money gives some countries the necessary breathing space to delay necessary policy reforms, is indeed operative.

27 The Bank's first report on adjustment lending as a whole (World Bank, 1988) emphasises at p. 103 that 'success in implementing reform programmes is strongly related to the government's commitment to the programme', but goes no further in discussing how such commitment may be built than to say that 'consensus must come from a genuine meeting of minds with the political leaders who will bear the risks of success or failure – and who will be committed only if they are persuaded the risks are worth taking' (ibid.). A Bank discussion paper on country commitment to *projects* (Heaver and Israel 1984) notes (p. 2) that

> there are differences in commitment between levels of the hierarchy, as when the Bank and policy-makers agree on a reform, but implementing staff are not committed to change; or the reverse situation, when the Bank can agree on a course of actions with officials at the technical level, but where change is unacceptable at the political level.

But whereas time in the field talking to project beneficiaries and sufferers is now a standard component of project planning, it is not a standard component of the planning of SALs and SECALs. As Heaver and Israel state later on in their paper (at p. 13), 'tranched, fast-disbursing loans may not on their own be the most suitable vehicle for building commitment to institutional reforms (e.g. in budgeting processes) which have long time horizons.'

28 The Bank is still involved in policy negotiations with the Kenya government over maize marketing (Volume 2, Chapter 16); but it has effectively devolved to the EEC the working out of the detail of institutional reform in this area.

29 The only countries in Table 4.8 to have been subjected to the 'tougher' conditions mentioned are: elimination of subsidies – Malawi, Pakistan; elimination of import quotas – Ivory Coast, Jamaica, Kenya, Philippines, Turkey; privatisation of agricultural marketing – Ivory Coast, Kenya. Of these seven countries, all except Ivory Coast, Jamaica and the Philippines are in the group for which the absolute number of conditions was highest, as shown in Table 4.8.

30 The practice of identifying 'key conditions' has been opposed by a number of desk officers within the Bank on the grounds that it would give recipient governments *carte blanche* to ignore all conditions not starred in this way.

5

IMPLEMENTATION AND SUSTAINABILITY

5.1 THE ANALYSIS OF SLIPPAGE ON LOAN CONDITIONS

We have now examined the World Bank's reasons for developing various types of adjustment lending in Chapter 2 and the process of negotiation of finance and associated conditions by the Bank and its borrowing countries in Chapter 3 and 4. In this chapter, we turn to the question of implementation – to Acts 2 and 3 of the 'game' described in Chapter 3 – and ask:

> to what extent have policy change conditions attached to adjustment loans been implemented, and to what extent has the degree of compliance with loan conditions about policy reform been caused by particular sorts of influences – historical, political and administrative?

Why are we asking these questions? It is not simply because we are interested in the ultimate impact of adjustment lending on the performance of the borrowing countries' economies. This is of great importance, and it is dealt with at length in Chapters 6 to 8. But the ultimate impact of adjustment lending is the product of three distinct things:

1 the policy reform changes actually implemented, i.e. the stipulated policy conditions in the loans minus any 'slippage' in their performance;
2 the disbursement of the associated loan finance;
3 the economic conjuncture within which both policy reform changes and loan finance are activated.

In this chapter, we concentrate our attention exclusively on the first of these. We do so because we are interested in the intermediate question of the mechanisms by which policy changes come about, or fail to come about. This, after all, is the novel element in adjustment lending, which demands analysis in its own right, before moving on to the broader and more comprehensive question of ultimate impact.

The Bank itself has been under some pressure from its Executive Board to evaluate policy reform conditionality, as part of its broader evaluation of adjustment lending. This was, therefore, included as one issue in the document 'Adjustment Lending: an Evaluation of Ten Years of Experience' (otherwise known as the 'Holsen Report', after John A. Holsen who led the team of authors) which the Bank issued in December 1988. The main findings were that 'at the completion of disbursements on the loans, about 60 per cent of the policy changes agreed as conditions in SALs and SECALs had been implemented fully or more than fully'[1] and 'the degree to which the conditions were met has differed substantially between policy areas' (McCleary, 1989: 32). There were also various refinements on these two major conclusions, which will be noted as appropriate in our later discussion. The main summary table of the Bank's results on the implementation of conditionality is reproduced as Table 5.1.

What do such figures really mean? How can compliance be quantified to the point where one can say confidently that overall compliance was 60 per cent? The basic evidence was some fifty-one SALs and SECALs involving

Table 5.1   Implementation of conditionality, fiscal years 1980–7: World Bank data (Percentage of conditions implemented)

	During the loan period		As of mid-1988	
	Conditions fully implemented (1)	(1) plus 'substantial progress'[1] (2)	Conditions fully implemented (3)	(3) plus 'substantial progress'[1] (4)
Exchange rate	70.0	90.0	62.5	87.5
Trade policies	54.9	84.2	63.4	89.3
Fiscal policy	53.2	78.3	69.8	95.3
Budget/public expenditures	68.0	78.0	71.7	84.8
Public enterprise reforms	61.3	86.7	70.0	90.0
Financial sector	71.4	85.7	73.5	89.8
Industrial policy (excl. restructuring)	53.3	93.3	42.9	85.7
Energy policy	79.2	83.3	83.3	88.9
Agriculture policy	57.1	81.6	58.1	83.7
All conditions	60.3	83.4	67.5	89.0

Source: World Bank (1988); based on an analysis of 51 SALs and SECALs in 15 countries.
Note 1 'Substantial progress' means that significant steps have been taken to move more than halfway toward full implementation.

fifteen different countries spread over sub-Saharan Africa, highly indebted countries and 'others'. For each condition of these fifty-one loans, a score of between 1 and 5 was given by an assessor – usually a junior person with little knowledge of the country or of the specific lending operation – to signify the degree of compliance. The initial scoring was reviewed by a few specialist consultants, and then the amended scores were aggregated into the summary statistics of Table 5.1. Evidently, the entire process is an exercise of judgement, much of it not at all expert, with a modicum of expert second-guesses and consistency checks to bring some coherence and discipline to its findings. In these circumstances, it would be rash to place very much confidence in a figure like 60 per cent. For what it is worth, the compliance scores emerging from the country case studies of Volume 2 have a lower average value – around 54 per cent – but with a wide dispersion around this average. The relevant data are set out in Table 5.2.

Table 5.2   Implementation of conditionality, 1980–8: case-study countries (percentage of conditions implemented on all SALs and SECALs at end of loan period)

Turkey	95
Thailand	70
Jamaica	63
Philippines	62
Ghana	58
Malawi	55
Kenya	38
Ecuador	28
Guyana	15

Source: Case Studies in Volume 2.
Note: Implementation rate as recorded here is 100 per cent less the slippage rate.

These figures substitute the authors' judgements, derived from the nine case studies in Volume 2, for those of the World Bank; but we have no means of knowing whether the slight difference between our results and the Bank's has any significance. Our figures come from a much smaller sample of countries than the Bank's fifty-one, but each one has been studied much more intensively. Our sample was not drawn by formal random sampling methods, so that the figures are non-comparable. All that it is possible to say, in the last analysis, is that quite a lot of the time the borrowers comply with the loan conditions, and that quite a lot of the time they do not. But to try to be more exact than that leads only to a spurious impression of precision.

That, however, is not the only reason for being unhappy with this style of quantification of compliance. A further reason is that it obscures some important aspects of the way in which loan conditions feed through, or fail to feed through, into real policy reform. This becomes clear once it is realised that the Bank's method implicitly equates implementation of conditions with commitment to the policies implemented, and that this can be a misleading assumption. The logic being used by the Bank here is analogous to the logic of plan fulfilment in centrally planned economies. Although plan fulfilment is often measured and statistics of it are often published by the government with feelings of pride or disappointment, the concept is crude and measurements of it (even when themselves quite accurate) often mislead about the nature of the underlying economic performance. So it is also with statistics of the implementation of loan conditions.

What then are the problems? One set of problems arises when the loan conditions are inappropriate to the economic context, either because they are the embodiment of badly designed policies, or because the context itself is changing in unforeseen ways, so that the implementation even of well-designed policies would be wrong in practice. Let us begin, however, by abstracting from the entire set of problems which arise from bad policies and/or bad forecasting of external economic conditions. They relate to the ultimate impact of adjustment lending, based on the interaction of implementation of conditions, injection of new finance and the economic conjuncture. Our analysis starts at a simpler level and with a narrower aim: that of understanding the relationship between the implementation of loan conditions and commitment to the Bank's preferred policies *when policies are sound and external trends correctly forecast*.

A diagram may help us to visualise this relation. The 2 x 2 matrix in Figure 5.1 has columns indicating the extent to which loan conditions are actually implemented, and rows indicating the degree of commitment of the borrowers to the aims and objectives of the agreed programme of policy reform.

Those countries whose policy reform experience places them in the top-left and bottom-right boxes represent the conventional cases which underlie the Bank's quantification exercise, namely that zero or partial implementation indicates low commitment, while full (and, in the Bank's terminology, 'more than full') implementation indicates high commitment. In many instances, this conventional view is not misleading. But there are two other cases to consider.

The top-right box is the situation when the full implementation of loan conditions is an indicator of low commitment. How can this be? This is the case when the letter of the conditionality is fulfilled, but not the spirit. In other words, all formal conditions are scrupulously performed, but at the same time, or shortly afterwards, other actions (which are not explicitly forbidden in the loan conditions) are taken, the effect of which is to neutralise the result of implementing the original condition. This may be called the case of countervailing action. The field of economic management is wide open to countervailing action. As noted in Chapter 1, it constitutes one of the major reasons why economic theorists of the Right have urged

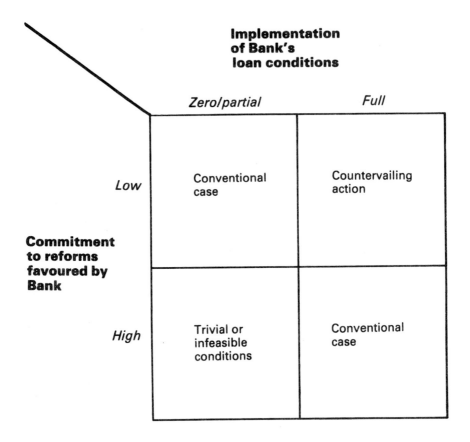

Figure 5.1   The relationship of condition implementation to commitment to agreed policy reforms

governments to desist from the use of fiscal policy to influence aggregate demand. The opportunity for countervailing action arises from the fact (once said by Joan Robinson to be the only thing necessary to learn about economics) that everything in economic life depends upon everything else. The economy does not consist of separate compartments, so that policy can be set in one with no fear of the consequences spilling over into all the others. Economic policy is not divisible. Consequently, the effect of loan conditions which are devised to regulate the use of one group of policy instruments can be undermined by the use or invention of other policy instruments which also impinge on the same dependent variables. In order to write loan conditions in a watertight way, one would have to outlaw an impossibly lengthy list of possible countervailing actions. Most economic

144

policy-makers know this, and know how to get the same kind of result by alternative methods.

It should be emphasised here that the use of countervailing action is not confined to devious Third World ministries of finance. The same phenomenon can be found in the United States, for example when the Gramm–Rudman–Hollings Act makes it mandatory to reduce the government budget deficit to a prespecified level. Some real cuts in public spending are made, but reductions in public spending are achieved by shifting other spending from the government budget to a variety of extra-budgetary funds. The resort to extra-budgetary funds is one mode of countervailing action that can be used to neutralise policies of structural adjustment. In Turkey after 1983, the extra-budgetary fund became an increasingly important phenomenon. Here the purpose was not merely to permit non-parliamentary spending on mass housing, in order to bolster the government's legitimacy. It was also designed to neutralise the effect of tariff liberalisation, by raising extra-budgetary levies on imports. A different instance of countervailing action was found in Jamaica, where a new Export Development Fund was set up, but was starved of hard currency because the government was not prepared to permit a unification of the foreign exchange rate and a significant devaluation, as urged by the IMF. Countervailing action is thus not a mere theoretical curiosity, a queer case. It is at the heart of a sophisticated response to the moral hazard created by adjustment lending. Yet the Bank's method of quantification ignores it. As a result, the commitment to reform of countries like Turkey and Jamaica would be exaggerated, if the Bank were to publish its compliance statistics for individual countries.

The bottom left-hand box of Figure 5.1 shows the situation when failure to implement loan conditions is compatible with high commitment to reform. This again cuts across the conventional view of the relationship between implementation and commitment. Two causes for this deviation can be found. The first, and least interesting, concerns trivial conditions. The common designation of conditions hides the fact that they are very variegated: some are broad in scope and fundamental in significance – energy prices, public investment programming or the marketing regime for a main export crop, for example. But others are peripheral, and concern matters of detail, such as the hiring of particular consultants, the design of a minor policy study or the reorganisation of a subdivision of a government office. Obviously, the breach of even a large number of such peripheral conditions is consistent with high levels of commitment to the main thrust of the policy reform. Alternatively, as happened with SAL I in the Philippines, high performance on non-crucial conditions gave a misleading impression of the (Marcos) government's basic stance towards economic reform. It seemed much more favourable than it really was. This point has been taken by the Bank and the Holsen Report has recalculated its compliance statistics for its fifteen chosen countries to determine the effect of excluding non-key conditions (World Bank, 1988). The level of compliance, as calculated, is raised thereby from 60 to 68 per cent. This rise is interesting because it tends to confirm the assertion in Chapter 2 that the early SALs were rather like Christmas trees, with conditions used as 'presents' for different divisions and departments of the Bank with a wide range of different policies to promote.

Apart from trivial conditions, failure to implement conditions is compatible with commitment to reform when the required conditions are infeasible or impossible. But how can both lender and borrower agree to conditions that are infeasible or impossible, it might be asked? Such a situation sounds wildly improbable. But on the other hand, given the complexity of some of the tasks of policy reform and the lack of knowledge of detail from which both short-term Bank missions and some departments of the developing country government themselves may suffer, an agreement to do the impossible cannot be ruled out of the question. The Ghana case study reveals one classic example: an agreement to meet a hopelessly ambitious target of state enterprises of which the government had to divest itself. At the time of this agreement, neither the Bank nor the Ghana government realised the depth of the problem of inter-enterprise borrowing and the impediment which inability to value each enterprise properly would place in the way of divestiture. So both agreed, in good faith but bad understanding, to an impossible target. Failure to fulfil this condition did not indicate any lack of commitment to reform on the government's part. On the contrary, it indicated an excess of zeal. So eager was the government to comply that it did not take basic steps to investigate the feasibility of the promised action, relying instead on the Bank's expertise − which in this instance was found wanting.

Even if the scoring of performance on individual loan conditions had been done with complete objectivity and consistency, the existence of unconventional cases means that the scores themselves are a defective guide to commitment. How defective? Do not these queer cases cancel each other out? If countervailing action leads us to overestimate commitment, does not the existence of trivial conditions and impossible conditions lead us to underestimate it? Would not the general assessment of reform remain much the same, therefore, even after allowing for these oddities? This argument has force. It may well be that the aggregate picture would not be vastly altered by taking them into account. Where it would make a difference is in understanding the compliance behaviour of individual countries. The Bank does not publish or make available to outside researchers its implementation scores for individual countries. It comments on the performance scores of *subgroups* of countries in its sample, but only to doubt the existence of 'any systematic differences in performance between the three (sub-) groups of countries' (McCleary, 1989: 32). The reader of this

146

statement may be left with the impression that deviations of country performance from the aggregate implementation score of 60 per cent are small or purely random. Looking at the unconventional cases shows us that any impression that country performance is either closely clustered or randomly distributed around an average is wrong. Looking only at the conventional cases obscures differences both in internal commitment and in the external pressures bearing upon recipient governments.

The effect of ignoring countervailing action is to make a basically non-committed borrower look more like an average performer with regard to the implementation of loan conditionality. The effect of ignoring trivial or impossible conditions is to make a basically committed borrower look more like an average performer. Thus the queer cases are significant precisely because they tend to blur the rather sharp differences between borrowing countries' basic stances towards the policy reforms that are tied to Bank programme finance. The evidence from our case studies suggests that, in the typical case, the borrower government either is firmly committed to pushing forward policy reforms of the kind desired by the Bank, or it is not. Governments are not particularly fuzzy in their attitudes, hesitant or undecided; even though a battle between pro- and anti-reform forces may be going on within each, the outcome of the conflict is usually clear. Usually the dominant groups within each government either want to see an economic reform package succeed, or they are fundamentally doubtful about it, even after they have formally espoused it – and they behave accordingly. In Thailand and Ghana, for example, the basic stance was always pro-reform, while in Guyana government implementation of SAL was initially 'characterised by a lack of urgency and commitment' and continued to be so in the second phase of the SAL operation. A country's basic stance can indeed change. Turkey moderated its strong pro-reform stance in 1983 and Jamaica moved to a much more committed stance after 1986. But there are usually clear political reasons for such shifts.

The clarity of the borrowing country's basic posture towards the reform package is obscured not only by the queer cases which have so far been discussed, but also by certain other factors. So far, the argument has deliberately abstracted from problems of implementation that are caused by bad policies and/or bad forecasting. But these can now be included. The distinction between impossible or infeasible conditions and bad policies is one of degree, rather than kind: if the design of policy is bad enough, the policy is simply impossible, but sometimes also design failures take time to become apparent, and for the policy to break down. An example of deficient policy design leading to implementation failure and breach of SAL conditionality is provided by the new Export Development Fund (EDF) set up by the Guyana government, using SAL finance in early 1982. Essentially, the problem with the EDF was the failure to build in enough incentives to encourage participation by exporters selling in hard currency areas. The EDF became a major drain on Guyana's scarce foreign exchange, and by September 1982, the Bank of Guyana was forced to suspend further disbursements to the EDF – in plain violation of the SAL agreement. The Bank accepted this breach of conditionality because it recognised that the original policy was flawed.

Bad policy design also affects implementation and conditionality in the opposite way. That is to say, it permits conditions to be fulfilled without the policy objectives which lie behind the conditions being satisfied. The Ecuador government's withdrawal of the maximum consumer price of wheat flour in early 1987 discharged one of the major conditions of its SECAL for the agricultural sector. But, it made little difference to the protection enjoyed by Ecuadorian cereal farmers, who continued to benefit from producer prices around 50 per cent above the price of wheat imports. Presumably the policy objective of the loan conditions was to eliminate the policy distortions in the market for wheat. If so, the policy change was badly designed, and the implementation of this condition gives no indication of the government's fundamental stance of commitment or non-commitment to policy reform.

Bad forecasting contributes another element of 'noise' in the policy implementation system which blurs the results of quantifying compliance in the manner of the Bank. Thailand's basic stance towards policy reform was highly positive, yet a variety of policy targets were missed in 1982 in the important areas of tariffs and taxation. But these failures occurred not because of any lack of will by the Thai government to achieve reform in these areas. Rather, the cause was a failure to forecast correctly the growth rate of the economy. An unexpectedly slow rate of growth produced a shortfall in government revenue. The government's response to the sudden prospect of a revenue gap was to slow down the implementation of changes in the foreign trade sector – the removal of export taxes and import levies. The interaction of trade liberalisation with stabilisation and the control of government deficits created a problem in the design of structural adjustment programmes which is being increasingly recognised and investigated (e.g. by Mosley and Toye, 1988: 407 and Greenaway and Milner, 1989). The Thai example shows that, even when the design problem is recognised, a forecasting error will lead to the violation of loan conditions, a poorer statistical measure of compliance and an obscuring of the government's fundamentally positive attitude to policy reform. The Philippine tax reforms of 1987–8 make an almost identical point. They were fully implemented ahead of time, but did not achieve the loan target for tax effort – because GNP grew faster than expected. This problem could perhaps be reduced by writing loan conditions only in terms of variables which the government in question fully controls.

Bringing into the argument these examples of bad policies and forecasting failures simply reinforces the basic point that has already been made. The attempt to quantify compliance will have the effect of disguising the strong contrasts between borrowing countries in the government's basic stance towards policy reform. Yet it is that basic stance – favourable or unfavourable – which largely determines whether policy reform will endure or fall apart. This is why the Bank itself has come in recent years to underscore what it terms the 'ownership' of policy reform programmes by the government undertaking them (World Bank, 1988: 58, Box 4.1 (4)). Whether one chooses to use the language of intellectual property rights or the more usual terminology of basic policy choice and political commitment does not matter much. What matters is whether or not it exists, and what are the political circumstances that create or destroy it. This will be discussed in section 5.2. But while government 'ownership' of, or commitment to, policy reforms may be necessary for them to succeed, it is by no means sufficient. The capability of the government machine is needed as well as the commitment of the government's leadership (Nelson, 1984). Over and above slippage caused by lack of genuine commitment by particular borrowing countries, slippage arises from administrative incapacity in countries which are basically favourable to the thrust of policy reform. The problems of bad policy design and bad forecasting, which we have just discussed, can be linked in a relatively straightforward way with weaknesses of the government administrative machine.

But whereas politically-induced failures of compliance would imply a random distribution of implementation failure across sectors and across types of condition, one might expect a particular sectoral or condition-wise pattern to emerge in the implementation failures caused by administrative incapacity. This is because different sectors or types of condition may exhibit differences in the intensity or complexity of administrative inputs. The Bank's own results on the sectoral pattern of implementation have already been presented in Table 5.1. They show a rather narrow band of variation around the average degree of implementation of 60 per cent, with a high of around 80 per cent for energy policy and lows in the mid-50s for trade, industry and agriculture policies. It seems plausible to argue that these sectoral results would be much more informative if they were disaggregated, by the separating out of the sample into two groups of borrowers, those whose basic stance was favourable to policy reform and those whose basic stance was not. Sectoral patterns should appear much more sharply focused in a sub-sample which included only the 'favourable' group. The Bank's reluctance to make available performance scores for individual countries suggests that it is unlikely to proceed in this way, presumably because it could hardly be done without Bank judgements on the attitude to reform of individual countries becoming apparent in the process.

The Bank believes that sectoral differences in implementation arise because reforms demanded in some sectors are administratively easier to implement than reforms demanded in others; and that some are more politically neutral than others, given a basic stance of commitment on the part of the borrower. On the first point, changes in prices are administratively easy whereas changes in the organisation and operation of institutions are administratively very difficult. On the second point, taxation and subsidies generally have a high level of political visibility, as does the industrial policy area because of accumulation there of politically created and sustained vested interests over the years.

Broadly speaking, our case studies in Volume 2 bear out these generalisations. Perhaps the clearest case is Ghana, because the attitude to policy reform was basically favourable, and the picture is not complicated by any change of regime. Here we see considerable success in reducing an overvalued exchange rate, raising the producer price of cocoa, decontrolling many consumer goods prices and raising domestic energy prices to parity with import prices. Also, the reduction of civil service payrolls and parastatal payrolls came quite close to targets set in loan conditions. By contrast, the reorganisation of the Cocoa Marketing Board has lagged behind schedule, the divestiture of state economic enterprises rapidly bogged down and planned programmes in the health sector had to be aborted. Perhaps because Ghana lost so much of its educated professional manpower by migration during the 1970s and early 1980s, the influence of administrative capacity on sectoral differentiation stands out very clearly.

In Kenya, matters were not quite so clear cut. The Bank's Project Completion Report for SAL I highlighted the sophistication and competence of the top administrative elite, and the scarcity of these virtues below the very top. Such a competence gap is obvious also in Ghana. Kenya, like Ghana, has made much progress in eliminating distortions in the prices of its crops, credit and foreign exchange, while allowing slippage on the administration-intensive tasks of land reform, decontrol of the maize trade and the rationalisation of the structure of protection. But, this evidence for the 'administrative ease' hypothesis on implementation is to some degree contaminated by the fact that various political inhibitions to the vigorous pursuit of those three measures were simultaneously present. Export promotion measures would have largely benefited multinational or Kenyan–Asian enterprises and may have had a low political priority for that reason; land reform and maize decontrol would have damaged the interests of large African farmers who form a major interest group in Kenya, and assisted the interests of Asian middlemen. So, in the Kenyan story, the explanatory waters remain muddied.

The Philippine experience, particularly in the period of the Economic Recovery Loan, 1987–9, at first sight appears to contradict the 'administrative ease' hypothesis on implementation. Here the most successful implementation occurred in the areas of tax structure reform and the reform of government financial institutions (GFIs). The tax measures consisted of a further rationalisation of tax incentives, a value added tax and studies for a capital gains tax and a property tax. The GFI reform required two major government development banks to be placed on a proper commercial basis after becoming bankrupt through granting non-performing loans to Marcos cronies. Successful implementation of these administration-intensive tasks was, however, the result of special factors. As in Kenya, politics intruded in a very obvious way, so one is not here looking at an administrative machine that is performing under normal circumstances. These reforms stripped of their rents holders of tax exemptions and of large non-performing loans. These people were the supporters of the Marcos regime: the new regime of Mrs Cory Aquino had no wish to favour her opponent's supporters with the same largesse used by the former President Marcos. The Philippine experience would seem to be an exception which does not disprove the administrative ease rule, once the effect of political factors is given due explanatory weight.

5.2 THE POLITICS OF IMPLEMENTATION

So far we have argued that countries which accept SALs and SECALs have relatively well-defined basic stances towards the implementation of the loan conditions. Typically, either a clear underlying commitment to implementation exists, or it is absent; and attempts at measuring compliance in statistical terms merely serve to blur at the edges the sharpness of this polarisation. We turn now to examine some questions about the political factors which influence the existence or otherwise of this commitment. The purpose here is to assess how much backing the empirical case studies provide for four different theories of the role which politics (that is to say, the domestic politics of the borrower country) plays in the process of economic reform. In order to do this, the first step is to state in outline the four theories which appear most plausible.

At a very broad level, one might want to argue that commitment to reform depends on the type of political regime which is in power in the borrower countries. A distinction is often made between democratic and non-democratic regimes in the belief that the latter are more effective in bringing about economic reform. As one neo-liberal economist, who worked in the Bank's research department in the early 1980s, has expressed it: 'a courageous, ruthless and perhaps undemocratic government is required to ride roughshod over . . . newly-created special interest groups' (Lal, 1983: 33). Democratic governments are seen as the source of irrational economic policies forced on them by their need to placate competitive interest groups. This is a characteristic and central proposition of the 'New Political Economy' which we analysed at some length in Chapter 1. In this light, the recent trend to democracy in Latin America (although, interestingly, not yet the same trend in Eastern Europe) is viewed as being economically problematic.

A contrasting view is that it is not the character of the regime – democratic or non-democratic, military or civilian, federal or centralised, etc. – that matters, but whether a new government administration has come to power. Even within the compass of an unchanging regime, a new government brings a fresh supply of ministerial energy and of popular credit. Starting without the handicap of past political compromises and the odium of previously failed policies to constrain their room for manoeuvre, governments still in their 'honeymoon period' can, it is asserted, inaugurate reforms most effectively. On this theory, it is new brooms that sweep cleanest, regardless of the kind of political structures within which the sweeping has to be done.

A third view puts the emphasis of explanation neither on structures nor on novelty, but rather on past history. Successful economic reform is interpreted as a learning experience in which past efforts in the same direction – even when unsuccessful, wholly or partially – contribute to building a consensus in favour of renewing the effort on a broader scale and with greater determination. That is the positive 'historical' interpretation. There is also a corresponding negative one. It says that, in the end, economic reform simply cannot be postponed. Attempts to back away from reform result in worse economic dislocations than those which the reforms were aimed to cure. The social learning occurs not through any beneficial effects of the (partially) failed episodes of reform, but from the increasingly distressing economic malfunctioning which occurs in the intervals between those episodes. This is a story about learning the hard way: effective commitment to reform becomes politically possible once the level of economic distress has become intolerable; and this is true of all regimes.

The fourth type of explanation concentrates directly on the analysis of the competitive struggle between interest groups. It sees the borrowing country's domestic politics as a reflection of the balance of power between different specific interest groups. Depending on the contents of the proposed reform package, groups will align themselves for or against reform according to its perceived impact on their interests. This approach has already been introduced in Chapter 4 (see Table 4.7). Where there is no basic commitment, the anti-reform groups will (by definition) be dominant. In order to bring about reform, the balance of power has to be changed. This is done by finding ways to undermine the solidity of the anti-reform coalition and by bringing the beneficiaries of the reforms more centrally into the political process. The necessary undermining is carried out both by advocacy and persuasion, and also by the supply of new foreign exchange through the loan itself which allows time for the reforms to work and for the anti-reform opposition to run out of steam.

The above selection of theories is by no means exhaustive: it merely lists the main variants which have entered the debate on the politics of implementation. Other refinements and sophistications could be provided. But this does not seem worthwhile before looking at the case-study evidence. It should also be emphasized that the four explanations outlined above are not presented as if they must all be mutually exclusive. Some form of the fourth may be compatible with any of the first three. Some account of the balance of power between interest groups may go alongside the story of a regime change, the arrival of 'new brooms' or the breaking of a 'final' economic crisis. Further, the theory of learning from experience can stand alongside that of a change of government, and the arrival of a new government can also coincide with a change in the nature of the regime. We must not look to the empirical evidence expecting only to find examples of pure cases. It is more likely that we will find evidence of several political influences in any one case, but mixed in different measures.

Turkey's experience seems, at first sight, to provide a pure example of the influence of regime type on the implementation of economic reform. Parliamentary democracy had produced two short-lived coalitions of ideologically divergent parties, neither of which was seriously interested in addressing the escalating balance-of-payments and budgetary deficits of the late 1970s. A period of military rule between 1980 and 1983 saw, by contrast, significant success in the growth of output and exports, the liberalisation of the trade and foreign exchange regime and the reductions of price controls over, and budget subsidies paid to, state economic enterprises. But when parliamentary democracy was reinstated in November 1983, extra-budgetary funds began to expand and budgeted public investment growth also accelerated, and an inflationary surge resulted. Some of the objects of the EBF expenditure were aimed at buying electoral support for the governing party: mass housing programmes were used for this purpose, for example. Do we not have in this vignette the classic vindication of the argument for strong, undemocratic government which can ride roughshod over sectoral interest groups?

Before jumping to this conclusion, one should incorporate some of the other facets of the Turkish experience, as evidenced by our case study. The change of the government's basic stance towards economic reform occurred just before the start of the period of military rule, and it was procured by Turkey's OECD partners for basically geopolitical reasons. After the fall of the Shah in May 1979, the instability and violence that accompanied the lead-up to elections in Turkey was interpreted as a possible prelude to a revolution like the Iranian one; and a large financial assistance package was put together by OECD countries. The Bank's role was largely instrumental and the large aid flows available greatly reduced some of the early problems of adjustment. All of this had happened before the military period began. The military government certainly maintained a reforming momentum that was already established. But it was not the creator of the change of course.

Nor, in sustaining it, did it play a particularly notable role (relative to the civilian regimes) in riding roughshod over vested interests. The case study makes it clear that, although there have been clear losers in the Turkish adjustment process, especially wage-earners and recipients of fixed incomes and those in the agricultural sector, a competitive struggle between social groups has not featured strongly. Turkish civil society has been dominated for many years by a strong state, whether civilian or military in complexion. The reforms of the 1980s have not changed that.

Ghana is a second country which appears on the surface to support the theory of the reforming efficacy of undemocratic regimes. The IMF and the World Bank were called in by Chairman J.J. Rawlings less than a year after he had overthrown the elected civilian government of Dr Hilla Limann. Ghana's Economic Recovery Programme has been steadily pursued through various phases by Rawlings' Provisional National Defence Council ever since the second half of 1982. The extent of democratization during this period has been minimal, the only example being the holding of district council elections at the end of 1988. Undemocratic government and fairly successful economic reform seem to be well correlated in Ghana.

But, as in Turkey, a wider perspective is needed. The story of Ghana in the 1980s is a complete reversal of the story of the 1970s. In the period 1969–72, the civilian government of Dr Busia made a brave attempt to straighten out Ghana's already failing economic development strategy, but was overthrown by Colonel Acheampong. It was the neglect and corruption of successive military governments over the next seven years which brought Ghana's economic crisis to a head. The brief democratic government of Limann certainly procrastinated, but was effectively paralysed by the insidious, and ultimately successful, threat of a coup by J.J. Rawlings. So the explanation in terms of regime type does not stick in Ghana, whose experience is better explained by a combination of our second and third theories. Rawlings was a new broom, bringing into government new men (with one important exception), sweeping aside alike military and civilian embodiments of past regimes. By the time of his arrival in power, the country had learned from its failures of economic policy that past patterns of behaviour were not sustainable. Although, unfortunately, the point below which a country's level of economic welfare cannot sink further never arrives, that level was low enough to convince Rawlings that resort to the Bank and Fund was the only hope – whatever his and his allies' initial ideological position. Ghanaian civil society, like Turkey's, has remained apathetic, quiescent and dominated by its government.[2]

Turkey and Ghana alike took a basic stance on the implementation of loan conditions that was favourable. But, it has been argued, the cause of this was not the undemocratic nature of the ruling regime. In Turkey's case, wider international considerations were the major determinant, while in Ghana, the arrival of a new broom at a point of deep crisis was the key feature. In Thailand, too, the government's basic stance on implementation of conditions was favourable. But after a largely successful first SAL, the second SAL which should have built further on it was implemented only indifferently. Slippage occurred on key energy, transport and utility pricing policies, and also on trade liberalisation, because the government was not willing to confront the party and popular opposition which it was believed that they would provoke. Since the regime was in the process in the early 1980s of moving gradually away from a military-dominated regime towards a more constitutional regime (albeit subject to ultimate military control by the ever present threat of a military coup), it could be argued that the indifferent implementation of SAL II in Thailand is consistent with explanation of performance in accordance with regime type.

As in the discussion of Ghana, a wider perspective suggests that this is a rather superficial view. The structural political problem in Thailand is a conflict within the ruling elite about its own future trajectory and that of the country, provoked by the strengthening of the social position of the urban middle class. In the 1970s and 1980s, the Thai elite has been torn between strategies of resistance and incorporation of this class. The student-led 'democratic revolution' of 1973–6, the tough military anti-communism of 1976–7 and the watered-down military regimes of Kriangsak and Prem and the abortive coups by Young Turks in the army in 1981 and 1985 are all symptoms of this underlying struggle. One should not, therefore, pay exclusive attention to which way the political pendulum was swinging at the precise moment of SAL II. The fact is that all the governments of the 1970s and 1980s in Thailand have been either weak or short-lived: governments whether civilian, military or some mixture of the two have lacked dynamism and the ability to engineer significant change, despite the basic alignment of Thai technocrats with the policy approaches of the Bank and the Fund. If one had to fit Thailand's SAL experience with any of our four initial theories, it would be the fourth. Social pressures (though not necessarily in the form of clearly defined interest groups) are strong, and governments – even when the military is heavily involved in them – do not have much room for manoeuvre.

The Philippine experience with SALs spanned what is often referred to as a 'change of regime', the transition in February 1986 from the Presidency of Ferdinand Marcos to that of Mrs Corazon Aquino. This change also marked a change in the basic stance of the Philippine government toward the implementation of structural adjustment. Marcos himself 'almost certainly adopted the language of liberalisation purely as a flag of convenience', according to our case study, whereas Mrs Aquino and her advisers were much more closely attuned to the Bank's economic philosophy, as evidenced by the 'Yellow Book' published as a prelude to the 1987–92 Development Plan, and also by greater zeal in implementation of tax reforms and reforms of government financial institutions. Does all this suggest that a regime change in favour of the 'more democratic' Mrs Aquino has been effective in advancing economic reform – the reverse of the conventional pro-authoritarian thesis?

It is easy to exaggerate, with rhetoric about a 'peaceful revolution', the differences between the Marcos and the Aquino governments. Aquino's social base in the old estate-owning oligarchy is no different from Marcos's and key figures moved straight from one government to the other. The Aquino government is more legitimate than its predecessor, because of a perceived greater commitment to human rights and a much lesser reliance on corruption and cronyism to build political support. Its weakness is its dislike of land reform and its failing struggle against rural insurgency – and its vulnerability to military coups when reform dries up the easy payoffs of the Marcos years. Economic reform since 1986 has largely been – as suggested at the end of Section 1 – the dismantling of Marcos's system of political patronage exercised through monopolies, industrial concessions, tax and tariff exemptions and privileged credit from government financial intermediaries.

The Philippines, like Thailand, has a weak authoritarian state, where on the one hand democratic institutions exist, but on the other the military is always in the background and often in the foreground of politics. In both, economic policy-making is weaker than in Turkey or Ghana, and draws back more readily in face of the opposition of vested interests. Marcos in the 1980–3 period was able to trim back his concessions to existing cronies in the hope of winning over previously excluded businessmen, but eventually ran into trouble with his planned liberalisation programme. Mrs Aquino was able to punish her political opponents, gain popular legitimacy and please the Bank for a while by her liberalisation programme. But, as in Thailand, it seems unlikely that this has been sufficient to revolutionise the economic or political outlook. Mrs Aquino has been the new broom, after the long period of increasing corrupt and repressive Marcos rule. She has also undermined anti-reform vested interests, especially in industry and finance. But that is a politically risky course to pursue and it is too early to claim that she has succeeded.

So far we have considered countries where, during the period of structural adjustment, episodes of military rule or marked military involvement in government have been evident. It has been difficult to find anything but superficial evidence that better implementation of loan conditions has resulted from these military episodes or involvements. But what of these countries where representative government is not disciplined (or threatened, depending on one's viewpoint) by the military forces? Is the competition of vested interests more intense, and does this militate against good performance in the implementation of loan conditions? Does not the electoral process confer sufficient power in a democracy to permit a government elected on a mandate of economic reform to carry through its own programme successfully?

The Jamaican case throws some light on these questions. Despite great expectations to the contrary in the minds of the Bank and the US government, the election victory of Edward Seaga's Jamaican Labour Party in 1980 over Michael Manley's Peoples National Party (PNP) did not constitute a critical breakthrough in the prospects for economic reform in Jamaica. Both the JLP and the PNP are based on trade union movements and support a state-led and interventionist development strategy. Both looked to the bauxite/alumina industry as a permanent major contributor to Jamaica's foreign exchange. Both feared a fluctuating exchange rate, a fall in the level of real wages and the growth of unemployment. Seaga's 1980 landslide in the polls was an endorsement of these attitudes and fears, not of the IMF stabilisation programmes which Manley had rejected at the end of the 1980s. Seaga was able to exploit the general failure to perceive this in the donor community. Politically, Seaga and Manley were much more like Tweedledum and Tweedledee than the Bank and others suspected. After 1980, Seaga was the new broom that was moving about, but not really sweeping.

Yet to conclude that, on the crucial issue of economic reform, democracy failed to provide a real alternative is also too glib. The PNP had boycotted the general election of 1983, but contested municipal elections in mid-1986 on the issue of the JLP's macroeconomic performance. It was the results of these elections which determined Seaga to enter into a new and more constructive policy dialogue with the Bank and the Fund, based on an explicitly Jamaican-designed programme. By 1987, it was clear that the government, the Bank and the Fund all accepted that they could learn from past failures. This less confrontational joint approach survived the re-election of Manley in 1989. Here we see not regime changes, not new brooms or the manipulation of vested interests, but just a general willingness to learn from experience.

In Guyana, it was the abuse of the democratic process, rather than the democratic process itself, which undermined any real possibility of the success of structural adjustment. In the course of decolonization, Britain managed to give political power after independence to the PNCP, the party of the Afro-Guyanese minority community led by Forbes Burnham. The PNCP retained power by electoral fraud and other devices like declaring all agencies of state the organs of the ruling party. By 1978, the economy had entered a serious crisis which provoked strikes and demonstrations by the opposition PPP (representing the Indo-Guyanese community) as well as by supporters of the PNCP. The Burnham government tried to further entrench itself constitutionally, and at a validating election in December 1980 was plausibly accused of massive electoral fraud. It is not surprising that the negotiation of a Bank SAL with the Guyana government at this juncture failed to elicit appropriate political commitment to the implementation of the reform conditions. These were, additionally, badly designed and the resulting level of compliance was very low. This episode has one thing to say about the effect of regime type on implementation: there is no guarantee that undemocratic and ruthless regimes can be persuaded to undertake economic reforms, even when welfare levels have sunk very low. They can prevent the emergence of new brooms, refuse to learn from experience and maintain themselves even in the face of widespread popular hostility.

Two cases which illustrate the power of vested interests to frustrate economic reform inside a broadly democratic framework are those of Kenya and Ecuador. Kenya, as a colony of European settlement, has long been economically dominated by large-scale agrarian interests; and although decolonization has Africanized the ownership of these interests to a considerable extent, the basic structure of the economy has not greatly changed. In Ecuador, too, the *latifundistas* in the sierra and the agro-exporting oligarchy have held a key economic position. In both countries, economic strength has been converted into political influence. In both countries, the Bank offered adjustment lending, with crucial conditions focused on the agricultural sector. In Kenya, in SAL II, one key condition was the dismantling of the system of controlled maize marketing, which had withstood repeated previous internal attempts at abolition or reform. In Ecuador, the Bank aimed at eliminating subsidies on agricultural credit and permitting free trade in food crops. In both cases, these objectives were not attained.

An odd similarity characterises the political circumstances of these failures. The general political and ideological climate at the time was not hostile to liberalisation efforts. Within each government a small group of enthusiastic technocrats was making a genuine effort to pursue liberalisation in the areas agreed with the Bank to be desirable. Ultimately, the Bank's good rapport with the Kenyan and Ecuadorian technocrats proved insufficient to procure the agricultural reforms. In both cases, the President of the country had a personal stake in agribusiness, and the 'distortions' objected to by the Bank formed an important part of the mechanism for ensuring political support for the President's party. It is ironical that some of the most recalcitrant vested interests in the path of economic liberalisation should be in the agricultural rather than the industrial sector, given that a frequent justification for policy reform is the need to remove the urban biasses which disadvantage rural producers.

In summary, this review of the political aspects of our case studies suggests a number of broad conclusions. The belief that ruthless and undemocratic regimes are especially helpful in securing good performance in implementation has little basis, for the perhaps intuitively obvious reason that such regimes can be weak as well as strong, economically ignorant as well as economically sophisticated. Countries do learn from past mistakes (as Jamaica appears to have done), but sometimes it takes a good long time to do, with much pain and misery experienced first. When this happens, new brooms (such as J.J. Rawlings or Cory Aquino) have a genuine opportunity for reform. The merit of democratic systems is that they can allow such new brooms to come out of the closet. But they do not always perform this function: they can also sustain parties built around vested interests – though oddly these seem stronger in agriculture than industry. And new brooms can suddenly materialise in the most unlikely of undemocratic settings, although we would have to go beyond our case studies to President Gorbachev's Soviet Union to find the most astonishing recent example.

It is clear from the foregoing that none of the first three hypotheses can be described as providing a political key to effective implementation even in the most literal sense of the latter word. The evidence is summarised in Table 5.3.

The dictatorship hypothesis is superficially plausible, and has been given additional currency by cases outside our sample such as Chile, but apart from the cases of effective reform under democratic governance such as Mauritius, it is clear from our case studies that the motor for economic reform was in all cases something additional to the ability of the

Table 5.3   Case-study countries: alternative explanations of implementation, I

Country	Dictatorship?	New government?	Standard of living 1980–2 more than 25% below average level of 1970s?	Level of implementation (%)
Turkey	Yes*	Yes	No	95
Thailand	Yes*	No	No	70
Ghana	Yes	Yes	Yes	58
Philippines	No* (post 1986)	No (yes post 1986)	No	62
Jamaica	No*	Yes	Yes	63
Malawi	Yes	No	No	55
Kenya	Yes*	No	No	38
Ecuador	No*	Yes	Yes	28
Guyana	No*	No	Yes	15

Notes and sources: A country is defined as a dictatorship if any of the following do not hold: regular elections for representative assembly and head of state; freedom of press and personal expression. In countries marked * there is an elective representative assembly. 'New government' denotes a change in political leadership during the two years preceding the grant of the first World Bank adjustment loan. 'Standard of living' is GNP per capita as set out in successive issues of World Bank *World Development Reports* (appendix table 1). Levels of implementation for each case-study country are as set out in Table 5.2.

government to transform desire into institutional change. The comparative study by Haggard and Kaufman (in Nelson, 1989: Chapter 2) makes it clear that in Latin America, in particular, there is no correlation between dictatorship and impulse towards reform.

The 'new government' explanation – that the new broom will be less beholden towards established rent-holders – has clear relevance to the progress of reform in Jamaica, Turkey, Ghana and Aquino's Philippines. But even this is neither a necessary nor a sufficient explanation of the degree of reform. Thorough-going programmes of reform have been undergone by elderly administrations (including Banda's Malawi and Pinochet's Chile) and one scarcely needs to add the counterpart that a change of government (Ecuador, Peru and many other examples across Latin America) is no guarantee of a reform programme.

The learning from misery viewpoint is also far from straightforward. Although this seems to have happened in Ghana, it is not the common case. Table 5.3 indicates an interesting paradox for this viewpoint. Within our sample, the rate of implementation of conditions has actually been higher in countries which *did not* experience a severe shock to standards of living at the beginning of the 1980s (with the exception of Ghana) than in countries which did.

We are therefore thrown back upon our fourth explanation, which at its most basic level looks suspiciously like a tautology: that the strength of the impulse towards reform depends on the outcome of the competitive struggle between pro- and anti-reform interest groups. If one widens the definition of 'interest groups' to include interest groups within government, the hypothesis is true by definition: obviously the relative progress of reform between countries depends on the relative power of pro- and anti-reform elements. The meaningful questions lie one step back from here. What caused the relative influence of different groups to diverge as between countries? Are there institutional differences which influence the way in which interest group conflicts are played out?

As a first step towards the answer, let us revert to the analysis of Table 4.7. This spelled out the *prima facie* orientation of different interest groups towards different types of reform, often at a level which itself did not rise far above tautology (e.g. farmers like higher prices). Reading down the columns, it tells us who the principal losers from structural adjustment are (urban wage-workers, who experience minus signs in respect of all measures except liberalisation of consumer goods imports) and reading across the rows, we learn something about why the different types of structural adjustment measures listed in Table 5.1 had different rates of implementation (public expenditure cuts and other fiscal reforms uniquely encounter universal minus signs because they are not supportive towards any interest group, and these reforms duly have the lowest implementation rate – 53 per cent – of all those listed in Table 5.1). But by definition the table tells us nothing about differences between countries, because the categories of gain and loss which it lists are the same across all countries. The entries for agricultural policy reform and import liberalisation, for example, read:

	Industrialists (manufacturing for home market)	Capitalist farmers/ workers	Urban wage- workers and salariat	Subsistence farmers
Increases in agricultural prices	–	+	–	+?
Removal of import restrictions	Inputs: + Outputs: –	+ (except on food)	+	–

If this is the balance of forces in every country, why, one may ask, did import liberalisation go further in Turkey than in Kenya, and agricultural marketing reforms make more progress in Ghana than in Ecuador?

Table 5.4 sets out the possible raw materials for an answer by asking of each such measure proposed by the Bank in our case-study countries: What was proposed? How were the gainers and losers organised? What was done to buy off the losers? What was the outcome?

As one looks at Table 5.4 three things become apparent. In the first place reform efforts worked better, *ceteris paribus*, if the gainers were organised in support of the proposed reform than if they were not. Typically, farmers in developing countries do not constitute an organised, let alone a powerful, interest group, and the most plausible of the Bank's claims for the progressivity of policy-based lending has been that it might redress the consequent urban bias. But in two of our case studies, Kenya and Ecuador, the *latifundistas* are indeed organised as a 'national farmers' union' whose members in addition have powerful representation in parliament. And in those countries (by contrast, for example, with Malawi) the Bank's *price-based* reforms have indeed been successful, and prices have been sustained above export parity levels. By the same token, their *marketing-based* reforms have been unsuccessful, since they attempted to remove the element of rent inherent in the price paid by the government marketing board, and no countervailing interest group was willing to help the government remove it. When one moves to the case of import liberalisation, the picture has to be disaggregated, since as revealed, for example, by Hirschman's pioneering study (1968) 'industrialists' nowhere constitute a unified pressure group on trade policy, except at the level that all of them would like to operate at lower cost, and therefore generally welcome liberalisation on the input side. On the output side, every attempt which we have examined to establish a coherent position on liberalisation

161

Table 5.4 Case-study countries: alternative explanations of implementation, II

Country	Import liberalisation					Agricultural pricing and marketing				
	Measure recommended	Government commitment? (extent of countervailing action)	Extra-govt support	Extra-govt opposition	Outcome	Measure recommended	Government commitment? (extent of countervailing action)	Extra-govt support	Extra-govt opposition	Outcome
Turkey	Progressive removal of quantitative import restrictions	Extra-budgetary levies raised on some imports	Strong support from foreign trade companies	Disjointed support from home market oriented industrialists, bought off by subsidies and by slow pace of reform	Majority of import restrictions removed; reduction in average tariff level	Not applicable				
Thailand	Removal of import restrictions and rationalisation of external tariff within band of 15–60%	Tariff increases in areas recommended by Bank for cuts (e.g. automobiles)	Thai Manufacturers' Association disunited concerning appropriate areas for tariff cuts	Some opposition from Chamber of Commerce	Little alteration of tariff structure	Privatisation of meat marketing				Implemented

Ghana	Extension of new foreign exchange auction system (introduced 1986) to consumer goods	No countervailing action	Export-oriented farmers and industrialists	Former licence holders	Accomplished 1988	Increases in producer price of cocoa	No counter-vailing action	Strong support from cocoa farmers		Implemented
						Privatisation of Cocoa Marketing Board	No explicit commitment	Little support; not seen as major issue	Board employees and allies	Not implemented
Philippines	Removal of import prohibitions from over 1,000 commodities between 1980 and 1988	Numerous *ad hoc* exemptions granted to specific importers even on restrictions which remained. Revaluation of real exchange rate 1980–4	Opponents of Marcos's 'cronies' keen to see special privileges removed	(a) Marcos cronies mostly swept away in 1986; (b) all home-market based manufacturers	Steady weakening in pace of reform after end 1987	Not applicable				
Jamaica	Removal of over 300 quantitative restrictions between 1980 and 1982	Revaluation of real exchange rate between 1980 and 1985; parallel rate maintained in being; Export Development Fund inoperative	Users of imported inputs	Former licence holders	Nominal implementation	Public sector production and marketing of sugar and bananas to terminate		Some support from banking sector	Large farmers mostly hostile	Sugar marketing transferred to Tate and Lyle; banana marketing continues in government hands

Country	Import liberalisation					Agricultural pricing and marketing				
	Measure recommended	Government commitment? (extent of countervailing action)	Extra-govt support	Extra-govt opposition	Outcome	Measure recommended	Government commitment? (extent of countervailing action)	Extra-govt support	Extra-govt opposition	Outcome
Malawi	Not applicable					(1981) Increase price of export crops by more, price of food crops by less, than prevailing inflation rate	Maize price (1981) increased over 60%, export crop prices just over 10%	Urban interests: export-oriented large farmers	Maize farmers	Not implemented
Kenya	Progressive removal of import restrictions; all except those on security-related items to be removed by 1990	No countervailing action	Export-oriented industrialists (many of them alien); urban consumers; market-oriented farmers	Home-market oriented industrialists; civil servants in receipt of kickbacks	Partially implemented (some 45% of quantitative restrictions remain) but with some successes e.g. fertilisers	Prices of major crops to be maintained at export parity level. National Crops and Produce Board to retreat to role of buyer and seller of last resort	No countervailing action. Controls on maize movement between districts persist	All market-oriented farmers, strongly organised. Private traders	Urban consumers. Large farmers in possession of maize movement permits	Implemented (but no discretionary action needed). Private traders admitted to grain market; now hold some 15% of grain market

Country	Reform	Gainers	Losers	Outcome
Ecuador	Remove prohibition on maize and wheat imports	Urban consumers	Large sierra farmers, well organised	Implemented after delay July 1988. Number of prohibitions *increased* during implementation period
	Privatisation of National Food Marketing Corporation	None	Urban consumers; cereal farmers protected by fixed buying prices.	Not implemented; Corporation extended to include new products.
	Remove maximum consumer price for wheat	Urban consumers	Wheat farmers	Implemented (during period of surplus 1986)

Source: Case studies in Volume 2.

within the Chamber of Industries or its equivalent ran into a welter of special pleading by manufacturers of particular products; and since a blocking coalition against each such proposal could always be constructed by manufacturers of other products, the *status quo* was generally invoked as a consensus-building instrument.[3] Consequently, the more successful of the Bank's liberalisation proposals have been those which featured a quick freeing-up of the import regime for key agricultural and industrial imports. No single programme amongst those discussed in Volume 2 exactly matches this ideal, but parts of them do: in particular, the Ghana government's introduction of a foreign exchange auction and the Kenya government's liberalisation of fertiliser imports, both in 1986, lowered the costs of a powerful producer group without setting up any countervailing opposition, and for that reason went through relatively smoothly.

The degree to which interest groups can succeed in constituting themselves as organized institutions is, nevertheless, only one part of the answer to why the interest group explanation seems to work better in some countries than in others. The other part of the answer is that countries differ in their formal political institutions and their informal ideological apparatuses and the 'thickness' or 'thinness' of such institutions determines the scope that any organized interest group has for exercising influence. A country without a free legislature, a free press or normal liberal civil rights is much less open to interest group influence than one with 'thicker' political and civic institutions. We have already noted that in Turkey and Ghana the sphere of action available to interest groups was highly circumscribed for these sorts of institutional reasons.

In the second place, the more successful reform programmes were those which were effective in buying the losers off. This could be done in two ways. One possibility – astonishingly rare in practice – was to design compensation explicitly into the reform programme by offering the losers a *quid pro quo*, as in the Philippines (Chapter 12) where manufacturers of textiles were compensated for the removal of import quotas by being offered an increase in the customs duty drawback (i.e. tariff exemption) in respect of their exports. The other, much commoner, expedient was to offer implicit compensation by using the proceeds of policy-based lending to make foreign exchange easier to obtain for all importers, in the hope of buying off dissent amongst consumers in general. Of all our case-study countries, Turkey alone suffered no import compression during the 1980–3 period (Table 11.1 in Volume 2) and Turkey was the most successful reformer. But if this form of non-specific 'compensation' is to be used, the resources must be adequate; and to see this is immediately to observe the contrast between the massive resources (4 and 9 per cent of GNP respectively) provided by the Bank in support of the reform programmes in Turkey and Ghana, and the minimal ones (0.5 and 1 per cent) provided in Ecuador and Guyana. Nothing, least of all the massive political risks associated with compliance with a SAL programme, can be bought for free.

In the third place, a dedicated and competent local technocracy is clearly a more effective vehicle for reform than an incompetent and self-doubting one, which brings us full circle to the question of government commitment. Being unobservable, commitment cannot be measured, and has to be inferred from the existence or otherwise of countervailing actions to those prescribed by the World Bank, such as the revaluations of the real exchange rate in Jamaica and the Philippines before 1985, or the five new parastatals created between 1982 and 1987 while the Kenya government was pretending to consider the divestiture of others. Using this criterion, the three countries in our sample where reform went farthest – Turkey, Ghana and Thailand – certainly had the advantage of governments whose commitment to reform was genuine. This is, of course, a necessary and not a sufficient condition. Ecuador, between 1985 and 1987, was governed by a technocracy entirely committed to reform, which achieved almost nothing in terms of the Bank's criteria.

Let us briefly pull the threads of this section together. The measured level of implementation may mean much or little, depending on the extent of countervailing government action and the extent of unforeseen change in the external environment. Out of four possible 'internal' explanations of government compliance, we find that two – previous economic experience and the presence or otherwise of military rule or dictatorship – have weak explanatory power. The arrival in power of a new government has often facilitated reform – by reducing the number of vested interests that need to be confronted – but is neither an essential nor an adequate precondition for effective reform. Finally, the balance between pro- and anti-reform elements appears susceptible, on the evidence studied, to the cohesiveness of pro-reform interest groups, to the resources applied to compensating the losers, and to the government's prior commitment, or otherwise, to reform.

Two loose ends remain untied. One of them is the importance of sheer skill in determining the outcome of Act 2; not only the political skill required to devise a compensation strategy for the losers, but also the economic expertise to see that if the government grain marketing board is already offering an efficient price to producers (as in Kenya and Ecuador) further efforts by the Bank to privatise it are purely quixotic. The influence of the adviser's technical competence, or otherwise, on the 'commitment' to reform of the advisee needs no underlining.

The discussion thus far, however, limits itself to the influence of internal political factors on the decision to carry out reform. The 'external' influence of the recipient government's bargaining relationship *vis-à-vis* the Bank, so far entirely ignored, constitutes the second loose end. It is considered in the following section.

167

5.3   THE 'ECONOMISTIC HYPOTHESIS': THE ROLE OF ALTERNATIVE SOURCES OF FINANCE IN RELATION TO THE DEPTH OF CRISIS

Let us recall the basic premiss of Chapter 3, namely that the conditional aid relationship is a game from which each player will extract what advantage he can. In particular, the more a recipient expects to need follow-on finance from a given donor in a subsequent period, the more risky the strategy of reneging on agreed conditions, and the less, we may suppose, is the likelihood that he will do so, whatever his willingness in principle to implement those conditions, as examined in section 5.2 above. People in glass houses, as the saying has it, shouldn't throw stones. We wish here to examine the hypothesis that the number of stones which recipients threw depended on the fragility of the financial house which they inhabited. We may call this an *economistic hypothesis* of recipient behaviour, since it posits that implementation was determined by the state of the economy rather than political structures or administrative competence; but the explanations we offer should be seen as linked rather than mutually exclusive. In particular, as explained earlier, the political balance between pro-reform and anti-reform elements is itself determined by the degree of perceived financial crisis.

In testing the hypothesis there are difficulties of measurement in relation to both the dependent and the independent variables. Any accurate assessment of *slippage* (or compliance), as we saw earlier, is bedevilled by the existence of ambiguity in the original conditions and by the possibility of neutralising any act of compliance either by countervailing measures or by simple reversal after the required finance has been secured. On the measurement of *financial vulnerability*, the difficulties are of a different nature. The key problem is that the recipient's actions are likely to be guided by his *expectation* of future financial flows in relation to his expected future requirements, to which current levels of Bank finance and balance-of-payments deficit give only an imperfect guide.

Having due regard to these difficulties, the available data on slippage and on financial dependence during the implementation period are as set out in Table 5.5.

From Table 5.5 it appears that, on average, low-slippage countries did indeed have more serious balance-of-payments problems than high-slippage countries, as the economistic hypothesis would predict, but the difference is not statistically significant. On the other hand, the level of a country's financial dependence on the Bank appears to have exercised no influence on slippage at all; a number of countries whose dependence on the Bank was very high, such as Kenya, Malawi and the Philippines, perpetrated serious slippage, and several which had ample access to alternative sources of finance, such as Turkey and South Korea, slipped relatively little; the

Table 5.5 Slippage on adjustment loan conditions: the 'economistic' hypothesis tested

Country	Implementation period	Indicators of slippage:		Indicators of financial predicament:	
		All adjustment lending (our estimate)	SALs only (Bank estimate)	Balance of payments during implementation period (% of GDP)	World Bank adjustment lending as % of gross external capital flow during implementation period
High-slippage countries:					
Bolivia	1980–2	80%	High	−3.0	11.3
Ecuador*	1985–8	72%		−7.0	
Guyana*	1981–4	85%	High	−2.6	22.9
Kenya*	1980–4		Medium	−5.6	20.3
	1980–8	62%		−5.4	
Malawi*	1980–7	45%		−11.6	38.4
Ghana*	1983–8	42%		−4.6	15.0
Average					
High-slippage countries		64%		5.6	21.9
Low-slippage countries					
Jamaica*	1982–6	37%	Low	−13.0	16.6
Philippines*	1980–4		Medium	−6.6	17.0
	1980–8	38%		(−3.6)	
Ivory Coast	1980–5	18%	Low	−12.7	12.8
Thailand*	1981–5	30%	Low	−6.3	11.1
Turkey*	1980–5	5%	Low	−4.5	14.6
South Korea	1980–3	25%	Medium	−5.3	4.5
Average					
Low-slippage countries		25%		7.7	12.4
t-statistic[1]		5.29**		1.11	2.11*

Sources: Slippage measures: Our measure of slippage on SALs only is from Mosley 1987, table 8, and on all adjustment lending it is from the case studies in Volume 2 (as summarised in Table 5.2 above). The World Bank's measure of slippage is from World Bank, 1986, Table 3.1, p.24.

Balance of payments as percentage of GDP: From statistical appendix to World Bank, 1988, except for Bolivia, Ecuador and Guyana, for which data are from IMF *International Financial Statistics*.

World Bank adjustment lending as percentage of capital inflow: Bank lending volumes from Nicholas (1988), updated from Bank internal records; total external capital inflow from OECD, Development Assistance Committee, *Geographical Distribution of Financial Flows to Less Developed Countries, various issues*.

Notes 1 Student's *t*-statistic = $(\bar{x}_1 - \bar{x}_2 / (\sigma_{\bar{x}_1 - \bar{x}_2})$ in all tables.
    * Denotes a country discussed in the case studies of Volume 2.

169

average level of dependence on the Bank for high-slippage countries was in fact 9 percentage points in excess of that for low-slippage countries, and so far as we can tell from the table, the relationship between slippage and financial independence is insignificantly *negative*. This may be because the current level of a country's financial dependence on the Bank is a good guide to its credit rating and therefore to its expected ability to borrow from alternative sources.

The performance of the economistic hypothesis as a predictor of implementation, is, therefore, poor; which is not to say that it is useless. In several countries it is clear that a continuing state of financial crisis played a large part in constraining governments which were by no means intellectually committed to the Bank's liberalising policies nonetheless to maintain a high level of nominal compliance with its recommendations. The two clearest cases from Table 5.5 are those of the Ivory Coast and Jamaica, both of whom suffered from double-figure levels of balance-of-payments deficit well into the middle 1980s and thus continued to be dependent on inflows of medium-term programme lending for a longer period than expected. Much of what they needed had to come from the Bank, hence in spite of an inclination to persist with controls – which in Jamaica went as far as an engineered *revaluation* of the currency in October 1985 – the governments in question were always careful to abide by the letter of the Bank's conditionality. The government of Thailand behaved in a similarly constrained way during the period to 1983 when its balance-of-payments problem was most severe: in 1984, when the pressure came off the current account and the government's access to Japanese financial markets improved, the level of slippage increased, as described in Chapter 13. A number of the cases of low slippage in the table are, however, by no means to be explained by a financial constraint. The good implementation record of Turkey and South Korea for example, clearly cannot be explained in this way. What happened there, rather, was that the Bank offered financial backing to a reform programme *whose details were already conceived and worked out within the recipient government*, so that the degree of coercion involved was minimal. Prior government commitment – as discussed in the previous section – was high. In such a situation, however, conditionality becomes unnecessary, since by hypothesis the programme would have been implemented with or without the Bank's intervention.

More interesting are the cases where, as we put it in Chapter 3, David outwits Goliath: that is, where the borrower fails to implement a large proportion of the conditions in spite of being in a state of economic crisis and continuing financial dependence. Of the countries in Table 5.5, this accurately describes the case of Kenya, Ecuador, and to a lesser extent Malawi and the Philippines. If one takes a 'naïve' game-theory viewpoint, such cases should not exist, since each of them was by virtue of its continuing economic dependence in a poor bargaining position during its implementation phase, and for this reason could not be recommended to put future financial flows at risk by allowing high levels of slippage. Two factors, however, make the actual position more complicated. In the first place, Kenya and, more especially, the Philippines enjoyed a sufficiently strong geopolitical relationship with the United States as to make it likely that, in the event of the policy dialogue between the Bank and that country running into difficulty, the United States Government would both use its influence within the Bank to persuade it not to take too harsh a view of slippage and, if need be, step up its own supply of bilateral assistance. In the second place, the expectation that 'borrowers in glass houses will not throw stones' will only be accurate if the said borrowers are risk-averse, and if in consequence they seriously fear that any slippage on their part will be punished by a withdrawal of future programme assistance. For if they are willing to take a gamble on the Bank not punishing them in this way, and the gamble comes off, they have the best of all possible worlds: finance *and* refinance without the associated political costs. This is case 3, 'slippage unpunished' in the notation of Figure 3.3; nor is it in any sense a theoretical curiosum. All of the four borrowers mentioned above constitute examples of the successful application of the strategy, in the sense that they have been successful in obtaining further adjustment loans from the Bank after demonstrating high levels of slippage on their previous one, as described in volume 2. And, as we shall see in the next section, there are many other such examples. The strategy may, on occasion, come unstuck, as is demonstrated by the cases of Senegal and Guyana (described in more detail in Chapter 18); flagrant non-compliance is sometimes punished. All that is being argued here is that a borrower who is willing to take a chance on the Bank's desire to disburse overcoming its desire to punish breach of contract may see its gamble rewarded. Other borrowers, on observing the behaviour being rewarded, will of course learn from the precedent, and in case of need use it to exculpate their own slippage in their own refinance negotiations. The fact that many borrowers have felt able to employ such a strategy, implementing only a small part of the promised reform programme in spite of the severity of their economic position, goes quite a long way to explain why the so-called 'economistic' hypothesis on implementation is weak in practice.

5.4   DONOR RESPONSE TO SLIPPAGE AND THE SUSTAINABILITY OF THE REFORM PROCESS

The Bank's principal device for enforcing implementation is ostensibly to divide adjustment loans into tranches, of which it is agreed that the second will only be disbursed if certain named policy actions have been carried out (see the example of an SAL agreement in the Appendix to Chapter 2). Of the loan transactions examined in our country case studies, all except the

Thailand SALs were divided into tranches; the normal practice is to have two tranches of equal value, but the Philippines Economic Recovery Loan of 1986 was divided into three equal portions.

A decision to release a second tranche is made by the Bank's Managing Directors (formerly the Senior Vice-President, Operations), on a recommendation from the country department responsible for the loan. The Executive Board is not involved, although a number of members of the Board would like it to be. The Bank's own account of the record makes it clear that, although there may be uncertainty about timing, there is in practice little uncertainty about *whether* a second tranche will be released. Even though 'almost all tranches are experiencing tranche release delays as a result of insufficient progress in fulfilling conditions', the Bank's review writes, 'almost all tranches have eventually been released' (World Bank 1988: 92). In practice there appear to be only two cases in the history of policy-based lending (Senegal in 1982 and Argentina in 1989) in which the second tranche has not eventually been released. Even in those cases where almost none of the second tranche conditionality has actually been fulfilled, such as the Ecuador Agricultural Sector Loan, the Structural Adjustment Loans to Guyana and Bolivia and the Second Structural Adjustment Loan to Kenya, all the money has eventually been handed over by the Bank. In cases where there has been substantial delinquency on loan conditions, a typical sequence has been as follows: a supervision mission, consisting mainly of Bank junior professional staff from Washington, flies out to the recipient country to inspect progress about a year from the date of release of the first tranche.[4] It decides that progress has been unsatisfactory. The recipient government is informed that the second tranche is being withheld. A Bank senior official (usually the relevant departmental director) now enters negotiations with the recipient government, indicating that although he is sympathetic to the difficulties that have caused the government's reform programme to lag behind schedule, he requires some earnest of the government's continued commitment to reform before he is able to secure release of the second tranche. The recipient government makes a conciliatory gesture (e.g. an increase in nominal interest rates in Ecuador; a promise to decontrol maize marketing in Kenya). The departmental director and regional vice-president, anxious about the rate of disbursement of their funds, seek to persuade the senior vice-president, operations, that the gesture is a sufficient one. Sooner or later (but possibly after one or two iterations) the senior vice-president gives way. What is being bargained about at this stage, therefore, is not whether the second tranche will be released, but when. Where delays have occurred in the release of the second tranche (which has occurred in over 75 per cent of cases) the length of the delay has varied between three and twelve months (Nicholas, 1988: 23). But it is quite clear from our interviews within the Bank that its junior staff of loan officers and country economists, who had been urged from above to be tough on conditionality at the stage of programme design and supervision mission, have felt traduced by the softness of the pledges which their seniors were willing to accept when it came to allowing the release of the second tranche. The cases instanced above illustrate this well: the Kenyan pledge of late 1983 to privatise maize marketing has not been implemented to date, and Ecuadorian interest rates, which had been raised in nominal terms in August 1986 in order to comply with the terms of the Agricultural Sector Loan, were already negative in real terms by the time that the second tranche was released in the following July. All parties now know that they are caught up in a ritual dance: Bank senior staff know that, bearing in mind what other countries have got away with, it will be neither just nor financially productive to make an example of one particular recipient who defaults on conditions by refusing the second tranche; Bank junior staff know that it will not be helpful to their careers to protest the decision to release; and the recipient knows that if it makes amicable noises, plus comparisons with other countries if necessary, it can expect the release of the second tranche within a year as surely as day follows night. The fact that so many conditions attached to Bank adjustment loans are phrased in terms which permit of a subjective assessment, such as 'substantial progress', 'satisfactory performance' and so forth (see page 123) merely helps to oil the wheels of the tranche release mechanism. The contrast with the IMF procedure, under which performance criteria are always defined in quantitative terms (e.g. 'growth of central bank net overseas borrowing between September and December 1989 may not exceed 8 per cent') and finance is always cut off, in the absence of a waiver, if a performance criterion is not satisfied, could scarcely be more graphic.

The battleground, then, is not the question of whether or not the second tranche is released but the question of whether subsequent adjustment loans can be obtained from the Bank even after slippage on a previous one. This is a much tougher fight, as witness the fact that although the Bank originally envisaged the structural adjustment lending process as being a medium-term relationship involving five structural adjustment loans over an equivalent number of years,[5] Turkey is the only developing country to have so far conformed to this pattern. Since the Bank switched the emphasis of adjustment lending from SALs to SECALs in the middle 1980s one's criterion for a smooth policy dialogue has to be amended somewhat, but the most casual scrutiny of the case histories of those countries which the Bank describes as 'adjustment-loan intensive' (such as Jamaica, Malawi and Kenya among the countries featured in Volume 2) quickly reveals that the process of follow-on finance has by no means proceeded as the Bank, or the recipient, planned. Is it possible, we may now ask, to explain the Bank's behaviour in granting refinance ('in Act 3', according to the language of Chapter 3) in terms of the determinants of bargaining strength discussed in preceding chapters?

Table 5.6 World Bank refinance behaviour in relation to slippage in previous periods

Country	First adjustment loan:			Second adjustment loan:			Subsequent adjustment lending by Bank to country
	Title and date	Level of slippage on conditions (%)	B of P deficit (as % of GDP) in final year of implementation period[1]	Title and date	Level of slippage on conditions (%)	B of P deficit (as % of GDP) in final year of implementation period	
High slippage countries (slippage on initial loan more than 40%):							
Bolivia	SAL I 1980	80	3.0	— — — none — — —	— — — none — — —	—	See Note 2
Guyana	SAL I 1981	80	2.6	— — — none — — —	— — — none — — —	—	none
Ecuador	Ag. Sec. Loan 1985	75	13.3	Fin. Sector Loan 1988	See Note 3	6.8	See Note 3
Malawi	SAL I 1981	45	11.9	SAL II 1983	30	8.3	One SAL One SECAL
Kenya	SAL I 1980	40	4.7	SAL II 1982	78	2.0	Two SECALs
Low slippage countries (slippage on initial loan less than 30 per cent):							
Jamaica	SAL I 1982	16	4.6	SAL II 1983	5	8.5	One SAL Three Export Devt Loans Two SECALs

Ghana	Export Rehab. 1983	30	6.1	Industrial sector credit 1986	25	2.9	One SAL Two SECALs
Philippines	SAL I 1980	30	8.4	SAL II 1982	45	4.7	One Economic Recovery Loan One SECAL
Pakistan	SAL I 1982	10	3.6	Energy Sector Loan 1985	20	2.1	One SECAL
Thailand	SAL I 1982	15	7.5	SAL II 1983	40	4.4	– – none – – Three SALs
Turkey	SAL I 1980	0	3.4	SAL II 1981	5	2.0	Three SECALs

Sources: For slippage data, country case studies in Volume 2 (slippage data by country are summarised in Table 5.2). For balance-of-payments data: IMF *International Financial Statistics*, various issues.

Notes:
1 'Implementation period' is defined as the two years following the grant of an adjustment loan.
2 In Bolivia, two Bank reconstruction loans were granted in 1986 and in 1987 after a change in government in the previous year. This must be interpreted as a completely separate adjustment episode from that analysed in the table.
3 Assessment of slippage on, and follow-up finance to, Ecuador Financial Sector Loan is not possible for lack of sufficient time elapsed since grant of this loan in January 1988.

Table 5.6 sets out the experience of our case-study countries, plus one or two others, in obtaining follow-on adjustment loans from the Bank in relation to the level of their slippage on the previous loan and various indicators of their economic predicament at the time the follow-on loan was requested. The data in the table need to be interpreted with care, since the adjustment-lending relationship may be broken off from either the supply or the demand side and a particularly successful exercise may enable a recipient to opt out of further injections of Bank adjustment finance earlier than planned, as in Thailand and South Korea. Once these cases have been removed, it is clear that there is some correlation between crime and punishment: all the countries in the low-slippage group were able to obtain at least one follow-up programme loan from the Bank, whereas two out of four countries in the high-slippage group were unable to do so. None the less, certain puzzles remain. Why is high (more than 40 per cent) slippage sometimes condoned (as in Ecuador), sometimes symbolically punished by the conversion of a SAL process into a sector-lending process (as in Malawi and Kenya) and sometimes genuinely punished by the withdrawal of adjustment lending even at a time of continuing external crisis (as in Guyana and Bolivia)? Why, if we move to these low-slippage cases in which a balance-of-payments problem did persist, was that low slippage sometimes rewarded (as in Turkey and Jamaica) and sometimes not (as in Pakistan)?

A clue towards the answer to these questions is offered by the analysis of Tables 4.8 and 4.9 in the previous chapter, from which it appears that the tightest loan conditions are negotiated with those countries which are in the worst bargaining position in the sense that they have a serious balance-of-payments problem, depended heavily on the Bank for finance, and yet only had small amounts of Bank capital already invested in the country, with the consequence that the potential for 'reverse leverage' by the recipient country was small. If we take only the four countries in Table 5.6 where slippage was 'high' (more than 40 per cent) we find from Table 5.7 that the two which were 'punished' by the refusal of further Bank programme loans – Guyana and Bolivia – were in a worse bargaining position on all the indicators mentioned than the two which were 'acquitted', Kenya and Ecuador. Kenya in addition benefited from its strong geopolitical links with the United States and from its reasonable claim, in spite of its disputes with the Bank, to be a well-managed economy by the standards of sub-Saharan Africa.

Various implications for recipient behaviour follow from Tables 5.6 and 5.7. The first is that if slippage is below 50 per cent, the probability of follow-up finance being refused by the Bank is virtually nil, providing that plausible enough reasons can be given. This observation now has such a solid empirical basis[6] that it is reasonable to expect every borrower country to believe, as it makes its implementation decision, that it can always get away with shortfalls of this magnitude. The second implication is that a borrower may sometimes be able to get away with shortfalls in excess of this magnitude, *even if hampered in its negotiation by economic crisis or a high level of financial dependence on the Bank*, if it holds a countervailing card, for example a large Bank stake already invested in the country or a good working relationship with the IMF.[7] The Bank, in other words, is some way short of being able to offer a credible threat against breaches of conditionality that a recipient feels to be in any way coercive. As suggested in Chapter 3, the threat which holds out the most hope of discouraging slippage might well be the random punishment of slippage above a certain random threshold rather than the present mild and inconsistent efforts to fit the punishment to the crime.

Table 5.7 High-slippage countries: comparison of bargaining parameters between the 'punished' and the 'unpunished'

	Balance-of-payments deficit (% of GNP)	Financial dependence on Bank[1]	Amount of Bank investment ($ million)
'Punished' countries:			
Guyana (1984),			
Bolivia (1982)	18.1	17.1	378
'Unpunished' countries:			
Kenya (1983),			
Ecuador (1988)	4.4	12.0	1474

Notes and sources: All data quoted are averages for the pair of countries mentioned in the year that the Bank made its decision on whether to offer follow-up finance, as quoted in the left-hand column. Balance-of-payments data are from IMF *International Financial statistics*; financial dependence on Bank is level of Bank policy-based lending (from World Bank, 1988) divided by total inward flow of public and private capital into the country (from World Bank, *World Development Reports*, various); amount of Bank investment from the Summary Statement of Loans and IDA credits contained in the appendix pages of the relevant World Bank *Annual Report*.

In conclusion, we explore the question of how far Bank-sponsored reforms have proved *sustainable*, that is, durable even in the absence of external pressure from the Bank. It was, of course, precisely the desire to make projects more durable which was the principal motive force behind the introduction of policy-based lending in the early 1980s, but any underpinning which is given to the productive structure by policy reform will clearly be short-lived if such reform is conceived purely as a temporary expedient to keep the Bank quiet. The analogy between projects and policy reform must not be stretched too far. Projects by definition are *structures*, investment in human or material capital designed to last a long time. Policy reform is not a structure, but a government action designed to influence the allocation of resources, hence the right duration for the implementation of a policy change will vary from case to case, and in some instances such as infant-industry tariffs or input subsidies the policy change will depend for its effectiveness on being transient. Sustainability of reform, then is not an end in itself, but a desirable objective in certain cases where structural change is sought through the long-term alteration of some policy pattern. In what follows we shall examine the sustainability of reform in three such areas: trade policy, agricultural pricing, and interest-rate policy. In most of the countries examined by our case studies the World Bank continues to maintain a conditional lending relationship with the recipient government, hence any conclusions that we are able to reach about the level of sustainability once that relationship is relaxed will be provisional even by the standards of the present study.

We may begin by examining what is necessary if an economic reform process is to be sustained. Essentially, a government, or sequence of governments, must believe that the maintenance of reform is in its interest: and for that to be the case, two conditions must be met. First, so long as policy dialogue with the Bank (or other lender) continues, *either* (a) the balance of domestic political forces between pro- and anti-reform elements must tilt in favour of the pro-reform elements *or else* (b) the government must be so convinced of the merits of continuing liberalisation – and of its power base[8] – that it is willing to override the advocates of a more controlled economy over a long period. Second, assuming that either (a) or (b) is satisfied during the period of policy dialogue with the Bank, the withdrawal of Bank adjustment finance must not weigh so heavily with the recipient government that, in the absence of this bribe, the continuance of the reform programme no longer appears attractive. It has been contended by a number of writers inside and outside the Bank (for example Krueger, 1974; Bhagwati and Srinivasan, 1982; Lal 1987) that condition (a) will be automatically satisfied through the initial implementation of liberalisation, since the removal of quantitative restrictions on importing, borrowing and agricultural marketing (for example) will put money and political power into the hands of those who benefit from an open market, and in general give all producers an incentive to increase their income by making themselves more competitive rather than by lobbying the government for the reintroduction of controls. On this analysis, the fundamental conflict which, we argued, confronts a recipient government at the beginning of a policy-based lending process – that between foreign resource inflows and the level of internal political support, as in Figure 3.1 – will gradually become less intense and finally melt away. Many of the minus signs of Table 4.7 – representing interest groups negatively affected by liberalisation and in a position to influence the stance of policy – will, in other words, gradually turn into plus signs, and in this way the momentum of structural adjustment can be sustained.

What empirical evidence is there of such processes among World Bank borrower countries in the 1980s? Table 5.8 summarises the evidence from our case-study countries in relation to the three instruments of trade policy, agricultural price and subsidy policy, and interest-rate policy. Whereas there is great variability in experience between countries and between policy instruments, it is apparent that even in those cases where initial implementation of policy reform was significant, there have been a number of cases of policy reversal, particularly in the area of trade policy. In the area of import restrictions there have been policy reversals in all the countries sample except Ghana and Turkey, but the move to a flexible exchange-rate regime has proved sustainable, except in Jamaica and Ecuador. In the area of agricultural prices there has been little fundamental change in policy in the sample countries, as earlier observed, but what has been achieved with the cocoa producer price in Ghana has so far been sustained. Positive real interest rates have so far been achieved in all countries in the sample except Ghana and Ecuador; in the remainder, they had already been achieved by the early 1980s (making it doubtful whether the movement to positive levels should be ascribed to the Bank's pressure) but were reversed in 1984–5 in Jamaica and the Philippines. Among the countries in our sample it is therefore only possible to speak of Turkey, and on a probationary basis Ghana and the Philippines post-Aquino, as states in which a sustained process of reform is under way; it is also notable that certain types of reform, notably exchange-rate and interest-rate reform, proved easier to sustain than others.

How are these variations in sustainability to be explained? The two countries in which a sustained reform effort is to be observed – Turkey and Ghana – were both governed by a technocratic group which was determined to push through a liberalisation programme on terms more or less consistent with what the World Bank was asking for (conditions 1(b) above). In Turkey the government twice demanded, and got, a popular mandate for its reform programme at a general election, an occurrence worthy of remark because it has scarcely been paralleled in any other developing country.[9] How much of the Turkish success was due to the commitment of the government and how much to the support which it got from (for example) export-oriented industrialists may be debated, but we recall that Turkey, uniquely among our case-study countries, was not subjected to an import squeeze during the 1980s. As a consequence much of the potential opposition to liberalisation, which elsewhere was responsible for policy reversals – in particular from influential importers – was bought off. Elsewhere, many of the political changes which in theory ought to have occurred as a consequence of liberalisation – specifically, an increase in the political leverage of export-oriented industrialists, large farmers and non-protected borrowers as import controls, agricultural prices and interest rates were liberalised – failed to occur on any lasting basis, not so much because those groups felt no benefit from liberalisation, but

Table 5.8 Trade policy, agricultural prices and interest rates: preliminary evidence on sustainability of reform

(i) Trade policy

	1980	81	82	83	84	85	86	87	88	89
Kenya										
Real effective exchange rate	−	−	+	−	+	−	−	−	−	−
Quantitative import restrictions	Minor	..	Reversal	..	..	Minor[1]	..	..	Minor	Minor
Ghana										
Real effective exchange rate	+	+	+	−	−	−	−	−	−	−
Quantitative import restrictions	..	..	..	..	..	Minor	..	..	..	..
Philippines										
Real effective exchange rate	+	+	+	−	−	+	−	−	−	−
Quantitative import restrictions	Minor	..	..	Reversal[2]	..	..	Major	Minor	..	Reversal
Turkey										
Real effective exchange rate	−	−	−	−	−	+	−	−	−	..
Quantitative import restrictions	..	Major	..	..	Minor	Minor	..	..	..	..

Thailand									
Real effective exchange rate	+	+	+	−	−	−	−	+	+
Quantitative import restrictions	..	Minor	Minor	Reversal	..	..	..	..	..
Jamaica									
Real effective exchange rate	+	+	−	−	−[3]	+	−	−	−
Quantitative import restrictions	..	Major	Minor	Minor	Reversal	..	..	..	..
Ecuador									
Real effective exchange rate	+	+	+	−	−	−	−	+[4]	+
Quantitative import restrictions	..	..	..	Minor	Minor	..	..	Reversal	..

Sources: For real exchange rates, World Bank (1988), appendix tables at end; for quantitative import restrictions, individual country studies in Volume 2. 'Major' denotes removal or relaxation of restrictions on over 10% of the import bill; 'minor' denotes relaxation or removal of restrictions on under 10% of the import bill; 'reversal' denotes a net increase in quantitative restrictions.

Notes: 1 Tariff cuts also in this year
2 Tariff increases also in this year
3 In spite of Central Bank *revaluation* of currency late in the year
4 Movement to a more restrictive foreign exchange regime in this year

Table 5.8 continued

(ii) Agricultural producer prices (as percentage of export realisation)

	1980	81	82	83	84	85	86	87	88	89
Kenya: coffee	98	86	82	94	77	87	96	94	83	103
maize	110	68	–	78	70	133	154	133	83	79
Malawi: tobacco, flue-cured	46	62	59	44	40	36	52	–	–	–
Ghana: cocoa	–	–	–	22	24	39	50	63	–	–
Ecuador: maize	–	85	92	90	87	91	90	86	92	88

Source: individual country case studies. For all African countries the original source is Lele, 1989, Table 13, p.25.

(iii) Real interest rates (commercial bank lending rates deflated by retail price index)

	1981	82	83	84	85	86	87	88	89
Kenya	8.6	-6.8	4.3	4.3	8.9	10.0	1.3	2.1	8.0
Malawi	6.7	8.7	4.8	-3.5	7.9	5.0	5.6	-12.0	-2.5
Ghana	-97.5	-3.3	-183.9	-18.5	-10.9	-4.6	-14.3	-5.0	..
Thailand	6.3	13.3	13.9	9.5	16.6	15.2	12.5	11.0	5.0
Philippines	..	3.6	3.4	-29.2	-4.2	10.4	4.5	2.7	7.1
Turkey	-1.8	5.2	2.7	10.0	8.6	18.8	11.2	-19.0	..
Jamaica	8.3	6.5	1.4	-11.0	-3.7	7.9	16.4	14.9	7.3
Ecuador	..	..	-13.0	-10.0	-9.8	-11.0	-33.0	-32.4	..

Source: IMF International Financial Statistics, various issues.

because they were unable to translate their common interest into collective action. The complaint of the Bank's Resident Representative in the Philippines, that 'the Philippines Exporters' Association is politically almost silent' (Chapter 12, page 50) could be paralleled for many of the other interest groups who stood to gain from liberalisation; the fact that in many cases these gainers were in a politically ill-favoured ethnic group (Asians in Kenya and Guyana, Lebanese in Ghana) or a geographically scattered occupational group (small cash-crop farmers elsewhere) did not help. It has to be added that the Bank, as discussed in Chapter 4, always explicitly eschewed the strategy of offering financial or other compensation to the losers from reform. The business of compensating the losers and organising the gainers was, until the beginning of the 1990s left to the market to arrange, and generally speaking, the market did not arrange it. Since 1991 the Bank has used 'social funds' open to competitive bidding by entrepreneurs, as a device to mitigate the social costs of adjustment in more than twenty countries.

From this it does not follow, of course, that reform did not occur, only that it had to be carried forward by the impetus of technocrats within government, usually swimming against rather than with the populist tide. Where those technocrats were able to retain power at least within the ministry of finance and central bank, they were often able to initiate a process of reform, *particularly in respect of policy instruments over which they had sole control*, such as the exchange rate and interest rates; the record of both initial implementation and sustainability is much better with these instruments than with others, and there are a number of polities – including Kenya, Jamaica, Thailand and the Philippines – which in the 1980s have experienced 'sustained but partial' liberalisation,[10] in the sense that the policy variables which lay under the thumb of these technocrats have been liberalised, and others not. Only in Turkey does one observe a reform process which was implemented on a broad front, and appears to have gathered popular support as it went. To the doubts which surrounded the permanency of the reform effort elsewhere has been ascribed much of its failure to exert any strong or sustained stimulus on the supply side, in particular on the level of private investment (Rodrik, 1989: 44). We examine these claims in our analysis of the effectiveness of policy-based lending in Part III.

NOTES

1 In the Bank's most recent evaluation of adjustment lending (World Bank 1990, paragraph 1.23) this percentage is raised to 66 per cent.

2 The 'dominated' nature of civil society in Ghana under the Rawlings regime has been well expressed by, among others, Hutchful (1989: 126), who says

State interest in Ghana has been conceived and elaborated to a large degree autonomously of, and in conflict with, not only the popular interests of labour and the peasantry, but with those of external and domestic capital, to which developmentalist rhetoric (and formal investment laws) otherwise pay lip-service.

3 For a first-hand account of this process at work in Thailand, see Chapter 13 below, Appendix C.

4 On early SALs the interval between the disbursement of the first tranche and the arrival of the Bank supervision mission was often very short, for example four months (September 1980 – January 1981) in the case of the first Philippines SAL and two months (June – August 1980) in the case of the Bolivia SAL. When the interval was this short, any slippage by the recipient country was almost bound to go undiscovered, since the recipient would not have had time to implement the reform in question. Now that the interval has lengthened (to about one year on average) this excuse has become less plausible, and the justifications which Departmental Directors have had to invent to secure second tranche releases have become more tortuous.

5 In the one case which appears to depart from this rule – Pakistan – the balance of payments improved so quickly in 1983 as to make follow-on finance, for the time being, unnecessary. Bank finance became necessary again, and was granted, in 1985 and 1986.

6 Relations with the Fund are of particular importance since the Bank's way of cutting off programme finance – as a general rule and certainly in the cases of Bolivia and Guyana here studied – is not to refuse it point-blank but rather to insist that the borrower comply with the conditions of an IMF stand-by before any further adjustment finance is granted. The ability of the Kenya government to defy the Bank's conditionality is spite of its exposed economic position – see Chapter 16 – owes a great deal to its excellent relationship with the Fund in the 1980s.

7 During the phase of policy dialogue with the Bank the 'merits of continuing liberalisation' include, of course, the increased probability that programme finance will be forthcoming from the Bank if such policies are pursued.

8 For cases where governments attempting strong and comprehensive reforms have been voted out of office (in 1988 and 1989 respectively), see within our sample the cases of Jamaica and Ecuador.

9 The World Bank's report on sustainability of *projects* (World Bank, 1985) discusses a number of factors determining the ability of projects to maintain viability after the termination of external donor support. Of these factors two ('adequacy of institutional capacity relative to the magnitude of responsibilities' and 'availability of sufficient finance following the termination of donor support' (World Bank, 1985: 25ff) have equal relevance to the sustainability of policy reform programmes.

10 Within these cases of 'sustained but partial liberalisation' the major achievement was usually the depoliticisation of the exchange rate, for which credit principally belongs with the IMF rather than with the Bank. For further discussion of this division of labour see section 4.3 above.

Part III

ASSESSMENT OF EFFECTIVENESS

6

EVALUATION METHODOLOGY: SIMPLE TABULAR COMPARISONS

6.1   ALTERNATIVE EVALUATION METHODS

We now turn to the second major question which this study tries to answer: to the extent that the policy conditions attached to World Bank programme loans were implemented, what difference did they make to the economies of the countries that received them? By contrast with the relatively sophisticated methods which exist for the appraisal and evaluation of financial transfers in project form, there is no readily available methodology which can be taken off the peg and applied to the *ex post* evaluation of policy-based lending. We shall need to devise our own.

In sequential order, the choices which have to be made are:

1   To identify *criteria* of evaluation − that is, indicators which may reasonably be accepted as measures of the success or failure of that action.
2   Once criteria of evaluation have been chosen, to identify a valid *procedure*, that is, a method which reliably defines the nature and extent of the links between the action being analysed and the criteria defined under 1 and eliminates the influence of extraneous factors.
3   Once the chosen procedure of evaluation has been carried out, to make valid *inferences* from the results, in particular concerning the direction of causation, and concerning the applicability of those results to policy-makers in similar situations.

In what follows we explain the choices we have made. These choices may be represented as forks in a many-branched tree, and Figure 6.1 gives a summary indication of which other branches of this particular tree have been explored and what fruit they have yielded.

Criteria of evaluation

In its various expositions of the rationale for policy-based lending the Bank has made it clear that its fundamental purpose is to improve levels of

187

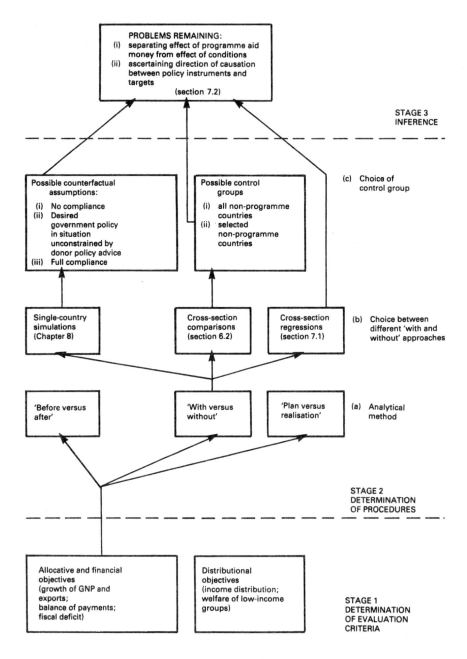

Figure 6.1 Programme lending: the 'tree' of possible evaluation procedures

output, exports, foreign finance and the balance of payments, rather than directly to influence distributional objectives. At the beginning of the Structural Adjustment Lending exercise in 1981, an exposition by a Bank staff member in the Bank/Fund magazine *Finance and Development* defined the purpose of Structural Adjustment Lending as

> to provide quick-disbursing finance to support measures designed to strengthen recipient countries' balance of payments within five to ten years without severely constraining demand in a manner that unnecessarily sets back economic and social development.
>
> (Landell-Mills, 1981: 17)

whereas in 1987, by which time the Bank's policy-based lending activities had broadened a great deal, one of his successors argued that

> the main purpose of Bank sector and structural adjustment loans is to facilitate the adjustment required to achieve sustainable growth and the mobilisation of external financing needed to support a country's adjustment efforts.
>
> (Michalopoulos, 1987: 8)

In the analysis which follows, therefore, there is only incidental discussion, until Chapter 8, of the influence of policy-based lending on income distribution and on the welfare of low-income groups, even though this influence is of fundamental importance. This is simply because we believe it to be fair to judge the Bank's efforts only in relation to the targets which it explicitly set itself. The distributional effects of adjustment (although not explicitly of adjustment *lending*) have in any case been thoroughly treated by Addison and Demery (1988) and by Cornia, Jolly and Stewart (1988). The World Bank's second report on adjustment lending (World Bank 1990) devotes a chapter specifically to the effects of adjustment lending on poverty.

Alternative evaluation methods

Any assessment of what happened to a target variable in a given period is a comparison – between what actually happened and some standard of performance, yardstick or 'control'. In principle, three such yardsticks are available:

1 what was expected to happen during that period (the 'plan target');
2 what happened in a previous period;
3 some estimate of what would have happened in the absence of the influence being assessed.

The plan target is a superficially attractive yardstick because it is chosen by the donor after making due allowance for the possible impact of external

189

events, but it is entirely arbitrary, since the methods by which targets are chosen by donors cannot usually lay claim to be a reasonable forecast of what a programme can be expected to achieve. Often, as in the case of the targets attached to World Bank Structural Adjustment Loans, they are simply guesses (Mosley, 1987; Table 4, and p. 6), and even if they are derived from modelling work such work cannot predict extraneous events bearing on economic outcomes (e.g. trends in the terms of trade or in weather conditions) with any reliability. In such a situation, economic performance which falls short of target during the period of a programme loan may be cited as evidence of poor programme design or implementation when it is the choice of target which is at fault; by the same token, performance during a loan period may exceed targeted performance for reasons which are in no way due to the loan. In other words, the relationship between performance and target tells us very little about the impact of Bank programme assistance, which is the basic thing we are trying to measure.

The 'before versus after' method of evaluation, objective and intuitively attractive though it is, is no better. If a programme loan is granted at time t, and the performance of exports and GDP (say) in time period $t+1$ is much better than in period $t-1$, it is tempting and natural to give the credit to the programme loan. In fact, such a difference may once again be due to any number of extraneous influences (increases in world prices, changes in world demand, improvements in the weather, the end of a war . . .) which had nothing to do with the programme loan under analysis. This problem is particularly serious if one attempts to compare the periods immediately before and after the major wave of programme lending in the early 1980s, which featured two major oil crises, a serious drought in sub-Saharan Africa, a world-wide depression, and wild fluctuations in interest rates. All of these had enormous impact on the variables we have chosen as criteria of evaluation – exports, GDP and the balance of payments – but no connection with programme lending by the Bank or any other agency. In consequence, as Goldstein stresses, 'the before-after approach can be useful to show what happened in programme countries, but not why it happened' (Goldstein, 1986: 3). In the last analysis we must therefore reject both the 'plan versus realisation' and the 'before versus after' approaches to evaluation. This is the second fork in the tree.

The only remaining approach, and the only approach, we would argue, which affords any hope of separating out the influence of programme loans from that of extraneous variables is the 'with versus without' method, in which what actually happened is contrasted with what, it is believed, would have happened in the absence of the programme loan. This is precisely the experimental procedure adopted, for example, by agricultural research stations which estimate the impact of a fertiliser treatment by comparing yields in two fields which are identical except for the level of

190

fertiliser applied (Casley and Lury, 1985: 20–5), or by medical researchers who estimate the effectiveness of a drug by comparing its effects on two samples which are identical in all respects except for the fact that one takes the drug and the other does not. In each case the evaluation hinges on a comparison between a 'treatment group' and a 'control group' which aims to eliminate the influence of extraneous variables by subjecting both groups to the same influences. The difficulty in the present case is that the 'control' consists not of a tangible thing but rather of the hypothetical counter-factual situation which could have been expected to materialise in the absence of programme lending. If this can be estimated with any reliability, then the principal problem associated with the 'plan versus target' and 'before versus after' approaches – namely the inability to control for the influence of non-programme influences on the recipient economy – disappears. In its place, however, we have the problem that the in-the-absence-of-loan situation is not directly observable and can therefore never be known with certainty. Let us persevere, however, and discuss various possible approaches towards the construction of plausible estimates of this hypothetical situation.

We may first of all distinguish between *aggregative* approaches, which examine the effect of programme lending in a number of countries, and *single-country* approaches, which concern themselves with one country case study only. At the aggregative level it is tempting to treat 'non-programme' countries as a control group: for example, in assessing the impact of World Bank Structural Adjustment Lending it would be possible to compare the performance of selected target variables in countries which had received SALs with the performance of those variables in countries which had not received them. This procedure, which one of us has tried out elsewhere (Mosley, 1987: 13), appears to be capable of holding extraneous influences constant as between programme and non-programme countries; but it is subject to at least four serious problems. First, it will give misleading results if the countries which receive programme finance are in any way unrepresentative of developing countries as a whole (for example, it has been suggested that countries which receive SALs have stronger economies than others (Mosley, 1987: 27–8)), since it will ascribe to the programme finance effects which are in fact caused by the intrinsic difference between the two groups of countries. Second, programme aid packages all come with policy conditions attached, but in some countries the degree of compliance with the conditions is far higher than in others, with the consequence that what is being evaluated is in some cases a financial flow plus quite radical changes in economic policy, and in other cases a financial flow only. Third, if the effects of programme finance 'spill over' into countries which have not received it – for example, through trade linkages – then the group of non-programme countries cannot, to the extent that spillovers have occurred, be treated as an uncontaminated control sample. Fourth, different packages of programme finance are increasingly becoming interlinked – for example, no World Bank Structural Adjustment Loan has ever been granted without an IMF stand-by agreement having been previously concluded,[1] and frequently packages of programme aid are contingent on the previous signing of an agreement with the Bank – with the consequence that it is very difficult to prise apart the independent influence of particular injections of finance and the associated policy reforms.

The first two of these problems can be dealt with more or less efficiently by segmenting the sample: that is, by making comparisons only between countries with economies of equivalent strength, and between countries with equivalent levels of slippage, and this is the approach which is adopted in the tabular comparisons conducted later on in this chapter. The fourth problem is more intractable, since as a consequence of the implicit agreement between the Bank and the Fund there is almost no country receiving programme finance from the Bank which has not immediately beforehand received conditional stand-by finance from the Fund. Hence, if the influence of the Bank and the Fund is to be disentangled, it cannot be by simple comparisons of 'programme' and 'non-programme' countries, but rather by regressions which contain both Bank and Fund disbursements as separate independent variables. This approach is attempted in the regression work of Chapter 7, which also considers explicitly, and attempts to hold constant, the influence of 'extraneous' influences on the success of programme lending operations (weather, terms of trade, etc.) by including them as independent variables in the regression equations. The third problem we see as almost insuperable, since there is no economy so closed that it can be categorised as unaffected by the giving of programme finance to other countries, and thus serve as a completely 'clean' control.

In summary, it is possible to extract some useful information from comparisons between programme and non-programme countries, but these comparisons need themselves to be restricted to appropriate samples if variations in slippage and in economic potential are to avoid contaminating the comparison. In the light of these imperfections, it would seem appropriate to supplement aggregative comparisons between programme and non-programme countries with single-country simulations if the 'with and without policy' approach is to be given a fair test. The problem here, of course, is that no ready-made estimate of the without-policy or 'counterfactual' situation is available for any country. Such an estimate has to be constructed from plausible assumptions about what would have happened in a given country in the absence of conditional programme assistance. The limiting cases are, of course, (i) *no adjustment*, i.e. no modification of policy instruments whatever, in spite of the crisis which promoted the programme assistance, and (ii) *full adjustment*, i.e. the recipient would have implemented the full set of policy reforms

192

recommended by the donor even in the absence of conditional programme aid, so that the influence of the aid package is identical with the impact of its cash component. The first of these assumptions, at any rate, seems particularly implausible since the policy of no adjustment to widening fiscal and balance-of-trade deficits would lead rapidly to inability to finance debt, and hence probably to a cessation of future credit; indeed, in the recent recession (1980–4) it has not been practised by any country known to the authors. One counterfactual assumption intermediate between (i) and (ii) is the hypothesis that programme countries, in the absence of programme finance, would have adopted the same economic policies as neighbouring non-programme countries; (for example, that Malawi would have managed its economy between 1981 and 1985 in the same way as Zambia); but this assumption, of course, takes us back into precisely the same problems as the aggregative-comparison approach. The best approach of all, in those countries where the government publicly articulated the economic programme which it would have liked to follow instead of the programme on which the donor insisted, is to use its own 'preferred' programme as the counterfactual;[2] but such an alternative view was not always articulated, and when articulated not always published. In Chapter 8 we present the results of two simulation exercises, one for Malawi and one for Morocco, in which the consequences of hypothetical 'full compliance' with Bank-recommended adjustment policies and hypothetical 'government-desired adjustment policies' are compared with what actually occurred, i.e. the partial compliance with Bank prescriptions which actually took place.

Finally, once statistical results have been obtained by each of these three methods – i.e. statistical comparisons between programme and non-programme countries, regression estimates and individual country simulation exercises – there remains the problem of inference; this is the third stage of the evaluation procedure. The essential problem is that even though any of the three methods proposed may expose a difference between 'with programme' and 'without programme' outcomes, the demonstration of this difference is not sufficient to prove that the programme caused the difference. It may be that the difference caused the programme: as the director of the principal development institute in one of the most successful 'adjusting' countries argues, 'it is not clear in South Korea to what extent liberalisation was responsible for economic growth, and to what extent economic growth produced the political conditions which made liberalisation possible' (Y. C. Park, Director of the Korea Development Institute, in Corbo, Goldstein and Khan, 1987: 96). The nature and direction of causation between programme lending and the variables it is intended to influence is explicitly considered in the concluding section of Chapter 7. The concluding section of Chapter 8 sums up the results, and considers whether it is possible to make a comparison between the 'yield' on programme aid and that on projects.

6.2 'PROGRAMME' AND 'NON-PROGRAMME' COUNTRIES: TABULAR COMPARISONS

In this section we apply the simplest possible version of the 'with and without' method, namely tabular comparisons of programme and non-programme countries. 'Programme countries' are those which have received one or more SALs since 1980 and 'non-programme' countries are a control group who have not received SAL packages.

The criteria of evaluation used are those most often used by the Bank itself, namely, the impact of SAL packages on GDP growth, real export growth, and the balance of payments on current account. Due to lack of data availability we have not been able to evaluate the impact of SALs on the inflow of private foreign finance. This evaluation criterion is, however, explicitly addressed in the regression work undertaken in Chapter 7. Trends in our chosen variables are compared between the SAL group and the non-SAL group in order to assess the impact of both the SAL financial flows and SAL conditionality. Changes in investment and consumption as a percentage of GDP, and in import growth rates, are also analysed for the two sets of countries, in an attempt to ascertain patterns and directions of causation associated with the impact of programme aid.

Selecting the 'with' and 'without' country groups

In all, twenty-five countries received SALs between 1980 and 1987 (Table 6.1). However, due to lack of data availability, the following countries have been excluded from the 'with SAL' group: Central African Republic; Gambia; Guinea; and Mauritius. South Korea has also been excluded due to lack of data on Taiwan, the country originally paired with it as a member of the non-SAL control group.

In selecting countries to form the 'without SAL' control group, a Non-SAL country has been paired with each SAL country. The objective of the pairing is to overcome the first problem associated with the aggregative 'with and without' method of evaluation, namely the possibility that misleading results may arise if SAL countries are in some way unrepresentative of developing countries as a whole. This problem of non-random programme-aid country selection has been shown to exist in the case of countries receiving IMF adjustment packages. In the period immediately prior to the implementation of IMF programmes, recipient countries systematically differed from non-recipients by having, on average, larger balance of payments and current account deficits as a proportion of GNP, lower rates of real output growth, and higher inflation rates (Goldstein, 1986: Table 4). In the following exercise, to ensure that like is being compared with like, countries receiving SALs have been paired with countries which experienced similar levels of GNP per capita and similar

194

Table 6.1 Structural Adjustment Loans approved as of May 1987

| Country | Amounts ($ m) | | | Total | Date of approval by Executive Board | SAL disbursement as % of disbursement-year GDP |
	IBRD	IDA	SFA/SJF[1]			
Bolivia[2]	50.0			50.0	Jun 1980	0.82
Burundi		15.0	16.2/19.3	50.5	May 1986	4.63
Central Afr. Rep		14.0	16.0/ –	30.0	Sep 1986	3.33
Chile I	250.0			250.0	Oct 1985	1.56
Chile II	250.0			250.0	Nov 1986	1.49
Costa Rica	80.0			80.0	Apr 1985	2.10
Côte D'Ivoire I	150.0			150.0	Nov 1981	1.73
Côte D'Ivoire II	250.7			250.7	Jul 1983	3.54
Côte D'Ivoire III	250.0			250.0	Jun 1986	3.47
Gambia I		5.0	11.5/ 4.5	21.0	Aug 1986	NA
Ghana		34.0	81.0/ –	115.0	Apr 1987	NA
Guinea		25.0	17.0/42.2	84.2	Feb 1986	NA
Guyana[2]	14.0	8.0		22.0	Feb 1981	NA
Jamaica I	76.2			76.2	Mar 1982	2.40
Jamaica II	60.2			60.2	Jun 1983	1.92
Jamaica III	55.0			55.0	Nov 1984	2.31
Kenya I		55.0		55.0	Mar 1980	0.92
Kenya II	60.9	70.0		130.9	Jul 1982	2.45
Korea I	250.0			250.0	Dec 1981	0.38
Korea II	300.0			300.0	Nov 1983	0.39
Malawi I	45.0			45.0	Jun 1981	3.17
Malawi II		55.0		55.0	Dec 1983	4.14
Malawi III		30.0	40.0/39.1	109.1	Dec 1985	11.25
Mauritius I	15.0			15.0	Jun 1981	NA
Mauritius II	40.0			40.0	Dec 1983	NA
Nepal		50.0		50.0	Mar 1987	NA
Niger		20.0	40.0/ –	60.0	Feb 1986	2.88
Pakistan[2]	60.0	80.0		140.0	Jun 1982	0.57
Panama I	60.2			60.2	Nov 1983	1.38
Panama II	100.0			100.0	Dec 1986	1.95
Philippines I	200.0			200.0	Sep 1980	0.56
Philippines II	302.3			302.3	Apr 1983	0.87
Senegal[2]	30.0	30.0		60.0	Dec 1980	2.26
Senegal		20.0	44.0/ 7.0	71.0	Feb 1986	1.90
Thailand I	150.0			150.0	Mar 1982	0.41
Thailand II	175.5			175.5	Mar 1983	0.43
Togo I		40.0		40.0	May 1983	5.56
Togo II		27.8	10.0/30.0	67.8	May 1985	9.69
Turkey I	200.0			275.0	Mar 1980	0.51
& supplement	75.0				Nov 1980	
Turkey II	300.0			300.0	May 1981	0.56
Turkey III	304.8			304.8	May 1982	0.61
Turkey IV	300.8			300.8	Jun 1983	0.63
Turkey V	376.0			376.0	Jun 1984	0.79
Yugoslavia	275.0			275.0	Jun 1983	0.59
					Group average	2.27
					Standard deviation	2.39

Notes: 1 Special Facility for Africa (SFA) and Special Joint Financing (SJF).
2 Programme discontinued.

195

GDP growth rates in the pre-SAL period. The pairing also tries, as far as possible, to match countries with similar economic structures, taking into consideration factors such as the level of industrialisation, the prevalence of commercial and subsistence agriculture, the degree of export concentration and the extent of state economic activity. In addition, in order to try to eliminate the effects of a major extraneous factor, in the form of changes in world market prices, countries have also been paired on the basis of having experienced similar trends in their terms of trade during both the pre-SAL and the SAL period.

Other possible pairing criteria, such as the level of non-SAL programme aid, the severity of internal and external imbalance in the pre-SAL period, strength of the political regime, and the impact of extraneous factors such as weather, have not been used, since the larger the number of criteria, the harder it becomes to find an acceptable country to pair with each SAL country. Hence these factors are not given any consideration in the crude aggregative statistical comparisons made between the SAL group and the non-SAL control group. However, some of them are explicitly contained in the regression analysis carried out in Chapter 7 and in the single country modelling work carried out in Chapter 8.

Table 6.2 shows the countries in the SAL group and those chosen to form the non-SAL control group, along with the terms of trade and GNP growth rate basis for the pairing. The first country in each pair (bold) is the SAL country and that immediately beneath it is the paired non-SAL country selected as a member of the control group.

Even using the limited criteria of terms of trade, GNP per capita, and GDP growth rates, no pairing is perfect. In particular, the pairings of Bolivia and Colombia, Costa Rica and Honduras, Côte d'Ivoire and Cameroon, Malawi and Zimbabwe and Philippines and Indonesia, are far from perfect, even though, using the chosen criteria, they are the best available. However, whilst some countries chosen to form the non-SAL control group (Colombia, Cameroon, Indonesia) had higher GDP growth rates in the pre-SAL period than the SAL country with which they are paired, others (Honduras, Zimbabwe) had lower growth rates than their SAL counterparts. Likewise, comparing trends in the terms of trade between members of a 'pair', the noticeably imperfect pairings are not systematically imperfect: some of the non-SAL countries faced more favourable terms of trade than their SAL counterpart country, others less favourable terms of trade. Hence, in the aggregative statistical comparisons between the SAL group and the non-SAL group which will be used to assess the impact of SALs, the effects of the presence of imperfectly paired countries in the non-SAL control group will, to some extent, cancel out.

Despite the above caveats, the pairing methodology used to construct a non-SAL control group is certainly an advance over the cruder method of simply comparing the economic record of SAL countries with that of the

Table 6.2 Comparison of SAL group and non-SAL control group countries

Country pairs	Change in terms of trade (%pa) 1975–81	Change in terms of trade (%pa) 1981–6	1976 GNP per capita (US $)	1981 GNP per capita (US $)	Real GDP per capita growth rate 1970–81 (%pa)
BOLIVIA*	7.9	−8.0	390	600	1.7
COLOMBIA*	0.6	3.7	630	1380	3.6
BURUNDI	NA	NA	120	230	1.3
RWANDA	−0.1	−4.3	110	250	1.6
CHILE	−7.4	−4.4	1040	2560	0.3
PERU	−6.4	−5.5	800	1170	0.5
COSTA RICA	−3.3	−0.5	1040	1430	2.4
HONDURAS	−5.7	−1.2	390	600	0.9
C.D'IVOIRE	−4.1	−1.4	610	1200	1.1
CAMEROON	−1.4	−1.4	290	880	4.0
GHANA	−2.2	−5.0	560	400	−3.2
ZAMBIA*	−5.6	−4.7	440	600	−2.6
GUYANA	−8.2	−4.0	NA	720	0.5
EL SALVADOR	−5.2	−3.1	490	650	0.2
JAMAICA	−3.6	−2.6	1070	1180	−2.6
NICARAGUA	−6.0	−2.9	750	860	−3.0
KENYA	−3.1	−1.1	240	420	2.1
TANZANIA	−0.9	NA	180	280	0.8
MALAWI	−4.3	0.8	140	200	2.5
ZIMBABWE	−7.1	NA	550	870	−1.4
NEPAL	NA	NA	120	150	−0.5
BURMA	3.4	−4.2	120	190	2.6
NIGER	−3.1	−3.0	160	330	−0.1
MAURITANIA	−6.0	−1.3	340	460	−0.6
PAKISTAN	−5.6	−2.0	170	350	1.9
EGYPT	−2.9	−4.6	280	650	4.9
PANAMA	−2.9	−2.5	1310	1910	2.2
GUATEMALA	−5.6	−1.6	630	1140	2.3
PHILIPPINES	−4.6	−2.0	410	790	3.4
INDONESIA*	6.9	−0.7	240	530	5.3

Table 6.2   continued

Country pairs	Change in terms of trade (%pa) 1975–81	Change in terms of trade (%pa) 1981–6	1976 GNP per capita (US $)	1981 GNP per capita (US $)	Real GDP per capita growth rate 1970–81 (%pa)
SENEGAL	−7.8	0.3	390	430	−0.7
SIERRA LEONE	−5.1	0.3	200	320	−0.8
THAILAND	−7.0	−1.9	380	770	4.6
MALAYSIA	−0.1	−6.3	860	1840	5.2
TOGO	−7.0	−3.5	260	380	0.7
BENIN	−4.6	−1.5	130	320	0.6
TURKEY	−6.6	NA	990	1540	2.6
GREECE	−2.4	NA	2590	4420	3.3
YUGOSLAVIA	−0.1	−0.6	1680	2790	4.9
HUNGARY*	NA	NA	2280	2090	4.6

Sources: Terms of trade 1975–81: World Bank, *World Tables* 3rd ed., Vol. 1, Economic Data Sheet 1
Terms of trade 1981–6, UNCTAD, *Handbook of International Trade and Development Statistics* 1987
1976 GNP per capita, World Bank, *World Development Report 1976*, Annex, Table 1
1981 GNP per capita, *ibid.*, Economic Data Sheet 2
1970–81 GDP per capita growth rate, *ibid.*, Comparative Economic Data Table 1

Note: Within each country pair the first country (in **bold** type) is a SAL recipient and the second is not. The non-SAL countries marked * did, however, receive other programme loans from the Bank (Sector Adjustment Loans, Trade Development Loans, etc.) during the period under review.

non-oil LDC group as a whole and attributing any difference in performance to the impact of SALs (Mosley, 1987; World Bank, 1986). Not only does the non-oil LDC group contain the group which received SALs within itself as a subset, but the methodology also makes no allowance for the possibly unrepresentative nature of SAL countries.

The comparative performance of annual average real GDP growth rates for the SAL group and the non-SAL control group is given in Table 6.3. This table provides an example of the type of data-set and aggregation procedure used to derive annual average values for the target variables used in the evaluation over different periods of time for the two groups of countries. The results for variables other than GDP growth rates are reported in the summary Table 6.4.[3] Taking 1976–9 as the pre-SAL period and 1980–6 as the SAL period, Table 6.3 shows that for both groups of countries annual average GDP growth rates fell significantly during the latter period. This is hardly surprising since the period was characterised by the effects of a second oil price shock, world economic recession, declining commodity prices, rising interest rates and severe drought in sub-Saharan Africa. However, given that programme aid in the form of SALs was introduced as a response to the effects caused by the above changes in the international economic environment, one would expect the decline in GDP growth rates to be less severe in the case of countries receiving SALs. Surprisingly, Table 6.3 shows the opposite results. Annual average GDP growth rates for the SAL countries fell from 4.5 per cent in the 1976–9 period to 2.0 per cent in the 1980–6 period, i.e. a growth rate decline of 56 per cent. By contrast, the annual average growth rates for the non-SAL control group fell from 3.8 per cent in the 1976–9 period to 2.7 per cent in the 1980–6 period, i.e. a decline of 28 per cent.

In principle, this problem could be due to bias in the selection of the sample, and in particular to the possibility that SAL countries had inherently weaker economies than their Non-SAL counterparts. In fact, the reverse is the case. The control group had an annual average GDP growth rate of 3.8 per cent in the pre-SAL period by comparison with 4.5 per cent for the SAL countries, a gap which reflects the degree of imperfection in the pairing methodology.

Nor is it likely that the better GDP performance of the non-SAL control group can be explained by the failure of a number of SAL countries to implement the prescribed conditions, since even in those SAL countries where compliance with SAL conditionality is minimal one would expect that the SAL financial injection itself would improve a country's GDP growth rate in contrast to the paired non-SAL country. Indeed, on average, SAL disbursements have accounted for over 2 per cent of the recipient country's GDP in the year of disbursement, as shown in Table 6.1.

However, it may be that the results are queered by a problem mentioned in the introduction, namely the existence of IMF arrangements in all countries receiving SALs. It is possible that the series of Fund programmes which were implemented in many countries receiving SALs resulted in a succession of deflationary effects, causing an adverse medium-term impact on GDP growth. The possibility that stabilisation effects more than outweighed the structural adjustment influence on medium-term GDP growth rates will be examined further in the regression work undertaken in Chapter 7.

In order to explore the effects of this second problem further, the SAL group has been disaggregated by isolating those SAL countries with low levels of slippage on SAL policy conditions. The countries which comprise the low slippage SAL group are: Chile; Côte d'Ivoire; Ghana; Jamaica; Malawi; Thailand; Togo; and Turkey.[4] The countries paired with these low slippage SAL countries are: Peru; Cameroon; Zambia; Nicaragua; Zimbabwe; Malaysia; Benin; and Greece, and they are used as the non-SAL low slippage control group. Comparing the low slippage SAL group with the associated control group provides an even more alarming result. Annual

Table 6.3 'Programme' and 'non-programme' countries: Real GDP growth rates (% per annum)

SAL countries	1976	1977	1978	1979	1980	1981	1982	1983	1984	1985	1986	1976–9	1980–6
BOLIVIA	6.8	3.5	2.8	1.5	−1.5	0.4	−2.8	−6.8	−0.9	−1.7	−2.9	3.6	−2.2
BURUNDI	8.2	7.0	9.1	1.9	3.3	10.3	−2.7	1.9	3.1	4.1	4.9	6.5	3.4
CHILE	4.1	8.3	6.0	8.5	7.8	5.5	−13.1	−0.5	6.0	2.4	5.4	6.7	1.9
COSTA RICA	5.5	8.9	5.7	4.3	0.8	−2.3	−7.3	2.7	7.9	0.9	4.4	6.1	1.0
C.D. 'IVOIRE	12.0	8.6	10.3	4.2	12.2	2.7	1.9	−3.5	−2.4	5.9	3.7	8.7	2.9
GHANA	−5.7	1.2	1.0	1.5	0.6	−2.9	−6.5	−4.5	8.7	5.4	4.3	−0.5	0.7
GUYANA	2.9	0.0	0.0	4.0	2.0	4.5	−10.8	−10.3	5.8	1.8	1.5	1.7	−0.7
JAMAICA	−6.7	−4.0	0.0	−1.7	−5.8	2.5	−0.2	1.2	0.0	−5.4	2.2	−3.1	−0.7
KENYA	5.1	9.2	6.7	3.5	4.8	2.9	2.5	3.2	0.9	4.1	4.0	6.1	3.2
MALAWI	4.1	5.9	7.2	5.6	0.6	−6.2	2.5	3.8	4.3	5.8	−1.1	5.7	1.3
NEPAL	4.4	3.2	3.3	2.4	−2.3	8.3.	3.8	−3.0	7.8	3.0	4.0	3.3	3.0
NIGER	17.7	6.5	10.0	4.7	4.8	1.2	−1.2	−1.8	−14.7	5.8	6.5	9.7	0.0
PAKISTAN	3.6	7.0	5.9	6.0	8.8	7.0	6.2	6.4	5.3	8.0	7.5	5.6	7.0
PANAMA	−0.3	3.4	2.7	4.9	15.1	4.2	4.9	−0.2	−0.4	4.1	3.0	2.6	4.3
PHILIPPINES	7.5	6.1	6.3	5.8	5.3	3.8	2.9	1.1	−6.3	−4.6	1.1	6.4	0.4
SENEGAL	7.3	0.7	−9.1	11.0	−3.1	−1.2	15.4	2.2	−4.0	3.8	4.5	2.4	2.5
THAILAND	9.8	5.8	8.4	6.6	5.8	6.3	4.1	5.9	5.5	3.2	3.5	7.6	4.9
TOGO	0.4	−4.2	5.8	3.6	14.5	−3.4	−3.3	−5.7	0.7	5.0	3.1	1.4	1.5
TURKEY	8.6	4.4	3.3	1.0	−0.7	4.4	5.0	3.7	5.7	5.1	8.2	4.3	4.4
YUGOSLAVIA	3.8	8.0	7.1	6.9	2.4	1.3	0.6	−1.1	1.8	1.0	3.4	6.4	1.3
SAL GROUP AVERAGE												4.5	2.0
STANDARD DEVIATION												3.1	2.2
LOW SLIPPAGE SAL GROUP, AVERAGE												3.8	2.1
STANDARD DEVIATION												4.2	1.9

Note: The growth rates are annual average growth rates of real GDP at constant market prices
Source: UNCTAD, *Handbook of International Trade and Development Statistics* 1981 and 1987, Table 6.2

average GDP growth rates for the low slippage SAL countries fell from 3.8 per cent in the 1976–9 period to 2.1 per cent in the 1980–6 period. Although this decline is less dramatic than that for the SAL country group as a whole, it contrasts very unfavourably with the annual average GDP growth rates for the non-SAL low slippage control group, which *increased* from 2.3 per cent in the 1976–9 period to 3.4 per cent in the 1980–6 period. The conclusion which must be drawn from the above analysis is that, despite having a stronger growth record in the latter half of the 1970s, and despite receiving programme aid, the SAL group of countries have performed significantly worse than their non-SAL counterparts, in terms of the GDP growth rate criteria, during the 1980s, i.e. the period when SALs were in place. In addition, for those SAL countries in which compliance with SAL policy conditionality was high, the performance of the GDP growth rate variable was even more unfavourable than performance in the relevant control group. To the best of the authors' knowledge, these results contradict those of other published exercises which use the aggregative 'with and without' method to evaluate the impact of

Non-SAL countries	1976	1977	1978	1979	1980	1981	1982	1983	1984	1985	1986	1976-9	1980-6
COLOMBIA	4.6	4.9	8.8	5.3	4.1	2.3	1.0	1.9	3.8	3.1	5.1	5.9	3.0
RWANDA	7.8	5.2	3.0	4.2	10.2	8.8	1.7	0.3	-6.0	7.5	4.9	5.0	3.9
PERU	2.0	0.0	-0.7	3.5	2.9	3.0	0.3	-11.8	4.7	2.5	8.0	1.2	1.3
HONDURAS	4.5	7.0	7.9	5.1	2.7	1.2	-1.8	-0.2	2.3	1.8	1.8	6.1	1.1
CAMEROON	6.2	4.9	5.5	4.3	11.2	15.5	7.8	6.9	7.6	6.9	5.3	2.2	8.7
ZAMBIA	8.3	-4.4	0.5	6.9	3.1	6.2	-2.8	-2.0	-0.4	1.5	0.5	2.8	0.8
EL SALVADOR	4.0	5.8	4.4	-3.1	-8.7	-8.3	-5.7	0.6	2.3	1.8	0.9	2.7	-2.4
NICARAGUA	5.0	6.3	-7.2	-24.8	10.0	5.3	-0.8	4.6	-1.6	-4.1	-0.4	-5.1	1.8
TANZANIA	6.4	6.5	5.6	3.0	3.3	-0.8	1.8	-2.0	3.2	2.3	3.8	5.3	1.6
ZIMBABWE	-1.6	-7.3	-3.6	1.5	6.0	15.8	-0.6	1.7	0.5	5.0	1.7	-2.7	4.3
BURMA	4.2	6.1	6.0	5.6	7.9	6.4	5.6	4.4	5.6	4.3	3.7	5.4	5.4
MAURITANIA	5.1	-2.0	-1.4	3.0	4.0	3.8	-2.1	6.5	0.3	0.0	4.9	1.1	2.4
EGYPT	8.0	8.8	8.0	8.6	14.3	6.7	6.0	5.2	5.2	1.6	-1.5	8.3	5.3
GUATEMALA	7.4	7.8	5.5	5.0	3.7	0.7	-3.4	-2.7	0.0	-0.6	0.2	6.4	-0.3
INDONESIA	6.9	7.4	7.2	6.0	9.9	7.9	2.2	4.2	6.2	1.9	3.2	6.8	5.0
SIERRA LEONE	1.4	0.3	1.7	0.8	3.1	5.5	4.9	-1.8	0.3	0.0	-0.3	1.0	1.6
MALAYSIA	11.1	7.6	7.6	8.5	7.4	6.9	6.0	6.4	7.9	-1.1	1.1	8.7	4.9
BENIN	3.4	2.1	5.5	4.1	6.5	9.0	6.8	-2.0	2.3	6.6	0.0	3.7	4.1
GREECE	6.5	3.4	6.2	3.8	1.8	0.0	0.4	0.4	2.8	3.0	1.3	4.9	1.3
HUNGARY	3.0	8.2	4.5	1.5	-0.9	2.5	2.6	0.3	2.5	-1.4	0.5	4.3	0.8
NON-SAL CONTROL GROUP AVERAGE												3.8	2.7
STANDARD DEVIATION												3.4	2.5
CONTROL GROUP FOR 'LOW SLIPPAGE' COUNTRIES, AVERAGE												2.3	3.4
STANDARD DEVIATION												4.5	2.6

Note: The growth rates are annual average growth rates of real GDP at constant market prices
Source: UNCTAD, *Handbook of International Trade and Development Statistics* 1981 and 1987, Table 6.2

programme aid in the form of SALs (Mosley, 1987; World Bank, 1986). Such studies, however, have used a cruder methodology which simply compares the performance of the SAL group of countries with that of all non-oil LDCs, indicating that misleading results may be obtained by the failure to construct an accurate control group.[5]

In order to investigate the channels through which SAL financing and conditionality may affect GDP, we now proceed to examine trends in the various components of national income – consumption, investment, exports, import and the balance of payments in Table 6.4. The table shows, first, that for the SAL countries consumption as a percentage of GDP increased from an annual average of 82.5 per cent in the 1976–9 period to 85.2 per cent in the 1980–6 period. However, for the non-SAL control group the increase was virtually identical over the same period – 80.8 per cent in 1976–9 to 84.2 per cent in 1980–6. Taking 1982–6 to define the SAL period, and excluding late SAL recipients from the SAL group, does not change the result. Consumption as a percentage of GDP increased by a similar magnitude for both the SAL and the non-SAL groups of countries.

201

Likewise, the experience of the low slippage SAL group and the relevant control group is much the same as for the SAL group as a whole. In short, consumption as a percentage of GDP increased slightly in the 1980s (with the exception of the non-SAL low slippage control group in the 1982–6 period). But since the trend affected both SAL and non-SAL countries equally, the hypothesis that it was the availability of SAL financing which enabled SAL countries to sustain their increased consumption expenditure finds little support.

Table 6.4 also shows trends in investment as a percentage of GDP. For the SAL group as a whole investment's share in GDP fell from an annual average of 24 per cent in 1976–9 to 20 per cent in 1980–6, a decline of 17 per cent. For the non-SAL control group, it fell from 20.7 per cent in 1976–9 to 19.9 per cent in 1980–6, i.e. a decline of 4 per cent. For the periods 1976–81 and 1982–6, the SAL group's share of investment in GDP fell from 27.1 per cent to 19.3 per cent, i.e. a decline of 29 per cent, whilst for the non-SAL control group the corresponding fall was from 21.1 per cent to 20.5 per cent, i.e. a decline of 2.5 per cent. The above results indicate that although investment as a share of GDP fell for all countries, the decline was much more severe for SAL countries, particularly when 1982–6 is defined as the SAL period. This finding is consistent with a number of macro-studies on the impact of aid, the results of which show a negative correlation between aid and savings as a share of GNP (Papanek, 1972; Mosley, 1980).

Confining the comparison of investment shares to SAL countries with low slippage on policy conditions, the result is even more unfavourable. Between 1976–9 and 1980–6, investment as a share of GDP fell from an annual average of 21.6 per cent to 17.2 per cent for low slippage SAL countries, i.e. a decline of 20 per cent, whilst for the control group the share of investment in GDP actually rose from 19.8 per cent to 22.0 per cent, i.e. an increase of 11 per cent. If 1982–6 is defined as the SAL period, investment as a share of GDP in the low slippage SAL countries fell from 27.8 per cent in 1976–81 to 19.2 per cent in 1982–6, i.e. a decline of 31 per cent, whilst for the non-SAL low slippage control group it rose from 22.0 per cent to 25.2 per cent, i.e. an increase of 15 per cent.

Our results show that during the 1980s the share of investment in GDP fell dramatically in those countries receiving SALs, with this experience contrasting very unfavourably with trends in the non-SAL control group.

Clearly, this could be coincidence. But, first, it is significant that the investment decline in the countries which received SALs was not only more serious than that in the control group, but was most serious in the low-slippage group – i.e. those countries which conscientiously implemented the reforms associated with SAL packages. Second, this decline became most apparent during the period after 1982 – when the worst of the recession was over and the adjustment lending phase had moved into full

Table 6.4 Aggregate comparison of 'SAL country' and 'non-SAL country' macro variables (bracketed figures = standard deviations)

	1976–9	1980–6	1976–81	1982–6
CONSUMPTION AS % OF GDP				
SAL country group average	82.5	85.2	81.9	85.7
	(7.0)	(6.8)	(7.6)	(5.8)
Low slippage SAL country group average	81.4	85.1	77.4	83.0
	(7.9)	(5.9)	(3.2)	(3.9)
Non-SAL country group average	80.8	84.2	81.8	84.4
	(6.4)	(9.2)	(7.7)	(11.4)
Low slippage non-SAL country group average	77.8	79.3	76.9	75.9
	(6.9)	(7.1)	(8.2)	(7.9)
INVESTMENT AS % OF GDP				
SAL country group average	24.0*	20.0	27.1*	19.3
	(7.0)	(6.3)	(3.6)	(4.0)
Low slippage SAL country group average	21.6	17.2*	27.8*	19.2
	(9.8)	(7.1)	(1.9)	(2.9)
Non-SAL country group average	20.7	19.9	21.1	20.5
	(3.6)	(5.8)	(3.7)	(7.3)
Low slippage non-SAL country group average	19.8	22.0	22.0	25.2
	(4.8)	(6.3)	(6.0)	(6.8)
BALANCE OF PAYMENTS CURRENT ACCOUNT AS % GDP				
SAL country group average	−6.5	−6.1*	−7.2*	−4.8*
	(2.8)	(4.1)	(2.6)	(4.6)
Low slippage SAL country group average	−5.0*	−6.2*	−7.1*	−6.0*
	(3.1)	(3.5)	(3.1)	(3.7)
Non-SAL country group average	−5.4	−8.7	−4.7	−6.7
	(6.7)	(7.1)	(4.4)	(5.5)
Low slippage non-SAL country group average	−2.3	−9.5	−4.1	−10.2
	(3.5)	(6.7)	(3.2)	(8.0)
REAL EXPORT GROWTH RATES				
SAL country group average	14.9*	4.9*	12.9	−0.4
	(11.1)	(8.2)	(7.9)	(6.2)
Low slippage SAL country group average	14.9*	7.9*	15.2	1.9
	(8.8)	(9.7)	(7.1)	(6.5)

Table 6.4 continued

	1976–9	1980–6	1976–81	1982–6
Non-SAL country group average	19.0	0.2	13.4	−1.3
	(9.7)	(7.1)	(5.5)	(7.5)
Low slippage non-SAL country group average	20.4	−2.6	13.5	−1.1
	(8.5)	(7.0)	(5.8	(7.3)
REAL IMPORT GROWTH RATES				
*SAL country group average	14.8*	1.8*	11.7*	−4.0
	(10.0)	(7.2)	(4.8)	(5.1)
Low slippage SAL country group average	14.8*	2.4*	12.1*	−4.3*
	(11.8)	(10.8)	(5.6)	(6.0)
Non-SAL country group average	11.0	3.4	15.6	−3.4
	(9.2)	(6.9)	(7.5)	(7.0)
Low slippage non-SAL country group average	7.7	5.7	17.6	−1.4
	(11.1)	(5.5)	(5.6)	(5.8)

Notes: Real export and import growth rates are for current US $ values.
* Difference between SAL and non SAL group means (t-statistic) significant at 5% level.

Sources: IMF, *International Financial Statistics*, 1987 Yearbook, series 96 Fr and 96 er and country tables; IBRD, *World Development Report*, 1978–88, Appendix tables 1 and 3; UNCTAD, *Handbook of International Trade and Development Statistics* 1981 and 1987, Tables 1.5 and 1.6.

swing, which suggests that what we see is neither a statistical freak nor a reflection of differences in the (IMF-inspired) *stabilisation* packages implemented during the recession, but a genuine reflection of the influence of World Bank adjustment lending as such.

World-wide, the decline in investment in countries which are poor and debt-distressed, for example sub-Saharan Africa, where the ratio of investment to GDP declined from 21.4 per cent in 1975–80 to 15.1 per cent in 1986–7 (World Bank, 1989c: Table 8.3) has greatly preoccupied the Bank as it seeks to move from a decade of 'adjustment' to a decade of 'sustainable growth'. But that this decline should be most serious precisely in those countries which are making most effort to set their house in order under its tutelage was clearly not an effect which it intended or desired. The effect is one to which we shall return after we have used alternative methodologies in the next two chapters to verify and interpret this initial finding. But at this stage we may set out some hypotheses concerning why it may have happened. These are:

1 *'Expenditure switching'*: Aid flows – as documented in Chapters 1 and 2

– were partly switched during the 1980s from *project aid*, which was directly linked to specific investments, to *programme aid* – including the World Bank's SALs and SECALs – which was provided for general import support according to the recipient country's preference. This gave recipient countries freedom, if they chose, to spend programme aid flows directly on imports of consumption goods, a freedom which had not previously existed.

2   *Compression of the development budget*:   All countries receiving SALs were required, as a prior condition, to conclude stand-by agreements with the Fund, which were invariably themselves conditional on measures to reduce the budget deficit. In principle, this can be done in three ways. But all measures to increase revenue – taxes, fees, user charges – take a long time to increase their yield, and measures to cut the government *recurrent* budget are politically most unpopular, since they involve either compulsory redundancies in the public sector or reductions in subsidies which may rapidly cause riots. This leaves the government *development* budget, which consists of *plans* to spend money on equipment and maintenance and hence can be altered in a manner which, in the short term, is both quick and politically invisible. Hence those countries which have chosen the path of strong economic reform in the 1980s have almost invariably done so by the route of cuts in government development spending which were out of proportion to the size of the overall macroeconomic adjustment[6] (Hicks and Kubisch, 1984; Mosley and Smith, 1989; see also Table 4.3).

3   *Private-sector knock-on effects*: It was hoped by the Bank in the early 1980s (e.g. Michalopoulos, 1987) that measures of macroeconomic adjustment, and specifically a reduction of the government's claim on aggregate resources, would stimulate private investment through two channels: in the first place, a reduction in aggregate demand would lower interest rates and thus stimulate domestic private investment (the so-called 'crowding-in' effect), and second, the award of the Bank/Fund seal of approval to those governments which concluded stand-by and SAL agreements would stimulate the confidence of foreign banks and private investors and bring back to these countries funds which they had repatriated during the debt crisis of the early 1980s. But although these mechanisms have been operative in more prosperous developing countries (e.g. Turkey, Thailand, South Korea: for the first two see Chapters 11 and 13) they have apparently been inoperative in poorer countries. In Ghana, Kenya, Jamaica and the Philippines, for example (see Volume 2, Chapters 12, 14, 16 and 17) reform has been carried out, and foreign investment has not revived. In these cases, very probably, a Keynesian mechanism, by which the decline in public-sector expenditure lowers aggregate domestic demand and the demand for private-sector output, appears to dominate any effects operating

through the interest rate (Taylor, 1988: 51). In addition, Rodrik (1988) and the World Bank's most recent report on adjustment lending (World Bank 1990) have suggested that uncertainty in the minds of domestic and foreign investors concerning whether reforms will be *sustained* – which the analysis of Chapter 5 suggests is well founded – may deter those investors from any immediate supportive response to a Fund – or Bank-inspired reform programme. Hence, in poorer countries, the net impact of reform on the private sector is to depress investment.

We shall return to the macro-effects of structural adjustment, and the effect on investment in particular, in Chapters 7 and 8. At this stage we simply note an implication of the decline of investment rates in many adjusting countries, which is that it may make the two main planks of a macroeconomic adjustment programme, namely, expenditure reduction and expenditure switching, mutually incompatible. These two planks were succinctly outlined in the introduction to the Bank's 1988 review of adjustment lending:

> Two types of policy response, both labelled adjustment, were called for. The first was stabilisation – managed reductions in expenditure to bring about an orderly adjustment of domestic demand to the reduced level of external resources. The second was structural adjustment – changes in relative prices and institutions designed to make the economy more efficient, more flexible, and better able to use resources and thereby to engineer sustainable long-term growth.
>
> (World Bank, 1988: 1)

When the burden of stabilisation, in the form of expenditure reduction, falls excessively on investment, the growth-enhancing objectives of expenditure switching, under the auspices of a Bank structural adjustment package, are often neutralised: for example, the elasticity of supply of industrial and, in particular, agricultural output to the relative price changes implemented through the medium of a SAL agreement may be reduced by the effect of prior public expenditure cuts on the infrastructure of transport links, institutional credit, and small-farmer services. In view of the disappointing GDP growth rate performance in many SAL countries, one is forced to conclude that an excessive part of the burden of expenditure reduction has indeed fallen on investment cut-backs.

Turning to the external account, Table 6.4 also shows trends in the annual average balance of payments on current account as a percentage of GDP. For the SAL group as a whole the current account deficit as a percentage of GDP remained fairly constant between the 1976–9 and 1980–6 periods, falling from 6.5 per cent to 6.1 per cent. By contrast, for the non-SAL control group, the deficit deteriorated quite sharply between the two periods, rising from 5.4 to 8.7 per cent. When 1982–6 is defined as the SAL period, the SAL country current account deficit as a percentage of GDP improved from 7.2 per cent in 1976–81 to 4.8 per cent in 1982–6, whilst for the non-SAL control group it rose from 4.7 to 6.7 per cent. If the analysis is confined to countries with low slippage on SAL conditionality, the comparison is even more favourable to SAL recipients. Between 1976–9 and 1980–6, the annual average current account deficit as a percentage of GDP for low slippage SAL countries increased slightly from −5.0 to −6.2 per cent, whilst for the non-SAL low slippage control group it increased sharply from −2.3 to −9.5 per cent. With 1982–6 defined as the SAL period, the low slippage SAL group deficit as a percentage of GDP fell from −7.1 per cent in 1976–81 to −6.0 per cent in 1982–6, whilst for the non-SAL low slippage control group it increased sharply from −4.1 to −10.2 per cent.

The above results indicate that, regardless of how the SAL period is defined, countries receiving SAL packages experienced considerably more favourable trends in their current account deficits compared to the non-SAL control groups. In addition, two further pieces of evidence lend support to the conclusion that this favourable relative current account performance was due to SAL policy conditionality:

1 The favourable performance of the SAL countries relative to the relevant control group is more marked when 1982–6, rather than 1980–6, is defined as the SAL period. This is to be expected if the improvement was brought about by policy conditions aimed at stimulating export production and curbing imports, where a lag between implementation and effect can be expected to exist.
2 The favourable current account performance, relative to the relevant control group, is most marked for those SAL countries in which compliance with SAL policy conditionality was greatest, i.e. the low-slippage SAL countries.

However, it should again be noted that we have not been able to isolate the SAL effect from the possible effects of IMF stabilisation packages, or from the programme lending activities of bilateral donors. Hence, it is possible that part of the favourable current account performance observed in SAL countries is due to the lending activities of other agencies.

A key question which arises from the above findings regarding balance-of-payments trends concerns the channels through which the favourable SAL country current account performance was brought about. Was it, for example, due to successful stimulation of the export side of the economy, or was it predominantly due to a curbing of imports − with possibly adverse effects on domestic production activities which use imported inputs and hence on investment and growth? If the latter, this might help to explain the disappointing investment trends and GDP growth rate performance in the SAL countries.

Table 6.4 shows annual average trends in real export and real import growth rates. Between 1976–9 and 1980–6, the average export growth rate in the SAL group fell from 14.9 to 4.9 per cent, i.e. a decline of 67 per cent. For the non-SAL control group the corresponding fall was from 19.0 to 0.2 per cent, i.e. a decline of 99 per cent. If 1982–6 is defined as the SAL period, real export growth rates for SAL countries fell from 12.9 per cent in 1976–81 to −0.4 per cent in 1982–6, i.e. a decline of 103 per cent, whilst for the non-SAL countries the corresponding fall was from 13.4 per cent to −1.3 per cent, i.e. a decline of 110 per cent. Confining the comparison to low slippage SAL countries, a similar pattern emerges, namely, the decline in real export growth rates is less severe for the SAL group than the non-SAL group both in the 1980–6 and the 1982–6 periods.

The above trends in annual average real export growth rates show that both the SAL and the non-SAL countries experienced a decline in their export growth rates during the 1980s. This is not surprising, given that the period was characterised by world recession and declining commodity prices. However, in the SAL group of countries, the decline in growth rates was significantly less severe than that experienced by the non-SAL control group, suggesting that SAL conditionality helped to stem what would otherwise have been a much more marked deterioration in export performance.

Regarding import growth rates, for the SAL group as a whole, the import growth rate fell from 14.8 per cent in 1976–9 to 1.8 per cent in 1980–6, i.e. a decline of 88 per cent, whilst for the non-SAL control group, it fell from 11.0 to 3.4 per cent, i.e. a decline of 69 per cent. If 1982–6 is defined as the SAL period, the SAL country import growth rate fell from 11.7 per cent in 1976–81 to −4.0 per cent in 1982–6, i.e. a decline of 135 per cent, whilst for the non-SAL control group the corresponding fall was from 15.6 to −3.4 per cent, i.e. a decline of 122 per cent. Confining the analysis to the low slippage SAL countries, the annual average real import growth rate for this group fell from 14.8 per cent in 1976–9 to 2.4 per cent in 1980–6, i.e. a decline of 84 per cent, whilst for the non-SAL low slippage control group it fell from 7.7 to 5.4 per cent, i.e. a decline of 26 per cent. With 1982–6 defined as the SAL period, import growth rates for the low slippage SAL countries fell from 12.1 per cent in 1976–81 to −4.3 per cent in 1982–6, i.e. a decline of 136 per cent, whilst for the non-SAL low slippage control group the corresponding fall was from 17.6 to −1.4 per cent, i.e. a decline of 108 per cent.

The above results indicate that annual average real import growth rates fell for all countries during the 1980s. However, in all cases, the decline was greater for SAL countries than for the relevant non-SAL control group, suggesting that SAL packages provided added impetus to the need of

208

developing countries to curb imports in response to the increasing current account deficits experienced during the 1980s. This finding is supported by the fact that the decline in the share of imports in SAL countries, relative to the relevant control group, is greater for the low slippage SAL countries than for the SAL group as a whole. Hence, although it is possible that the disbursement of SAL finance may, in the short run, aggravate the current account deficit by providing credit for otherwise unaffordable imports (Mosley, 1987: 28), the net impact of SAL financing *together with* conditionality, over the SAL period as a whole, has had the opposite effect. This leads us to the conclusion that the relatively favourable performance of SAL country current account balances during the 1980s was the combined result of successful SAL conditions aimed at stimulating export performance in the face of an adverse external trade environment and of SAL conditions which helped to curb import growth rates.

In the Bank's recent internal review of adjustment lending (World Bank, 1988) a 'with versus without' method of evaluation was also used to assess the effectiveness of adjustment lending. The Bank's study, however, differed from ours in several respects. First, its scope was wider since it covered all forms of adjustment lending (i.e. SALs, SECALs, and other programme loans such as trade development credits) whereas the present analysis is confined to Structural Adjustment Loans strictly defined. The methodology used by the Bank for their 'with versus without' evaluation was also slightly different. As in our study, countries who have received adjustment loans, referred to as AL countries by the Bank, were each paired with a non-recipient, 'NAL', country (although the latter countries are not explicitly named in the report and the basis for the pairing is not described). However, rather than carrying out comparisons between aggregated data for each group of countries, as we have done in this study, the Bank study compares the performance of each individual AL country directly with that of its NAL comparator. The proportion of AL countries who performed better than their NAL control country, in terms of various criteria of evaluation, is then calculated. The time period used in the Bank study also differs from our own. Individual country comparisons between the AL and NAL countries were made for the three years immediately after the AL country in question received its adjustment loan. This contrasts to our use of two generalised time periods, namely, 1980–6 and 1982–6, to define the SAL period for aggregative country comparisons.

We have transformed the data contained in Tables 6.3 and 6.4 so that it provides a direct comparison between our results and those obtained by the Bank from their individual country pair comparisons. The two sets of results are given in Table 6.5. Despite various differences between the two studies, i.e. in the country pairings, the time periods, the types of adjustment loans covered, and the data sources, there is a remarkable similarity between the two sets of results shown in Table 6.5. Both sets of

Table 6.5 Effectiveness of adjustment lending: comparison of World Bank results with those based on data used in this study

(Figure in each cell is percentage of AL countries who performed better on the stated indicator than their NAL comparator country)

Study:	This Study	World Bank (1988b)
Coverage:	Structural Adjustment Loans 1980–7	All Programme Aid Loans 1980–7
Period of Measurement:	1982–6	Three years following Loan Disbursement
Indicators:		
Growth of real GDP	50	53
Investment as % of GDP	36	37
Growth of real exports	65	57
Current account balance as % of GDP	79	70

Sources: World Bank, 1988: Table 2.4a; Tables 6.3 and 6.4 above.

results suggest that a majority of adjustment loan recipients had *better* trade performance (balance of payments and export growth), *worse* investment performance, and *little difference* in growth rates in relation to their 'non-adjustment loan' comparators.

Even more significant is the fact that both sets of results contained in Table 6.5, which are based upon a 'with versus without' methodology in which comparisons are made between individual pairs of countries, support the results contained in Tables 6.3 and 6.4 above, in which a different form of 'with versus without' methodology is used, namely, one which makes comparisons on the basis of aggregated 'with-programme' and 'without-programme' country groups. This similarity of results, we may hope, adds weight to the conclusions we have reached so far.

The aggregate 'with and without' evaluation exercise has produced some interesting, and occasionally unexpected, results regarding the impact of SALs on the variables chosen by the Bank as criteria for SAL evaluation. In addition, it has pointed us in the direction of certain questions which need to be addressed in the two following chapters.

These results can be summarised as follows:

1 If 1980–6 is defined as the SAL period, SALs appear to have had an adverse effect on GDP growth rates, particularly for those SAL countries with low slippage on SAL policy conditionality. When

210

allowance is made for the medium-term nature of SAL packages – by defining 1982–6 as the SAL period – and when late SAL recipients are excluded from the group, we find a favourable, although very weak, impact of SALs on GDP growth rates. However, the results also suggest that this was due to the SAL financing rather than SAL policy conditionality. In order to explore this finding further, regression work is required in which the SAL financial disbursement and the SAL policy conditions are treated as *separate* independent variables. This regression work will be conducted in Chapter 7.

2   We have found no evidence to support the view that the availability of SAL finance has enabled an otherwise unsustainable level of consumption expenditure in recipient economies.

3   It appears that SAL conditionality, in conjunction with IMF demand-related conditionality, has given rise to a decline in SAL country investment as a share of GDP. This result is particularly alarming, given that the central objective of the Bank's SAL programme is the achievement of adjustment with growth. Further work needs to be done, via regression analysis, in order to separate and quantify the impact of Bank conditionality and IMF conditionality on the investment variable. In addition, it seems worth exploring the extent to which the relatively disappointing GDP growth rate performance amongst SAL countries can be explained by the impact of SAL conditionality on the investment variable.

4   Our results indicate that SAL conditionality has had a marked beneficial impact on SAL country current account deficits as a percentage of GDP. SAL policy conditionality appears to have worked through two channels to bring this about:

(a) it has helped to stem what would otherwise have been a much more severe deterioration in SAL country export performance;

(b) and it has given rise to a stronger curbing of import growth rates in SAL countries.

Our findings, which have contradicted some of the results of other aggregative 'with and without' evaluation exercises, have indicated that the definition of both the control group and the pre-SAL and SAL time periods, can have a crucial impact on the results obtained from such exercises. Given that our own construction of a control group is far from perfect, the results reported here should be treated with some caution, at least until supported by alternative evaluation techniques. Despite this caveat, it is encouraging to see that the results obtained from our aggregate 'with and without' evaluation are compatible with those obtained by the World Bank in a similar evaluation exercise.

A further caution relates to the fact that the evaluation work undertaken in this section has not been able to isolate the impact of the Bank's

Structural Adjustment Loans from that of programme lending activities of other agencies, and in particular, IMF stabilisation programmes. Hence it is possible that part, and possibly all, of our reported results are due to the effects of non-Bank programme loans. Firm conclusions must therefore be suspended until we have carried out the regression and modelling work of Chapters 7 and 8.

Finally, it should be noted that the standard deviations reported in Tables 6.3 and 6.4 are, in most cases, quite large. This is not surprising, given that our results are based on highly aggregated data. The large standard deviations indicate that there is considerable diversity of performance *within* both the SAL and non-SAL group of countries. For example, the fact that our results show, for example, that SAL packages are associated with lower investment levels does not mean that this has occurred in all SAL countries. Rather, some SAL countries have experienced favourable investment trends, whilst others have experienced trends considerably more unfavourable than those indicated by our aggregated data. The standard deviation figures lead us to conclude that donors such as the World Bank need to exercise considerable caution against any tendency to prescribe 'standard' adjustment packages across a wide range of countries, a point reinforced by the case studies of Volume 2. The major elements of variation in response between countries which received World Bank finance are summarised in Chapter 10 of that volume.

NOTES

1 None of the Bank's Structural Adjustment operations to end fiscal year 1987, and only 3 of its 70 sectoral adjustment operations, had been initiated without an IMF stand-by agreement having been signed beforehand. More recently, in September 1988, a large ($500 million) policy-based lending package (not a SAL) was assembled for Argentina without prior agreement between the Argentinian government and the IMF. See Chapter 2.

2 This has been done for Malawi by Harrigan (1988); see also Chapter 8.

3 The full data-set for these other variables and notes on the statistical definitions and derivations can be found in Mosley and Harrigan, 1989. Certain SAL countries appear in the GDP growth rate table but not in subsequent tables. They are excluded from the latter, along with the relevant paired non-SAL control group country, due to lack of data availability.

4 The Bank, in an internal review of the SAL experience (World Bank 1988, Table 3.1) takes ten countries who have received SALs and ascribes a SAL policy implementation rating to each, using the following scale:

1 = negligible
2 = fell short of expectations
3 = largely successful

Within each group, Côte d'Ivoire, Jamaica, Thailand and Turkey were the only countries awarded a 3 rating. Hence, these countries are included in our low slippage SAL group. The other countries included in our group, namely Chile, Ghana, Malawi and Togo, were not covered in the above Bank report. We have classified them as low slippage on the basis of assessments contained in the Bank's Project Performance Audit Reports (PPARs) and on the basis of research carried out by one of the authors elsewhere (Mosley, 1987).

5   In all tables, the following SAL countries, along with the paired control country in brackets, are excluded from the 1976–81 and 1982–8 comparisons due to the fact that their first SAL was received in 1985 or later:

Burundi	(Rwanda)
Chile	(Peru)
Costa Rica	(Honduras)
Ghana	(Zambia)
Nepal	(Burma)
Niger	(Mauritania)

It should in addition be noted that if allowance is made for the fact that many policy changes concluded under a SAL agreement are intended to be long term in effect and a lag is inserted in consequence, the results of the comparison between programme and non-programme countries change. If the 'pre-SAL period' is taken as 1976–81 and the 'SAL period' as 1982–6 the comparison of GDP growth rates becomes:

	1976–81	1982–6
All countries in sample		
Countries receiving SALs	3.9	1.8
Countries not receiving SALs	4.3	2.0
'Low slippage countries'		
Countries receiving SALs	4.2	2.7
Countries not receiving SALs	3.5	2.5

In both the programme countries and the control group, in other words, the growth rate now halves when the 'new' post-SAL period is compared with the pre-SAL period; the greater rate of decline which is apparent in SAL countries under the previous comparison disappears when a two-year lag is inserted.

6   In Malawi, Zambia and Tanzania the real value of government development spending in 1984 was less than half the 1980 value (Mosley and Smith, 1989: Table 6).

7

REGRESSION-BASED RESULTS

7.1 THE RELATIONSHIPS TO BE ESTIMATED

The tabular comparisons undertaken in Chapter 6 provide useful information concerning the 'yes/no' question: was the influence of Structural Adjustment Loans positive or not? However, this approach cannot tell us the precise quantitative influence of programme lending in relation to other influences; nor can it explicitly isolate the influence of exogenous non-policy variables, such as that of the weather and terms of trade movements, from the influence of programme lending; nor, within the category of programme lending, can it isolate the influence of Bank SALs from other Bank programme lending and Fund programmes, or the influence of policy changes attached to SALs from the influence of the money which they provide. To answer such questions we need a technique which will tell us what proportion of the variance in the Bank's chosen target variables is accounted for by specific independent variables. The appropriate technique for this purpose is multiple regression, and in this section we apply these methods to the same sample of SAL countries examined in Chapter 6, but now incorporating the influence of all policy-based lending rather than SALs alone. The five relationships which we wish to estimate each express the major targets of World Bank policy-based lending as a function of three groups of variables: *financial flows* from the IMF and World Bank, plus domestically financed investment; degree of compliance with Bank *policy conditionality*, as analysed in Chapter 5; and *extraneous* (i.e. non-aid) variables believed to have an influence on growth and the Bank's other policy targets. In its simplest terms this can be seen as a variant of the fundamental Harrod-Domar growth relationship: the growth rate equals savings, times the productivity of capital. The financial flow variables represent different components of savings; the level of compliance with conditionality and the extraneous variables represent obvious potential influences on the productivity of capital. In symbolic form the relationships we wish to estimate are:

1   $gGDP_t = \text{constant} + a_1\ IMF_t + a_2\ SAL_t + a_3\ SAL_{(t-1)} + a_4\ SAL_{(t-2)} + a_5\ INV_t$

$$\underbrace{\hspace{6cm}}_{\text{financial flows}}$$

$+\ a_6\ CI_t + a_7\ CI_{(t-1)} + a_8\ CI_{(t-2)}$

$$\underbrace{\hspace{4cm}}_{\text{compliance with conditionality}}$$

$+\ a_9\ W_t + a_{10}\ ToT_t + a_{11}\ gEX_t.$

$$\underbrace{\hspace{4cm}}_{\text{extraneous variables}}$$

2   $gEX_t = \text{constant} + b_1\ IMF_t + b_2\ SAL_t + b_3\ SAL_{(t-1)} + b_4\ SAL_{(t-2)} + b_5\ INV_t$

$$\underbrace{\hspace{6cm}}_{\text{financial flows}}$$

$+\ b_6\ CI_t + b_7\ CI_{(t-1)} + b_8\ CI_{(t-2)}$

$$\underbrace{\hspace{4cm}}_{\text{compliance with conditionality}}$$

$+\ \underbrace{b_9\ W_t + b_{10}\ EPI_t}_{\text{extraneous variables}}$

3   $gIM_t = \text{constant} + c_1\ IMF_t + c_2\ SAL_t + c_3\ SAL_{t-1} + c_4\ SAL_{t-2} + c_5\ INV_t$

$$\underbrace{\hspace{6cm}}_{\text{financial flows}}$$

$+\ c_6\ CI_t + c_7\ CI_{t-1} + c_8\ CI_{t-2}$

$$\underbrace{\hspace{4cm}}_{\text{compliance with conditionality}}$$

$+\ c_9\ W_t + c_{10}\ ToT_t.$

$$\underbrace{\hspace{4cm}}_{\text{extraneous variables}}$$

4   $INV_t = \text{constant} + d_1\ IMF_t + d_2\ SAL_t + d_3\ SAL_{t-1} + d_4\ SAL_{t-2}$

$$\underbrace{\hspace{6cm}}_{\text{financial flows}}$$

$+\ d_5\ CI_t + d_6\ CI_{t-1} + d_7\ CI_{t-2}$

$$\underbrace{\hspace{4cm}}_{\text{compliance with conditionality}}$$

$+\ d_8\ W_t + d_9\ ToT_t$

$$\underbrace{\hspace{3cm}}_{\text{extraneous variables}}$$

5   $FF_t = \text{constant} + e_1\ IMF_t + e_2\ SAL_t + e_3\ SAL_{t-1} + e_4\ SAL_{t-2} + e_5\ INV_t$

$$\underbrace{\hspace{6cm}}_{\text{financial flows}}$$

$$+ e_6\, CI_t + e_7\, CI_{t-1} + e_8\, CI_{t-2}$$

$$\underbrace{\phantom{+ e_6\, CI_t + e_7\, CI_{t-1} + e_8\, CI_{t-2}}}$$

compliance with conditionality

$$+ e_9\, W_t + e_{10}\, ToT_t$$

$$\underbrace{\phantom{+ e_9\, W_t + e_{10}\, ToT_t}}$$

extraneous variables

where:

$gGDP$	=	growth rate of GDP
IMF	=	drawings of IMF finance as a percentage of GDP
SAL	=	SAL and SECAL finance as a percentage of GDP
CI	=	compliance index on SAL policy conditions
W	=	weather index
ToT	=	terms of trade
gEX	=	growth rate of export values
EPI	=	export price index
gIM	=	growth rate of import values
INV	=	investment as a share of GDP
FF	=	inflows of private foreign finance

$\left.\begin{array}{l} a_1 \ldots a_{11} \\ b_1 \ldots b_{10} \\ c_1 \ldots c_{10} \\ d_1 \ldots d_8 \\ e_1 \ldots e_{10} \end{array}\right\}$ = coefficients

$t;\ t-1;\ t-2$ = annual time periods

Note: Full data arrays and details of sources are provided in the Appendix to this chapter.

The Bank finance variable and the compliance variable also enter each equation with one and two period lags. The rationale behind the use of lags is the belief that the injection of Bank finance into an economy may have multiplier effects on the dependent variables (for example, a multiplier effect on GDP growth rates may come about via the financial flows enabling higher import and investment levels) with the impact of such multiplier effects taking several years to emerge. Likewise, in the case of compliance with Bank policy conditions, many of these conditions relate to reforms designed to influence medium-term supply-side variables such that their effects may take several years to materialise.

The equations represent somewhat crude hypotheses regarding the determinants of the five dependent variables. There are many other independent variables which could have been included as explanatory variables in the equations. In addition, lags could have been introduced to more of the independent variables, such as IMF finance and investment shares. However, since it is specifically the impact of Bank finance and policy conditions which we wish to quantify, we have refrained from more complex specification of the equations.

7.2 RESULTS

The five equations are estimated using the ordinary least squares regression technique. In order to maximise the number of observations, a hybrid cross-section/time-series data set is used. For each variable, observations run from 1980 to 1986 and cover each of the nineteen SAL recipient countries analysed in Chapter 6, thus providing 133 observations. The data set is given in the Appendix to this chapter. Where possible, data definitions and sources are the same as those used in Chapter 6.

In addition to estimating the equations for the entire sample of nineteen SAL countries, estimates are also made for two sub-groups of countries: sub-Saharan countries receiving SALs and middle-income countries receiving SALs. This is done in order to ascertain whether Bank programme lending activities have different effects according to the type of country in which they are implemented. In particular, several commentators (e.g. Taylor, 1986; Green, 1988) have noted that sub-Saharan economies face many unique adjustment problems and hence require different types of structural adjustment packages as compared to non sub-Saharan countries. The sub-Saharan countries include: Côte d'Ivoire, Ghana, Kenya, Malawi, Niger, Senegal and Togo, thus giving a data set with 49 observations on each variable. The middle-income countries include: Bolivia, Chile, Costa Rica, Côte D'Ivoire, Guyana, Jamaica, Kenya, Korea, Panama, Philippines, Senegal, Thailand, Turkey and Yugoslavia, thus giving 96 observations on each variable. Countries are defined as middle-income if so classified in the Bank's *World Development Report 1983*. The regression results for each of these three groups of countries are presented in Tables 7.1, 7.2 and 7.3.

GDP growth

The estimation of the GDP growth rate equation for the three groups of countries produces mixed results in terms of the impact of Bank SAL and SECAL finance. For the group containing all SAL countries (Table 7.1) inflows of finance in the current period, t, and in the period $t-2$, have a weak positive impact on GDP growth, whilst inflows in period $t-1$ have a weak negative impact. None of the coefficients, however, possess statistical significance. In the case of both the sub-Saharan group of countries (Table 7.2) and the middle-income group of countries (Table 7.3) Bank financial flows in periods t and $t-1$ have a negative effect on GDP growth rates, whilst flows in periods $t-2$ have a positive effect.

The general trend which emerges from these results is that for all three groups of countries, Bank financial flows in the previous period ($t-1$) have a *negative* impact on GDP growth rates, which is statistically significant at the 1 per cent level in the case of middle-income countries. This negative impact of Bank financial flows is unexpected. A possible explanation relates to a temptation inherent within programme lending, namely, the possibility of using the financial flows provided by programme lending to stave off pressure to implement immediate policy reform. If this hypothesis

217

Table 7.1 Results of regression analysis: all SAL countries

Dependent variable	Regression coefficients on independent variables (Student's t-statistics in brackets beneath coefficient)													
	Constant	IMF_t	SAL_t	SAL_{t-1}	SAL_{t-2}	CI_t	CI_{t-1}	CI_{t-2}	W_t	ToT_t	EPI_t	INV_t	gEX_t	r^2
GDP growth	−24.65** (−5.65)	−0.11 (−0.46)	0.03 (0.05)	−1.85* (−2.54)	0.98 (1.30)	0.23 (0.53)	1.35** (2.87)	0.23 (0.52)	0.12** (4.54)	0.16** (4.07)	N/A	0.01 (0.16)	0.04* (2.57)	0.40
Export growth	−0.51 (−0.02)	2.64 (1.83)	−10.03** (3.08)	3.72 (0.84)	1.69 (0.41)	9.63** (3.96)	−6.04* (−2.15)	1.72 (0.64)	−0.15 (−0.97)	N/A	0.20 (0.94)	−0.25 (−0.71)	N/A	0.17
Import growth	24.84 (0.93)	2.91* (1.99)	−6.13 (−1.86)	−2.07 (−0.46)	3.57 (0.77)	6.69** (2.71)	−4.58 (−1.61)	0.34 (0.13)	−0.18 (−1.13)	−0.15 (−0.63)	N/A	0.12 (0.34)	N/A	0.13
Investment as % of GDP	−16.37* (−2.42)	0.00 (0.00)	−0.70 (−0.83)	0.53 (0.46)	−0.72 (−0.60)	−0.33 (−0.60)	0.49 (0.67)	−0.20 (−0.28)	0.10* (2.39)	0.32** (6.03)	N/A	N/A	N/A	0.25
Private foreign finance	−1269.71* (−1.97)	−61.81 (−1.76)	−30.62 (−0.39)	−16.16 (−0.15)	−108.64 (−0.97)	−25.46 (−0.43)	−2.04 (−0.43)	62.43 (0.96)	8.17* (2.15)	6.67 (1.17)	N/A	16.99* (2.01)	N/A	0.18

Note: ** denotes significance of a coefficient at the 1% level and * at the 5% level.
For variable definitions, data sets and sources see the Appendix.
Short definitions of each variable are given at page 210.

Table 7.2 Results of regression analysis: sub-Saharan countries

Dependent variable	Constant	IMF_t	SAL_t	SAL_{t-1}	SAL_{t-2}	CI_t	CI_{t-1}	CI_{t-2}	W_t	ToT_t	EPI_t	INV_t	gEX_t	r^2
					Regression coefficients on independent variables (Student's *t*-statistics in brackets beneath coefficient)									
GDP growth	-31.87** (-4.82)	-0.04 (-0.08)	-1.47 (-1.33)	-0.87 (-0.72)	1.55 (0.89)	-0.16 (0.16)	2.13* (2.03)	-0.34 (-0.30)	0.19** (4.70)	0.19** (3.16)	N/A	0.02 (0.26)	0.03 (1.35)	0.53
Export growth	14.35 (0.29)	7.23 (1.84)	-21.30* (-2.50)	18.93 (2.00)	5.81 (0.41)	20.22* (2.58)	-20.72* (-2.64)	4.07 (0.43)	-0.23 (-0.71)	N/A	-0.02 (-0.03)	-0.32 (-0.42)	N/A	0.35
Import growth	78.67 (1.44)	5.80 (1.47)	-16.69 (-1.95)	7.41 (0.78)	20.13 (1.39)	16.29* (2.08)	-15.57 (-1.95)	-4.05 (-0.42)	-0.48 (-1.44)	-0.54 (-1.09)	N/A	-0.07 (-0.09)	N/A	0.31
Investment as % of GDP	-7.36 (-0.63)	-0.02 (-0.02)	0.13 (0.07)	0.47 (0.23)	-1.44 (-0.47)	-0.68 (-0.41)	0.48 (0.28)	-0.48 (-0.23)	0.07 (1.02)	0.24* (2.37)	N/A	N/A	N/A	0.18
Private foreign finance	-166.09 (-0.44)	-27.27 (-0.99)	-76.30 (-1.29)	-69.10 (-1.05)	96.99 (0.97)	47.03 (0.87)	43.27 (0.79)	49.40 (0.74)	2.24 (0.97)	0.99 (0.29)	N/A	-0.25 (-0.05)	N/A	0.23

Note: ** denotes significance of a coefficient at the 1% level and * at the 5% level.
For variable definitions, data sets and sources see the Appendix.
Short definitions of each variable are given at page 210.

Table 7.3 Results of regression analysis: middle-income SAL countries

Dependent variable		Constant	IMF_t	SAL_t	SAL_{t-1}	SAL_{t-2}	CI_t	CI_{t-1}	CI_{t-2}	W_t	ToT_t	EPI_t	INV_t	gEX_t	r^2
						Regression coefficients on independent variables (Student's t-statistics in brackets beneath coefficient)									
GDP growth		-23.94**	0.16	-0.21	-2.86**	1.27	0.08	1.32*	0.35	0.12**	0.13*	N/A	0.07	0.06*	0.43
		(-3.73)	(0.59)	(-0.30)	(-3.26)	(1.57)	(0.18)	(2.47)	(0.70)	(3.23)	(2.44)		(1.00)	(2.45)	
Export growth		-70.54**	-1.07	-4.71	-1.96	2.33	4.54**	-1.21	1.58	0.23	N/A	0.72**	-0.44	N/A	0.26
		(-3.01)	(-1.02)	(-1.78)	(-0.57)	(0.73)	(2.63)	(-0.58)	(0.81)	(1.56)		(3.66)	(-1.57)		
Import growth		-42.09	0.17	-1.54	-5.90	3.60	2.79	-0.58	-1.95	0.19	0.21	N/A	0.27	N/A	0.14
		(-1.45)	(0.14)	(-0.49)	(-1.46)	(0.97)	(1.36)	(-0.24)	(-0.86)	(1.17)	(0.88)		(0.85)		
Investment as % of GDP		-20.20*	0.05	-0.86	0.37	-0.54	0.15	0.95	-0.29	0.09	0.36**	N/A	N/A	N/A	0.28
		(-2.10)	(0.11)	(-0.82)	(0.27)	(-0.43)	(0.22)	(1.15)	(-0.38)	(1.67)	(5.09)				
Private foreign finance		-2116.82	-87.54	-33.02	-46.24	-148.46	-52.45	5.20	86.09	12.00	13.00	N/A	17.22	N/A	0.20
		(-1.90)	(-1.88)	(-0.28)	(-0.30)	(-1.04)	(-0.67)	(0.06)	(1.00)	(1.89)	(1.41)		(1.42)		

Note: ** denotes significance of a coefficient at the 1% level and * at the 5% level.
For variable definitions, data sets and sources see the Appendix.
Short definitions of each variable are given at page 210.

is correct, the Bank finance variable, by retarding the pace of policy reform, could be expected to have a negative one-period lagged impact on GDP growth rates of the type shown by our results. Several of the country case studies of Volume 2 lend support to this theory regarding the negative correlation between the level of programme aid finance and the level of both policy reform compliance and GDP growth. For example, large flows of Bank and Fund policy-based lending into the Philippines in 1980–1, and into Jamaica a year later, were followed by *appreciation* of the real exchange rate which in turn led to a decline in export growth and growth of GNP; not an intended effect, but a 'Dutch disease' effect that was only made possible by inflows of external finance. Similarly, in Thailand an interviewee reported that:

> losses in some state enterprises required some forms of financing from the central government, which worsened the budget deficit. The SAL recommendation of raising service charges of these state enterprises was one solution to solve their losses. However, the implementation of this measure slipped because doing so might trigger public unrest and consequently destabilise the government. (Hence) part of the SAL money was used to help finance the losses of some state enterprises.
>
> (Volume 2, Chapter 13, Appendix C, Table C4, interviewee B)

Such cases do not necessarily show up in the regressions with a low value of the compliance index, *CI*: in those cases where the commitment to reform was low and finance was used to postpone many essential policy changes, governments were none the less often able, as we saw in Chapter 5, to comply with the letter of the conditions set, because those conditions did not address the fundamental problem. In Jamaica and the Philippines in the early 1980s, for example, the fundamental problem was an overvalued exchange rate, but neither Bank nor Fund conditionality effectively attacked this problem until 1984, so that their respective governments were able to claim that compliance was high even though external finance was serving to postpone the most urgently-needed reforms.

Our regression results suggest that the effect of compliance with Bank policy conditions on GDP growth rates was favourable. For all three groups of countries, compliance in periods t, $t-1$, and $t-2$ has a positive impact on GDP growth (with the exception of compliance in period $t-2$ for sub-Saharan countries). In addition, the $t-1$ compliance variable possesses statistical significance in all three cases – at the 5 per cent level for sub-Saharan and middle-income countries and at the 1 per cent level for the group containing all SAL countries. This is a robust and encouraging result, suggesting, as it does, that compliance with Bank-guided adjustment reforms has a positive effect on GDP growth rates which emerges most strongly in the year following reform implementation. However, it should be noted that in evaluating the *overall* impact of SALs

221

Table 7.4   Net impact of Bank programme loans on GDP growth rates

	All SAL *countries*			Sub-Saharan			Middle-income		
	t	$t-1$	$t-2$	t	$t-1$	$t-2$	t	$t-1$	$t-2$
Bank finance (SAL)	0.03	−1.85	0.96	−1.47	−0.87	1.55	−0.21	−2.86	1.27
	(a_2)	(a_3)	(a_4)	(a_2)	(a_3)	(a_4)	(a_2)	(a_3)	(a_4)
Bank conditions (CI)	0.23	1.23	1.35	0.16	2.13	−0.34	0.08	1.32	0.35
	(a_6)	(a_7)	(a_8)	(a_6)	(a_7)	(a_8)	(a_6)	(a_7)	(a_8)
Net effect	+	−?	+	−?	+?	+?	−?	−?	+

Note: The figure in each cell is the value of the coefficient produced by our estimation results with the relevant symbol given in brackets beneath. Where the two coefficients (*SAL* and *CI*) possess the same sign, the net effect can be unambiguously classified as positive or negative. Where the two coefficients have opposite signs, we have tentatively ascribed the sign of the larger of the two coefficients to the net effect.

and SECALs, i.e. finance plus policy reform, that the positive GDP growth rate effects of compliance with policy reforms in the period $t-1$ are counterbalanced by the negative effects of Bank financial flows in the period $t-1$. The net GDP effect of Bank programme lending is shown in Table 7.4, which indicates a very weak overall positive effect – a result which is compatible with the findings of the tabular comparisons carried out in Chapter 6.

The regression results concerning the impact of the IMF finance variable on GDP growth rates are disappointing. The coefficient is negative in the case of the group of all SAL countries and the sub-Saharan group of SAL countries and positive in the case of the middle-income group. However, in each case the effects are very weak and statistically insignificant, recalling the similar results obtained by Khan and Knight (1985: 19–23). The weakness of effects may be due to the fact that we have no independent variable in the equation which captures the effects of the policy conditions attached to IMF stabilisation programmes, so that the IMF finance variable is also serving as a proxy for these conditions. It is possible, therefore, that any positive influence of IMF finance on GDP is being neutralised by negative effects of recessionary, demand-reducing conditions associated with the finance, so producing a coefficient close to zero. It should also be noted that we have not introduced any lags to the IMF finance variable and this may also explain the disappointing results.

The estimation of the GDP growth rate equation produces, as expected, strong results in terms of the impact of two exogenous independent variables, namely, weather and the terms of trade. For all three groups of countries, favourable weather and improvements in the terms of trade have a positive effect on GDP growth rates which is statistically significant at the 1 per cent level (with the exception of terms of trade movements for the middle-income group of countries, where statistical significance is obtained at the 5 per cent level). Results concerning the effect of investment on GDP growth, however, are disappointing. The coefficient on the investment variable is close to zero and statistically insignificant for all three groups of countries. This result is undoubtedly due to the fact that we have not introduced lags to the investment variable. Similarly, growth of exports appears, surprisingly, to have little effect on the GDP growth rate, with the coefficient close to zero in all cases and possessing statistical significance, at the 5 per cent level, only in the case of the group containing all SAL countries.

In summary, our estimation of the GDP growth rate equation indicates that compliance with policy conditions attached to Bank programme lending has a positive effect on GDP growth rates which emerges most strongly in the year after policy implementation, whilst the inflow of finance provided by the programme loans has an unexpected negative impact on GDP growth in the year following loan disbursement. When these two effects are taken together, the overall impact of programme lending on GDP growth rates is positive, but very weak. In addition, two exogenous variables, weather and the terms of trade, were found to be important determinants of GDP growth. These results hold regardless of whether the SAL recipient is a sub-Saharan country or a middle-income country.

Export growth

Estimation of the export growth rate equation indicates that inflows of Bank SAL and SECAL finance in the current period have a very strong *negative* effect on export growth for all three groups of countries, with the coefficient being statistically significant at the 1 per cent level for the group containing all SAL countries, and at the 5 per cent level for the sub-Saharan group. However, the inflow of finance lagged two years has a positive effect on export growth rates for all three groups of countries, although none of the coefficients possess statistical significance. The strong, immediate negative response of exports to Bank finance is a surprising response, which reinforces the view that the disbursement of programme aid finance, by reducing the immediate pressure to adjust to a balance of payments financing gap, may retard the recipient's pace of adjustment, hence resulting in a negative impact on variables such as GDP and export growth rates in the short term.

Compliance with Bank policy reform conditions in the current period has a strong positive, and statistically significant, impact on export growth rates for all three groups of countries. This suggests that compliance with Bank adjustment packages, most of which contain reforms designed to liberalise the trade regime and to provide export incentives, leads to an immediate and favourable export growth response. However, this favourable result of compliance appears to be somewhat short-lived. For all three groups of countries, compliance with Bank policy conditions in period $t-1$ has a negative impact on export growth rates. This lagged negative effect is statistically significant at the 5 per cent level in the case of both the group containing all SAL countries and the sub-Saharan group and is very strong in the latter case. This lagged negative result may be explained by the findings of some of our country case studies, in particular those for Jamaica, Kenya, and Philippines, and the findings of Chapter 6, namely, that compliance with Bank policy reforms has an adverse negative effect on both public and private sector investment levels, which may in turn give rise to a lagged negative impact on export growth rates. Work carried out by one of the authors elsewhere (Mosley and Smith, 1989) indicates that this negative investment effect resulting from compliance with adjustment packages is particularly strong in sub-Saharan economies – the same group of economies for whom our regression results revealed the strongest negative correlation between compliance in period $t-1$ and export growth rates, with a significant regression coefficient on CI_{t-1} of -20.72 (Table 7.2).

The negative impact of compliance in period $t-1$ on export growth rates contrasts with its effect in the GDP growth rate equation, where compliance in period $t-1$ was found to have a positive impact on GDP growth. This suggests that the lagged adverse effects of compliance, caused, we speculate, by reductions in investment levels, specifically affects the export sector of the economy, as opposed to all components of GDP. In terms of the sub-Saharan group of economies, for whom the negative lagged effect of compliance on exports was found to be the strongest, agriculture constitutes the main export activity. Hence we can hypothesise that for such countries compliance with Bank-guided adjustment programmes has a negative effect on investment in the agricultural sector, leading to a lagged negative response in agricultural output which translates into a disappointing export performance. This scenario is consistent with results produced by other studies (Table 7.3) and with the results of the Malawi modelling exercise (Chapter 8).

Results concerning the impact of IMF finance on export growth rates are mixed and disappointing. The impact is positive for the group containing all SAL countries and the sub-Saharan group, and negative in the case of the middle-income countries. None of the coefficients, however, possess statistical significance. The reasons for such results are likely to be the same as those advanced for the disappointing results in terms of the impact of IMF finance on the GDP growth rate variable.

Surprisingly, the impact of two important exogenous variables, weather and the export price index, on export growth rates are found to be statistically insignificant, close to zero, and often with an unexpected negative coefficient. The exception is the case of the export price index for middle-income countries, where a weak positive and statistically significant impact on export growth rates is revealed. These generally disappointing results may be due to the fact that we have not introduced lags to these two independent variables. The same factor probably explains the unexpected results concerning the impact of investment on export growth – in all cases, the coefficient on the investment variable is negative, weak, and statistically insignificant.

In summary, the results derived from the estimated export growth rate equation indicate that the inflow of Bank finance has a strong negative effect on export growth rates in the immediate period, but a positive lagged effect which emerges between one and two years later. By contrast, compliance with Bank policy conditions attached to this finance has a strong positive effect on exports in the immediate period but in the year following policy implementation we find a negative lagged effect on export growth which is particularly strong in the case of sub-Saharan countries. Taking the *net* impact of Bank programme loans, i.e. loan finance plus loan conditions, we find that for all three groups of countries the net impact of loans on export growth in periods t and $t-1$ is possibly negative, whilst the net impact of loans made available in period $t-2$ is definitely positive (Table 7.5).

Table 7.5 Net impact of Bank programme loans on export growth rates

	All SAL *countries*			Sub-Saharan SAL *countries*			Middle-income SAL *countries*		
	t	$t-1$	$t-2$	t	$t-1$	$t-2$	t	$t-1$	$t-2$
Bank finance (SAL)	-10.03 (b_2)	3.72 (b_3)	1.89 (b_4)	-21.30 (b_2)	10.93 (b_3)	5.81 (b_4)	-4.71 (b_2)	-1.96 (b_3)	2.83 (b_4)
Bank conditions (CI)	9.63 (b_6)	-6.04 (b_7)	1.72 (b_8)	20.22 (b_6)	-20.72 (b_7)	4.07 (b_8)	4.34 (b_6)	-1.21 (b_7)	1.50 (b_8)
Net effect	$-?$	$-?$	$+$	$-?$	$-?$	$+$	$-?$	$-$	$+$

Note: The figure in each cell is the value of the coefficient produced by our estimation results with the relevant symbol given in brackets beneath. Where the two coefficients (*SAL* and *CI*) possess the same sign, the net effect can be unambiguously classified as positive or negative. Where the two coefficients have opposite signs, we have tentatively ascribed the sign of the larger of the two coefficients to the net effect.

Import Growth

Estimation of the import growth rate equation produced disappointing results, in that only three coefficients possessed statistical significance. For the group containing all SAL countries and the middle-income group of countries, the disbursement of Bank SAL and SECAL finance in periods t and $t-1$ has a negative effect on import growth rates, whilst disbursement in period $t-2$ has a positive effect. For the sub-Saharan group of countries, finance in period t has a negative impact on import growth rates, whilst finance in periods $t-1$ and $t-2$ has a positive impact. None of the coefficients on the Bank finance variable, however, possess statistical significance. This immediate negative impact of Bank finance on import growth rates, followed by a lagged positive effect, is unexpected since it contradicts the expectation that the provision of hard-currency finance immediately relaxes the balance-of-payments constraint on imports. One recalls, however, the finding of Table 4.1 that Bank structural adjustment programmes were frequently interrupted by a stabilisation episode, and it may be this extraneous influence, rather than the intervention of the Bank as such, which was responsible for the temporary drop in import values.

Compliance with Bank policy conditions in period t has a positive impact on import growth rates in all three groups of countries, which is statistically significant at the 1 per cent level for the group containing all SAL countries and at the 5 per cent level for the sub-Saharan group. This is consistent with the findings of many of our country case studies (e.g. Kenya, Ghana, Jamaica), where compliance with Bank policy conditions, such as removal of quantitative restrictions on imports, reform of the tariff regime, and the liberalisation of foreign exchange allocation mechanisms, were found to result in an immediate increase in import levels. Our results also indicate that compliance in periods $t-1$ and $t-2$ has a lagged negative effect on import growth rates for all three groups of countries (with the exception of compliance in period $t-2$ for the group containing all SAL countries), although none of the coefficients are statistically significant. This lagged negative effect suggests that increased import levels are a short-term phenomenon of compliance with Bank-guided adjustment packages, occurring only in the first year of policy implementation when producers take advantage of a liberalised trade regime in order to import capital goods and restock before the reorientation of productive activities towards the export sector.

The IMF finance variable has a positive effect on import growth rates for all three groups of countries, which is statistically significant at the 5 per cent level in the case of the group containing all SAL countries. This result indicates that the availability of IMF finance, unlike Bank finance, enables an immediate increase in imports which more than counterbalances the negative effects of IMF demand-deflationary and import-reducing conditions, for which the IMF finance variable serves as a proxy.

Results concerning our two exogenous variables, namely weather and the terms of trade, are disappointing, in that none of the coefficients possess statistical significance. In the case of the sub-Saharan group, improvements in weather have a negative effect on import growth, which is expected since good rains reduce the need for imported food, particularly in the case of the sub-Saharan countries. For the middle-income group, however, improved weather has the reverse effect on import growth rates. Similarly, improvements in the terms of trade have a negative effect on import growth for the group containing all SAL countries and the sub-Saharan group and the reverse effect for the middle-income group. The investment variable also produces erratic results – increased investment has a positive effect on import growth rates for the SAL countries taken together and for the middle-income group, and a negative effect for the sub-Saharan group. However, since none of the coefficients have any statistical significance, and since we have not introduced lags to the investment variable, it is not possible to draw conclusions from this miscellany of results.

In summary, the estimation of the import growth rate equation produced unexpected results regarding the effects of Bank finance, which was found to have an immediate negative impact on import growth rates followed by a lagged positive effect. By contrast, the provision of IMF finance had an immediate positive effect on imports. Compliance with Bank policy conditions produced the expected combination of an immediate positive effect on import growth rates, followed by a lagged negative effect. The remaining variables in the import growth rate equation produced mixed and statistically insignificant results.

Investment as a Share of GDP

Estimation of the equation with investment as a share of GDP as the dependent variable also produced inconclusive results, with very few coefficients possessing statistical significance. For the group containing all SAL countries and the middle-income group, the provision of Bank finance in periods t and $t-2$ has a negative impact on investment, whilst finance in period $t-1$ has a positive impact. For the sub-Saharan group of countries, Bank finance in periods t and $t-1$ has a positive impact on investment, whilst finance in period $t-2$ has a negative impact. However, in all cases, the coefficient values are low and statistically insignificant. The only general result which emerges is that for all three groups of countries, Bank finance has a two-period $(t-2)$ lagged negative effect on investment. This result contradicts the expectation that Bank programme aid finance is used to finance higher investment levels.

For the group of all SAL countries and the sub-Saharan group, compliance with Bank policy conditions in period t has a negative effect on investment

227

and compliance in period $t-1$ a positive effect. For the middle-income group compliance in periods t and $t-1$ has a weak positive effect on investment levels. For all three groups of countries, however, compliance in period $t-2$ has a weak negative impact on investment as a share of GDP. This latter result supports the findings of Chapter 6, namely that the implementation of Bank adjustment packages has a lagged adverse effect on investment. It should be noted, however, that none of the coefficients on the compliance variable possess statistical significance, and in all cases the coefficient values are low, implying that the effects are weak.

The provision of IMF finance, and the associated stabilisation conditions, appear to have no effect on investment, although once again this neutral result may be due to the fact that we have not introduced lags to the IMF variable.

For all three groups of countries, improvements in the terms of trade have a positive and statistically significant impact on investment as a share of GDP, whilst effects of weather improvements are close to being neutral and are statistically insignificant.

In summary, results from the estimation of the investment equation are, on the whole, inconclusive. The provision of SAL and SECAL finance and compliance with attached policy conditions both have a two-period lagged negative effect on investment as a share of GDP. Although this result supports the findings of Chapter 6, lack of statistical significance did not provide us with the robust result we had expected in view of the strength of evidence elsewhere suggesting a negative correlation between Bank programme lending and investment levels (Chapter 6; Volume 2, Jamaica, Kenya and Philippines country studies; Mosley and Smith, 1989: Table 6; World Bank, 1988, Table 2.6; World Bank, 1990, Tables 2.6 and 2.7).

Inflows of private foreign finance

Estimation of the determinants of inflows of foreign private finance produced virtually no statistically significant results. For all three groups of countries, the provision of Bank SAL and SECAL finance has a negative effect on flows of foreign private finance (with the exception of Bank finance in period $t-2$ for sub-Saharan countries, where a positive effect occurs). But the lack of statistical significance is itself significant, as noted below.

Compliance with Bank policy conditions has varying effects on the inflow of foreign private finance according to country type. For the group containing all SAL countries compliance in periods t and $t-1$ has a negative effect on the flow of foreign private finance, whilst compliance in period $t-2$ has a positive effect. For sub-Saharan countries compliance in all three periods has a large positive effect on flows of private foreign finance, whilst for the middle-income group of countries, compliance in period t has a negative effect and in $t-1$ and $t-2$ positive effects.

Taking the net effect of Bank programme lending (i.e. Bank finance plus Bank policy conditions), only in the case of sub-Saharan countries do we find any evidence of a positive net impact on the inflow of foreign private finance. However, none of the coefficients on either the Bank finance variable or the compliance variable possess statistical significance, such that even this tentative result must be treated with caution. In all country groups, the provision of IMF finance and the attached stabilisation conditions has a negative and statistically insignificant impact on inflows of foreign private finance.

Increases in investment as a share of GDP appear to have a *positive* impact on private foreign financial flows for the group containing all SAL countries and the middle-income group, with statistical significance at the 5 per cent level in the former case. This contradicts the 'crowding out' hypothesis that public and private investments are negatively related, a result supported by the researches of Taylor (1988: 51). However, since we have not introduced lags to the investment variable, this correlation tells us nothing about the direction of causation between these two variables; a general discussion of causation in relation to all of our results is provided in the next section of this chapter. It is possible that causation runs in the reverse direction from that suggested by our equation since inflows of foreign private finance can be expected to finance investment rather than consumption expenditures, such that it is foreign private finance flows which cause investment as a share of GDP to increase, rather than vice versa.

In summary, our estimation of the private foreign finance equation suggests that neither loan finance nor loan conditions of either Bank adjustment programmes or Fund stabilisation programmes have had any significant impact in terms of attracting higher levels of foreign private capital flows, with the possible exception of the sub-Saharan group of countries. This is a disappointing result, since the stimulation of foreign commercial finance has often been proposed by the architects of such programmes as an anticipated beneficial effect of their reform packages. For example, the Bank's Senior Vice-President for Finance, Ernest Stern, has argued that a major objective of the original structural adjustment lending programme was to 'act as a catalyst for the inflow of other external capital to help ease the balance of payments situation' (Stern, 1983: 89), and more recently its Director of Economic Policy Analysis and Co-ordination, Constantine Michalopoulos, has stated that 'the main purpose of Bank sector and structural adjustment loans is to facilitate the adjustment required to achieve sustainable growth and the mobilisation of external financing needed to support a country's adjustment efforts' (Michalopoulos, 1987: 8).

Our statistical results, taken together with the case studies of Volume 2, indicate that *as a rule*, and with distinctive exceptions such as Turkey, Bank adjustment loans have failed to have this catalytic effect of attracting increased flows of foreign private finance and investment in response to, and in support of, an improved macroeconomic environment. The claim that the Bank and the Fund could rekindle international capital flows to developing countries by placing a seal of approval on select LDC governments (Taylor, 1988: especially 50–2) has, so far, proved to be unfounded. There is indeed, as we saw in Chapter 3, evidence of the reverse process taking place, with the Bank helping by its programme loans to hold open the door for the exit of the commercial banks and the IMF from countries to which they had over-exposed themselves during the boom of the late 1970s and subsequent debt crisis.

7.3 THE DIRECTION OF CAUSATION

The results we have obtained so far suggest that compliance with the conditions attached to World Bank policy-based lending is positively associated with improvements in macro variables, such as GDP and export growth, only in certain countries. In such countries, however, all we know is that an association exists; we do not know whether the direction of causation is (as the World Bank argues) from compliance with conditions, i.e. liberalisation, to growth, or from growth to liberalisation. It is entirely possible that the higher rate of economic growth has caused the liberalisation, rather than vice versa, since increased growth makes it easier for a government to 'buy off' interest groups who would otherwise suffer a welfare loss from the implementation of liberalisation conditions attached to programme assistance. We now consider explicitly which way the line of causation runs.

The simplest way of addressing the causation issue is to graph the two variables which are known to be correlated. If the graph indicates that a peak in export growth, for example, occurred before a peak in trade liberalisation, then the former cannot have been caused by the latter. The four quadrants of Figure 7.1 plot the graphs of GDP and export growth in relation to both the disbursement of World Bank programme finance and to measures of liberalisation associated with this programme finance. The graphs are constructed for two sub-Saharan countries, Kenya and Malawi, which have been the subject of detailed simulation exercises carried out by the authors elsewhere (for Malawi, see Chapter 8) and for two Asian countries, Thailand and the Philippines, for which we have case study material (Volume 2). GDP and export growth rates are measured by the percentage growth rate per annum of real GDP and real exports. For Kenya, Thailand and the Philippines, liberalisation is defined as the proportion of all export and import controls *removed* (or if the index is negative, *imposed*) in a given year. Although this liberalisation index does not fully reflect the whole range of adjustment reforms implemented under Bank programme loans, it is an easily and accurately quantifiable measure which serves as a useful proxy for the level of adjustment reform undertaken in each country. In the case of Malawi, where removal of export and import controls did not feature as a major component of Bank-guided liberalisation, we have used the compliance index from the previous section as a proxy for the level of adjustment reform.

The four quadrants of Figure 7.1 provide varied evidence regarding the direction of causation. In the case of Malawi and Thailand, the evidence suggests that causation does run, as the Bank argues, from programme finance-associated liberalisation to increased GDP and export growth rates. In the case of Kenya and the Philippines, however, the evidence is ambiguous.

In both Kenya and the Philippines, the programme finance (and liberalisation in the case of the Philippines) of 1980–1 is followed, with a one year lag, by a collapse of exports and a continued decline of GDP growth. Hence, it is clearly not the case that programme aid has caused an improvement in export and GDP performance. In both countries, however, the 1984 peak in export growth follows, with a one year lag, increased liberalisation and the provision of Bank finance, suggesting a causal link running from programme aid to export growth. The same causal evidence does not apply to GDP growth rates which reached a trough in 1984, i.e. the year following the wave of liberalisation and Bank finance. The improvement in GDP and export growth rates which occurred in the Philippines in 1986 follows upon a period in which trade controls were reimposed, such that we cannot attribute the cause of the improvement to liberalisation associated with Bank lending. It is possible that this surge in growth was caused by an external factor, namely an influx in foreign investment consequent on a change in political regime. In Kenya, 1986 witnessed a peak in the export growth rate and a slight improvement in GDP growth. This coincided with trade liberalisation measures and the provision of Bank finance, making it impossible to ascertain the direction of any possible causal links. Again, there is strong reason to believe that the surge in growth was mainly caused by an external factor in the form of a boom in coffee prices. Overall, the evidence from both Kenya and the Philippines is ambiguous, with the only exception being the improved export performance of 1984 in both countries which clearly followed a wave of liberalisation associated with Bank programme lending activities.

Malawi and Thailand provide stronger evidence for a positive causal link running from programme aid to improved GDP and export growth rates. In Malawi, the 1984 peak in export growth rates and the 1984–5 improvement in GDP performance followed a major episode of liberalisation under SALs I and II which occurred between 1982–4. Likewise in Thailand, the 1984 peak in export growth and the end of GDP decline followed a period of sustained liberalisation and provision, in rapid succession, of two Structural Adjustment Loans.

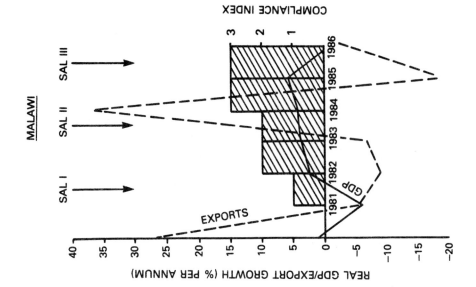

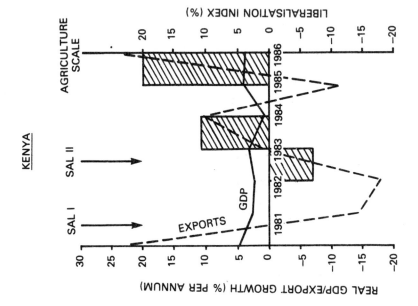

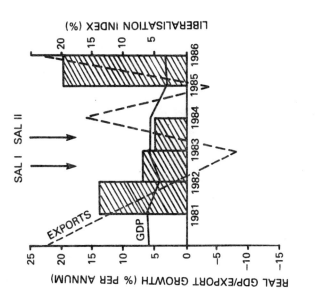

Figure 7.1 Direction of causation between liberalisation and growth: graphical analysis of four country cases

The combined evidence from the four countries analysed above indicates that in many, but not all, cases the correlation between SAL/SECAL loans and improved performance of macro indicators results from causal links which run from the former to the latter. We can, however, supplement this evidence with information provided by the regression work carried out in the previous section. The regression equations summarised in Tables 7.1 to 7.3 included Bank finance (SAL) compliance with liberalisation measures (*CI*) as lagged independent variables with one $(t-1)$ and two $(t-2)$ period lags. A positive and statistically significant regression coefficient on these lagged variables would provide evidence that causation runs from Bank finance and liberalisation to improvement in the independent variables which we have used as criteria for the evaluation of Bank programme lending.

Table 7.6 summarises the regression in terms of statistical significance obtained for the lagged independent variables. Although lags were introduced to the regression equations in order to specifically address the issue of causation, the results are somewhat disappointing. Despite the fact that our equations estimate forty-five coefficients for the lagged SAL and CI variables, in only seven cases do we find a statistically significant coefficient. One causal trend does, however, emerge from Table 7.6. The compliance variable lagged by one period (CI_{t-1}) has a statistically significant effect on both GDP and export performance for all groups of countries (with the exception of export growth in middle-income countries). It appears, therefore, that the evidence in favour of the proposition that *compliance with conditions* caused an improvement in GDP and export performance is stronger than the evidence in favour of the proposition that the *finance* associated with policy-based lending caused such an improvement.

Overall, our analysis of the causation issue indicates that in some cases the direction of causation does seem to run, as argued by the Bank, from programme aid to improvements in macro variables. In particular, our regression results suggest a favourable causal link between compliance with liberalisation and improvements in GDP and export growth. This is further supported by the graphical evidence presented for Malawi and Thailand. Nevertheless, as our graphs for the four countries illustrate, the causal evidence varies greatly between different countries. In addition, the type of evidence we have presented uses the criterion of 'precedence' to establish the direction of causal links. We have used the fact that programme aid precedes, in time, improvements in macro variables as evidence that the direction of causation runs from former to latter. Although such precedence is a necessary condition for causal links, it is not a sufficient condition to conclusively prove that the correlations constitute causal relations. Hence, at best, we have found weak and necessary, but not sufficient, evidence to support the Bank's argument that programme aid has caused improvements in such variables as GDP and export growth.

Table 7.6 Regression causation tests

Dependent variables	Lagged independent variables			
	SAL(*t*−1)	SAL(*t*−2)	CI(*t*−1)	CI(*t*−2)
All SAL countries:				
GDP growth	5%	–	1%	–
Export growth	–	–	5%	–
Import growth	–	–	–	–
Investment	–	–	–	–
Foreign finance	–	–	–	–
Sub-Saharan countries:				
GDP growth	–	–	5%	–
Export growth	–	–	5%	–
Import growth	–	–	–	–
Investment	–	–	–	–
Foreign finance	–	–	–	–
Middle-income countries:				
GDP growth	1%	–	5%	–
Export growth	–	–	–	–
Import growth	–	–	–	–
Investment	–	–	–	–
Foreign finance	–	–	–	–

Note: 1 per cent and 5 per cent denote the level of statistical significance, whilst – denotes a statistically insignificant regression coefficient.

7.4 CONCLUSIONS

It is time to draw together the threads of our discussion so far. Table 7.7 compares the influence of the adjustment lending provided by the World Bank, as measured in this chapter and the previous one, both with the World Bank's own estimates of these responses and with previous estimates of the effect of IMF stabilisation lending made by Killick *et al.* (1984).

If the broad consensus of effects reported in Table 7.7 is telling a true story, the effect of the adjustment programmes of the Bretton Woods institutions on the world economy in the 1980s has been very different from that which was planned. The intention was that the IMF would persuade borrowing countries to administer a dose of deflation to the macroeconomy, which would close the balance of payments and fiscal deficits; the Bank would then build upon this foundation to stimulate the supply side. The outcome appears to have been that the IMF administered only an insignificant deflationary blow, whereas such stimulus as the Bank has been able to impart to the supply side appears to have been confined to the exportables sector. The measured effect of Bank adjustment lending on

235

Table 7.7 Tabular and regression methods: summary of results

Indicators of performance	Real GDP growth	Real export growth	Investment GDP	Balance of payments	Private foreign finance
a. World Bank adjustment loans					
Tabular comparisons with control:					
This study (Ch. 6)	weak −ve	+ve	−ve	+ve	. .
World Bank (1988, 1990)	neutral	+ve	−ve	+ve	. .
(1992)	weak +ve (−ve in Africa)	neutral	neutral	. .	. .
Multiple regression:					
This study (Ch. 7)	weak +ve (finance only: weak −ve)	+ve	weak −ve	+ve	neutral
b. IMF stand-by credits					
Killick *et al.* (1984)	neutral	. .	. .	weak +ve	neutral
This study (Ch. 7)	neutral	+ve	neutral	. .	weak −ve

Notes and sources: . . denotes not measured. 'Weak' denotes not statistically significant. Results for this study are from Tables 6.3, 6.4 and 7.1 to 7.3; for World Bank (1988) from Table 2.4a and 2.6; for Killick *et al.* (1984) from vol. 1, Ch. 7.

growth varies according to the method of analysis chosen and is in any case weak; but there are cases in which adjustment lending appears to be associated with, and to have caused, subsequent growth. There is little systematic relationship between Bank adjustment lending and subsequent inflows of private foreign finance, and possibly as part consequence, investment levels appear to be lower in adjusting than in non-adjusting countries.

In all of this the most striking results on the Bank side are the weak growth effect and the negative investment effect, and at this point it is interesting to relate the discussion to the original intentions of policy-based lending and to the existing literature on the effectiveness of overseas aid. Reduced to its essentials, the purpose of all overseas aid is to augment the volume of resources available to a developing country or in the language of microeconomics to push its consumption frontier outwards, for example from *CD* to *HJ* on Figure 7.2. The resources supplied by aid can be used either for consumption or for investment (i.e. consumption in future periods); assuming that a recipient government does not wish to reduce either, the 'menu' for a country which receives the aid inflow described is defined by the points *F* and *G* on the post-aid consumption possibility curve.

For many years, extending into the 1980s, a debate persisted between 'aid pessimists' (e.g. Bauer) who styled the 'typical developing country government' as likely to allocate incremental resources mostly to wasteful

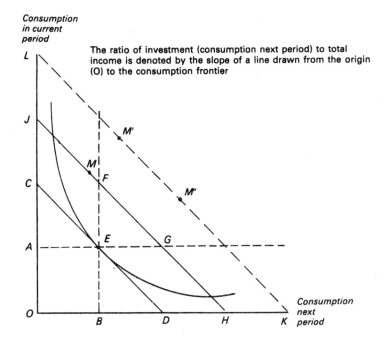

Consumption in current period

The ratio of investment (consumption next period) to total income is denoted by the slope of a line drawn from the origin (O) to the consumption frontier

Consumption next period

Figure 7.2 Present versus future consumption: aid allocation choices facing a recipient government

consumption (ending up at or near point *F*) and 'aid optimists' (e.g. Chenery, Cassen) who expected it to allocate its aid inflows in the vicinity of point *G*, so that aid inflows provided a significant increment to investment. The range of potential government behaviours between these extremes is clearly infinite; but in any case, as a series of writings of the 1980s illustrated, the effectiveness of aid is not only a question of how the recipient government uses it but also of its effects on relative prices. Like any other financial inflow (e.g. an oil boom) aid flows, in the absence of countervailing action, may, for example, buoy up the real exchange rate to the point of making industry uncompetitive (the effect known as 'Dutch disease'; see Mosley, Hudson and Horrell, 1987) or push up the cost of non-tradable goods such as labour, building materials and transport: the consequence recently described by Collier (1989) as the 'construction boom effect'. But of course not all relative-price effects of aid are malign.

This is where policy-based lending enters the picture. For the promise which this form of aid offered was to raise the effectiveness of aid by automatically combining a financial flow with an increase in the productivity of capital achieved through *beneficent* changes in relative prices, i.e. distortion-reducing policy interventions. On this view, a flow of aid,

EG, would push out the consumption frontier from *CD* to *JH* if it came merely as a sum of money, but could increase the economy's productive potential further − say to *KL* − if tied to a package of policy measures designed to 'get the prices right'. What the analysis of this chapter suggests is that the influence of the money provided by policy-based lending on its own was immediate and growth-depressing, whereas the influence of the conditions, *if* they were implemented, was lagged and positive. Some governments, then, starting at point *E*, took the money and ran, landing up at a point such as *M* with lowered investment and expanded present consumption (Guyana, Ecuador); others were able to enlarge their production possibilities through policy reforms, but still characteristically landed up at a point such as *M'*, with a lower ratio of investment to national income (Philippines, Jamaica, Kenya). There were others whose investment ratio increased, say to *M''* (Ghana, Turkey) but these are atypical. As commented by Helleiner (1990: 3), the tendency of policy-based lending to depress investment places a high premium on the expected efficiency gains from price-based reforms, which as the country case studies show have been slow and uncertain to materialise.

APPENDIX   DATA AND SOURCES

a.   REGRESSION DATA SET

	1980	1981	1982	1983	1984	1985	1986
gEX							
BOLIVIA	21.0	−5.1	−8.6	−9.0	−5.5	−12.9	−19.8
CHILE	20.0	−16.4	−5.0	3.4	−4.7	4.5	10.4
COSTA RICA	7.3	0.6	−13.6	−0.6	12.9	1.1	3.7
C.D'IVOIRE	24.9	−19.3	−11.8	−7.5	30.5	8.9	8.9
GHANA	15.4	−7.4	−17.9	213.2	−79.4	9.8	39.9
GUYANA	32.8	−11.1	−30.3	−21.6	11.1	−1.4	5.3
JAMAICA	17.7	1.1	−21.3	−4.6	2.0	−24.5	5.7
KENYA	25.5	−14.5	−17.8	0.6	10.2	−11.5	25.3
KOREA	16.3	21.4	2.8	11.9	19.6	3.5	14.6
MALAWI	27.8	−5.3	−8.9	−6.9	36.7	−19.5	−3.6
NIGER	26.3	−19.6	−27.0	−9.9	−23.7	−2.2	16.6
PAKISTAN	25.9	11.3	−16.8	28.4	−15.0	4.0	21.6
PANAMA	19.7	−9.6	−3.1	−1.6	−15.8	19.5	6.9
PHILIPPINES	25.8	−1.1	−12.3	−0.3	6.3	−14.6	6.6
SENEGAL	−11.0	4.8	9.6	−0.9	−1.7	−24.7	34.3
THAILAND	23.0	8.2	−1.3	−8.3	16.4	−3.9	22.9
TOGO	53.7	−37.0	−16.1	−8.5	17.9	−0.5	5.3
TURKEY	27.1	61.6	20.9	0.2	24.4	11.7	−6.5
YUGOSLAVIA	63.1	1.5	−6.1	−3.6	−0.8	8.5	−32.3

	1980	1981	1982	1983	1984	1985	1986
EPI							
BOLIVIA	100	80	71	74	67	66	56
CHILE	100	82	73	75	67	67	66
COSTA RICA	100	81	77	75	62	60	85
C.D'IVOIRE	100	86	76	70	76	75	81
GHANA	100	71	60	58	63	53	60
GUYANA	100	94	88	83	78	65	68
JAMAICA	100	91	84	82	77	64	66
KENYA	100	93	90	82	65	83	79
KOREA	100	97	94	92	89	89	90
MALAWI	100	104	96	105	105	94	95
NIGER	100	83	84	82	71	72	71
PAKISTAN	100	102	93	87	87	83	75
PANAMA	100	103	87	79	77	73	72
PHILIPPINES	100	92	79	79	85	77	73
SENEGAL	100	104	87	79	88	88	83
THAILAND	100	101	80	81	82	75	74
TOGO	100	86	79	72	77	76	68
TURKEY	100	89	83	73	74	73	70
YUGOSLAVIA	100	96	93	90	88	87	87

	1980	1981	1982	1983	1984	1985	1986
FF							
BOLIVIA	16	6	65	0	0	0	0
CHILE	2694	4103	1378	234	114	86	162
COSTA RICA	102	54	75	0	0	0	20
C.D'IVOIRE	262	271	676	441	895	978	900
GHANA	0	0	0	0	0	0	0
GUYANA	0	0	0	0	0	0	0
JAMAICA	25	0	35	35	10	10	7
KENYA	87	16	92	189	31	169	50
KOREA	551	1009	449	1558	1102	1601	2336
MALAWI	0	0	0	0	0	0	0
NIGER	113	123	65	34	24	29	66
PAKISTAN	9	15	18	7	4	13	19
PANAMA	0	0	0	0	0	0	0
PHILIPPINES	472	608	564	269	70	285	100
SENEGAL	0	3	0	0	0	6	5
THAILAND	1288	790	707	950	1417	784	587
TOGO	0	0	0	0	0	0	0
TURKEY	75	50	51	55	81	42	180
YUGOSLAVIA	3223	2003	1489	1348	878	554	140

	1980	1981	1982	1983	1984	1985	1986
gGDP							
BOLIVIA	−1.5	0.4	−2.6	−6.6	−0.9	−1.7	−2.9
CHILE	7.8	5.5	−13.1	−0.5	6.0	2.4	5.4
COSTA RICA	0.8	−2.3	−7.3	2.7	7.9	0.9	4.4
C.D'IVOIRE	12.2	2.7	1.2	−3.5	−2.4	5.9	3.7
GHANA	0.6	−2.9	−6.5	−4.5	8.7	5.4	4.3
GUYANA	2.0	4.5	−10.8	−10.3	5.8	1.8	1.5
JAMAICA	−5.8	2.5	−0.2	1.2	0.0	−5.4	2.2
KENYA	4.8	2.9	2.5	3.2	0.9	4.1	4.0
KOREA	−3.0	7.4	5.7	10.9	8.6	5.4	11.9
MALAWI	0.6	−6.2	2.5	3.8	4.3	5.8	−1.1
NIGER	4.8	1.2	−1.2	−1.8	−14.7	5.8	6.5
PAKISTAN	8.8	7.0	6.2	6.4	5.3	8.0	7.5
PANAMA	15.1	4.2	4.9	−0.2	−0.4	4.1	3.0
PHILIPPINES	5.3	3.8	2.9	1.1	−6.3	−4.6	1.1
SENEGAL	−3.1	−1.2	15.4	2.2	−4.0	3.8	4.5
THAILAND	5.8	6.3	4.1	5.9	5.5	3.2	3.5
TOGO	14.5	−3.4	−3.3	−5.7	0.7	5.0	3.1
TURKEY	−0.7	4.4	5.0	3.7	5.7	5.1	8.2
YUGOSLAVIA	2.4	1.3	0.6	−1.1	1.8	1.0	3.4

	1980	1981	1982	1983	1984	1985	1986
IMF							
BOLIVIA	1.15	0.00	1.00	0.57	0.00	0.00	2.70
CHILE	0.00	0.00	0.00	3.21	1.38	1.24	1.74
COSTA RICA	0.41	2.36	0.00	3.89	0.00	0.92	0.00
C.D'IVOIRE	0.00	4.34	1.68	2.34	0.63	1.17	0.31
GHANA	0.00	0.00	0.00	7.58	4.86	2.51	0.66
GUYANA	10.00	3.73	1.64	0.00	0.00	0.00	0.00
JAMAICA	0.00	8.11	5.72	3.62	4.33	2.63	0.00
KENYA	1.30	0.50	3.11	2.81	0.91	2.49	0.00
KOREA	1.07	1.03	0.17	0.27	0.70	0.16	0.14
MALAWI	2.25	2.55	0.91	2.78	3.58	2.37	0.00
NIGER	0.00	0.00	0.00	2.46	1.03	1.01	0.72
PAKISTAN	0.64	2.26	2.04	1.18	0.00	0.00	0.00
PANAMA	0.00	2.35	0.00	2.65	2.27	0.74	1.02
PHILIPPINES	1.11	0.61	0.00	0.89	0.26	0.99	0.88
SENEGAL	2.11	2.92	2.35	1.32	1.34	2.23	1.02
THAILAND	0.00	1.70	0.19	0.70	0.00	0.89	0.31
TOGO	1.60	1.02	0.00	2.92	2.54	2.14	1.43
TURKEY	1.19	0.88	0.66	0.77	0.36	0.00	0.00
YUGOSLAVIA	0.71	1.03	1.11	1.26	0.74	0.58	0.26

	1980	1981	1982	1983	1984	1985	1986
gIM							
BOLIVIA	−25.6	37.9	−39.6	−4.0	18.6	21.2	15.0
CHILE	21.5	24.2	−39.8	−22.5	17.2	−13.6	5.0
COSTA RICA	9.1	−20.7	−26.1	10.6	9.8	1.2	2.9
C.D'IVOIRE	20.9	−20.9	−12.3	−13.5	−16.4	15.3	9.1
GHANA	32.5	−2.0	−36.3	207.5	−73.2	26.0	7.1
GUYANA	24.5	10.1	−35.8	−17.9	9.6	1.2	−2.0
JAMAICA	18.0	25.8	−6.2	10.8	−25.1	−3.1	−11.6
KENYA	56.2	−20.1	−22.0	−15.8	13.9	−7.1	12.2
KOREA	9.6	17.2	−7.2	8.0	16.9	1.6	1.4
MALAWI	10.6	−20.5	−11.1	0.0	−13.5	5.6	−11.3
NIGER	28.6	−14.1	−8.6	−30.5	1.9	21.2	−7.5
PAKISTAN	31.9	3.7	−3.0	−0.8	10.0	0.3	−8.8
PANAMA	21.3	8.0	1.1	0.4	0.8	−2.2	−8.3
PHILIPPINES	25.4	−4.2	3.9	−3.3	−24.2	−13.1	2.5
SENEGAL	13.0	−18.2	15.2	4.7	−2.8	−38.6	21.0
THAILAND	28.1	8.0	−14.1	20.3	1.1	−11.1	−1.1
TOGO	6.2	−21.3	−9.7	−27.4	−4.6	6.3	−30.6
TURKEY	40.8	18.5	−0.1	4.8	15.8	5.3	−2.2
YUGOSLAVIA	38.1	−13.5	−15.6	−9.3	−4.7	5.4	−31.6

	1980	1981	1982	1983	1984	1985	1986
INV							
BOLIVIA	13	13	7	7	18	17	8
CHILE	18	22	10	8	14	14	15
COSTA RICA	25	28	23	21	25	23	23
C.D'IVOIRE	27	27	24	18	13	13	12
GHANA	6	6	1	8	6	9	9
GUYANA	30	33	26	27	23	21	21
JAMAICA	16	20	20	22	22	23	19
KENYA	30	25	22	21	22	19	26
KOREA	31	26	26	27	29	30	29
MALAWI	22	23	20	23	16	16	10
NIGER	29	27	26	25	14	14	11
PAKISTAN	18	17	17	17	17	17	17
PANAMA	27	29	29	21	18	15	17
PHILIPPINES	30	30	29	27	18	16	13
SENEGAL	15	17	20	17	15	14	14
THAILAND	27	28	21	25	23	23	21
TOGO	26	31	26	23	26	26	28
TURKEY	27	25	21	21	20	20	25
YUGOSLAVIA	35	32	34	35	29	39	38

	1980	1981	1982	1983	1984	1985	1986
SAL							
BOLIVIA	0.41	0.32	0.00	0.00	0.00	0.00	4.19
CHILE	0.00	0.00	0.00	0.00	0.00	0.78	1.49
COSTA RICA	0.00	0.00	0.00	0.41	0.35	1.05	0.94
C.D'IVOIRE	0.00	0.87	0.99	1.77	1.87	0.00	1.71
GHANA	0.00	0.00	0.00	0.54	1.29	1.82	1.65
GUYANA	0.00	3.14	3.74	0.00	0.00	0.00	0.00
JAMAICA	0.59	0.63	1.76	2.65	3.05	1.39	0.00
KENYA	0.46	0.40	1.23	1.32	0.00	0.00	0.50
KOREA	0.00	0.19	0.18	0.20	0.18	0.13	0.11
MALAWI	0.00	1.64	1.70	2.26	2.75	5.62	4.96
NIGER	0.00	0.00	0.00	0.00	0.00	0.00	1.44
PAKISTAN	0.12	0.10	0.28	0.27	0.00	0.32	0.41
PANAMA	0.00	0.00	0.00	0.69	0.66	0.00	0.98
PHILIPPINES	0.28	0.26	0.00	0.44	0.69	0.23	0.00
SENEGAL	1.13	1.29	0.00	0.00	0.00	0.00	0.95
THAILAND	0.00	0.00	0.20	0.40	0.21	0.00	0.00
TOGO	0.00	0.00	0.00	2.78	2.82	4.84	3.46
TURKEY	0.26	0.53	0.60	0.65	0.71	0.69	0.57
YUGOSLAVIA	0.00	0.00	0.00	0.29	0.47	0.10	0.00

	1980	1981	1982	1983	1984	1985	1986
CI							
BOLIVIA	1	1	0	0	0	0	3
CHILE	0	0	0	0	0	3	3
COSTA RICA	0	0	0	2	2	2	2
C.D'IVOIRE	0	3	2	2	2	0	2
GHANA	0	0	0	3	3	3	3
GUYANA	0	1	1	0	0	0	0
JAMAICA	1	2	2	2	2	1	0
KENYA	2	2	1	2	0	0	2
KOREA	0	3	3	3	3	3	3
MALAWI	0	1	2	2	3	3	3
NIGER	0	0	0	0	0	0	2
PAKISTAN	3	3	3	3	0	3	3
PANAMA	0	0	0	2	2	0	2
PHILIPPINES	3	3	0	2	2	2	0
SENEGAL	1	1	0	0	0	0	3
THAILAND	0	0	3	2	2	0	0
TOGO	0	0	0	3	3	3	2
TURKEY	3	3	3	3	3	3	3
YUGOSLAVIA	0	0	0	2	2	2	0

	1980	1981	1982	1983	1984	1985	1986
ToT							
BOLIVIA	100	85	77	82	77	75	59
CHILE	100	85	78	82	75	75	75
COSTA RICA	100	84	82	83	92	90	95
C.D'IVOIRE	100	89	81	77	86	85	90
GHANA	100	73	84	63	71	59	68
GUYANA	100	97	93	92	88	73	77
JAMAICA	100	92	69	91	87	73	83
KENYA	100	93	92	88	92	90	93
KOREA	100	98	100	101	98	99	108
MALAWI	100	108	102	116	118	104	103
NIGER	100	86	90	91	79	81	82
PAKISTAN	100	104	98	94	96	92	88
PANAMA	100	104	90	86	85	81	85
PHILIPPINES	100	93	82	86	94	85	87
SENEGAL	100	108	95	90	102	102	100
THAILAND	100	101	82	87	89	82	87
TOGO	100	91	84	81	66	86	80
TURKEY	100	67	88	94	92	92	102
YUGOSLAVIA	100	101	100	100	99	97	95

	1980	1981	1982	1983	1984	1985	1986
WEATHER							
BOLIVIA	99	102	106	94	110	109	115
CHILE	120	109	97	115	120	116	107
COSTA RICA	102	106	93	111	119	100	97
C.D'IVOIRE	101	99	86	72	102	106	98
GHANA	87	88	75	62	101	104	99
GUYANA	104	101	98	96	102	97	116
JAMAICA	100	108	96	109	103	94	118
KENYA	83	74	79	85	64	90	101
KOREA	104	102	96	108	92	100	104
MALAWI	71	51	80	78	65	84	58
NIGER	51	53	68	75	43	78	102
PAKISTAN	100	97	102	90	86	108	103
PANAMA	99	104	103	102	95	90	100
PHILIPPINES	90	88	100	91	86	78	90
SENEGAL	69	71	102	70	61	85	88
THAILAND	94	97	104	106	96	94	93
TOGO	102	104	96	96	81	104	102
TURKEY	96	95	102	104	94	99	97
YUGOSLAVIA	94	97	99	106	99	95	106

b. DATA DEFINITIONS AND SOURCES

gEX = Annual average growth rates of export values in curent US$. Source: UNCTAD *Handbook of International Trade and Development Statistics*, 1981 and 1987, Table 1.5.

EPI = Index of export unit values i.e. current value of exports (fob) converted to US$ and expressed as a percentage of the average for the base period (1980). The data series is the annual average percentage change of this index over the specified time period. Source: UNCTAD *Handbook of International Trade and Development Statistics*, 1989, Table 7.2, except Turkey, for whom the data are from IMF *International Financial Statistics 1987 Yearbook*, Table 74.

FF = Annual average absolute value in (current US$ millions) of private non-guaranteed long-term debt disbursed in a given year by official and private creditors (suppliers, financial markets, parent companies overseas). Source: World Bank, *World Debt Tables*, 1987–8 edition, Vol. II, *Country Tables*.

gGDP = Annual average growth rates of GDP at constant market prices (1978=100). Source: UNCTAD *Handbook of International Trade and Development Statistics*, 1981 and 1987, Table 6.2.

IMF = IMF finance as a percentage of GDP. IMF finance to a country is defined as purchases, i.e. total drawings, by the country from the

244

General Resources Account, excluding drawings on the Reserve Tranche, in a given year. The General Resources Account includes most major components of the Fund's programme finance – Stand-bys, the Compensatory Finance Facility, the Buffer Stock Financing Facility, the Extended Facility and the Oil Facility. However, the General Resources Account does not include drawings from: the Special Disbursements Account (from which Structural Adjustment drawings are made); from the IMF's Trust Fund and from the Supplementary Financing Subsidy Account. The Structural Adjustment Facility was not established until March 1986, and for this reason is not included in our data series. The Trust Fund and Supplementary Financing Subsidy are legally separate from the resources of the IMF, and since they are not part of the Fund's ordinary resources, are excluded from our data. Source: IMF finance data from World Bank, *World Debt Tables*, 1987–8. GDP data as above.

gIM   =   Annual average growth rate of import values in current US$. Source: UNCTAD, *Handbook of International Trade and Development Statistics*, 1981 and 1987, Table 1.6.

INV   =   Gross domestic investment as a percentage of GDP. Source: World Bank, *World Development Report*, various issues, Table 5.

SAL   =   Structural adjustment loan and sectoral adjustment loan finance as a percentage of GDP. It is assumed that 50% of a loan is disbursed in the year of loan approval by the Bank Board and 50% in the subsequent year. Although this assumption does not always reflect the disbursement pattern of SAL and SECAL loans, the generalisation is supported by the Bank's own assessment of tranche release:

> . . . about three-quarters of all adjustment loans are experiencing delays in tranche release as a result of delays in fulfilment of agreed conditions. Nonetheless, . . . they are rarely abandoned altogether. Less than one in ten loans are suffering delays of more than one year.
>
> (World Bank, 1988, Report no. R86–15, p. iv)

Source: GDP data in US$ from World Bank, *World Development Reports*, 1981 to 1988, except Guyana, for whom GDP data is from World Bank, *World Debt Tables*. Data on the annual value of SAL and SECAL disbursements are from World Bank Country Policy Division (now called the Strategic Planning and Research Division).

CI   =   Index of compliance with conditional policy reforms attached to programme loans. The index is defined as follows:

     0 = no compliance with Bank policy condition since no SAL or SECAL loan is in place.
     1 = low compliance with Bank policy conditions
     2 = moderate compliance with Bank policy conditions
     3 = high compliance with Bank policy conditions

This index is derived from the Bank's own compliance index given in

Structural Adjustment Lending: A First Review of Experience, Table 3.1. World Bank (1986) in the bibliography. For countries not covered in this report compliance is based on the authors' own subjective estimates. The compliance index is explicitly calculated for SAL policy conditions, and each country is assumed to display the same level of compliance with conditions attached to SECAL loans.

ToT   =   The net barter terms of trade, defined as the ratio of the export unit value index to the import unit value index (1980 = 100). The data series is the annual average percentage change of the terms of trade index. Source: as for export price index.

WEATHER   =   Weather index proxied by the average rainfall in capital city for period stated as a percentage of the 25-year average 1961–86. Source: United Nations *Statistical Yearbook*, various issues.

8

MODEL-BASED RESULTS

[In collaboration with François Bourguignon, Christian Morrisson and Akiko Suwa.]

8.1 INTRODUCTION

Within the set of 'with versus without' methodologies proposed for the evaluation of policy-based lending in Figure 6.1, there remains one branch of the tree still unexplored, namely the possibility of simulating the impact of policy packages on a model of the economy in specific countries. In principle, this approach has three advantages over the analytical methods used in Chapters 6 and 7. First, the individual components of a conditionality package (e.g. removal of quotas, agricultural price increases etc.) can be separately analysed, which is not possible with the regression or control-group approaches. Second, the 'without programme lending' case consists no longer of a cluster of non-programme countries or a dummy variable set at zero, both of which imply the possibility of biased results, but simply a model of a specific country run in the absence of the finance the World Bank would have supplied and the policy changes which it recommended. Third, the single country approach greatly reduces the problem of causal inference, since causal structure has been embodied in the construction and estimation of the model.

These advantages of the single-country modelling approach are, however, gained at a cost which goes beyond the money and time required to build the model. In the first place, the 'without programme aid' situation is no longer an observable construct, such as a group of non-programme countries, as was the case in Chapter 6, but rather the imaginary situation in which the country under analysis received no adjustment finance from the Bank and made no associated policy changes. But this situation is not easy to define with absolute accuracy, since *some* adjustment to economic crisis is invariably made by recipient countries whether or not the Bank intervenes, and the question of what kind of policy change would have been carried out in the absence of a deal with the Bank cannot be resolved with certainty. In addition, the choice between models is a subjective matter. Even a model which has predicted well in the past may be rejected by the user on the grounds that its structure does not square with his intuitive belief about how the economy works.[1]

The Philippines desk of the World Bank, for example, commissioned a couple of modelling exercises in 1986 as a preparation for the programme of new lending to the Aquino government (discussed in Volume 2, Chapter 12). One of these was an econometric model designed by a member of the Bank's Economic Analysis and Projections Department (Hwa, 1986). It was rejected, *not* on account of its ability to forecast the Philippines economy (which was quite good) but rather because:

(a) it was unstable (i.e. any external disturbance drove it further and further away from macroeconomic equilibrium)[2] and thus mathematically inconvenient;

(b) it exhibited certain counter-intuitive features. One was a negative response of the demand for money to the interest rate, which accounted for the instability above described; the other was a price elasticity of demand for demand for exports well below one. Hence, as an internal Bank commentary on the model put it, 'an export-led growth strategy is incompatible with balance of payments equilibrium. Clearly then, this elasticity is another key parameter on which more work must be done before simulation results can be accepted' (Kharas, 1986: 12).

What all of this illustrates is that model-based findings, however well founded they may be econometrically, will not convince if they attack a fundamental principle of the reader's belief system, for example that the World Bank's fundamental belief that an export-led growth strategy is compatible with balance-of-payments equilibrium. It is not, however, a function of this book to question such beliefs *a priori*, but rather to follow through their logic and to examine the effectiveness of Bank policy packages *using the Bank's own chosen models*. We shall do this using one model of the agricultural sector only (for Malawi) and one of the entire economy (for Morocco). Both of these are computable multi-market models which are calibrated to data for one year only rather than econometric models which are estimated against time-series data for a run of years; but econometric models have not been widely used in policy analysis by the Bank. Given the unreliability of estimates made against short runs of data during a period of structural change, this bias in analytical method is probably sensible. The two sections which follow are rather technical and readers mainly interested in the conclusions are invited to skip to section 8.4 on pages 281–2.

8.2 RESULTS FROM A MULTI-MARKET AGRICULTURAL SECTOR MODEL: MALAWI*

In the early 1980s, the World Bank's own Economic Policy Management Support Unit (EANEM) developed a micro-computable multi-market agricultural pricing model for Malawi's smallholder agricultural sector (Singh and Squire, 1984). This sectoral model was designed to be used in the SAL policy debate between the Bank and the Malawi government on issues relating to pricing policy in this sector. It has been transferred by the authors to an IBM-compatible microcomputer disk, and is available from them in this form.

The Malawi multi-market agricultural pricing model developed by EANEM built upon the tradition of farm-household models which incorporate both production and consumption decisions (e.g. Barnum and Squire, 1979). Supply and consumption responses were derived from underlying production and utility functions in which optimisation and technology choice were treated implicitly. Responses to exogenous price changes were first calculated at the micro level of the representative household and then aggregated to generate responses at the market level. A detailed specification of the model is provided in Appendix I to this chapter.

The micro-computable reduced form of the model only covers the smallholder subsector and incorporates five principal crops – maize, tobacco, cotton, groundnuts and rice, and one input – fertiliser. The model is able to simulate a wide range of price policy packages and measures their impact on multiple indicators, such as agricultural production, consumption and resource allocation (efficiency), smallholder incomes (welfare), food production (self-sufficiency), balance of payments (external balance), and the government budget (internal balance). Hence the model provides an analytic tool which allows for *multiple* policy objectives. Policy trade-offs can be clearly specified, and the opportunity costs of different policy packages are quantifiable.

In using the EANEM Malawi model for our single country modelling exercise we are, however, accepting certain limitations in this approach to the evaluation of SAL impact. First, the model restricts us to a partial equilibrium approach since we are only able to evaluate the impact on one sector of the economy, namely, the smallholder agricultural sector. Second, the model has been specifically designed to capture the impact of price policy changes. Although pricing policy constituted the key area of Bank policy conditionality in the smallholder sector, non-price policies relating to market liberalisation and institutional reform were also implemented and the model does not enable us to quantify the impact of such reforms. In addition, it cannot assess the effects of the injection of SAL finance, which

*Warm thanks are due to Geoffrey Mulagha of the Ministry of Economic Planning and Development, Malawi, for help in adapting and running this model.

has, on average, comprised 1.5 – 2.0 per cent of Malawi's GDP per annum between 1981 and 1987. An important advantage of restricting analysis to the impact of price policy, however, is that it enables us to isolate the impact of Bank programme lending from that of the Fund's programmes, since pricing policy was an area exclusive to the Bank's activities.

Policy Scenarios for Simulation

In our evaluation exercise the model is used for retrospective policy analysis. Three policy scenarios are simulated, each scenario consisting of a time series of annual producer and input prices covering the years 1981–8. Scenario one consists of the actual policies implemented over the period and hence represents the government's *partial compliance* with SAL agricultural pricing conditionality. Scenario two consists of counter-factual price policies representing the hypothetical case of *zero compliance* with SAL conditionality i.e. the government's own first best policies. The fact that in Malawi policy-makers publicly articulated an alternative economic pro-gramme which the government would have preferred to follow in the absence of external pressure from the Bank helps us to be confident in choosing this counter-factual case, and is one reason for choosing Malawi as a case for analysis of this type. Scenario three also consists of counter-factual price policies, this time representing the hypothetical scenario of the government's *full compliance* with SAL conditionality, i.e. the Bank's own first best policies.

Table 8.1 provides the crop and input prices used under each scenario. Counter-factual scenario three, which represents full compliance with the Bank's first-best set of policies, reflects the Bank's belief that structural weaknesses in the smallholder sector took the form of: inadequate price incentives offered by the Agricultural Development and Marketing Corporation (ADMARC), the state marketing board, for smallholder exportable crops (tobacco, cotton, rice and groundnuts); allocative inefficiencies resulting from distorted, i.e. subsidised, input prices; and excessive policy emphasis on the production of food crops. Hence, the Bank's first-best policy prescriptions involve the attainment of export parity prices for exportable crops by 1985, via regular annual price increments starting in 1981, and the maintenance of parity prices after 1985. Input subsidies on fertiliser are also removed over a four-year period, again via constant annual price increments, with fertiliser selling prices being determined by current economic costs from 1985 onwards. Finally, in order to redress the incentive imbalance between export and food crops, maize price increases are limited to 5 per cent per annum throughout the period.

The second policy scenario of 'zero compliance' assumes that the government implemented its own first-best price policy. Food self-sufficiency is the top policy priority, giving rise to frequent increases in the

Table 8.1 Malawi: price policy scenarios for simulation exercise

	1981	1982	1983	1984	1985	1986	1987	1988
Scenario 1:	**Partial compliance**							
Maize	66.0	111.10	111.10	122.20	122.20	122.20	122.20	166.60
Tobacco	443.90	520.80	756.40	837.40	1018.20	1020.30	1015.20	1100.00
Cotton	230.00	285.00	380.00	420.00	460.00	500.00	550.00	650.00
Rice	100.00	100.00	115.00	150.00	170.00	190.00	220.00	270.00
Groundnuts	330.00	370.00	550.00	600.00	700.00	750.00	750.00	750.00
Fertiliser	184.00	235.00	250.00	294.00	338.00	405.00	412.00	454.00
Scenario 2:	**Zero compliance**							
Maize	66.0	111.10	111.10	122.20	122.20	133.30	155.50	166.60
Tobacco	443.90	466.10	489.40	513.87	539.56	566.54	594.87	624.61
Cotton	230.00	253.00	278.30	306.13	336.74	370.42	448.20	493.03
Rice	100.00	110.00	121.00	133.10	146.41	161.05	177.16	194.87
Groundnuts	330.00	363.00	399.30	439.23	483.15	531.47	584.62	643.08
Fertiliser	162.00	272.16	272.16	299.38	299.39	326.32	381.79	409.52
Scenario 3:	**Full compliance**							
Maize	66.0	69.30	72.77	76.40	80.22	84.24	88.45	92.87
Tobacco	443.90	526.47	624.39	740.52	879.30	1171.2	2871.19	2871.19
Cotton	230.00	283.36	349.10	430.09	529.30	536.33	583.39	779.44
Rice	100.00	110.00	121.00	133.10	146.80	230.00	102.31	304.70
Groundnuts	330.00	363.99	401.48	442.83	488.37	659.9	702.39	733.69
Fertiliser	184.00	229.54	286.35	357.22	445.73	524.88	542.72	586.19

Note: 1981 refers to the 1980/81 cropping season, and similarly for other years.

maize producer price throughout the period. In order to pay for the resulting subsidisation of maize production and distribution, it is assumed that the government continues with its policy of the 1970s, i.e. implicitly taxing smallholder export crops, particularly tobacco, by offering farmers prices well below export parity levels. Hence, tobacco producer prices are only allowed to increase by 5 per cent per annum, whilst the prices of rice, cotton and groundnuts are allowed to increase by 10 per cent per annum. The government also maintains its policy of subsidising fertiliser, with increases in fertiliser prices linked to increases in the producer price of maize.

Scenario one reflects partial compliance with SAL price policy conditionality, as incorporated in the actual price policies implemented during the period. In the early 1980s the government pursued its own desired policies, in direct defiance of Bank conditions. For example, large maize price increases were implemented, fertiliser continued to be heavily subsidised, and smallholder export crops were implicitly taxed, via low producer prices, in order to finance maize production and distribution. However, under SAL II and the first tranche of SAL III, i.e. 1984–7, government compliance with conditionality was high – the maize price was held constant, export crop prices were increased considerably and subsidies on fertiliser were rapidly removed. In 1988 slippage again increased – a large maize price increase was announced and fertiliser prices contained a subsidy of well over 20 per cent.

Simulation results

When the relevant prices under each scenario are fed into the model, the model predicts yearly outcomes for the following variables: Net ADMARC cash flow and net Smallholder Fertiliser Revolving Fund (SFRF) cash flow (these two together giving rise to the net overall budgetary effect); smallholder real income; maize production (including a separate analysis of improved maize production); non-maize cash crop production; maize imports and exports; and the net balance of payments effect. The results for each variable are presented in Table 8.2.

It must be stressed that since the model is based on a large number of assumptions for which the empirical evidence is weak, predictions about *absolute* changes are subject to a large margin of error. The model's use is essentially to make *comparative* predictions regarding the relative impact of different price policy packages.

Net budgetary effects

A policy of zero compliance with Bank pricing conditionality has a detrimental impact on the government budget throughout the period (part (a) of the table). Despite the fact that zero compliance involves suppressing the producer price of exportable cash crops (tobacco, groundnuts, rice and cotton) to levels well below export parity, the resulting profits made by ADMARC on these crop trading activities are insufficient to cover the costs of increased subsidisation of maize production, procurement and distribution and the costs of subsidising fertiliser. Hence, a government policy of placing top priority on food self-sufficiency, via increases in the maize producer price and subsidised fertiliser, has a high opportunity cost in the form of worsening internal imbalance. Successful Bank opposition to the government's policy of food crop and fertiliser subsidisation, which led to the temporary abandonment of the policy during the period 1984–7, was based upon the concern that such policies were placing an intolerable financial burden on parastatal finances and hence the government budget. The modelling results suggest that the Bank's concerns were well founded.

Smallholder real income

The zero compliance scenario, placing top priority on food self-sufficiency, in addition to having an adverse effect on the government budget, also has

252

Table 8.2 Malawi: Simulation results

(a) *Net budgetary cost (1000 Malawi Kwacha per year)*

	1981	1982	1983	1984	1985	1986	1987	1988
Partial compliance	13	−12.710	13,851	14,525	12,696	28,895	−52,549	−110,528
Zero compliance	−2,214	−14.998	633	175	−2,343	9,042	−76,740	−117,215
Full compliance	675	7,417	18,894	43,426	40,137	27,433	−69,843	−71,324

(b) *Smallholder real income* (Malawi kwacha per hectare per year)

	1981	1982	1983	1984	1985	1986	1987	1988
Partial compliance	219.91	226.62	237.64	337.96	343.55	342.23	385.58	397.80
Zero compliance	220.31	223.73	220.56	329.68	329.66	326.43	375.57	387.66
Full compliance	219.90	224.42	226.97	322.36	328.20	347.80	410.33	428.18

(c) *Total smallholder maize production* (1000 metric tonnes per year)

	1981	1982	1983	1984	1985	1986	1987	1988
Partial compliance	1,751	1,321	1,213	1,418	1,406	1,310	1,294	1,434
Zero compliance	1,262	1,340	1,263	1,475	1,473	1,403	1,352	1,467
Full compliance	1,248	1,227	1,146	1,337	1,316	1,217	1,217	1,266

(d) *Improved maize production* (metric tonnes per year)

	1981	1982	1983	1984	1985	1986	1987	1988
Partial compliance	244,093	311,232	271,706	277,293	272,968	242,734	236,237	313,198
Zero compliance	252,532	326,122	303,891	309,753	311,423	303,214	275,937	328,340
Full compliance	242,267	231,508	210,059	204,844	195,740	171,307	170,439	180,957

(e) *Smallholder export crop production* (thousand metric tonnes per year)

	1981	1982	1983	1984	1985	1986	1987	1988
Partial compliance	194,185	181,767	224,159	122,063	134,858	151,077	139,763	144,021
Zero compliance	192,905	182,114	193,942	99,558	105,425	115,444	111,726	122,810
Full compliance	194,669	207,335	223,061	119,749	129,575	173,406	142,375	177,535

(f) *Net balance of payments* (thousand Malawi kwacha per year)

	1981	1982	1983	1984	1985	1986	1987	1988
Partial compliance	23,973	24,441	59,921	64,400	65,474	68,734	−22,633	−30,504
Zero compliance	22,572	23,587	30,010	51,595	48,351	50,550	−32,955	−36,444
Full compliance	24,333	34,254	43,978	62,737	61,891	47,805	−16,918	−35,251

Table 8.2 continued

(g) *Maize exports* (metric tonnes, − = Imports)

	1981	1982	1983	1984	1985	1986	1987	1988
Partial compliance	−56,063	−1,153	−1,153	179,565	179,565	179,565	−28,800	−28,800
Zero compliance	−56,063	−1,153	−1,153	179,565	179,565	179,565	−28,800	−28,900
Full compliance	−56,063	−56,063	−56,063	179,565	179,565	66,341	−72,142	−50,789

a detrimental impact on smallholder real incomes (part (b) of the table). This trend, however, does not begin to emerge until fairly late in the period (i.e. 1986 onwards), when the zero compliance scenario gives rise to unfavourable smallholder income effects in comparison to both the partial and full compliance scenarios.

Between 1986 and 1988, the higher export crop prices under the full compliance scenario more than compensate for the adverse income effects of the scenario's lower maize prices and higher fertiliser prices such that full compliance has the most favourable effect of the three scenarios on smallholder income levels. However, the fact that the full compliance scenario only gives rise to comparatively favourable income effects in the last three years of the period rebuts the Bank's argument that parity pricing for both export crops and fertiliser would unambiguously improve average smallholder income levels. In addition, this highly aggregated result obscures important distributional effects *within* the smallholder sector. Although average smallholder real income improves in the latter years of the full and partial compliance scenarios, this is at the cost of a worsening income distribution within the smallholder sector (see Harrigan, 1988b, for a discussion of this distributional issue).

Maize production

The modelling results fully support the government's constantly reiterated concern regarding the impact of Bank price policy prescriptions on the central objectives of the government's development strategy, namely, increasing maize productivity and production via promotion of the uptake of high-yielding maize varieties. Full compliance with Bank pricing conditionality, i.e. improving the prices of export crops relative to maize and removing the subsidy on fertiliser, results in the least favourable outcome in terms of both total maize production (part (c) of the table) and, in particular, improved maize production (part (d) of the table). In contrast, the government's own first best policy of zero compliance has the most favourable outcome in terms of these two variables.

Export crop production

The cost of zero compliance and the resulting higher maize production, however, not only takes the form of deterioration in the government's budget deficit and lower smallholder income levels in latter years, but also lower production of smallholder exportable cash crops (part (e) of the table). In view of the fact that a central objective of the SAL process was to diversify the country's export base, through promotion of smallholder exportable cash crops, the Bank's concern at the low level of prices offered for such crops appears, at first sight, to be reasonable in light of the unfavourable impact of zero compliance on the export crop variable.

However, the Bank's fears were grounded in a concern regarding the effect that a narrowing export base was having on the balance of payments. Indeed, throughout the entire SAL process, the potentially beneficial impact on the balance of payments was used as the main (and sometimes the only) justification for the prescription of parity pricing for exportable crops.

Net balance of payments:

The simulation results indicate that implementation of the Bank's prescribed conditions had a far from favourable impact on the balance of payments. In all years except one (1981) a policy of full compliance results in an unfavourable balance-of-payments outcome, by comparison with the actual policy of partial compliance followed throughout the period (part (f) of the table). Despite increased exports of smallholder cash crops under the full compliance scenario, the impact on the balance of payments is more than offset by lower maize exports in maize surplus years and higher maize imports in maize deficit years (part (g) of the table). In addition, in 1986 and 1987, the full compliance scenario compares unfavourably, in terms of balance-of-payments effects, not only with the partial compliance scenario, but also with the zero compliance scenario.

Conclusions

The modelling results indicate a clear and unambiguous trade-off between the government's first-best pricing policies, as represented by zero compliance, and the Bank's first-best pricing policies represented by full compliance, that is, between the 'with' and 'without' SAL scenarios. This takes the form of a negative relationship between the country's internal imbalance (government budget deficit) and the country's external imbalance (balance-of-payments deficit).

The government's favoured ('zero compliance') policy scenario has advantageous effects on the balance of payments, brought about by the achievement of the national food self-sufficiency objective. The opportunity cost of this success, however, is a deterioration in the government budget deficit, caused by the need to subsidise both fertiliser sales and the production, procurement and distribution of maize.

The Bank's favoured ('full compliance') policy scenario brings about an improvement in the budget deficit due to the fact that the two parastatals which trade smallholder crops and inputs are allowed to move towards market-orientated pricing policies in the form of import and export parity pricing for fertiliser, maize and exportable cash crops. The opportunity cost, however, is high in terms of a worsening of the balance-of-payments deficit, resulting from the failure to achieve national food self-sufficiency.

An analysis of the policy bargaining and dialogue between the Bank and the government throughout the duration of Malawi's three SALs indicates that neither party was fully aware of the nature of the above trade-offs. This is unfortunate, given that considerable investment had been made *within the Bank* in developing the Malawian Multi-Market Agricultural Pricing Model, the main aim of which was to provide an analytic tool able to clearly quantify the impact and trade-offs of alternative pricing packages on *multiple* policy objectives. As this exercise has shown, the model performs well in terms of its ability to meet these aims. Had greater use been made of the model, both the Bank and the government would have had a clearer picture of the opportunity costs of their differing policy objectives, namely, the government objective of obtaining food self-sufficiency and the Bank objective of rectifying the budget deficit. In addition, Bank staff would have become more aware of the adverse balance-of-payments effects of the policies they were prescribing to the Malawi government.

The type of results generated by our single-country modelling exercise are very different from those produced by the aggregated evaluation exercises of Chapters 6 and 7. The single-country modelling approach has enabled us to evaluate the impact of Bank programme lending using *country-specific* criteria of evaluation. In the case of Malawi, differences between the Bank and the government centred on the impact of SAL policies on policy objectives related to food crop production, export crop production, smallholder incomes, the government budget and the balance of payments. It is in terms of these variables, therefore, that the model has been used to evaluate the outcome of various policy scenarios. This level of detail is not possible in the aggregated approaches of Chapters 6 and 7, where we were dealing with a large number of countries often with very different policy objectives. Aggregate approaches, as a consequence, are therefore forced to concentrate evaluation on a small number of macro-variables, such as GDP growth, export and import trends, and investment levels.

There is, however, one area of overlap between the aggregate work of Chapters 6 and 7 and the single country modelling work of this chapter.

All three approaches have used the balance of payments as a criterion of evaluation. Whereas the aggregate evaluation results indicated that Bank programme lending has a favourable effect on the balance of payments via a lagged stimulation of exports and a lagged curbing of imports, the Malawi modelling exercise produced the reverse result – compliance with Bank conditions adversely affected exports and imports in the sector under analysis. These conflicting results serve to reinforce our earlier caution regarding the considerable diversity of individual country experience concealed within the aggregated outcomes of macro variables. Such diversity suggests that donors should be aware of the potential dangers of applying standard policy packages across a wide range of countries. Certainly, within the sub-Saharan countries, the Bank has displayed a tendency to adopt a blanket approach to agricultural price policy, with most of its policy-based lending agreements entailing a standard package of export parity pricing and input subsidy removal. However, as our Malawi modelling exercise has shown, this uniformity of approach can result in unexpected adverse outcomes on crucial variables, such as food crop production and the balance of payments, in certain countries.

In view of the diversity of individual country experience, the single-country modelling approach to evaluating the impact of programme lending is probably the most fruitful of the three approaches we have adopted, particularly when the evaluation exercise is seen as the first step in the attempt to design better policy packages for the future. It is also, however, the most costly and time-consuming of the three approaches. Despite this latter drawback, it is encouraging to note that in recent years, the Bank itself has invested considerable resources in the development of a large number of individual country models which go beyond the single-sector analysis of the Malawi model. Such models are being used increasingly for both retrospective policy analysis and for forecasting work in the dialogue with recipient governments (see for example Braverman and Hammer, 1988). This new trend indicates a growing Bank awareness of the importance of allowing for the country-specific nature of responses to policy prescriptions. It also suggests that increasing importance is being attached to the ability to accurately evaluate the impact of past Bank policies and the ability to forecast the impact of future policy packages, not just on the macro-variables of concern to the Bank, but also on variables of concern to the recipient government such as food security whose achievement may conflict with the fulfilment of those macro-objectives.

8.3   RESULTS FROM A CGE WHOLE-ECONOMY MODEL: MOROCCO*

Background

In the case of Morocco, likewise, ambiguities are inevitable concerning the path which the economy would have followed in the absence of the policy-based lending package negotiated with the World Bank. The crisis there started with a collapse in the terms of trade, adverse climatic conditions and a growing foreign debt, the service of which became impossible when world interest rates soared in 1982. The several policy packages adopted after negotiations with the IMF and the World Bank included an impressive list of measures aimed at restoring the main macroeconomic balances, and at increasing the efficiency of the resource allocation process – e.g. financial market liberalisation, tariff reduction and harmonisation, abolition of price controls, of credit rationing, etc.

This adjustment process has apparently been successful in several respects. The current account was close to equilibrium three years later, the budget deficit had been reduced, and a satisfactory rate of growth seemed to have been re-established. What is not clear, however, is whether some other policy package would have been equally successful on the macroeconomic front, and whether the policy package actually implemented was the least costly in social terms. These are the questions one would like to answer in order to draw all the lessons from an experience like that of Morocco, and, in particular, to judge whether that experience could be generalised to other countries.

It is precisely at that stage that counterfactuals become indispensable, and relying on some kind of economic modelling becomes unavoidable. This is attempted in the present section, extending some previous modelling work conducted within the OECD Development Centre Research Program on 'Adjustment and Income Distribution' (Bourguignon, Branson and de Melo, 1989). Instead of the predominantly macro approach followed in that project, we get here into the more 'structural', or microeconomic oriented measures that were included in the initial adjustment package.[3] The analysis is confined to the effects of eight of the most important quantifiable measures included in the SAL agreement signed between Morocco and the World Bank in 1985, as set out in Table 8.3. We begin with a brief summary of the recent evolution of the Moroccan economy, spelling out the adjustment policies which have been implemented. We then outline the model used for the simulation of these policies, followed by a summary of the simulations themselves. A

* This section is based on research carried out by François Bourguignon and Akiko Suwa of the Ecole Normale Supérieure, Paris, and Christian Morrisson of OECD. Thanks are due to the OECD for making their model of the Moroccan economy available to us.

comparison of the results and an evaluation of some combinations of these policy measures is undertaken in the concluding subsection, where it is suggested that 'structural' adjustment measures have been less effective than the conventional IMF stabilisation package initiated in 1983 in improving Morocco's economic situation.

Disequilibrium and adjustment in Morocco

Unbalanced growth: 1976–83

As in some other developing countries at the time, unbalanced growth in Morocco largely resulted from a 'Dutch disease' phenomenon. The sudden increase in the price of phosphate in 1974 (tripling in real terms), was at the origin of this process. As the main beneficiary of the revenue surplus, the government embarked on an ambitious spending programme. Real public investment was multiplied by a factor of 3.4 from 1974 to 1977, civil servants' wages were raised by 26 per cent in 1974 and basic food subsidies were introduced in 1975. According to the typical 'Dutch disease' pattern, prices increased faster for non-tradable goods than for tradable goods and production switched from exports to domestic demand. When the export boom abruptly ended in 1976 with a 47 per cent fall in phosphate prices, the government felt able neither to cut investment expenditures nor to rescind the subsidies given in the boom years to civil servants or consumers. The collapse of phosphate revenues without any diminution of public spending was the origin of the huge fiscal deficit (18 per cent of GDP) that opened up as early as 1976.

Thereafter, Morocco's growth relied on foreign credit. After 1976, fiscal revenues practically remained at the same level as public current expenditures, so that all incremental public capital expenditures were financed by borrowing from abroad. The government attempted twice to implement adjustment programmes, aimed at stopping the growing disequilibria. The 1978 programme included a civil servants' wage freeze, a rise in tax rates and a cut in public investment. But several exogenous factors interrupted the application of the programme in 1979: the second oil shock, bad crops due to a drought, and a social uprising. In response to the latter, the government went back on its decisions and raised public sector wages by 10 per cent, the minimum wage by 30 per cent and increased food subsidies. The second attempt at adjustment took place in October 1980 with a three-year programme approved by the IMF which included a slow-down in credit growth and a reduction in subsidies. The enforcement of the latter measure in the spring of 1981, involving a 50 per cent increase in food prices, led to violent riots in Casablanca. The stabilisation programme, in consequence, was postponed. Because of unfavourable exogenous factors (drought, revaluation of the US dollar and increasing foreign interest rates), it was cancelled in 1981.

Morocco's growth between 1976 and 1983 was therefore achieved at the cost of widening imbalances. Over that period, the fiscal deficit fluctuated between 10 and 17 per cent of GDP, whereas the current account deficit varied between 8 and 16 per cent of GDP. This deficit was financed by the foreign debt, which rose from $2.3 billions in 1976 to $11.2 billions in 1983. The debt service/exports ratio reached 45 per cent in 1982 (before diminishing in 1983 thanks to a debt rescheduling). In 1983, foreign exchange reserves had almost vanished and the government imposed drastic import controls. This crisis led to the negotiation of an adjustment programme with the IMF and the World Bank.

The adjustment and its impact

This new adjustment programme involved two sets of measures: on the one hand, measures aiming at a sharp reduction in total demand (as defined in the stand-by agreement with the IMF signed in September 1983); on the other hand, medium-term supply-oriented measures included in the two SAL agreements with the World Bank in March 1984 and July 1985. The measures agreed with the World Bank, which are the subject of the present analysis, are summarised in Table 8.3.

Demand-side measures

The agreement with the IMF included the following measures:

- reduction in food subsidies;
- bringing the fiscal deficit down to 7 or 8 per cent of GDP, from 14 per cent in 1982;
- limiting public sector recruitment;
- reduction in the rate of domestic credit expansion from 20 to 15 per cent.

The wages of civil servants were frozen and recruitment into the service was limited to 10,000 employees per annum for three years. Food subsidies were reduced so that sugar, oil and flour prices went up by 30, 52 and 87 per cent respectively between 1982 and 1985. Other food subsidies (butter, milk, high quality flour) were fully eliminated. The most drastic cuts hit public investment, which fell by half in real terms between 1983 and 1986. Finally, the current account deficit was reduced through a series of devaluations. The effective real exchange rate depreciated by 23 per cent from 1982 to 1986.

Supply-side measures consisted of a whole package of measures meant to liberalise external trade, and several measures in the monetary and tax fields.[4] In order to encourage exports, the 'statistical tax' (at a rate of 0.5 per cent) was eliminated and all the export licensing requirements, set up

Table 8.3 Morocco: Conditionality attached to World Bank Industrial and Trade Policy Adjustment Loans (March 1984 and July 1985)

Policy area	*Conditionality*
Reform of protection	– Reduction of special import tax from 15% to 5%.
	– Elimination of import licensing requirements on an agreed list of products.
Tariff reform	– Reduction of maximum normal tariff ceiling from 200% to 45%.
Exchange rate management	– Maintenance of a flexible exchange rate policy.
Export promotion	– Elimination of statistical export tax.
	– Elimination of export licensing requirements on virtually all products.
	– Completion of a study on export marketing of fresh fruits and vegetables.
	– Rationalisation of special customs regime.
Foreign trade procedures	– Creation of a committee for the simplification of foreign trade procedures.
Public investment programme and public enterprises	– Introduction of new investment budgetary techniques to keep commitments in line with available resources.
	– Updating of arrears matrix for public enterprises, preparation of arrears reduction programme and reduction of net government arrears by DH 1 billion.
Tax reform	– Approval of enabling legislation to rationalise existing sales tax (TPS) and elimination of anti-export bias.
Price controls	– Liberalisation of price controls on 60 product categories.
Interest rates	– Increased flexibility in establishing interest rates at levels dictated by market forces.
Development of money market	– Increased competition between Treasury and their borrowers for available supply of loanable funds.
Efficiency of the banking sector	– Promotion of a more competitive interbank environment.
Foreign exchange risk	– Establishment of a foreign exchange risk scheme.

in the early 1980s so as to provide enough supply for the domestic market, were removed (except for two or three mining products). Export taxes were eliminated on virtually all goods but mining products.[5] Agricultural exports were to be encouraged by abolishing the monopoly of the state marketing board (Office de Commercialisation et d'Exportation). Lastly, the functioning of the customs service was improved: the processing time was reduced by 50 per cent and the temporary admission scheme was broadened.

On the import side, the system of high tariffs and quantitative restrictions, which had isolated the Moroccan market from the rest of the world, was lifted. The share of goods whose import was strictly prohibited or required a prior licence fell from 100 per cent in March 1983 to 37 per cent in February 1986, when all import prohibitions were suppressed. The special tax on imports was reduced from 15 per cent to 5 per cent and the maximum tariff rate limited to 60 per cent in July 1984 and 45 per cent in the beginning of 1986, instead of 200 per cent in 1983. Consequently, the average nominal rate went down from 36 per cent in 1983 to 23 per cent in 1986. After addition of the special import tax and the stamp duty, the average rate of nominal protection was thus reduced to 36 per cent in 1986.

Other measures were meant to improve the efficiency of the tax system, and encourage savings and production. In order to rationalise the tax system, eliminate anti-export biases and raise revenue, sales taxes were replaced by a VAT after 1 April, 1986. Financial savings were encouraged through the suppression of reserve requirements on time deposits. The access to Treasury bonds was extended to the non-financial private sector. Nominal interest rates were raised so that real interest rates, which were negative in 1982–3, became positive. Special foreign currency accounts earning a higher interest rate were created to attract emigrant workers' savings. On the whole, this policy has brought interest rates to levels close to those likely to result in a free market system.

Agricultural output was encouraged by systematic increases in producer prices. Price distortions were limited by a 40 per cent reduction in fertiliser subsidies, an increase in the water supply fee and an improvement in crop collection. The private sector was permitted to sell fertilisers, produce or buy seeds, which used to be a public monopoly.

Manufacturing incentives included the liberalisation of some prices (controls were completely lifted for sixty products) and the introduction of a new investment code. The possibility of faster depreciation was eliminated, which resulted in a significant increase in the cost of capital. Such a rise was meant to prevent firms from adopting increasingly capital-intensive production techniques because of a rising relative cost of labour as happened in the 1970s.

Several attempts were also made at improving the efficiency of the public sector: a settlement of payment arrears, reform of the relationship between state enterprises and the government and new and more restrictive public investment criteria.

The impact of the adjustment programme

As of 1986, the results of the programme can be summarised in three points:

- satisfactory growth performance, although this was partly due to favourable exogenous factors;
- a reduction of the fiscal deficit, that was in fact more apparent than real;
- a significant reduction of the external deficit, thanks to export growth and a successful trade liberalisation.

Contrary to the experience of other countries, the negative impact of adjustment on growth was limited. GDP growth, after coming down in 1984 (1.7 per cent), climbed to 7.7 per cent in 1985 and 6.3 per cent in 1986. But this successful performance partly resulted from a single exogenous factor, namely the uncommon rains that produced a 17 per cent boom in agriculture during 1985–6. With half of the growth in GDP coming from agriculture, it is clear that without this climatic advantage, the GDP growth rate would have been less than 2.5 per cent, which would have implied a small decrease in GDP per capita.

No general trend is apparent in the other sectors. The building sector was severely affected. On average, the public investment reduction led to a 5 per cent drop in that sector over 1984–5. However, a small recovery started by the end of 1985 because of an increase in housing construction fuelled by emigrant workers' remittances and investment growth in exporting sectors. Manufacturing output stagnated during 1984–5 before a slight recovery in 1986. Domestic trade also stagnated during that period because of the general slow-down in activity and price deregulations which reduced mark-up rates.

The fiscal deficit, in terms of actual spending, remained stable between 1982 and 1985, thus implying growing payment arrears by the government, which had been hardly noticeable in 1981–2 but amounted to 4 per cent of GDP in 1985. This situation changed after 1986, when both expenditure commitments and disbursements were controlled.

However, the adjustment programme was an undeniable success in reducing the current account deficit, which went down from 12.7 per cent of the GDP in 1982 to 7.2 per cent in 1985, despite a lower degree of protection. This resulted from the outstanding performance of industrial exports (fertilisers and phosphoric acid, textiles, clothing, footwear, etc.), sales of which doubled over the period, and tourism, where revenues increased by 145 per cent in three years. Clearly, the policy of real devaluation has done a great deal for tourism and manufactured exports, the price elasticity of which with respect to the real exchange rate is around 1.6 in the long run. The trade reforms, supported by the first sectoral adjustment loan ever granted by the World Bank, thus appear as a genuine success. The revenue surplus in foreign currency resulting from the reform exceeded by far the repayment of the loan.

A disaggregated simulation model applied to Morocco

Model outline

The model used in the counterfactual analysis of some of the preceding measures integrates a standard computable general equilibrium (CGE) model and fully fledged macroeconomic closures. Special emphasis has been given to the financial sector. A full description of the 'maquette'[6] can be found in Appendix 2; see also Bourguignon et al. (1988, 1989). We just sketch here its main characteristics.

The economy has four kinds of agents: firms (6 sectors), households (6 socio-economic groups), the government and financial intermediaries. These agents intervene on four types of markets: goods and services, labour, money and bonds, and foreign exchange. Clearing on all these markets, under alternative specifications of the equilibrium conditions or 'closures', defines the state of the economy during a given unit-period – i.e. the year.

Markets for goods and services

Firms' short-run supply decisions result from profit maximisation. Technology is given by a Leontieff function for intermediate products and a constant elasticity of substitution (CES) production function for factors of production (capital, labour, land, and a specific factor used in primary exports). On the demand side, there is imperfect substitutability between domestically produced and imported goods. Domestic demand is defined in terms of composite goods which combine imported and domestic goods, according to the Armington specification. However, some composite goods are pure imports whereas some others are pure domestic products. Consumption is specified, for each group of households, as a linear expenditure system (LES) defined on incomes net of taxes and savings. Investment demand in each productive sector is determined by a profitability criterion reminiscent of Tobin's q. Exports depend on relative domestic/foreign prices and on exogenous foreign demand.

In a given unit-period, market-clearing may be specified in two ways:

(i)   competitive Walrasian price adjustment;
(ii) non-competitive mark-up pricing and quantity adjustment, through flexible utilization of existing capacities.

264

Labour market

Wages and self-employment earnings define household incomes, and the distribution of incomes, in addition to remittances from abroad, government transfers, interest payments, dividends and, possibly, rents arising from various market imperfections. Labour earnings are determined on labour-markets – one market for each type of labour – under alternative specifications:

(i) full wage flexibility;
(ii) partial wage flexibility (Phillips curve);
(iii) nominal or real wage rigidity (with a variable rate of indexation over the cost of living in the case of real wage stickiness).

Together with quantity adjustments in markets for goods and services, the last two assumptions about the labour market allow for a full 'Keynesian' closure of the model, as an alternative to the standard Walrasian framework.

Money and financial markets

After payment of wages, indirect and income taxes, interest charges and dividends, firms' borrowing requirements are determined by the intended change in their working and physical capital. As a short cut to the equity market, these requirements are partly and directly met by that share of their savings that households do not invest in financial assets. The remaining deficit is covered by domestic or foreign loans.

The domestic credit market is directly affected by the budget deficit (or surplus) of the government and how it is financed. Fiscal revenues come from various taxes: on sales, incomes, payrolls, foreign trade. Government spending includes subsidies to exports or specific sectors, transfers to households, civil servants' wages, debt service, investment and current expenditures. Its deficit may be financed by borrowing from the domestic financial market, from abroad, or from the Central Bank (money creation).

There are thus three types of financial assets in the model: money, domestic and foreign bonds. Households' portfolio allocation results from arbitraging between the various assets. They first decide about money holdings on the basis of their income and the domestic interest rate, then the share of savings invested directly in productive sectors is determined on the basis of the relative rates of return on physical capital and financial assets. Finally, their remaining wealth is allocated between domestic public bonds and foreign assets, on the basis of their relative yields. Current savings may also be affected by capital gains (or losses). Firms arbitrage similarly between foreign and domestic debt.

The macroeconomic closure of the model depends on market-clearing assumptions on the money and the domestic bond markets meant to represent a variety of situations in developing countries. In particular, the model is equipped to deal with:

1 Credit rationing with an exogenous ceiling on the interest rate and a discretionary allocation of credits to productive sectors.
2 No issuing of public bonds.
3 Partial or full sterilisation of private capital movements (in case of no foreign exchange control).

The foreign exchange market

Foreign exchange operations include the trade balance, net current transfers abroad by households, interest payments, net profit repatriation, private and public capital movements. Three closures are available:

1 fixed nominal or pegged real exchange rate: the government sets its foreign borrowing so as to meet foreign exchange requirements.
2 flexible exchange rate: public foreign borrowing is now exogenous.
3 import rationing: government foreign borrowing is exogenous, the official exchange rate is fixed, but import consumers pay a premium on auctioned import licenses.

Dynamics

All the preceding market-clearing rules apply to the unit period. The dynamics of the model correspond to a sequence of 'temporary' equilibria. These equilibria are linked to each other through changes in capital stocks, population, technology, and, possibly, expectations. Note though that the model is not truly dynamic in the sense that individual maximising behaviours are not inter-temporal.[7]

Capital is fixed during any one year. It changes only through depreciation and investment. Productivity growth is exogenous, as are expectations of inflation and devaluation. The overall rate of demographic growth is exogenous, but the breakdown of the population into socio-economic groups results from an endogenous Harris-Todaro type migration mechanism.

Application to Morocco

The model is applied to Morocco over the period 1980–6. Special care was given, if not to bring out the exact aggregate values, at least to replicate the features and the broad evolution of the economy.

266

The main model specifications

The Moroccan economy has been divided into the six sectors and six socio-economic groups shown in Table 8.4. The six sectors are: primary exports (phosphates), agriculture, light industry (foods, beverages, textile, paper), heavy industry (oil, metallurgy, machinery), services, informal sector. The socio-economic groups are: capitalists, large farmers, small farmers, modern workers, agricultural workers, informal workers. Capitalists own the factor specific to primary exports and most capital in other sectors. They are the only group to hold foreign assets (up to 30 per cent of their financial wealth). Large and small farmers are distinguished by the size of farms. Unlike small farmers, large farmers' portfolios include public bonds.

Table 8.4: The disaggregated structure of the Moroccan model

Sectors	% share in total production
Primary exports	6.1
Agriculture	15.4
Light industry	19.8
Heavy industry	16.3
Services	31.8
Informal sector	10.6
Total	100.0

Households	% share in total production
Capitalists	26.1
Large farmers	39.3
Small farmers	12.3
Modern workers	12.1
Agricultural workers	2.9
Informal workers	7.3
Total	100.0

Households provide three types of labour: agricultural, urban modern and urban informal. Agricultural labour is fully employed with an endogenous market-clearing wage. Nominal wages are rigid downwards, both in the modern private and the public sectors. Urban informal workers' income is given by the GDP per capita in the informal sector. There is some mobility across the three groups of workers from one year to the next, depending on relative expected incomes (defined as a moving average of incomes times the unemployment rate).

267

The base run

A complete description of the calibration method is found in Morrisson (1989). The various closures have been set according to the basic features of the Moroccan economy during the period under analysis (1980–6).

Markets for goods and services clear with mark-up pricing and quantity adjustment in the non-agricultural formal sectors, and through prices in other sectors. The wage rate ensures full employment in the rural labour market and is downwardly rigid, at a constant nominal level, in the modern sector labour market. The exchange rate is fixed at each point of time in accordance with observed nominal devaluations; import rationing is enforced in 1983–4 in order to replicate the adjustment policy used at that time. Credit is rationed in the event that the market-clearing interest rate is above 8 per cent. Rationing is imposed proportionally to the capital stock in each sector. There is no formal foreign exchange control but the arbitrage elasticity between domestic and foreign bonds is assumed to be fairly low.

These basic assumptions are summarised in Table 8.5(a). Exogenous policy or foreign environment variables are shown in 8.5(b). The comparison of the base-run predictions and the actual values of a few macroeconomic aggregates depicted in Figure 8.1 illustrates the ability of the model and the base-run specifications to track the actual evolution of the Moroccan economy during the early 1980s.

Simulation of the individual reforms included in the 1985–6 SAL agreement

The SAL agreement signed with the World Bank in 1985 involved a large number of reforms. However, some of them are too much concerned with microeconomic issues to be analysed with the simulation model presented in the previous section, whereas others, as shown in Table 8.3, are mere statements of intention, such as 'Promote a more competitive inter-bank environment', rather than quantifiable changes in policy.

This section reports on two sets of simulations. The first set refers essentially to tax reforms and includes the proposed reduction, and uniformisation, of tariffs, the reduction in export taxes and the increase in direct taxation. Because the simulation model is not equipped to deal with alternative indirect taxation schemes, it has not been possible to investigate the possible effects of a switch to a generalised VAT system.

The second set of simulations is concerned with the financial liberalisation measures included in the agreement, namely the adoption of a flexible exchange rate system, involving the creation of a foreign exchange market, abolition of import quotas, and liberalisation of foreign capital movements – including incentives for the repatriation of foreign workers'

Table 8.5(a) Basic behavioural elasticities and exogenous growth rates

Households	Elasticity	%growth
Labour supply growth		
Average growth		2.5
Capitalist and large farmers'		
population growth		1
Small farmers' population growth		1.5
Consumption		
Expenditure elasticity (e_e)	$0.34 < e_e < 1.3$[1]	
Frisch parameter (F)[2]	$1.25 < F < 2$	
Capital gain effect on consumption[3]		10
Portfolio		
• Money demand:		
Semi-elasticity with respect to		
interest rate	2	
Income elasticity	0.6	
• Arbitrage between physical and		
financial savings:		
Physical/financial saving elasticity	1	
Average share of physical saving	0.93	
• Arbitrage between domestic and		
foreign assets	5	
Domestic/foreign bonds elasticity	5	
Average domestic share of total		
financial wealth (W_d)	$0.45 < W_d < 1$	

Firms	Elasticity	% growth
Technology		
Elasticity of substitution in		
production function (Cobb-Douglas)	1	
Technical progress (P_t)		$0 < P_t < 3$
Depreciation		4
Portfolio		
Sales elasticity of working capital	0.5	
Domestic/foreign loans elasticity	5	
Foreign trade (prices elasticity)		
export demand elasticity (e_{ex})	$3 < e_{ex} < 4$	
import demand elasticity (e_{im})	$0.6 < e_{im} < 1.5$	

Notes: 1 These figures give the limits of the expenditure elasticity across different household groups.
2 Parameter of the LES, which is equal to income/income above the minimum consumption level.
3 Proportion of wealth change consumed.

Table 8.5(b) Main exogenous annual variables

Year	Fiscal and money policy						
	1980	1981	1982	1983	1984	1985	1986
Employment	4.6	4.9	5.36	5.83	5.85	5.88	6.07
Wages	1.9	2.2	2.24	2.27	2.37	2.55	2.69
Expenditure	4.73	5.38	6	6.34	6	7	7.5
Investment	4.6	5.15	6.67	4.28	5.77	4.83	5.06
Money supply	32.53	37.41	41.15	46.5	50.68	52.68	55.86

(billions of dirhams; employment in 10,000)

Year	Foreign parameters						
	1980	1981	1982	1983	1984	1985	1986
Interest rate	12%	14%	13%	10%	12%	10%	7%
Import prices (growth rate)	15%	0%	0%	2%	5%	5%	

Year	Export prices (growth rate)					
	1981	1982	1983	1984	1985	1986
Primary exports	20	−3.3	−9.5	0	23.8	3.8
Agriculture	10	11.8	−12.0	0	11.1	12.5
Light industry	10	10.9	−12.3	9.3	2.6	12.5
Heavy industry	17	6	−13.7	4.7	7.1	12.5

overseas bank deposits. It would have been rather contradictory to analyse all these liberalisation measures while maintaining the credit rationing closure selected for the money market in the base run. All the preceding measures are thus simulated under the assumption that all types of restraints on the credit market are simultaneously eliminated.

It must be kept in mind, moreover, that all these measures come in addition to the more macroeconomic aspects of adjustment in Morocco, that is the reduction in public expenditures, the various devaluations of the currency, and the monetary tightening recommended by the IMF, all measures included in the base run. A full evaluation of the adjustment-stabilisation package put to work in Morocco would thus require additional simulation work, with some thought being given to what would have been the adjustment process, had the Moroccan authorities decided not to follow the recommendations of the IMF and the World Bank.

If fully implemented, all the preceding measures would necessarily lead to some changes in the current account and in the net indebtedness of the country. As it would make little sense to compare the evolution of the economy in situations where the level of overseas borrowing differed between cases, a normalisation rule had to be selected which would standardise the level of government borrowing. The rule selected is that

270

(a) GDP (constant prices, 1980 = 100)

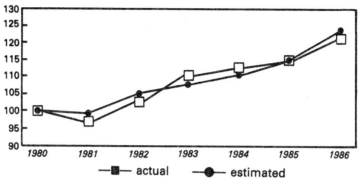

(b) *fiscal deficit* (share of GDP, %)

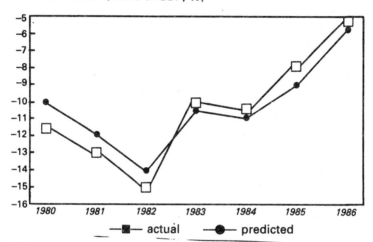

(c) *current account* (share of GDP, %)

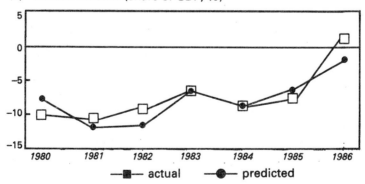

Figure 8.1 Morocco: simulations of model predictions in relation to actual levels

271

foreign borrowing is constrained to be, in all simulations and for every year, at the level actually observed. As the move toward a flexible exchange rate system is one of the simulations we wanted to consider, the most simple way to meet the foreign borrowing constraint at each point of time was to keep the exchange rate flexible throughout all the remaining situations.

In order to evaluate the separate effect of each simulated measure in this section, it is thus necessary to analyse them in a specific order – a summary of the various experiments is given in Table 8.6. This order is as follows:

E-1 The reference simulation   presented in the previous section includes credit rationing, import quotas in 1984 and 1985 and a fixed – although subject to successive devaluations – exchange rate.

E-2 Foreign exchange liberalisation   This simulation is E-1 plus a flexible exchange rate, no import quotas, and foreign borrowing being constrained to that observed every year in E-1.

Then come three simulations aimed at replicating financial market liberalisation measures:

E-20 Credit market liberalisation   This is essentially E-2 with a freely determined rate of interest and no credit rationing.

E-3 Domestic financial market development   This is E-20 with an increase in the elasticity of the demand for money with respect to the rate of interest, a shift of the financial portfolio allocation schedule toward domestic bonds, and a reduction in budget deficit money financing by the government.

E-4 International financial market liberalisation   This is E-20 with an increase in the substitution elasticity between domestic and foreign bonds and loans in households' and firms' portfolio allocation behaviour.

The next four simulations are concerned with reforms of the tax system, all of them leading to the same (absolute) change in total tax receipts.

E-5 Tariff reform   Simulation E-2 with a reduction and uniformisation of tariff rates.

E-6 Reduction in export tax rates   This is E-2 where export tax rates have been scaled down.

E-7 Income tax reform   This is E-2 with a progressive increase in the personal income tax.

272

E-8 The corporate tax reform   This is E-2 with an increase in corporate tax rates in the modern sectors of the economy (light and heavy manufacturing, modern services).

E-9 Complete financial liberalisation   This is a blend of the separate financial reforms (E-20), (E-3) and (E-4), i.e. a combination of financial liberalisation on internal and external account.

E-10 Comprehensive tax reform   This is a combination of all the separate tax reforms above listed, namely (E-2), (E-5), (E-6), (E-7) and (E-8).

A glance back at Table 8.3 will show that the conditionality analysed here, that of the Bank's Industrial Sector and Trade Policy Adjustment Loans, consisted of liberalisation of the foreign exchange market plus the removal of the export tax. As earlier discussed, the quantifiable proposals of Table 8.3 were almost completely implemented, thus the actual case corresponds quite closely to (E-6). (E-1) is the zero compliance case, (E-9) represents comprehensive financial liberalisation and (E-10) represents comprehensive tax reform. The last two cases represent cases of 'more than 100 per cent compliance', that is, hypothetical extensions of what the Bank has so far attempted in these two major fields of reform. (E-20), (E-3) and (E-4) are intermediate stops on the road to full financial deregulation and (E-5) to (E-8) are intermediate stops on the road to full tax reform.

   We now analyse those various simulations in turn. Their main characteristics, relative to some reference simulation, are summarised in a set of figures and in Table 8.6.

Impact of tax reforms

As may be seen from the comparison between E-1 and E-2 in Figure 8.2, the effects of abolishing import quotas and adopting a flexible exchange rate system are limited to the years 1983–4. In both years, additional import rationing has been imposed by the Moroccan government as a way of meeting the foreign payment constraint while avoiding a drastic devaluation of the currency. Import quotas were present before then, and, to a lesser extent, afterwards, but their actual effect on foreign trade was certainly much weaker than during the crisis years. As no information is available on the respective role of quotas and tariffs in effective protection outside that period, the former were not included in the model.[8] However, the effects of those 'permanent' quotas is likely to be small in comparison with the temporary 'overrationing' imposed in 1983–4. In any case, the fact that no change has been introduced outside the 1983–4 period, and that net government foreign borrowing is constrained to be the same in the

Table 8.6 Morocco: main simulation results

	Financial liberalisation						Tax reform				
	E-1 ('zero compliance')	E-2	E-20	E-3	E-4	E-9 (full financial liberalization)	E-5	E-6 'actual'	E-7	E-8	E-10 (full tax reform)
GDP growth	3.3	3.2	3.5	3.5	3.6	4.3	3.6	3.7	3.3	3.2	3.8
fiscal deficit[2]	-10.6	-10.1	-9.8	-12.0	-10.6	-9.3	-11.3	-11.1	-9.2	-9.3	-10.7
current account[3]	-1.3	-1.4	-1.4	-1.6	-1.3	-1.3	-1.4	-1.3	-1.4	-1.4	-1.3
unemployment rate (%)[4]	8.0	7.7	7.6	8.0	7.9	6.5	7.5	7.8	7.6	7.7	7.5
utilization rate (%)[4]	94.0	94.0	95.0	95.0	95.0	96.0	95.0	95.0	94.0	94.0	95.0
money growth	9.4	9.4	9.4	4.2	9.1	10.1	9.4	9.4	9.4	9.4	9.4
CPI inflation	7.2	7.2	7.9	6.6	6.9	8.6	7.1	6.8	7.1	7.1	6.6
devaluation	5.9	5.9	6.8	4.7	4.9	6.4	6.1	5.0	5.8	5.7	5.3
public foreign debt[5]	42.5	42.5	42.4	42.3	42.5	42.6	42.6	42.4	42.4	42.5	42.4
public domestic debt[6]	1.3	1.3	1.5	14.0	0.9	14.1	1.3	1.2	1.3	1.3	1.3
household consumption[7]	1.9	1.8	1.9	2.5	2.3	3.2	2.2	2.4	1.8	1.8	2.5
export growth	9.7	9.7	9.8	8.3	8.3	7.6	10.3	110.3	9.6	9.5	111.0
investment growth	-6.0	-6.2	-3.5	-3.4	-1.2	2.6	-5.4	-5.7	-5.3	-5.5	-5.8
import growth	-0.1	-0.2	0.2	0.8	1.0	2.2	0.7	0.4	-0.1	-0.1	1.0

Summary of experiments:

E-1: the base run.
      Credit rationing, interest ceiling set to 8%, import quotas in 1983–4, fixed exchange rate.

E-2: foreign exchange liberalization.
      (E-1) + flexible exchange rate. Elimination of import quotas. (The public foreign borrowing is set to the base-run value).

E-20: credit market liberalization.
      (E-2) + freely determined rate of interest. No credit rationing.

E-3: Domestic financial market development.
(E-20) + reduction of money supply growth : 0% in 1981 and 5% afterwards.
Increase in the interest semi-elasticity of money demand.
Partial substitution of money demand for domestic bonds.

E-4: International financial private capital movements liberalization.
(E-20) + elimination of sterilization of the money supply.
Increase in the substitution elasticity between domestic and foreign bonds.

E-5: Tariff reform.
(E-2) + Tariff uniformization and lowering of the average rate to 14.5% instead of 19%.

E-6: Reduction in export tax rates.[8]
(E-2) + reduction of export tax.

E-7: Income tax reform.
(E-2) + progressive increase in the personal income tax.

E-8: Corporate income tax reform.
(E-2) + progressive increase in corporate tax.

E-9: Financial liberalization package.
(E-20) + (E-3) + (E-4).

E-10: Tax reform package.
(E-2) + (E-5) + (E-6) + (E-7) + (E-8).

Notes: 2   Average share of GDP.
3   Average value, in billions of 1980 US dollars.
4   Average rate, over 1980–6.
5   1986 level, in foreign currency (exogenous).
6   Average share in GDP.
7   Average growth rate.
8   In E-5, E-7 and E-8, tax rates are computed so as to keep the same absolute value of tax revenue changes as in E-5 (lowering of tariff).

All changes begin in 1981 and last until 1986.

(a) GDP in constant prices (percentage change in relation to E–1)

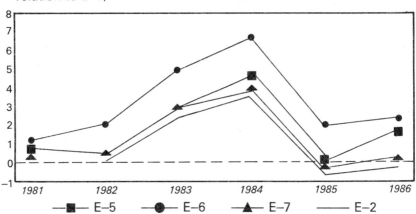

(b) Fiscal deficit (percentage share in GDP)

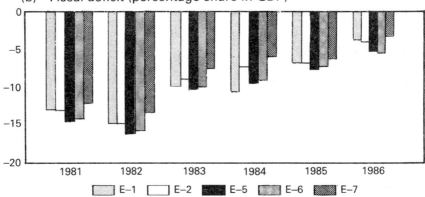

(c) Current account (billions of 1980 US dollars)

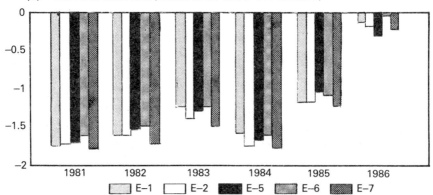

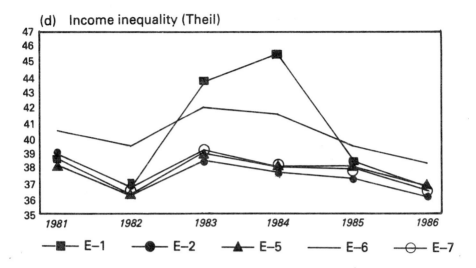

(d) Income inequality (Theil)

—■— E–1   —●— E–2   —▲— E–5   ——— E–6   —○— E–7

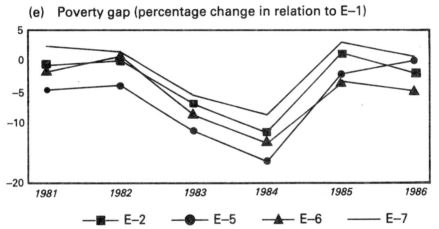

(e) Poverty gap (percentage change in relation to E–1)

—■— E–2   —●— E–5   —▲— E–6   ——— E–7

Figure 8.2   Morocco: simulated effect of tax reforms

present simulation as in the base-run explain why the latter coincides with a flexible exchange rate scenario.

Replacing import rationing by a further devaluation of the currency in order to meet the foreign exchange constraint has major effects. As could be expected, exporters benefit from higher domestic prices for their product. The resulting increase in exports permit a faster growth of GDP, since more goods can be imported while satisfying the foreign payment constraint. Accordingly, GDP increases by 3 per cent on average in 1983 and 1984, whereas exports increase by 13 per cent thanks to a 6 per cent additional devaluation. Because the current account now adjusts on both the export and the import sides, the additional exports due to the replacement of import quotas by a devaluation also permit larger imports of investment goods than before. However, the period is too short to see the subsequent effects on growth.

The social effects of using devaluation rather than import rationing to equilibrate the balance of payments are impressive. Inequality goes down in a considerable proportion, whereas poverty falls quite significantly, as illustrated in parts (d) and (e) of Figure 8.2. The first effect is essentially due to our (reasonable) assumption in the base run that the quasi-rents associated with import rationing were appropriated by the class of 'capitalists'. The drop in poverty is due to the increase in the overall level of activity in the economy and the resulting fall in urban unemployment. It is also associated with the fact that a devaluation in Morocco benefits exporters in the rural sector of the economy, and, through the labour market, agricultural workers.

The possible effect of *permanent* import quotas, as opposed to those temporarily imposed in 1983–4, can be readily inferred from the present experiment. It may be computed from the base run, and additional simulations, that the import rationing implemented in 1983–4 was equivalent to a reduction of imports by approximately 15 per cent. If an equivalent estimate were available for permanent quotas, their effect could be estimated through proportional corrections of the preceding figures.

Financial liberalisation

The first step in the liberalisation and the development of financial markets in a country like Morocco is probably to free the interest rate and to abolish credit rationing. Such a measure could have two kinds of effect. At the microeconomic level, the allocation of investment funds across sectors may be more efficient in comparison with the initial situation where the allocation of credit rationing is largely discretionary or results from mere lobbying. At the macroeconomic level, the resulting increase in the lending rate of interest may have two effects. On one hand, it may directly increase savings, if savings are assumed to be interest-elastic, which they are not in the present model.[9] On the other hand, a higher domestic interest rate may induce a reallocation of households' and firms' portfolio. However, the only thing which matters for the real side of the economy is the extent to which that part of the portfolio which was initially invested abroad will be reduced.[10]

It is difficult to take properly into account the intersectoral micro-economic allocation effects with the present model, because of a lack of information about the rationing scheme, if any, that was actually implemented. That scheme in the base run is essentially proportional, so that reallocation effects when freeing the interest rate are likely to be

278

limited.[11] On the contrary, the macroeconomic effect is relatively easy to account for.

As may be seen from the comparison of simulations E-2 and E-20 in Figure 8.3, the lifting of credit rationing seems to foster growth. However, the only significant effect concerns the last year of the simulation period and it must be interpreted as a short-run effect of an expansionary increase in investment during that year rather than a genuine acceleration in growth. Credit rationing is important – given our initial assumptions – only during years 1982 and 1986 in the base run.[12] As no direct observation of the extent of credit rationing was available, this essentially results from the various calibration assumptions made for that run.

As mentioned above, the effect of lifting credit rationing depends on the reallocation that a rise in the domestic interest rate will imply between domestic and foreign (net) assets. In 1982, the foreign interest rate is extremely high and after freeing the domestic credit market, the equilibrium domestic rate of interest reaches a level close to that ruling abroad. It follows that the cost of capital remains approximately the same for firms which were constrained to borrow from abroad in the situation of rationing.[13] No significant macroeconomic effect is thus observed during that year. In 1986, however, the foreign rate of interest is lower, and freeing the domestic rate of interest leads to a much wider gap with respect to foreign capital markets. The impact on private investment and, through multiplier effects, on GDP is then quite substantial: −20 and 2 per cent respectively. Note on the other hand that, because the lifting of credit rationing induces capital flows to and from the rest of the world, the exchange rate is affected. Basically, firms import, and households export, less capital from abroad. This leads to a faster devaluation and an improvement in the current account. Finally, the fiscal deficit is reduced because the gain in GDP increases tax receipts. This favourable evolution will then be transmitted to the following years because of the higher growth potential made possible by the increase in investment.[14]

Several lessons may be drawn from this experiment. First, analysing the effects of freeing the domestic credit market logically requires a precise knowledge of the initial extent of credit rationing and the allocative effects of the rationing scheme. This information is seldom available, though, so that microeconomic allocation effects cannot be correctly identified and only qualitative, rather than quantitative, macroeconomic consequences may be put into evidence. Second, the latter effects appear to be strongly dependent upon the whole macroeconomic environment. This is illustrated in the present simulation by the prominent role of the foreign capital market, which determines the opportunity cost of capital, even though capital mobility may be limited, and of the exchange rate regime.

Experiment E-3 attempts to replicate what could be the consequences of pushing financial liberalisation further, by developing an attractive

(a) GDP (percentage change in relation to E–2)

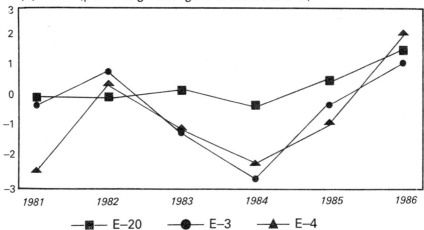

(b) Fiscal deficit (percentage share in GDP)

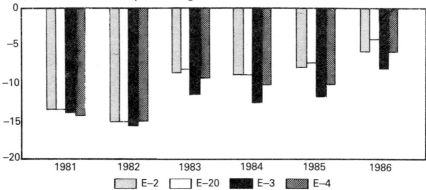

(c) Current account (billions of 1980 US dollars)

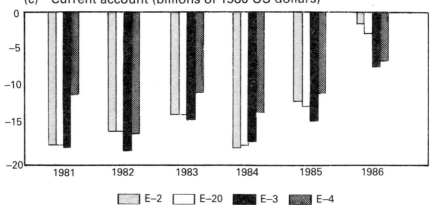

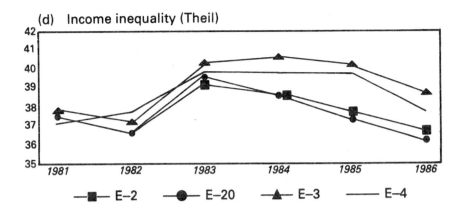

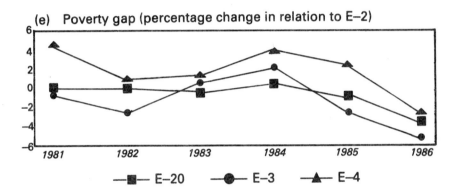

Figure 8.3 Morocco: effects of financial reforms

domestic financial market. It is assumed therefore that households' money demand falls and becomes more elastic with respect to the relative return on domestic and foreign financial assets. Finally, the initial money supply and its rate of growth are reduced so that a larger share of the budget deficit is financed by bonds.

This modification of the initial system, in which government bonds were issued in limited amount and only as a counterpart to households' time deposits, this being a consequence of credit rationing, raises the equilibrium nominal and real interest rate – because of the contractionary

281

monetary policy – and reduces investment. It also significantly reduces inflation and increases real wages in the modern sector, because money wages are kept at their base-run values. The result is a slight fall in GDP and a limited slowdown in growth, due to a crowding-out effect on private investment – despite the expansionary increase in real wage rates. The budget deficit increases because of the drop in the level of economic activity, the increase in debt service and the lower inflation tax. The current account deteriorates because the increase in real wages induces a real appreciation of the currency, an evolution that is consistent with the larger capital imports resulting from the increase in domestic interest rates.

Changes in the income distribution do not compensate for these negative results. Unemployment increases, partly because of the increase in the real wage rates in the modern sector, and partly because of the drop in GDP, whereas the terms of trade deteriorate in the agricultural sector.

The last simulation undertaken under the heading of financial liberalisation (E-4) consisted of raising the substitution elasticity between domestic and foreign assets, or, in other words, of increasing capital mobility. To appreciate the relevance of this implicit weakening of foreign exchange control, it must be kept in mind that a country like Morocco, where emigrant workers' remittances represent approximately 5 per cent of GDP, cannot be totally isolated from foreign capital markets. 'Compensation' practices, whereby residents export capital by shortcutting wage remittances from abroad, are widespread. This is the reason why the calibration assumptions selected for the base run allowed for some limited capital mobility, despite the quite restrictive initial official foreign exchange controls pertaining in Morocco in the early 1980s.

As foreign interest rates are higher than in Morocco for 1981, 1983, 1984 and to a lesser extent 1985, in the reference simulation E-20, higher capital mobility leads to substantial capital outflows during those years, and to a slower growth of money supply. The opposite occurs in 1982 and 1986. As a consequence, the domestic interest rate and the exchange rate are directly influenced by the evolution of the international capital markets. The level of economic activity reflects that dependence, and substantial year-to-year departures from the reference simulation are noticeable in the evolution of GDP and other macroeconomic aggregates.

Whether Morocco would have fared better with higher capital mobility over the early 1980s, and whether it will do better in the future if that measure is enforced, is difficult to say on the basis of the present experiment. Capital mobility involves not only the absence of foreign exchange controls at home but also the absence of an overseas borrowing constraint abroad. Practically, however, such constraints arose from the difficulties experienced by the country and its adjustment needs. To a large extent, ignoring those constraints thus is equivalent to dismissing altogether the problem of adjustment. A more convincing experiment would therefore consist of considering capital movements in gross rather than in net terms, maintaining some borrowing constraints – or a premium on the debtor foreign rate of interest – while freeing investments abroad, and capital repatriation, by domestic residents.

The simulation model is not equipped to deal with this asymmetric situation. However, given the limited role of the latter flows in simulation E-4, it is quite likely that such an experiment would have led to almost negligible departures from the reference experiment.

All in all, it appears from the preceding simulations that the potential impact of a financial liberalisation in Morocco, as accounted for by the present model – and despite the rather extended scope of that model – is limited, and in any case highly dependent on the accompanying fiscal, monetary and wage policy measures. True, freeing the interest rate on the domestic credit market has been shown to potentially enhance investment and growth. But this was obtained mostly through a modification of the limited capital movements to and from the rest of the world. True, making the domestic financial market more attractive to residents allows a contractionary monetary policy, in simulation E-3, to produce disinflation at a low cost in terms of economic activity. But, with a flexible exchange rate and limited capital mobility, the same result could have been achieved with fiscal instruments. Finally, a higher capital mobility has been shown to be of limited effect when restricted to the creditor side of the market, or to be inconsistent with the actual working of the international market when extended to the debtor side.

Taxation reforms

The first simulation undertaken under this heading concerns the reform of tariffs. Following the World Bank recommendations, it is assumed here that the average effective tariff rate is brought down, from 1981 until the end of the simulation period, from 19 per cent in the base run to 14 per cent, and made uniform, at that rate, across sectors. It is assumed that the resulting changes in foreign payments are met through changes in the exchange rate. The reference experiment therefore is E-2.

The drop in tariffs initially increases imports and depresses domestic production through substitution effects. The resulting deterioration of the current account is compensated by a faster devaluation of the currency – from 3 to 4 per cent, that is significantly less that the drop in tariffs. This real devaluation in turn increases exports and the overall level of demand, overcompensating the initial depressive effect of tariff reductions.

Not surprisingly, this partial reduction of existing distortions has positive overall effects on the economy, as shown in Figure 8.2. The average annual growth rate of GDP rises from 3.2 to 3.6 per cent and the average level of investment increases by 8 per cent. Nonetheless, the increase in tax receipts resulting from a higher GDP and a higher GDP growth rate cannot compensate for the drop in government revenues due to the reduction in tariffs. Accordingly, the fiscal deficit increases substantially. It is covered by the increase in savings left over once additional investments have been paid for, the rise in savings resulting itself both from the higher degree of capacity utilisation every year and from faster growth.

The distributional consequences of the tariff reduction are also favourable. Unemployment is reduced in the urban sector of the economy, whereas agricultural workers and peasants benefit from the higher relative price of their products induced by the devaluation.

Reducing export taxes has slightly more favourable effects, although the change in export tax rates in E-6 has been calibrated so as to produce the same overall drop in government receipts as in E-5. The fall in the export tax rate increases the producer price and reduces the final price of exports. The resulting rise in the volume of exports increases foreign exchange receipts and leads to a real appreciation of the currency in comparison with the reference simulation, E-2. The consequent fall in the relative price of imports boosts the domestic level of activity in the rest of the economy and makes investment less expensive. An acceleration of growth follows.

The last two reforms analysed in this paper concern income taxation. In simulation E-7, the personal income tax on the two richest groups of individuals in the economy – the group of capitalists and that of large farmers – is raised by an amount approximately equal to the change in tax receipts in the preceding two simulations. Reversing the signs of the effects shown in Figure 8.2 and in Table 8.6, thus permits a direct comparison of income and trade taxation. Increasing the income tax without modifying public expenditures may be shown to have an ambiguous effect on the level of output in the basic Keynesian model. On one hand, effective demand is reduced. On the other hand, the demand for money also shifts downward. Thus, if no monetary contraction comes along with the increase in taxation – a reduction in money supply being justified by a lower level of deficit financing – the rate of interest goes down with an expansionary effect on investment and output. In the short run, one should thus find that, with a constant money supply, an increase in income taxation reduces the rate of interest and has an ambiguous effect on output. Things would obviously be different in the long run with a balanced public budget. The dominant effect would then be a drop in the average propensity to save, and a lower rate of growth.

The results found with simulation E-7 are in accordance with the preceding argument, as shown in Figure 8.2. The output effect is slightly positive, the rate of interest is lower than in the reference experiment E-2, and the increase in the investment rate overcompensates the drop in household consumption. Thanks to a higher level of investment, the growth potential of the economy is now larger, whereas, of course, the budget deficit is reduced. Another obvious consequence is a drop in income inequality: the increase in poverty appearing in part (e) of Figure 8.2 corresponds to a temporary drop in the income of the informal urban sector directly hit by the fall in the consumption of those households whose income tax has increased.

Increasing the corporate tax – simulation E-8 – rather than the personal income tax has slightly different effects. Basically, the drop in dividend payments which should have the same impact as an increase in the personal income tax is now compensated by a drop in investment demand, itself due to the increase in the cost of capital. In the Keynesian framework the resulting output effect is practically negligible. The volume of investment slightly declines, whereas that of household consumption increases moderately. As before, this substitution goes through the money supply. The initial drop in investment causes a fall in output and the demand for money. The rate of interest goes down and compensates somewhat the initial drop in investment. The fall in effective demand brings the price of those goods exchanged on competitive markets downward with a positive effect on real wages and household consumption.

In summary, the scope for an efficient taxation reform in extension of the measures prescribed in the 1986 SECAL agreement seems substantial. Combining the reform of tariffs and an increase in the income tax, for instance, should produce, according to the present simulation model, significant improvements in the allocation of resources and the distribution of income with an unchanged budget deficit. Note, moreover, that these favourable effects are not essentially long run. With the typically short-run semi-Keynesian macroeconomic closures selected for all the preceding experiments, a reduction and a uniformisation of tariffs coupled with an increase in the income tax should have immediate positive effects on the level of activity and employment. This would remain the case even if both the wage rate in the modern sector and public expenditures were specified in real rather than in nominal terms, and if the wage rate were allowed to respond to changes in the level of unemployment.

Conclusions

The analysis of the Moroccan economy conducted in this section goes beyond that conducted in the previous section in three ways: first, it is based on a model of the whole economy rather than a partial model of the agricultural sector; second, it breaks up the Bank's policy package into its separate components, and examines the possibility of going beyond the packages so far recommended by the Bank; third, it goes beyond the analysis of the output indicators so far considered and examines also the influence of distributional variables. A bare summary of the relationship

Table 8.7 Morocco: effects of alternative policy packages by comparison with 'zero compliance' (E-1)

Package Effect on target variable	Actual World Bank package (E-6)	Actual Bank package plus liberalisation of external capital controls (E-4)	Actual Bank package plus liberalisation of all capital controls (E-9)	Actual Bank package plus tax reforms (E-10)
Output and financial indicators:				
GDP growth	rise	neutral[1]	rise	rise
Fiscal deficit	neutral	neutral	improve[2]	neutral
Current account	neutral	neutral	neutral	neutral
Export growth	rise	fall	fall	rise
Investment	neutral	fall	rise	rise
Social indicators:				
Unemployment rate	neutral	neutral	improve[2]	improve[2]
Theil inequality index	. .	worsen[2]	. .	. .

Notes: 1 A policy package is described as 'neutral' in relation to a particular indicator if that indicator differs by less than 10 per cent from its value under the base run.

2 A reduction in the fiscal deficit, unemployment rate or Theil inequality index is described as an 'improvement' and an increase as a 'worsening'.

between the different simulations is set out in Table 8.7.

Already we can see how sensitive the Moroccan economy is to the manner in which reforms are brought in. Whereas the policy package actually implemented by the Moroccan government appears to have increased GDP and exports, further liberalisation of capital controls appears to have an export-depressing effect, and if such liberalisation is done without simultaneous development of the *internal* financial market, the result is in addition both a fall in investment and an increase in inequality. This finding from Morocco echoes experience from the Southern Cone of Latin America, where liberalisation of external capital movements in the absence of deepening of the internal financial structure led in the early 1980s to massive outflows of capital and increases in unemployment (Foxley, 1983; Toye, 1987: 67–8). But it is specific to this particular type of liberalisation package, and as earlier demonstrated the distributional effects of foreign exchange liberalisation (simulation E-2) on their own appear to be positive.

Table 8.8 Effect of Bank policy-based lending. All evaluation methods: summary of results

Evaluation method	Real GDP growth	Real export growth	Investment/ GDP	Balance of payments	Private foreign finance	Unemployment and poverty
Tabular comparisons with control:						
This study (Ch. 6)	weak –ve	+ve	–ve	+ve	..	..
World Bank (1988, 90)	neutral	+ve	–ve	+ve	..	neutral
(1992)	weak +ve (–ve in Africa)	neutral (–ve in Africa)	neutral	..	..	..
Multiple regression:						
This study (Ch. 7)	weak +ve (finance only: weak –ve)	+ve	weak –ve	+ve	neutral	..
Model-based simulations (from present chapter):						
Malawi	..	ambiguous	..	–ve	..	..
Morocco	+ve	+ve	neutral	neutral	..	neutral

Sources: as for Table 7.7, plus Tables 8.2 and 8.7.

8.4 COMPARISON OF ALTERNATIVE EVALUATIVE METHODS

It remains to bring together the model-based results of this chapter with the conclusions on effectiveness derived from the different approaches used in Chapters 6 and 7. This is done in Table 8.8.

Many of the results obtained from Chapters 6 and 7 are reinforced, in particular the apparent positive effect of conditional policy packages, *if and only if the conditions are implemented*, on export growth and GNP. However, certain new findings emerge from these model-based studies only, in particular:

(from Malawi) the trade-off between packages which take the economy towards external balance and those which take it towards internal balance;

(from Morocco) the threat to investment if external capital controls are loosened on their own;

(from Morocco in particular) the extreme sensitivity of the income distribution effect to the manner in which liberalisation is introduced. On balance, however, it appears from the Morocco study that the negative trend in social indicators such as literacy and infant mortality that has occurred in the 1980s in many parts of the Third World (Cornia *et al.*, 1987) may be associated more with deflation and stabilisation than with Bank-inspired structural measures.[15] In Morocco, certainly, trade liberalisation on its own appears to do low income groups nothing but good.

The pattern of policy reform pursued by the Bank in Morocco contrasts greatly with that employed in Malawi. The Moroccan package consisted largely of 'whole-economy' measures such as trade and tax reforms, whereas the Malawi package consisted largely of changes to agricultural prices and subsidies. Comparison of the two studies suggests strongly that comprehensiveness of approach does not imply bigness of impact. Most of the qualitative effects reported for Morocco in Table 8.3 are quite modest − even with reforms going far beyond what the Bank has so far been able to achieve, the balance of payments does not change by more than one percentage point from its base run, nor unemployment by more than two percentage points. The magnitude of response of the Malawian economy to much more partial reforms (Table 8.3) is far greater. Our comparison is in no sense scientific, but it appears to suggest that the Bank's shift in the middle 1980s from a whole economy-based to a sector-based strategy of reform may have been a wise one.

APPENDIX 1 THE MALAWI MULTI-MARKET AGRICULTURAL SECTOR MODEL

This appendix outlines the structure of the model used in the analysis of section 8.2. A copy of the model calibrated to 1988 data for Malawi suitable for use on an IBM or IBM-compatible microcomputer is available from the authors.

The model invokes the assumption that smallholder farmers, on average, tend towards a profit-maximising solution, subject to three constraints: satisfying subsistence consumption requirements; technological possibilities and fertiliser availability. Hence, it is assumed that a representative, national 'average' farmer attempts to maximise the following:

$$\text{Max } \pi = \sum_{i=1}^{n} P_i Y_i A_i - (R + W) \sum_{i=1}^{n} F_i A_i - C \tag{1}$$

where: π = total farm profits from production of various crops, i.e. unfertilised local maize, fertilised local maize, composite maize, hybrid maize, tobacco, groundnuts, cotton and rice

P_i = crop price
Y_i = crop yield per unit of land
A_i = land area under various crops
R = price of fertiliser
W = other costs (mainly labour) associated with fertiliser use
F_i = fertiliser use for unit of land
C = all other production costs

The technological possibilities constraints take the form of fertiliser response functions:

$$Y_i = a_i + b_i F_i - c_i F_i^2 \tag{2}$$

where a_i, b_i, c_i are parameters.

The constraint on total fertiliser use, which results from the country's fertiliser import supply programme, is specified as:

$$\sum_{i=1}^{n} F_i A_i < \bar{F} \tag{3}$$

where: F is the quantity of fertiliser available to the representative farmer. The value of $\bar{F}$ is determined by the total amount of fertiliser sold by ADMARC and a leakage function. The latter captures the amount of fertiliser leaked i.e. sold unofficially, by smallholders to estates. This leakage results from the differential between ADMARC's subsidised fertiliser price and the price at which estates can buy fertiliser from the commercial company Optichem. The leakage function is specified as:

$$L = M \left[\theta_i + \theta_2 (\hat{R} - R)^\beta - \theta_3 \left(\sum_{i=1}^{n} P_i \right)^\alpha \right] \tag{4}$$

289

where: L = leakage to estates
M = total ADMARC fertiliser imports
P_i = smallholder crop prices
R = ADMARC's fertiliser price
$\hat{R}$ = Optichem's fertiliser price
θ_i, θ_2, θ_3, β, α are parameters.

Hence,

$$\bar{F} = M - L \qquad (5)$$

A third constraint exists in the form of a subsistence consumption requirement for local maize. The fact that Malawian smallholders grow local maize primarily for own-consumption, and hybrid and composite maize for sale, means that the profit maximising motive only applies to hybrid and composite varieties. The subsistence constraint takes the form of:

$$Y_iA_i + Y_2A_2 \geqslant \bar{C} \qquad (6)$$

where: Y_iA_i = production of fertilised local maize
Y_2A_2 = production of unfertilised local maize
$\bar{C}$ = minimum consumption requirement.

In all simulations the subsistence constraint is binding.

The amount of fertiliser, F_i, used on local maize, can be derived directly from equations (2) and (4). The amount of fertiliser available for other crops is therefore:

$$\bar{F} - A_iF_i$$

and its allocation is determined by the profit maximising solution, subject to the technological constraints and the revised constraint on fertiliser availability. The solution gives the following set of demand curves for fertiliser use on all crops other than local maize:

$$F_i = \frac{1}{2c_i} - \left(b_i - \frac{R + \lambda}{P} \right), \quad i = 2 \ldots n \qquad (7)$$

where λ is the Lagrangian multiplier on the constraint defining fertiliser availability. The value of λ corresponds exactly to the scarcity premium on fertiliser i.e. the extent to which the true value exceeds market price. The model determines the value of λ as a function of F. Equation (7) possesses all the usual properties of a demand curve: the demand for fertiliser is negatively related to the fertiliser price and positively related to crop prices.

Equations (1) to (7) are the core of the model. Once the model has been solved for a particular set of prices (R and P) and fertiliser imports M, information can be obtained regarding the impact of the price package on variables of relevance to government policy objectives, such as total fertiliser use, total crop production and changes in farm profits. The budgetary cost of a particular price and import policy package, in terms of input trading activities, can also be assessed:

$$NFE = (\sum_{i=1}^{n} F_i + L)(R - C) - MX - A$$

where: NFE = net profits/loss on ADMARC's fertiliser trading account

$\sum_{i=1}^{n} F_i + L$ = ADMARC's total fertiliser sales

$\quad\;\; R$ = ADMARC's fertiliser selling price

$\quad\;\; C$ = average transport and handling costs

$\quad\;\; M$ = quantity of ADMARC's fertiliser imports

$\quad\;\; X$ = c.i.f. cost of fertiliser imports

$\quad\;\; A$ = overheads associated with fertiliser trading.

The model also calculates ADMARC's net profits/losses from various crop trading activities. This depends on total procurement, domestic demand and domestic selling prices, export demand and export selling prices, transport and handling costs and overheads. For example, assuming all maize procurements are sold for domestic consumption:

$$NPM = Q(\hat{P} - P - T) - A$$

where: NPM = net profit/loss on maize account

$\quad\;\; \hat{P}$ = ADMARC maize selling price

$\quad\;\; P$ = ADMARC maize buying price

$\quad\;\; T$ = average transport and handling costs

$\quad\;\; Q$ = total maize procurement

$\quad\;\; A$ = overheads.

Maize procurement is estimated as follows:

$$Q = \sum_{i=1}^{4} Y_i A_i - \bar{C}Z \tag{8}$$

where: $\sum_{i=1}^{4} Y_i A_i$ = total procurement of fertilised local maize, unfertilised local maize, hybrid maize and composite maize

$\quad\;\; \bar{C}$ = subsistence consumption per smallholder

$\quad\;\; Z$ = number of smallholders.

291

For all other crops, procurement is assumed to equal total production.

Assumptions regarding minimum and maximum ADMARC procurement requirements can also be used to calculate the revenue effects of a policy package in terms of maize imports and stock run down, or maize exports and stock accumulation.

The total budgetary cost of a given fertiliser supply and input and output price package i.e. ADMARC's net revenue/loss on crop and input trading is:

$$R = NPF + NPM + NPO$$

where: NPO = net revenue/loss on all non-maize crop trading.

The model calculates the change in revenue for alternative policy scenarios:

$$\Delta R = R_i - R_0 \tag{9}$$

where: R_0 = revenue in base case
  R_i = revenue in policy simulation.

APPENDIX 2   THE MOROCCO CGE MODEL

This appendix describes the model outlined in section 8.3. It draws on an earlier paper (Bourguignon *et al.*, 1989) where a more complete dicussion of the model is available. To simplify notation, the presentation is made for a one-sector model, but the reader should think of accompanying subscripts for goods markets, labour markets, and household consumption and financial decisions. As a rule, no subscripts appear for sectors, nor for labour markets, but a subscript h is used to denote a variable indexed over households and a subscript t to indicate time is used in the description of dynamic linkages. A subscript -1 indicates a one-period lag for the value of that variable and expectations about inflation and exchange rate changes are denoted by $\hat{P}^e$ and $\hat{e}^e$. As before, variables expressed in foreign currency units have an asterisk superscript and Δ is the first difference operator.

In the description of the selected functional forms, the following conventions are used: A *CES* function with arguments X_1, X_2 is denoted: $Y = CES\ (X_1,\ X_2;\ A,\ \alpha,\ \sigma)$ with parameters following the semi-colon. The corresponding dual is denoted $P_y = CESD\ (PX_1,\ PX_2;\ A,\ \alpha,\ \sigma)$; the same convention is followed for Leontief (*L*) and LES (*LES*) functions. Non-competitive imports are denoted by a subscript 0 and foreign currency denominated assets (prices) are denoted by an asterisk.

Model equations

Technology

(A.1) $X^S = A(t) \, L(VA, V_2)$

Leontief production function for gross output and value-added

(A.2) $V_1 = CES_1(V^d, V^m; \sigma_c, \gamma)$

CES intermediate aggregation function

(A.3) $V_2 = L(V_1, M^{NC})$

Leontief intermediate technology

(A.4) $VA = CES_2(L_S, \bar{F}, U, \bar{K}; \sigma_p, \alpha)$

CES aggregation function for value-added. (F = sector specific factors; U = capacity utilization rate; $0 < U < 1$)

Commodity demand definitions

(A.5) $X^d = D^d + E^d$

Total demand

(A.6) $D^d = V^d + I^d + G^d + C^d$

Domestic effective demand

(A.7) $M^c = V^m + I^m + G^m + C^m$

Import demand for competitive imports

(A.8) $Q = CES_1 \, (M^c, D^d; \bar{A_2}, \gamma, \sigma_c)$

Composite demand

Prices

(A.9) $P^m = P^*_m e \, (1 + \bar{tm})$

Import price (competitive imports)

(A.10) $P^m_0 = P^{m*}_0 e \, (1 + \bar{tm}_0)$

Import price (non-competitive imports)

(A.11) $P^e = P^*_e e \, (1 + te) = P^d$

Export price

(A.12) $P^d = \bar{P}^d \, (1 + \bar{tx})$

Tax inclusive domestic price

(A.13) $P^n = P^d - a_x P^c - a_0$

Value-added price

(A.14) $P^c = CESD \, (P^d, P^m)$

Composite price

293

Factor demand, wage determination, and expectations

(A.15)　$L_s^d = g_2\left(\dfrac{W}{P^n}; U, \bar{F}, \bar{K}\right)$ — Labour demand for category s from short-run profit maximization

(A.16)　$\bar{L}_s^s = L_s^d + \bar{L}_G$ — Wage determination; neo-classical full employment

(A.17)　$W_{s,t} = \bar{W}_{s,t-1} + \Omega \hat{P} + (1 - \Omega)(1 + \hat{P}_e)$ — Wage indexation; s denotes a labour category

(A.18)　$P^e = \hat{P}_{-1}; \hat{e}^e = \hat{e}_{-1}$ — Adaptive price expectations (P is GDP deflator)

Commodity demands

(A.19)　$E^d = \bar{E}_0\,(P_e^\bullet/\bar{P}_w^\bullet)^{-z}; z > 0$ — Export demand

(A.20)　$\dfrac{D^d}{M^c} = g_1\left(\dfrac{P^d}{P^m}; \gamma, \sigma_c\right)$ — Domestic use ratio

(A.21)　$I_t = a\left(\dfrac{p^n MP_k U}{q(\sigma + J^F)} - 1\right) = \left(\dfrac{B}{C} - 1\right)$ — Investment demand

　　　　$I_t \geqslant 0$ — (see text)

(A.22)　$J^F = \theta i + (1 - \theta)(1 + \hat{e}^e)i^\bullet - b\hat{p}^e$ — Opportunity cost of credit (θ is share of domestic component; b, a parameter)

(A.23)　$M^{NC} = a_0 X$ — Non-competitive imports

(A.24)　$C = \text{LES}(P^C, Y^H, \mu, \phi); \mu \equiv 1 - s$ — LES consumption demand (μ is marginal propensity to consume)

(A.25)　$GE = \bar{G}\bar{P}^C + \bar{w}_G \bar{L}_G + \bar{I}_G P^C$ — Exogenous government expenditures

(A.26)　$I = k\Delta K$ — Investment by sector of origin (k is vector describing composition of capital across sectors)

(A.27)　$q = k'P^c$ — Price of capital goods

Flexible and fix price commodity market

(i) Price adjustment

(A.28) $X^S = X^d$ Market-clearing price

(ii) Quantity adjustment

(A.29) $P^{d,min} = \{ (p_T^m - 1_{-1}w_{-1})m$ Mark-up pricing;
                                                        1 = unit labour
        $+ 1_{-1}w_t + ap_{-1}^d \} (1 + \hat{p}^e)$ requirement;
                                                        m = minimum share of
                                                        period $t-1$ profit
                                                        margins required for
                                                        period t;
                                                        a = input-output
                                                        coefficients

$$\begin{cases} X^S U = X^d \text{ if } P^d = \bar{P}^d \\ \text{or} \\ X^S(1) = X^d \text{ if } P^d > \bar{P}^d \end{cases}$$

Utilization rate
adjustment in case of
excess supply

Price adjustment in case
of excess demand

Household income and saving

(A.30) $Y_h = w_s L + \bar{w}_G \bar{L}_G + (PNX^S - W\bar{L}_S)(1 - \omega)$ ω is distributed share of
                                                        profits

(A.31) $S_h = sY_h - a_s \hat{W}e$ Household savings (a_s is
                                                        semi-elasticity of savings
                                                        with wealth)

(A.32) $P^C C = P^C \bar{C} + (Y_h - S_h - P^C \bar{C})$ Household consumption;
                                                        $\bar{C}$ is exogenous
                                                        consumption

(A.33) $W = H_h + B_h/i + eF_h/i^* + P_E^k$ Household wealth
                                                        constraint

Portfolio determination (g_i):

(A.34) $\dfrac{g_1}{1 - g_1} = \psi_1 \left[\dfrac{1 + r}{J_F} \right] \varepsilon_1$ Allocation between
                                                        physical and financial
                                                        assets

(A.35) $J_F = g_2(1 + i) + (1 - g_2)(1 + i^*)(1 + \hat{e}^r)$ Average nominal return
                                                        on bonds

(A.36) $\bar{r} = PN \times U \times \dfrac{\partial X}{\partial K} \times \dfrac{K}{\bar{K}}$ Average nominal return
                                                        on physical assets

295

(A.37) $\dfrac{g_2}{1 - g_2} = \psi_2 \left\{ \dfrac{(1 + i)}{(1 + i^*)(1 + \hat{e}^c)} \right\}^{\varepsilon_2}$

Allocation between domestic and foreign bonds

(A.38) $\ln H_h = \ln p^c + \alpha r + \beta \ln(Y_h/P^c) + \ln \bar{B}$

Money demand; $\alpha < 0$; $\beta > 0$ $r \equiv (1 + i)/(1 + \hat{p}^c) - 1$

(A.39) $g_3 = \dfrac{\Delta H_h}{S_h}$

Household saving allocated to money

Household savings allocation

(A.40) $S_{h,k} \equiv S_h - \Delta H_h$

Household savings allocated to non-monetary assets

(A.41) $S_{h,k} = S_{h,k} +$

Household savings allocated to non-monetary assets

$g_1 S_{h,k} +$

Physical capital

$g_2(1 - g_1) S_{h,k} +$

domestic bonds

$(1 - g_2)(1 - g_1) S_{h,k}$

foreign bonds

Firm's investment financing

(A.42) $H_f = \beta^F \left(\dfrac{J_F^t}{1 + \hat{p}^c} \right) \gamma_F \times P^d X^s$

Working capital requirements; $\gamma_F < 0$

Where $J_F^t = (1 + i)\theta + (1 + i^*)(1 + \hat{e}^c)(1 - \theta)$

(A.43) $S_f = \omega PN \, X^S - DP$

Firms' savings (undistributed profits)

(A.44) $BF = q^t + \Delta H_f - S_f - g_1 S_{h,k}$

requirements to finance investment expenditures; $BF = \Delta L_b + e \Delta L^*_w$

(A.45) $DP = (\varrho + i_{0-1})L_b + (\varrho + i^*_{-1})eL^*_w$

Repayment of debt (ϱ is exogenous repayment rate)

Firm borrowing allocation and credit rationing

(A.46) $\dfrac{g_4}{1 - g_4} = \psi_4 \left[\dfrac{(1 + i)}{(1 + i^*)(1 + \hat{e})} \right]^{-\varepsilon_4}$

Borrowing allocation between domestic and foreign bonds

296

(A.47) $\Delta L_b = g_4 BF - \varrho L_b$ Firm domestic net borrowing

(A.48) $\Delta L_w^{\bullet} = \dfrac{1}{e}(1 - g_4)L_w^{\bullet} - \varrho L_w^{\bullet}$ Firm foreign net borrowing

Credit rationing

(A.49) $q\, I^R = q^I - \mathrm{Inf}(0, g_4 L^F - \bar{B}^R)$ Effective demand for investment under rationing (see below)

Government revenue and deficit financing

(A.50) $GR = \bar{P}^d tx\, X^S + \bar{P}_0^{\bullet} M^{NC} + \bar{P}_m^{\bullet} tm\, M$ Tax receipts

(A.51) $GD \equiv GE - GR \equiv \Delta B_b + \Delta B_h + e\Delta B_w^{\bullet}$ Financing of government deficit (implied by monetary and national income identities)

Market equilibria

(A.52) $X^S = X^d$ Goods market

Financial markets

(A.53) $\Delta H \equiv \Delta B_b + \Delta L_b + \theta e\, CA$ Money supply definition ($\theta = 0$, full sterilization; $\theta = 1$, no sterilization)

(A.54) $\Delta H = \Delta H_f + \Delta H_h$ Money market equilibrium

(A.55) $\Delta B_h = 0$ No domestic bond market

(A.56) $\Delta F_h^{\bullet} = L_w^{\bullet} = B_w^{\bullet} = 0$ Foreign exchange control

(A.57) $i_0^R = i_0 = + i_\gamma; i_\gamma > 0$ Credit rationing (shadow interest rate determination used to evaluate notional credit demands)

Foreign exchange market

(A.58) $CA = P_e^{\bullet} E^d - \bar{P}_0^{\bullet} M^{NC} - \bar{P}_m^{\bullet} M^C + i_{-i}^{\bullet}(F_h^{\bullet} - L_w^{\bullet} - B_w^{\bullet})$ Current account

297

(A.59) $KA = \check{K}\check{F} - \Delta F_h^* + \Delta L_w^*$

Capital account ($\check{K}\check{F}$ is
exogenous capital flows)

Floating exchange rate (ΔB_w^* fixed)

(A.60) $CA + KA = 0$

Fixed exchange rate (ΔB_w^* endogenous)

(A.61) $\Delta B_w^* = -CA - \check{K}\check{F} + \Delta F_h^* - \Delta L_w^*$

Dynamics

Factors of production

(A.62) $\check{K}_t = K_{t-1} + I_{t-1}$

Capital stock definition

(A.63) $\check{L}_{s,t} = L_{s,t-1}(1 + g_s)$

Labour force growth

(A.64) $\check{A}_t = A_{t-1}(1 + g_a)$

Technical progress

Note: All elasticities are constant elasticities and are defined as positive numbers. Elasticities (ε_i) entering the asset demand functions are share elasticities, i.e.:

$$\text{e.g. } \varepsilon_1 \equiv \left(\frac{\hat{g}_1}{1 - g_1}\right) / (\hat{f}_F / r)$$

Firms', households' and government decisions in goods markets are presented first. Next, asset market behaviour by firms and households. Finally the market for foreign exchange which derives from goods and portfolio decisions. Alternative closures and dynamic linkages close the discussion.

The representative firm makes decisions about output supply and investment demand. Output decisions derive from the maximisation of short-run profits. Technology is given by a constant returns to scale production function with short-run diminishing returns to labour, the only variable factor along with intermediate demand. Capital is putty-clay: once installed, it can only be varied through capacity increase or through depreciation.

Technology for gross output is given by a Leontief function between value-added VA_i and intermediate demand with intermediate demand a Leontief function for each supplying sector. Thus there is no substitution between the various components of intermediate demand. However, within a given sector, domestically and foreign-produced goods are imperfect substitutes according to a CES aggregation function between the domestically and foreign-produced components (equation A.2). As shown by the block of equations defining commodity demands, the same functional form and elasticities apply for all components of final demand (equations 6–8).

The price block includes the definition of tax and tariff inclusive domestic prices, and the value-added and composite prices which result from cost minimization (equations A.13 and A.14). The factor demand and wage determination block indicates the two alternatives in the labour market: (i) neo-classical wage determination and, (ii) wage indexation. Also note that government employment (and the government wage) are exogenous. Finally price (and exchange rate) expectations are taken to be adaptive with a one-period lag.

Commodity demands come next. The domestic use ratio (equation A.20) results from cost minimization under the CES functional form described in equation (A.8) and export demand has a constant foreign price elasticity of demand. Consumption demand by each household class results from the familiar LES after household savings have been deducted from disposable income (see equations A.31 and A.32 below). Government expenditures are fixed in nominal terms and the composition of a unit of capital is assumed to be identical across sectors (equation A.26 and A.27).

Investment demand is determined by the profit rate (equation A.21). Such a functional form is consistent with formulations of investment demand in which there are costs of adjustment and investment decisions are irreversible (Nickell, 1978: Chapter 4). However, with this specification, the model exhibits extreme fluctuations to changes in the relative profitability of investment caused by interest rate or expectation changes. For this reason, real investment is given by the quadratic expression:

$$\frac{I_t}{K_t} = q\gamma_1\left\{\left(\frac{B}{C}\right)^2 + \gamma_2\left(\frac{B}{C}\right)\right\}$$

where γ_1 and γ_2 are suitable selected parameters so that in equilibrium when $B/C = 1$, investment will be at a level which will ensure a rate of growth of net capital stock equal to g. The elasticity of investment with respect to a change in profitability. $\partial I/\partial(B/C)$, evaluated at $B/C = 1$ is equal to a predetermined value, e. The resulting shape of the investment function is a quadratic function passing through the origin. Also note from equation A.22 that the expectation of a change in inflation is not fully incorporated in the investment decision if $b < 1$.

Equations A.28 and A.29 describe the two market clearing mechanisms for commodity markets: (i) Walrasian price adjustment (equation A.28) and; (ii) Keynesian mark-up pricing (equation A.29) with endogenous capacity utilization. When there is full capacity utilization (i.e. $U_i = 1$), then prices adjust as under (i).

Household income includes labour income and the share of capital income after firms accounting for firms' retained earnings. In addition to factor income, households receive income from their asset holdings (equation A.30). (The details on the mapping from functional to household income are described below.) Household savings rates adjust to changes in wealth, so the marginal propensity to consume is endogenous (equation A.31). The savings rates are not assumed to be responsive to interest rates. This assumption reflects the conflict between income and substitution effects of changes in interest rates on saving, and the resulting ambiguity in the empirical literature. Analytically, the assumption is not important, because investment is assumed to depend negatively on the interest rate. So in the maquette, excess private saving depends positively on the interest rate via investment.

The wealth constraint shows that households hold money domestic bonds and foreign bonds in their portfolio. Portfolio determination follows the multi-level determination discussed above. All elasticities entering the asset demand functions, ε_i, are share elasticities. The allocation of household savings is in two stages: first households allocate savings to money, then to non-monetary assets. Within non-monetary assets, the allocation rules described in equations (A.34)–(A.39) reflect the allocation structure described above. The allocation satisfies the financial wealth constraint (equations A.40–41).

Firms' investment financing is for working capital requirements and for investment expenditures. Equation (A.44) shows that firms can borrow domestic bonds and foreign bonds with the allocation between domestic and foreign bonds similar to the allocation decision by households (equations A.46–48). When there is credit rationing (equation A.49) investment is residually determined from the national income identity (equation A.66) with shadow interest rate determination given by equation (A.58).

The government collects tax revenues and the government deficit is assumed to be met by borrowing from the Central Bank (ΔB_b), abroad (ΔB_w^*) and domestically (ΔB_h) (equation A.51).

Equilibrium in the money market takes place under different financial market closures. For example, if there are foreign exchange controls, no foreign asset holdings are allowed for firms or households (equation A.57). Also note that varying degrees of sterilization are accommodated in the money supply definition (equation A.53).

The foreign exchange market includes the net demand for foreign exchange resulting from demand for goods and assets. The alternatives of a fixed and a floating exchange rate are given by equations (A.61) and (A.62).

300

NOTES

1 For a discussion of the United Kingdom case, where a group of competing models was judged by government sponsors not on forecasting accuracy but rather on a prior government opinion concerning what type of structure was econometrically acceptable, see the article by Weir (1982).

2 In the Hwa model the demand for money is positively, rather than negatively, associated with the interest rate, the *LM* curve is downward-sloping and as a consequence the model is macroeconomically unstable.

3 A thorough analysis of the macroeconomic package implemented from 1983 on, including its structural and distributional consequences, is provided by Morrisson (1989).

4 Most of these supply-oriented measures were included in the 1985 SAL agreement with the World Bank. A summary is given in Table 8.3.

5 As this concerns phosphates, for which Morocco enjoys some monopoly power on world markets, the tax burden is in fact partly transferred to importing countries.

6 This term may be more appropriate than the term 'model' because of the extreme flexibility that has been built in, which allows for applications to a large variety of countries and institutional settings. This maquette considerably enlarges the scope of the usual CGE models, as described, for instance, in Dervis, de Melo and Robinson (1982). Recent attempts at introducing the financial and monetary sector in a CGE framework also include Fargeix, de Janvry and Sadoulet (1989) and Lora (1989). Recent developments of CGE in that direction are surveyed in Robinson (1989).

7 Recent examples of truly dynamic CGE models include Auerbach and Kotlikoff (1987), Goulder and Eichengreen (1989).

8 In particular, the extent to which those permanent quantitative constraints on imports are actually binding is quite ambiguous.

9 Savings are modelled according to the usual Keynesian fashion, rather than in an intertemporal framework where the interest rate would obviously be an essential determinant of savings. However, changes in the interest rate may have transitory (positive) effects on the savings rate through changes in the value of wealth.

10 As savings are interest inelastic, except for capital gains or losses, the change in domestic private savings is essentially determined by changes in capital movements.

11 Of course, things would be totally different if strong initial biases had been arbitrarily assumed in the base run. Note also that the model does not allow for the existence of a 'curb market' which would correct part of those biases.

12 The 'shadow' rate of interest which indicates the rate of interest at which the market demand would be equal to the actual supply of credit.

13 In the case of rationing, firms decide about the allocation of their loans between domestic and foreign creditors on the basis of a 'shadow' domestic rate – i.e. the implicit price of credit in presence of rationing – and the foreign interest rate. In the case of strong rationing, the shadow domestic interest rate is much higher that the official rate and the share of foreign loans is accordingly larger.

14 But at a lower rate of interest than with no change in the money demand.

15 This is certainly the claim of the Bank's latest evaluation of policy-based lending, which argues (World Bank 1990:39) that 'the available data do not suggest that adjustment lending has on average increased poverty'.

Part IV
CONCLUSIONS

9

SUMMARY OF ARGUMENT AND POLICY PROPOSALS

9.1 SUMMARY OF ARGUMENT

This study has sought to answer two fundamental questions. First, does the giving of aid confer power on the donor, in particular, power to change the recipient's economic policies? Second, has the exercise of such power as exists been of any help to the developing countries? The answer, to both questions, is 'a little, but not as much as the Bank hoped'. It will be useful to recapitulate the main steps in the book's argument at this point as a prelude to an attempt to state what lessons the experience of policy-based lending holds for policy-makers in the late 1990s and beyond.

The 1980s, as we saw, was a period in which a balance of payments crisis of unprecedented magnitude was superimposed on a slowing-down of growth in all areas of the world except the Far East. Policy-based lending was a weapon designed by the Bank to kill two birds with one stone. First, to provide quick-disbursing finance to deal with the crisis, and second, to demolish those structures of policy which it blamed both for the increasing incidence of failure on its projects, and also for the widening gap in economic performance between the Far East and the rest of the developing world. One instrument with two policy objectives is necessarily problematic: a trade-off inevitably arises and the Bank has not decided where on this particular trade-off to locate itself.

The exercise was a leap in the dark, in three senses. First, in terms of economic theory – which provided no guideline on how much liberalisation, if any, would be appropriate in a 'distorted' developing economy. Second, in terms of politics – for the Bank now found itself at the top negotiating table in developing countries without any explicit strategy for disarming the forces opposed to its suggested reforms. Third and last, in terms of relations with the IMF, which after many years of sharp separation of functions suddenly found itself supplying medium-term policy-based loans in the same market as the Bank. Notwithstanding these difficulties, and the initial opposition of the Bank's Executive Board, the principle of policy-based lending quickly took root, and now accounts for over a quarter of all lending by the Bank. Most other multilateral and bilateral donors now disburse some of their aid in policy-based form.

One rationale behind the Bank's conditionality, then, was to persuade recipient countries to rid themselves of policy structures which it believed to be prejudicial to development. Characteristically these structures were seen as protective walls designed to shelter special interest groups ('rent-seekers') from the pursuit of efficiency through competition in the market. In fact, as our case studies show, they served other functions as well. They consisted of a mixture of protection for the inefficient, intervention with a perfectly good economic rationale (e.g. infant-industry tariffs) and intervention with a social rationale (e.g. food subsidies). One of our conclusions is that there are more justifications for government intervention than the Bank has generally been prepared to accept and that further work to determine the appropriate form and levels of such intervention is now urgent.

But whatever the justification for state controls, the Bank encountered political opposition in attempting to overcome them, reflecting the fact that the losers from structural adjustment feel their loss sooner, and can express it more effectively, than the gainers. The Bank thus became involved, however reluctantly, in a multistage bargaining game. Often, opposition to the Bank was not effectively expressed at the negotiation stage of a policy-based lending agreement, since at that stage both parties have everything to lose and nothing to gain from delaying the transfer of the associated money. As a consequence, the Bank often succumbed to the temptation to prescribe policy reform even in markets where its own analysis had revealed no significant distortion and to ride into battle, like Don Quixote with his lance tilted, even in fields where there were no noble deeds to be done. In some cases the Bank's SAL conditionality even ran counter to the policy changes which its own staff were trying to bring in at project level, as in Malawi where the team negotiating SAL3 attempted to remove a fertiliser subsidy for small farmers which was fundamental to the success of the National Rural Development Programme, which the Bank's own project division was itself financing. Political opposition, and a government's willingness or lack of willingness to override it, becomes more apparent at the implementation stage, either through sins of omission or more typically, in countries which expect their relationship with the Bank to continue into the medium term, through countervailing actions. Both overt evasion and covert avoidance of conditionality can be the more readily contemplated by a recipient because it is aware of what we have called the Bank's 'disbursement dilemma' – that is, its reluctance to put its disbursement and its financial position at risk by too rigorous an insistence on compliance with conditions. As a consequence, even overt slippage on conditions has been substantial – over 40 per cent, according to the evidence of our case studies.

The case studies also reveal, however, how wide has been the dispersion of experience around this mean level, from Turkey, which implemented almost everything that was asked of it, to Guyana or Ecuador, which implemented almost nothing. Our discussion in Chapter 5 showed that some of this variation can be explained in terms of the recipient's economic predicament: those who live in glass houses know that it is unwise to throw too many stones, and compliance was somewhat higher among those who continued to be locked into economic crisis throughout the 1980s than among those who escaped. Some plausible political explanations, including the proposition that dictatorships and 'new brooms' will be relatively effective agents of reform, turn out to be wrong as often as they are right, but an obviously fundamental determinant of reform was the willingness and ability of the group which negotiated the conditionality agreement with the Bank to overcome the inevitable opposition. Different issues come into play here for each country and policy reform that is studied, but one factor remains constant: where there is articulate opposition to policy reform, as there usually is, that opposition must be overcome somehow if implementation is to take place. If it is to be overcome without compulsion, that requires either persuasion or financial compensation by the group pleading the case for such reforms. Failure to implement, in our case studies, can often be ascribed to the fact that the group within government which had signed the agreement with the Bank did not deploy either strategy effectively, and was as a consequence unable to deliver. We return to this issue in our final section.

Implementation, then, was partial; with some exceptions, it was more complete in respect of price-based policy instruments, which could be quickly altered by a few staff in the ministry of finance or central bank, than in respect of institutional changes which required widespread consent and the support of the legislature. Chapters 6, 7 and 8 above represent a three-pronged attack on the question of what these policy changes achieved. The three different analytical methods used there come to similar conclusions, namely:

1   the implementation of structural adjustment programmes under Bank guidance was almost always favourable to export growth and the external account;
2   the influence of structural adjustment programmes on aggregate investment is almost everywhere negative;
3   the influence of structural adjustment programmes on national income and on financial flows from overseas is, on balance, neutral. However, the regression analysis of Chapter 7 suggests that neutrality in respect of national income consists of two mutually cancelling effects, namely a positive lagged response to implementation of conditions, where that occurred, balanced by a *negative* and immediate response to the receipt

307

of SAL money. The negative coefficient may reflect the tendency of some countries to use SAL money as a substitute for painful reforms.

4 Although the major objective of this study has been to evaluate the Bank's policy-based lending in terms of its own chosen criteria and hence not to go too far into distributional impact, the Morocco study suggests that compliance with Bank conditions has been distributionally neutral. Probably this is again a question of mutually cancelling effects, e.g. the progressive effect of increases in farm prices balanced by the regressive effect of withdrawal of food subsidies. Living standards of the poor have evidently fallen in many developing countries, including those which have undergone structural adjustment (Cornia *et al.*, 1987). This appears to be partly in response to cuts in public expenditure, for which both the Bank and the Fund bear responsibility, and partly due to the impact of price reforms advocated by the Bank.

These results describe general patterns only, and the further insights which emerge from analysis of individual countries are described in the opening chapter of Volume 2, but we are encouraged by the consistency between the results emerging from the various analytical methods we have used, and between the results summarised above and those reported by the World Bank in its own internal investigations of adjustment lending (World Bank, 1988, 1990, 1992c).

9.2 IMPLICATIONS

In relation to the expectations placed upon policy-based lending when it was first conceived, the results reported above are bound to appear disappointing. By contrast with the Bank's generally acknowledged success in project lending (e.g. an average *ex post* rate of return of 17 per cent across all projects between 1960 and 1980; Mosley (1987: 153)), it is not even clear whether the net return, in terms of growth of gross national product, on the $35 billion which the Bank has so far invested in policy-based lending is positive or negative. But we do not need to take refuge in the Bank's frequent insistence that policy-based lending is a medium-term process, many of whose results are not yet apparent, to question the superficial appearance. The point, as earlier noted, is that policy-based lending seeks to kill two birds (quick-disbursing finance and enforcement of conditionality) with a single stone. It is our view that these objectives are fundamentally in conflict, and that although the quick-disbursement objective is less emphasised by the Bank, it is the one most likely to prevail. This in turn derives from the financial imperatives which have confronted the Bank during the debt crisis of the 1980s. For during that period the Bank has been faced not only with the spectre of default on its own loans, but also with insistent appeals from the US government, amongst others, to relieve financial pressure on the IMF and American commercial banks by lending into the arrears of the most heavily debt-distressed developing countries. (The cases of Jamaica, Ecuador, Philippines and Kenya are considered in detail in our case studies.) The appropriate response to both pressures was the same, namely to pump out money on demand. Any protracted wrangle with a recipient government over the speed with which its marketing boards were being privatised or its structure of import controls rationalised could not but hinder the achievement of this solution. The World Bank, it must not be forgotten, is a bank, and in the last analysis it must protect its financial stability before it does anything else.[1] In the event it has protected the financial stability of other institutions as well. The erection of a safety net under the international financial system, then, is the hidden benefit which must be added to the rather meagre benefits catalogued above before any balance sheet is drawn up. As the international financial community, at the end of the 1990s, finds itself increasingly drawn into lending to Eastern Europe on terms at least as risky as the last great wave of commercial lending to Latin America in the late 1970s, it is more than likely that the safety-net function of the Bank's adjustment lending will need to be extended in the coming decade.

But if adjustment lending has hidden benefits, it also has a hidden cost. This is the downward pressure which it has exerted, in conjunction with IMF stabilisation programmes, on the level of investment in developing countries. The 1980s has been a decade of preoccupation with the short term, during which both the concern of the previous decade with distributive justice and the more ancient wisdom that development does not happen without appropriate levels of investment in human and material capital have been submerged by pressure to 'get the macroeconomic balances right first'. As we emerge from what the Bank has called 'a decade of adjustment' into a decade of 'sustainable growth' it has become clear that the manner in which those balances are got right has implications for the long term. In particular, the shift from project assistance to a mixture of hard-conditionality IMF finance and soft-conditionality Bank programme lending has led to a squeeze on public-sector development spending. The fact that both domestic and overseas private investment, especially in the poorer developing countries, have often fallen rather than risen in response to cuts in public development expenditure has compounded the problem.

It is in these poorer developing countries that we encounter the kernel of the World Bank's adjustment-lending dilemma. For both economic theory and the evidence of our case studies suggest that the Bank's chosen package of reforms has more relevance to Thailand and Turkey, say, than to Malawi or Guyana. A policy of trade liberalisation works better if industry is already competitive on export markets; price incentives to commercial farmers work better if those farmers have access to credit, fertiliser and

309

good roads; privatisation works better if there exists a private sector able and willing to take over the public sector's assets. At this point it becomes relevant to see matters in historical perspective. Both in Europe and Japan in the nineteenth century, and since the Second World War in countries such as Taiwan and South Korea, it is possible to see the level of state intervention in the economy over time describing a reverse U-shape as state support is first given to infant industries to enable them to gain a foothold in world markets, then progressively withdrawn (with cycles around the trend) as this support becomes unnecessary and 'the market mechanism that regulates the exchange behaviour among economic actors is gradually depoliticised' (Fei and Ranis, 1988: 16). The point is that structural adjustment policies of the Bank's chosen variety constitute in very poor countries a gratuitous obstruction, just as in the NICs they constitute a welcome acceleration, of the policy evolution above described. The Bank is at pains to stress that it does not impose a uniform policy package on its borrowers (cf. Table 2.3); and a simple comparison of the Kenya and Ghana case studies will show how much it has learned over the 1980s about the art of phasing and appropriate policy design. But it still has to grasp the point that in very poor countries, privatisation and removal of infant-industry protective structures are at best an irrelevance. True structural adjustment requires the building up of the country's export sectors and associated infrastructure, which in the short term may require more rather than less state intervention.

9.3 POLICY PROPOSALS

Baldwin's recent essay on economic statecraft has usefully warned us against the making of superficial judgements on the success of initiatives in international relations. Such initiatives, he stresses, should only be judged 'in terms of the goals of the policy-makers, not in terms of the policy preferences of the analyst' (1985: 250) and in relation to the costs of achieving the same goals by alternative means (ibid.: 149–50). The difficulty in the present case is that we are dealing with two sets of policy-makers ('donor' and 'recipient'), each with multiple goals. But it will be useful if we categorise the lessons of experience emerging from the preceding experience according as they appear to hold out the promise of benefit for the lender, the recipient, or both parties:

(i) Proposals of benefit to the lender

1 The case for *shorter lists of 'key conditions', tailored to cases of genuine distortion only*, has already been eloquently put by the Bank's own internal review of policy-based lending (1988: 15, para. 41), although

there is, as yet, little sign of its implementation. Such a pruning exercise would save a great deal of staff time in the donor agency; increase the credibility of the threats it does make; and most important, increase the likelihood that it can disburse the money it wishes to disburse at a planned rate without the inevitable symbolic delay when first-tranche conditions are not met.

2   We feel that the Bank's policy on granting refinance to recipients who have committed some slippage on conditions should either be consistent (in the interests of equity) or explicitly governed by chance. As demonstrated in the Appendix to Chapter 3, *Random punishment (through refusal of refinance) of recipients who fail to comply with conditions* would be the most effective means of making the donor's threat credible while maintaining a planned rate of disbursement. Alternatively, the Bank could practice a policy of strict equity as between recipients who commit a given level of slippage, a policy which is a long way from its present practice (Table 5.6).

(ii)   Proposals of benefit to the recipient

3   *Particularly in the poorer countries, the 'structural adjustment' policies on which programme lending is contingent should embrace, where appropriate, policies to expand the economic role of the state (infant-industry protection, credit for low income groups, expansion of infrastructure . . .)* in addition to measures to remove harmful state interventions. This proposal follows on directly from the concluding observation of the previous section, and from our case studies of low-income countries such as Ghana, Malawi and Guyana. The essential point is that a failure to allocate resources efficiently, and hence a supply bottle-neck, may arise as much from endogenous market failure as from market failure induced by policy intervention. The poorer the country, the more likely is such endogenous market failure (e.g. under-utilisation of productive land, inability of small businessmen to borrow on commercial terms, lack of access to the market by producers of tradables . . .) to constitute a constraint on production.

4   The policy changes on which programme finance is contingent *should be introduced where possible on an experimental basis* (e.g. a recommended privatisation of food-crop marketing could be introduced initially in one province only) in order to enable the recipient to see that a given policy change will indeed have the merits that its sponsor claims for it. In the event that his forecast is wrong, he can retreat without having inflicted too much damage.

5   The models which the Bank uses for the forecasting of the macroeconomic impact of its recommended policy changes *should be lodged with the recipient in the form of a micro-computer disc, in order that the*

311

recipient can simulate the effect of his own preferred policies. (This can be done now for Malawi and Morocco, for example, using the models set out in the Appendices to Chapter 8). This should make for a policy dialogue whose outcome is determined more by the intellectual merits of the policy proposals under discussion than by the sheer bargaining power of the two protagonists. The provision of technical assistance to policy analysis divisions of recipient governments to enable them to carry out simulations of this type would be an appropriate use for aid funds.

6   The present *modus operandi* of structural adjustment lending militates against making full use of available information on the local economy, society and politics. A large number of short missions, with very different personnel on each mission, prevents the Bank from accumulating much country-specific knowledge that is relevant to policy implementation. Apart from what is contained in each mission report, knowledge of the local context is restricted to what accumulates in the local resident representative's office. This has little time to assemble much information, as it is largely occupied as a manager of the short-term missions. Bilateral donor agencies however often prove to be repositories of a considerable local knowledge, on agriculture, health, etc. *The Bank should find ways of tapping these sources more effectively.*

7   Country models require the input of crucial information about the world environment if they are to produce sensible and realistic results. We have found some reasons to criticise the over-optimism of the Bank's own Commodity Price Forecast and believe that *the Bank should make much greater use of price forecasts made by forecasters who have no interest in the future price being either high or low.*

8   The device of Policy Framework Papers, setting out an internally consistent policy structure agreed between Fund, Bank and recipient government, *should be extended to those (mainly middle-income) countries not currently in receipt of Fund SAF or ESAF credits,* as an instrument for increasing co-ordination between the Fund and the Bank. Such agreements should in future contain *covenants protecting the level of real government development expenditure,* thereby setting up a defence against the problem of depressed investment described in the previous section. A corollary of this approach will be that fiscal balance would have to be sought by way of increasing government revenue to match the level of desired expenditure, rather than by seeking to pull down expenditure to the level of available revenue.[2]

9   Policy-based loans aimed at a particular sector *should where possible be offered in kind,* as a means of increasing the sense of 'ownership' of the reform programme felt by the ministry whose sector the proposed reforms affect: for example, agricultural sector loans in the form of

fertiliser. (The Bank's recent introduction of 'hybrid lending', i.e. programme loans whose policy conditionality is linked to the performance of a new capital project also financed by the donor, makes a similar link between conditionality and the interests of the operating agency).

(iii)   Measures offering benefit to both donor and recipient

10   The losers from policy-based reform programmes *should be identified and compensated out of the sum budgeted for the loan.* Naturally, since the purpose of such reform is to remove distortions to the price system, such measures should avoid introducing new distortions, and the Bank is now well aware that this need not happen. It is not difficult, in fact, to think up ways offering compensation in a non-distortive way, for example,

(a)   manufacturers who lose quota protection can be compensated by a reduction in payroll tax, or by an increase in the customs duty drawback available on exports (actually implemented in the Philippines – see Volume 2, Chapter 12);

(b)   Farmers who lose a fertiliser subsidy can be compensated by a programme of labour-intensive rural road building;

(c)   Poorer urban workers who lose a food subsidy can be compensated by the setting up of a special loan fund for informal-sector businessmen;

(d)   Borrowers who are hurt by the shift to market-determined interest rates can be compensated by the provision of additional services financed from the proceeds of higher rates and more intensive supervision – for example, compulsory crop, livestock or asset insurance.

The Bank has now begun to implement these ideas by making resources available for Social Funds and for the extension of the social safety net, as in the recent Indian operation of November 1992.

The above recommendations take it as given that the Bank and other development agencies decide to continue with policy-based lending, rather than, as has been suggested, reverting to the project mode entirely. Our own view is that policy-based lending as such represents an imaginative response by donor agencies to the global economic crisis of the early 1980s, and that the problems which remain are design problems susceptible to reform, as described above, rather than problems which undermine the entire original concept. The besetting sin of development policy throughout its life has been vulnerability to fashion, so that when a new idea is introduced the valuable elements in previous practice are rejected

313

rather than assimilated. These modifications to existing practice are suggested in the hope of grafting on to the valuable concept of policy-based lending the more ancient, and equally valuable, ideas of protecting vulnerable groups and protecting the ultimate springs of economic growth during periods of adjustment. If the result is a movement towards 'a kinder, greener and gentler World Bank' at the end of the twentieth century, we shall be more than happy.

NOTES

1 Bowing to the pressure to disburse, however, at the cost of foregoing Government commitment to reform, may lead to a vicious circle of disbursement, in which disbursement which is not followed by growth creates pressure for the disbursement of further loans in order to make possible the repayment of the original credit.

2 Although such recommendations might sound straightforward, in practice, their implementation will often be complex and lengthy. If the attempt to increase Government revenue is to be accomplished without conflicting with Bank/Fund trade liberalisation policies, the burden of taxation will need to be shifted from external to domestic sources. Again, the use of PFP's may help to ensure such compatibility between the various aims of stabilisation and adjustment programmes, but this will often need to be supplemented with technical assistance, and a slow-down of the reform process, to enable the necessary institutional tax reforms to be undertaken.

It should also be noted that privileging the level of real Government development expenditure should not be undertaken regardless of additional reforms of the budgetary mechanism to improve the selection of priority areas for expenditure. The Bank previously gave technical assistance to draw priority expenditure budgets. The problem has been linking these 'priority' expenditure plans into the actual spending system. Our Malawi case study illustrates a successful marriage of prioritisation with real spending. But in several other adjusting countries the Bank has not been able to arrange this marriage and has had difficulty recruiting advisers with practical understanding of budgeting systems rather than a theoretical understanding of optimal expenditure patterns.

BIBLIOGRAPHY

Addison, Tony and Demery, Lionel (1987) 'Alleviating poverty under structural adjustment', *Finance and Development* 24 (December): 41–3.
———— (1988) *The Alleviation of Poverty Under Structural Adjustment.* Washington DC: World Bank.
———— (1989) 'The economics of rural poverty alleviation', in S. Commander (ed.), *Structural Adjustment and Agriculture* London: Overseas Development Institute.
Agarwala, R. (1983) *Price Distortions and Growth in Developing Countries,* World Bank Staff Working Paper 575, Washington DC: World Bank.
Amsden, Alice H. (1989) *Asia's Next Giant: South Korea and Late Industrialisation,* Oxford: Oxford University Press.
Ayres, R.L. (1983) *Banking on the Poor: the World Bank and World Poverty,* Cambridge, Mass.: MIT Press.
Baldwin, David A. (1985) *Economic Statecraft,* Princeton, NJ: Princeton University Press.
Baran, Paul A. (1975) *The Political Economy of Growth,* Harmondsworth: Penguin.
Barnum, H. and Squire, L. (1979) *A Model of an Agricultural Household: Theory and Evidence,* World Bank Staff Working Paper 27.
Berg, Elliot and Batchelor, Alan (1984) *Structural Adjustment Lending: a Critical Analysis,* unpublished paper, Alexandra, Virginia: Elliot Berg Associates,
Bhagwati, Jagdish and Srinivasan, T.N. (1975) *Foreign Trade Regimes and Economic Development: India,* New York and London: Columbia University Press for the National Bureau of Economic Research.
———— (1982) 'The welfare consequences of directly-unproductive profit-seeking (DUP) lobbying activities: price versus quantity distortions', *Journal of International Economics,* 13: 33–44.
Bolnick, Bruce R. (1975) 'Interpreting Polak: monetary analysis in "dependent" economies', *Journal of Development Studies* 11 (July).
Bond, Marian (1983) 'Agricultural responses to prices in Sub-Saharan Africa', *IMF Staff Papers* 30 (December): 703–26.
Bourguignon, Francois, Branson, William and de Melo, Jaime (1988) *Macroeconomic Adjustment and Income Distribution: A Macro-Micro Simulation Model,* OECD Technical paper No 1.
———— (1989) *Adjustment and Income Distribution,* unpublished paper, Ecole des Hautes Etudes en Sciences Sociales, Princeton University and World Bank.
Braverman, A and Hammer, J. (1988) 'Computer models for agricultural policy analysis', *Finance and Development* June.
Bruno, Michael (1993) *Crisis, Stabilisation and Economic Reform: therapy by consensus,* Oxford: Oxford University Press.

315

Bulow, Jeremy and Rogoff, Kenneth (1989) 'A constant recontracting model of sovereign debt', *Journal of Political Economy*, 97: 155–78.

Carty, Anthony (1988) 'Liberal economic rhetoric as an obstacle to the democratisation of the world economy', *Ethics* 98 (July): 742–56.

Casley, Dennis J. and Lury, Denis A. (1982) *Monitoring and evaluation of agriculture and rural development projects*, Washington DC: Johns Hopkins University Press.

—— (1985) *Monitoring and Evaluation of Agricultural and Rural Development Projects*, Baltimore: Johns Hopkins University Press.

Cassen, Robert et al. (1986) *Does Aid Work? Report to an Intergovernmental Task Force*, Oxford: Oxford University Press

Chang, H-J. (1993) 'The political economy of industrial policy in Korea', *Cambridge Journal of Economics*, 17, no. 2 (June).

Cleaver, Kevin (1985) *The Impact of Price and Exchange Rate Policies on Agriculture in Sub-Saharan Africa*, World Bank Staff Working Paper 728, Washington DC.

Collier, Paul (1989) *Trade Shocks in Africa: A Review of the New Macroeconomics of External Shocks*, paper presented at conference on Policy Adjustment in Africa, Nottingham, 18 September.

Commonwealth Secretariat (1986) *Co-operation Without Cross-conditionality: an Issue in International Lending*, London.

Colclough, C. and Manor, J. (eds) (1990) *States or Markets: Neoliberalism and the Development Debate*, Oxford: Oxford University Press.

Corbo, Vittorio, Goldstein, Morris and Khan, Mohsin (1987) *Growth-oriented Adjustment Programmes*, Washington DC: IMF and World Bank.

Cornia, Andrea (1994) 'Income distribution, poverty and welfare in transitional economies: a comparison between Eastern Europe and China', *Journal of International Development*, 6, 569–608.

Cornia, Andrea, Jolly, Richard and Stewart, Frances (1987) *Adjustment with a Human Face*, Oxford: Oxford University Press.

Dervis, K., de Melo, J., and Robinson, S. (1982) *General Equilibrium Models for Development Policy*, Cambridge: Cambridge University Press.

De Swan, A. (1988) *In Care of the State*, Oxford: Polity Press.

Downs, Anthony (1960) 'Why the government budget is too small in a democracy', *World Politics* (July): 541–63.

Edwards, Sebastian (1984) *The Order of Liberalisation of the External Sector in Developing Countries*, Princeton NJ: Princeton Papers in International Finance 156.

—— (1986) *The Sequencing of Economic Liberalisation in Developing Countries*, World Bank Staff Working Paper.

Evans, D. and Alizadeh, P. (1984) 'Trade, industrialisation and the visible hand', *Journal of Development Studies* 21 (October): 221–45 (supplement).

Faber, Michael (1990) 'Debt: new treatment of the chronic but repentant', *Journal of International Development* 2 (April): 232–42.

Faber, M. and Seers, D. (1972) *The Crisis in Planning*, London: Chatto and Windus for Sussex University Press.

Fei, John C.H. and Ranis, Gustav (1988) *The Political Economy of Development Policy Change: a Comparative Study of Thailand and the Philippines*, unpublished paper, Economic Growth Center, Yale University.

Feinberg, Richard (1986) *The Changing Relationship Between the World Bank and the International Monetary Fund*, unpublished paper, Washington DC. Overseas Development Council.

Feinberg, Richard et al. (1986b) *Between Two Worlds: the World Bank's Next Decade*, Washington DC: Overseas Development Council.

Foxley, Alejandro (1983) *Latin American Experiments in Neo-conservative Economics*, Berkeley: University of California Press.

316

Friedman, James W. (1989) *Game Theory with Applications to Economics*, 2nd edn, Oxford: Oxford University Press.

Genberg, Hans and Swoboda, Alexander K. (1986) *The Medium-term Relationship between Performance Indicators and Policy*, Country Economics Department Working Paper no. 1986–2, Washington DC: World Bank.

George, S. and Sabelli, F. (1994) *Faith and Credit: The World Bank's Secular Empire*, London: Penguin.

Goldstein, Morris (1986) *The Global Effects of Fund-supported Adjustment Programmes*, Occasional Paper 42, Washington DC: IMF.

Goulder, L. and Eichengreen, B. (1989) *Trade Liberalisation in General Equilibrium: Integrated and Inter-industry Effects*, Working Paper 2814, Washington DC: National Bureau of Economics Research

Green, Reginald H. (1988) 'Ghana: progress, problematics and limitations of the success story', *IDS Bulletin* 19 (January): 7–16.

Griffith-Jones, Stephany (1988a) 'Debt crisis management in the early 1980s: Can lessons be learnt?', *Development Policy Review*, vol 6 (January): 3–28.

—— (1988b) 'Cross-conditionality, or the spread of obligatory adjustment', unpublished paper, University of Sussex, Institute of Development Studies.

Grindle, Merilee S. (1989) 'The new political economy: positive economics and negative politics', unpublished paper, Cambridge, Mass.

Gulhati, Ravi (1987) *Recent Economic Reforms in Africa: a Preliminary Political Economy Perspective*, Washington DC: EDI Policy Seminar Report Series, No. 8.

Harrigan, Jane (1988a) 'Alternative concepts of conditionality', *Manchester Papers on Development* 4 (October): 451–71.

—— (1988b) 'Malawi: the impact of pricing policy on smallholder agriculture 1971–88', *Development Policy Review* 6 (December): 415–34.

Hayter, Teresa (1971) *Aid as Imperialism*, Harmondsworth: Penguin.

Hayter, Teresa and Watson, Catharine (1985) *Aid: Rhetoric and Reality*, London: Pluto Press.

Heaver, Richard and Israel, Arturo (1984) *Country Commitment to Development Projects*, Discussion Paper 4, Washington DC: World Bank.

Helleiner, Gerald, K. (1983) *The IMF and Africa in the 1980s*, Princeton Essays in International Finance, no 152.

—— (1990) *Structural Adjustment and Long Term Development in Sub-Saharan Africa*, unpublished paper.

Hexter, J.H. (1979) *On Historians: Reappraisals of some of the Masters of Modern History*, Cambridge, Mass.: Harvard University Press.

Hicks, Norman, and Kubisch, Anne (1984) 'Cutting government expenditure in LDCs', *Finance and Development* 21, 35–42.

Hindess, Barry (1988) *Choice, Rationality and Social Theory*, London: Unwin Hyman.

Hutchful, E. (1989) 'From "Revolution" to Monetarism: the economics and politics of the adjustment programme in Ghana' in B.K. Campbell and J. Loxley (eds), 1989, *Structural Adjustment in Africa*, Basingstoke: Macmillan.

Hwa, Erh-Cheng (1986) *Simulating Economic Recovery Strategies for the Philippines*. World Bank, Economic Analysis and Projects Department, unpublished paper.

Kenny, Charles (1994) *Risk and the World Bank*, unpublished MA thesis, SOAS, University of London.

Khan, Mohsin S. and Knight, Malcolm D. (1985) *Fund-supported Adjustment Programmes and Economic Growth*, Occasional Paper 41, Washington DC: IMF.

Kharas, Homi (1986) 'An assessment of the Philippines macroeconomic modelling exercise', unpublished paper, East Asia Department, World Bank.

Killick, Tony (1989) *A Reaction Too Far: Economic Theory and the Role of the State in Developing Countries* (2 vols), London: Overseas Development Institute.

Killick, Tony *et al.* (1984) *The Quest for Economic Stabilisation: the IMF and the Third World*, London: Heinemann Educational.

Krueger, Anne O. (1974) 'The political economy of the rent-seeking society', *American Economic Review* 64: 291–310.

—— (1983) *Trade and Employment in Developing Countries*, New York: National Bureau of Economic Research.

Krugman, Paul (1988) 'Forgiving vs. financing a debt overhang', *Journal of Development Economics* 29, 253–68.

Lal, Deepak (1983) *The Poverty of 'Development Economics'*, Hobart Paperback 16 London: Institute of Economic Affairs.

—— (1987) 'The political economy of economic liberalisation', *The World Bank Economic Review* 1 (2) January.

Landell-Mills, Pierre (1981) 'Structural adjustment lending: early experience', *Finance and Development* 18 (January): 17–21.

Leff, Nathaniel (1985) 'The use of policy science tools in public sector decision-making: social benefit–cost analysis in the World Bank', *Kyklos* 38.

Lele, Uma (1989) *Agricultural Growth, Domestic Policies, the External Environment and Assistance to Africa: Lessons of a Quarter Century*, Washington DC: World Bank.

Lewis, Sir W.A. (1966) *Development Planning: the Essentials of Economic Policy*, London: Allen and Unwin.

Lipton, Michael (1977) *Why Poor People Stay Poor: Urban Bias in World Development* London: Maurice Temple Smith.

—— (1987) 'Limits of price policy for agriculture: which way for the World Bank?', *Development Policy Review* 5: 197–215.

Lipton, Michael and Toye, John (1990) *Does Aid Work in India? A Country Study of the Impact of Official Development Assistance*, London: Routledge.

Little, Ian, Scitovsky, Tibor and Scott, M.F. (1970) *Trade and Industry in Some Developing Countries*, Oxford: Oxford University Press for OECD Development Centre.

McCleary, William (1989) 'Policy implementation under adjustment lending', *Finance and Development* 26 (March): 32–4.

Meier, Gerald M. (ed.) (1987) *Pioneers of Development Economics*, vol. 2, Washington DC: World Bank.

—— (1989) 'Do development economists matter?' *IDS Bulletin* 20 (July): 17–25.

Michalopoulos Constantine (1987) 'World Bank programmes for adjustment and growth', Chapter 3 in V. Corbo, M. Goldstein and Mohsin S. Khan, *Growth-Oriented Adjustment Programmes*, Washington: World Bank and IMF.

Morawetz, David (1977) *Twenty-five Years of Economic Development 1950–1975*, Baltimore: Johns Hopkins University Press for the World Bank.

Morrisson, Christian (with assistance of A. Suwa and S. Lambert) (1989) *Ajustement et distribution des revenus: application d'un modèle micro-macro au Maroc*, Paris: OECD, Document Technique No. 7.

Morss, Elliot (1984) 'Institutional destruction resulting from donor and project proliferation in sub-Saharan African countries', *World Development* 12: 465–97.

Mosley, Paul (1980) 'Aid, savings and growth revisited', *Oxford Bulletin of Economics and Statistics*, 42 (May): 79–95.

—— (1983) 'The politics of evaluation: a comparative study of World Bank and UKODA evaluation procedures', *Development and Change*, 14: 593–608.

—— (1987) *Conditionality as Bargaining Process: Structural Adjustment Lending 1980–1986*, Princeton, NJ: Princeton Essays in International Finance, no. 168.

—— (1989) 'Review article: effective stabilisation policy in less developed countries', *Journal of International Development* 1 (April): 273–80.

——(1992) (ed.) *Development Finance and Policy Reform*, London: Macmillan.

Mosley, Paul and Harrigan, Jane (1991) *World Bank Policy-based Lending 1980–87: an Evaluation, Journal of Development Studies*, 27 (April).

Mosley, Paul and Smith, Lawrence (1989) 'Structural adjustment and agricultural performance in sub-Saharan Africa 1980–87', *Journal of International Development* 1 (July): 321–55.

Mosley, Paul and Toye, John (1988) 'The design of structural adjustment programmes', *Development Policy Review*, 6 (December): 395–413.

Mosley, Paul, Hudson, John and Horrell, Sara (1987) 'Aid, the public sector and the market in less developed countries', *Economic Journal* 97 (September): 616–42.

Naim, M. (1994) 'From supplicants to shareholders: developing countries and the World Bank', in United Nations (1994) *International Monetary and Financial Issues for the 1990s*, Vol. IV, New York for UNCTAD, Geneva.

Nelson, Joan (1984) 'The political economy of stabilisation: commitment, capacity and public response', *World Development* 12 (December): 983–1006.

—— (ed.) (1989) *Fragile Coalitions: the Politics of Economic Adjustment*. Washington DC: Overseas Development Council.

—— (ed.) (1990) *Economic Crisis and Policy Choice: The Politics of Adjustment in the Third World*, Princeton, NJ: Princeton University Press.

Nicholas, Peter (1988) *The World Bank's Lending for Adjustment: an Interim Report*, Discussion Paper 34, Washington DC: World Bank.

Olson, M. (1971) *The Logic of Collective Action: Public Goods and the Theory of Groups* (revised edition), New York: Schocken Books.

—— (1982) *The Rise and Decline of Nations: Economic Growth, Stagflation and Social Rigidities*, New Haven and London: Yale University Press.

Oppenheimer, Franz M. (1987) 'Don't bank on the World Bank', *American Spectator*, October issue: 46–8.

Overseas Economic Cooperation Fund of Japan (OECF) (1993) *Issues Related to the World Bank's Approach to Structural Adjustment: Proposal from a Major Partner*, Occasional Paper No 1, Tokyo: OECF.

—— (1993a) 'The intellectual awakening of a sleeping partner: an OECF view of structural adjustment', *OECF Research Quarterly*, no. 1.

—— (1993b) *The East Asian Miracle: Proceedings of a Symposium*, Tokyo: OECF.

Papanek, Gustav (1972) 'The effect of aid and other resource transfers on savings and growth in less developed countries', *Economic Journal* 82: 934–50.

Please, Stanley (1984) *The Hobbled Giant: Essays on the World Bank*, Boulder, Colo.: Westview Press.

Pearson, L.B. *et al.* (1969) *Partners in development: Report of the Commission on International Development*, London and New York: Praeger.

Prawer, S.S. (1978) *Karl Marx and World Literature*, Oxford: Oxford University Press.

Rapoport, Anatol and Chammah, Albert M. (1965) *Prisoner's Dilemma: a Study in Conflict and Cooperation*, Ann Arbor: University of Michigan Press.

Rasmusen, Eric (1989) *Games and Information*, Oxford: Blackwell.

Rodrik, D. (1988) 'Liberalisation, sustainability and the design of structural adjustment programmes', unpublished paper, Harvard University and World Bank.

—— (1989) 'Notes on credibility and sustainability of trade reform', unpublished paper, Harvard University and World Bank.

SDA Steering Committee (1993) *The Social Dimensions of Adjustment Program: A General Assessment*, Washington DC.

Seers, Dudley (1979) 'The congruence of Marxism and other neo-classical doctrines' in K.Q. Hill (ed.) *Toward a New Strategy for Development*, New York: Pergamon Press.

Singer, H.W. (1965) 'External aid: for plans or projects?', *Economic Journal* 75 (September).

Singh, I. and Squire L. (1984) *Malawi: Agricultural Policy Model*, unpublished paper, Economic and Management Support Unit, World Bank.

Smith, Lawrence and Spooner, Neil (1989) *Sequencing of Structural Adjustment Measures*, unpublished report for the FAO.

Srinivasan, T.N. (1989) 'Political economy of foreign trade regimes', unpublished paper, University of California at Berkeley.

Stern, Ernest (1983) 'World Bank financing of structural adjustment', chapter in Williamson (1983).

Stern, Nicholas (1989) 'The economics of development: a survey', *Economic Journal* 99 (September): 597–686.

Stewart, F. (1994) 'Education and adjustment: the experience of the 1980s and lessons for the 1990s' in Prendergast, R. and Stewart, F. (1994) *Market Forces and World Development*, Basingstoke: Macmillan.

Streeten, Paul (1989) 'A survey of the issues and options', in S. Commander (ed.) *Structural Adjustment and Agriculture* London: Overseas Development Institute.

Taylor, Lance (1988) *Varieties of Stabilisation Experience: Towards Sensible Macroeconomics in the Third World*, Oxford: Oxford University Press.

Toye, John (1976) 'Economic theories of politics and public finance', *British Journal of Political Science* 6: 433–48.

—— (1987 2nd ed. 1993) *Dilemmas of Development: Reflections on the Counter-revolution in Development Theory and Policy*, Oxford: Basil Blackwell.

—— (1989) 'Can the World Bank Resolve the Crisis of Developing Countries?', *Journal of International Development* 1 (April): 261–72.

Wade, Robert (1989) *Unpacking the World Bank: Lending versus Leverage*, unpublished paper, Washington DC, March.

—— (1990) *Governing the Market. Economic Theory and the Role of Government in East Asian Industrialisation*, Princeton: Princeton University Press.

Wallich, C.I. (1994) 'What's right and wrong with World Bank involvement in Eastern Europe', *Journal of Comparative Economics*, forthcoming.

Wapenhans, W. (1994) 'The political economy of structural adjustment: an external perspective' in Van der Hoeven, R., and Van der Kraaij, F. (eds) *Structural Adjustment and Beyond in Sub-Saharan Africa: Research and Policy Issues*, The Hague: Ministry of Foreign Affairs (DGIS) and London: James Currey.

Weir, Stuart (1982) 'The model that crashed: how the Cambridge economic forecasting groups have been pushed out into the cold', *New Society*, 12 August: 251–3.

Williamson, John (1983) *IMF Conditionality*, Washington DC: Institute for International Economics.

World Bank (1978) *Rural Development Projects: a Retrospective View of Bank Experience in Sub-Saharan Africa*, report no. 2242, Washington DC: World Bank.

—— (1981) *Accelerated Development in Sub-Saharan Africa: an Agenda for Action*, Washington DC: World Bank.

—— (1986) *Structural Adjustment Lending: a First Review of Experience*, Report No. 6409, Washington DC: World Bank Operations Evaluation Department.

—— (1988) *Report on Adjustment Lending*, Washington DC: World Bank, Country Economics Department.

—— (1989) *Sub-Saharan Africa: from Crisis to Sustainable Growth: a Long-term Perspective Study*, Washington DC: World Bank.

—— (1990) *Report on Adjustment Lending II: Adjustment Lending Policies for Sustainable Growth*, Washington DC: World Bank Country Economics Department.

—— (1990a) *Structural Adjustment: a Conceptual, Empirical and Policy Framework*, Report No. 8393 – AFR, Washington DC: World Bank.

—— (1990b) *World Development Report*, Washington DC: World Bank.

—— (1991) *Assistance Strategies to Reduce Poverty*, Washington DC: World Bank.

—— (1992a) *Poverty Reduction Operational Directive*, O.D. 4.15, Washington DC: World Bank.

—— (1992b) *Poverty Reduction Handbook*, Washington DC: World Bank.

—— (1992c) *Report on Adjustment Lending III: Adjustment Lending and Mobilization of Public and Private Resources for Growth*. Washington DC: World Bank.

—— (1992d) *Effective Implementation: Key to Development Impact*, [Wapenhans Report], Washington DC: World Bank.

—— (1993) *The East Asian Miracle: Economic growth and Public Policy*, Oxford: Oxford University Press.

—— (1994a) *The World Bank Annual Report 1994*, Washington DC: World Bank.

—— (1994b) *Making Development Sustainable*, Washington DC: World Bank.

—— (1994c) *Adjustment in Africa. Reforms, Results and the Road Ahead*, Oxford: Oxford University Press.

—— (1994d) *Poverty Reduction and the World Bank. Progress in Fiscal 1993*, (Mimeo dated March 21st, 1994) Washington DC: World Bank.

Yagci, Fahrettin, Kamin, Steven and Rosenbaum, Vicki (1985) *Structural Adjustment Lending: an Evaluation of Program Design*, Staff Working Paper 735, Washington DC: World Bank.

321

INDEX

The suffix n after an index entry, thus (87n) denotes a reference to the Notes at the end of each chapter.